HOME IMPROVEMENT
HOME REPAIR

HOME IMPROVEMENT HOME REPAIR

RICHARD V. NUNN

CREATIVE HOMEOWNER PRESS®   A DIVISION OF FEDERAL MARKETING CORPORATION, 24 PARK WAY, UPPER SADDLE RIVER, NEW JERSEY 07458

COPYRIGHT © 1980 CREATIVE HOMEOWNER PRESS®
A DIVISION OF FEDERAL MARKETING CORP., UPPER SADDLE RIVER, NJ

Manufactured in United States of America

Current Printing (last digit)
10 9 8 7

Editor: Shirley M. Horowitz
Art Director: Léone Lewensohn
Proofreader: Marilyn M. Auer
Technical Assistance: Edward Giese

Library of Congress Cataloging in Publication Data

Nunn, Richard V.
  Home Improvement/Home Repair

80-66637
ISBN: 0-932944-17-5
ISBN: 0-932944-18-3 pbk

CREATIVE HOMEOWNER PRESS®
A DIVISION OF FEDERAL MARKETING CORPORATION
24 PARK WAY, UPPER SADDLE RIVER, NJ 07458

Contents

(Continued on Pg. 6)

1 Tools and Workshops

The more expensive tools will repay the added cost in safety and durability. This is especially true of hammers, saws, chisels, planes, measuring and marking tools, and most power equipment.

Quality is not as important for tools such as screwdrivers, pliers, files, snips and similar tools, only because these items are often lost or borrowed, or become worn, dull, or rusted and have to be replaced. This is not to say that the equipment should be cheap; it should not be. But if your tool budget does not permit the best of everything, then skimp on these smaller items and invest in the capital equipment that will be used for years.

You do not have to be a tool expert to know the difference between cheap tools and expensive ones once you have compared them. Quality tools not only make any job easier, but will last a lifetime. Good pipe wrenches grip steel pipe firmly, even through galvanizing. Cheap ones will slip because the serrations in the jaws become dull — and they slip just when your hand is where it will hit a concrete wall.

The price tag is the first clue, but also pay attention to how well the tool has been manufactured. It should be smoothly machined and balanced — especially in the case of hammers, saws and hand-held power tools. Beware of tools that are painted. Paint is used to hide bad machining and flaws and rough spots in the metal castings.

WORKSHOP LAYOUT

If you have the room in your home for a separate workshop, you are lucky indeed — regardless of its size. But you still can have a working "shop," even if you do not have much space.

The key is organization of tools and materials — not necessarily space — although you do have to have a place to work.

This may sound like a paradox, but remember that you can always take the tools to the job, instead of bringing the job to the tools. In fact, for many home repair projects, you probably will take the tools to the job.

You may have workshop space and not know it. Consider these sometimes-overlooked places:

- a basement room — perhaps in back of the furnace or laundry area;
- under basement stairsteps that have a landing;
- in a large storage or utility closet;
- in your garage;
- in your next door neighbor's garage (rent or a trade);
- above the collar beams in your garage — you can usually add joists and floor the area if you have adequate head room down from the ridge of the roof and rafters;
- a spare bedroom;
- in the attic;
- the storage area in a carport;
- a garden shed you can build, or buy prefabricated.

If these areas are now nonexistent or not practical, you will have to settle for a tool box that serves as a portable work area. Tool boxes that you buy, like the metal ones you often see in gas station lube areas and full-time garages where your car is repaired, are the best long-run bargain. The wood and time it takes to fabricate your own tool box is almost prohibitive.

Tool boxes will hold hammers, chisels, screwdrivers, and so on. Hand saws, levels, and carpenters' squares are too large to be included in most of the small portable cases. Therefore, you

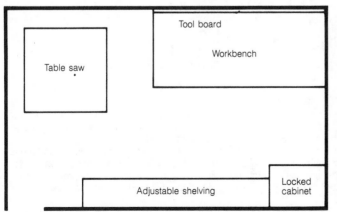

A small 8x10-ft. shop packs lots of work area into a small space. The table saw on casters can be rolled into the room to help support large projects on the bench. The locking cabinet could be placed near the bench to free up space for lumber.

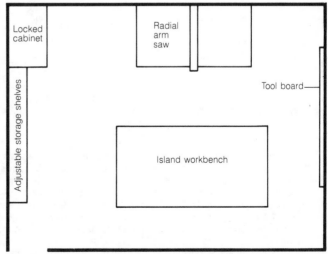

An island workbench offers four workable sides but requires lots of space. Unused floor space along one wall can accommodate stationary power equipment such as a jigsaw, drill press, jointer. Materials will fit here, as well.

will have to find wall-hanging space for these large tools. This should not be too difficult.

The idea of a workshop, work area, or tool box simply is to keep your tools organized and in a place where you will know where to find them. If you throw the tools in a drawer you may lose the tools, and certainly nick and dull the sharp cutting edges.

Workshop Setup

There are no cast-in-concrete rules of workshop planning. There are suggestions to help the work area function more smoothly.

Size. Start with the largest space available. Minimum space would be 8x10 feet; all considerations listed in this chapter are based on this area. An 8x10-foot space gives you room to turn and stack 4x8-ft. sheets of plywood and hardboard and other materials.

Paint. Paint the walls and ceiling of the room a light color such as off white, light green or light blue — any light color that you like and that will help reflect light. The paint job also will help keep the room cleaner. Sawdust clings less to painted surfaces than to unpainted surfaces, especially if walls are concrete block or brick.

Light. Add plenty of light to the room. The area should have

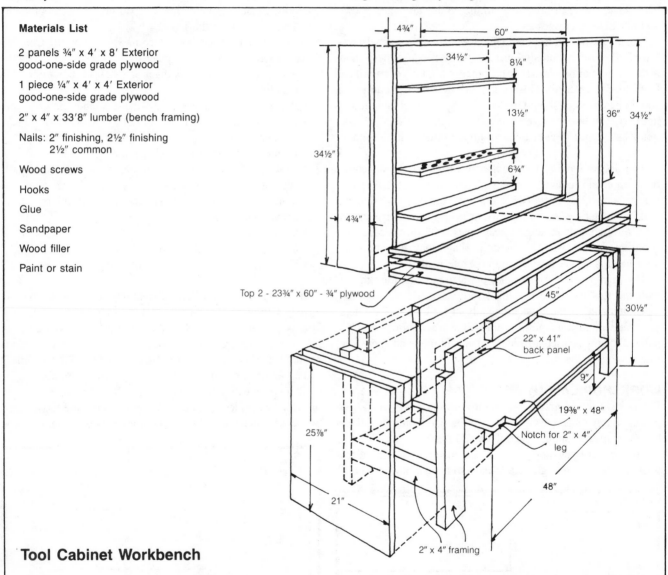

Materials List

2 panels ¾" x 4' x 8' Exterior good-one-side grade plywood

1 piece ¼" x 4' x 4' Exterior good-one-side grade plywood

2" x 4" x 33'8" lumber (bench framing)

Nails: 2" finishing, 2½" finishing
        2½" common

Wood screws

Hooks

Glue

Sandpaper

Wood filler

Paint or stain

Top 2 - 23¾" x 60" - ¾" plywood

22" x 41" back panel

19⅜" x 48"

Notch for 2" x 4" leg

2" x 4" framing

Tool Cabinet Workbench

This workbench and cabinet combination gives room to store tools and to work comfortably. Before cutting, lay out all parts on the plywood panels. Allow for blade widths (saw kerfs) between parts. Cut parts to the exact sizes. Cut the 2x4 bench framework to the lengths given in the materials list. Notch one end of each 2x4 leg for cross rails, as shown. Smooth edges of parts with sandpaper.

Using glue and nails, assemble the 2x4 lower shelf framing. Fasten the ¾ in. plywood shelf to the frame. Set up the legs, the end cross braces, and the top rails. Nail and glue the ½ in. plywood back and end panels to the 2x4 framing. Glue the two ¾ in. plywood panels for the top, back-to-back, using screws or clamps that are driven into the underside; clamp until glue sets. True the edges of the top, rounding the corners slightly with sandpaper or a block plane. Fasten the top of the bench framework with glue and wood screws. Countersink and plug the screw heads.

Now assemble the tool cabinet: nail and glue the side and end strips to the back panel. Drill holes for screwdrivers, chisels, and so forth. Drill the holes in the first shelf before fitting the vertical divider and shelving. Paint the understructure of the bench and the tool cabinet for protection and for easier cleaning. Fill nail holes and sand, prime the wood with enamel undercoat or resin sealer. Apply two finish coats. (Line art and instructions courtesy of Georgia-Pacific Corp.)

at least one 40-watt, 2-tube fluorescent light fixture over the workbench area or in the center of the room. If your budget permits, use three such fluorescent units in the shop area. These cost less to operate than incandescent units, and give an even, nonglaring light. You can, when your budget permits, use spotlights to increase the light output in special work areas.

Ventilation. The work area should be heated and well ventilated. Heating probably will not be a problem, but ventilation might be. If you cannot open a window or outside door for ventilation, you can install an exhaust fan in a window or through a duct installed in an outside wall. Exhaust the air outside, not into another adjoining room or the attic.

Flooring. At least paint the workshop floor. A painted floor is easier to keep clean than an unpainted floor. If you have the money to spend, tile the floor. Tile is even easier than paint to maintain, and it offers some comfort to your feet.

Safety for Kids. Install a workshop door that can be locked. This is a *must* if you have children in the house. Kids love tools; tools can be dangerous.

Ceilings. If you have adequate ceiling height, cover the ceiling with acoustical ceiling tile. The ceiling, from the top of the floor to the bottom of the tile, should be from 7½ to 8 ft. Any measurement less than 7½ ft. may not provide adequate head room with ceiling tile. The acoustical tile will absorb about 60% of the sound that strikes it. Batt or blanket insulation provides some — not a lot — sound conditioning.

Versatility. Don't plan the workshop just around home maintenance and repair jobs. As your tool skills improve, you may want to add woodworking, furniture repair and refinishing, metal working, wood turning, and mechanics to the basic workshop area. At that point you will also want to think about future expansion. You may not have a lot of space at this time, but ask yourself if the present available space could someday be expanded by removing a partition wall, moving a laundry area, or adding an addition to the room.

BASIC WORKSHOP FURNISHINGS
Your workshop should have a workbench, storage cabinet, lumber bin or storage rack, and a large scrap box for sawdust and general junk.

If your interest in home maintenance and woodworking is from necessity only, you can buy a prefabricated workbench for about $50. Assemble it according to the manufacturer's instructions. If you are a serious do-it-yourselfer, it is recommended that you build your own workbench. The bench can be simple, but tailor-made to your needs.

Workshop Shelving
You can create shelving using 1x10 or 1x12-inch boards, or buy either steel shelving that you bolt together or adjustable track shelving that you attach to the wall with toggle bolts (for hollow walls) or lead anchors (for masonry walls). We suggest the ready-made shelving simply because it is less costly in the long haul.

If you have children, or there will be children in the workshop, consider a metal locking cabinet for paints and thinners and sharp cutting tools such as razor knives and chisels.

Most lumber and sheet materials should be stored flat. This takes floor space, so you'll probably buy this material as the

work demands it. However, you may want to store short lengths of lumber up off the floor. Adjustable metal shelves are adequate for this; buy rugged steel shelving. A three or four strip unit will hold considerable weight, since most of the weight is "sheer" and the pressure will be on the shelving connectors.

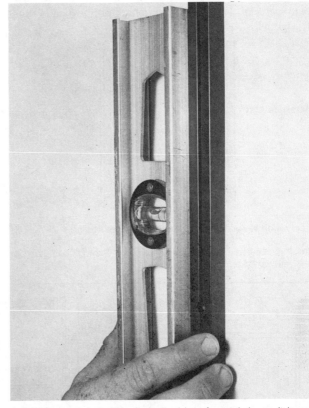

Adjustable metal shelving is a good buy for workshops; it is rugged enough to hold a fairly good load of materials. Plumb the brackets and hang them on studs with long wood screws. Do not use toggle bolts here.

Tool Display Boards
The tool display board can be fabricated from perforated hardboard or plywood, whichever you prefer. If you choose hardboard, use only tempered hardboard to deter moisture. The ¼-in. thick hardboard is best, since the hardboard tool hooks tend to seat better in the holes. If you decide on plywood, it should be at least ½-in. thick, A/C faces, and exterior grade — to block moisture. The hardboard or the plywood should be painted both sides, plus the edges, for moisture control and to help reflect light in the shop.

You can buy a wide range of hangers for almost any type of tool manufactured: hammers, chisels, screwdrivers, planes, saws, and so forth. Some people like to paint the shapes of the tools on the tool board so replacement of tools after use is quick and easy.

If you decide on perforated hardboard, buy anchoring clips for the hooks. These clips are tiny wirelike devices that snap over the hooks and into the hardboard perforations, keeping the hooks firmly attached to the hardboard surface. Regular metal clips for plywood are usually screwed to the surface of the plywood.

Installation. A plywood tool board may be applied directly to the studs, or to studs over gypsum wallboard, or to masonry walls with lead anchors and screws. A perforated hardboard tool board must be installed on furring strips for best results. The furring creates a ¾-in. space in back of the hardboard and the wall so that the tool hooks may be inserted freely into the perforations. You can attach the furring — 1x3 or 1x4 in. boards — to studs or over finished walls with Molly bolts and anchors. The strips may be fastened with lead anchors and screws to masonry. The sheet of hardboard or plywood is sim-

ply nailed or screwed to the furring strips in any position you want.

If you use toggle or Molly bolts, first bore the holes for the anchors in both the wall and in the furring strips or plywood. Then insert the fasteners through the furring or board to be hung, and into the hole. You should barely countersink the holes in the furring or plywood so the fasteners are below the surface of the board. This way, the screws will not interfere

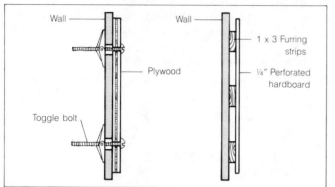

Hang a plywood toolboard directly to the wall after sealing the wood at sides and edges. Perforated toolboard has to go over furring, which also should be sealed against moisture damage. The toolboard can be any size you want it.

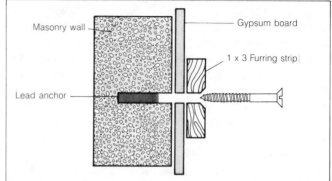

To fasten the toolboard to a masonry wall, drill holes with a masonry drill. Plug the hole with lead or fiber anchors. Then drive screws through the furring strips into the anchors. Fasten the toolboard to the furring strips.

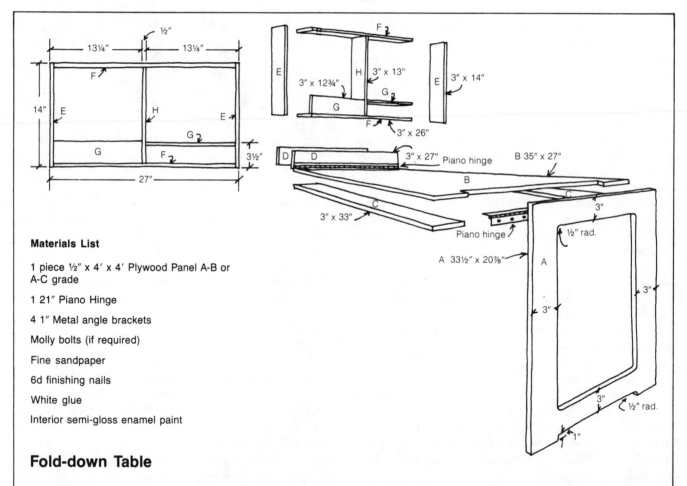

Materials List

1 piece ½" x 4' x 4' Plywood Panel A-B or A-C grade

1 21" Piano Hinge

4 1" Metal angle brackets

Molly bolts (if required)

Fine sandpaper

6d finishing nails

White glue

Interior semi-gloss enamel paint

Fold-down Table

Measure and cut all the necessary pieces from the plywood panel. Assemble cabinet pieces (E, F, G, H) using both glue and nails. Next, notch section B (the table top), so that the upright base (A) fits snugly into place. Then glue and nail the braces (C) into place. Now attach the table top to the support brace and the wall brace (D) using the piano hinges. To finish, attach the remaining wall brace (D) directly to the wall using molly bolts or by screwing directly into the studs. Attach the wall brace (D) on the table top to the now secure wall piece (D). To fold against wall, use hook-and-eye or friction catch. Finish as desired. (Line art and instructions courtesy of Georgia-Pacific Corporation.)

with the tool hangers or board. At this point there is enough flexibility to position the strips or plywood so that both will be level and plumb (vertical level) when the anchors are tightened with a screwdriver.

Future Workshop Planning

As you settle into new workshop space and build the basics, you shouldn't overlook other niceties that are fairly inexpensive, but which add to the smooth operation of any workshop area.

A shop vacuum. A canister-type specially made vacuum can save you countless hours of cleaning up sawdust and dirt.

Sawhorses. Lower than a workbench, sawhorses come in handy for all kinds of workshop operations — sawing, drilling, and even painting, staining, and finishing work.

You can build your own from scratch with 2x4 or 2x6 lumber. Or you can buy metal sawhorse brackets into which you insert 2x4s for the legs and cross-members of the horses. The big advantage of metal brackets is that the sawhorses fold shut, taking a minimum of workshop storage space. And you can fold them to transport to any job in a car or station wagon.

Stationary power tools. This equipment is very expensive. However, if you are a serious do-it-yourselfer, it probably won't be long until you buy a bench or table saw, drill press, radial arm saw, grinder, or jointer. The tops of many of these tools may be used as work tables and can help support heavy objects that overflow from the workbench. Keep these additional "benches" in mind when you figure the height of your main workbench or work table surface.

Casters. These rollers can be put onto stationary power tools and are a boon to small workshops. Equipped with casters, heavy tools may be stored out of the way against a wall, and then easily moved to the center of the shop when you have a large project underway and need table support.

HAND AND POWER TOOLS

Go into any good, well-merchandised hardware store or home center outlet and you will be impressed by the array of hand and power tools for sale. You don't need them all, but every homeowner or tenant does need several basic tools to handle occasional household breakdowns. Here is the basic list:

    13-ounce claw hammer
    8 or 12 point crosscut saw
    screwdriver set (Phillips and standard blade)
    adjustable wrench
    25-ft. tape measure
    pliers
    two C-clamps
    mill bastard file
    hand drill and assorted drills
Additional helpful tools include:
    ripsaw
    hacksaw with assorted blades
    coping saw and blades
    chisels
    block and jack plane
    brace and wood bit assortment
    tinsnips
    vise

    file assortment
    sharpening stone
    stapler

At this point, you'll probably start thinking power tools. It is strongly recommended that you buy just two power tools at the outset: a ¼- or ⅜-inch variable speed portable electric drill, and a variable speed portable electric jigsaw with a blade assortment. With just these two power tools you can handle nearly all home maintenance and repair jobs.

Later you will probably want to add to both your hand and power tool collection. When you do, your experience with the basic tools will enable you to choose the additional tools you need. You will find that you will be continually purchasing tools and equipment as projects dictate. For example, when a drain clogs, you will buy a plumber's snake to open the drain. When a copper pipe bursts or leaks, you will probably buy a propane torch outfit to "sweat" in a new length of pipe.

Hammers and Their Use

There should be three hammers in your life, purchased in this order: a 13-ounce claw hammer with a composition grip; a tack hammer that's magnetized on one end, and a rubber or plastic mallet.

A 13-ounce claw hammer is much easier to swing than its 16-ounce cousin — especially if you are not constantly involved in repair and remodeling projects or when you are pounding at something above your head. However, if you do a lot of hammering, buy a 16-ounce claw hammer in addition to the lighter one. The big tool will stand up to a lot of punishment and hard usage. A composition handle is better than a plain wooden handle because the composition handle is easier to grip, will not slip out of your hand as easily when your hand sweats, and can be used to tap paneling and finish boards into position without damaging their surfaces.

To drive tacks, use a tack hammer. It is lightweight so it won't bend brads and tacks when they are driven. If you buy a tack hammer with a magnetized end, you can use the magnetized end to start brads and tacks into the work.

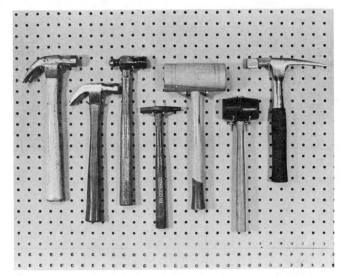

The ideal hammer collection includes 13 and 16 oz., claw hammers, ball-peen, tack, wooden mallet, rubber hammer, and masonry hammer. Your first buy should be claw hammer, then tack hammer and rubber or wooden mallet for chisels.

The faces of quality hammers are slightly crowned. You can feel this crown by rubbing your fingers over the face. Quality hammers also have a finished, machine appearance. Cheap hammers look like they have been stamped out of metal.

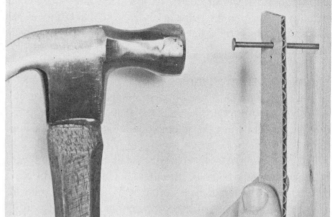

Start nail in tight quarters by first putting it through a piece of light cardboard. Hold the cardboard up, and drive the nail. Once it has been started, you can jerk the cardboard off the nail and continue pounding. Another method is to hold the nail in place with pliers.

A tack hammer with a magnetic feature lets you start small nails and tacks without mashing your fingers. After you start the nail, turn the hammer over and use the other hammer head to drive in the fastener.

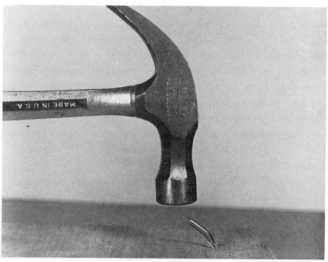

To clinch a nail, hit the very tip of the nail at an angle. Then bend it down and over so the point goes into the wood. For a real strong clinch job, alternate the directions of the nails as you sink them into the wood.

To get more leverage when you pull nails using a hammer, insert a wooden block or piece of scrap wood under the hammer handle. If the nail does not pull easily with the hammer, switch to a pry bar or regular nail puller.

"Toenailing" means driving a nail into the material at an angle. This technique is used most often in fastening studs to headers and sills, on rafters and joists to sill plates. Try to hit the nail as squarely as possible.

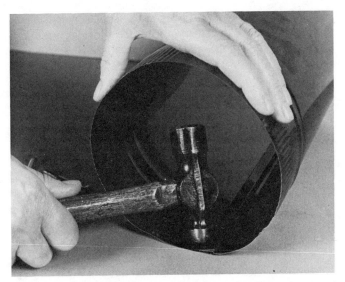

The rounded end of a ball-peen hammer is designed for metal work and for flattening rivets in metal and other materials. The hammer also may be used for striking metal, but use a baby sledge hammer to drive star drills or cold chisels.

To drive chisels, use a rubber, plastic, or wooden mallet, not a metal hammer. Chisels have wooden or plastic handles that can be easily damaged by a metal hammer. Rubber, plastic, and wooden hammer heads are softer and are purposely manufactured for driving chisels.

For metal projects, use a ballpeen hammer. This hammer has a rounded head on one end for peening over rivets and forming bends and creases in sheet metal such as aluminum.

For masonry projects, always use a masonry hammer or sledge hammer. Both of these hammers are especially made for working with concrete and stone. The heads are oversized and heavy. Some hammers have a pointed end for breaking brick and block; this end also may be used as a pry. You can, of course, use a regular claw hammer for masonry work. However, you can damage the face of the hammer by striking it against masonry.

Safety. When working with hammers, you should observe these safety rules.

(1) Do not use one hammer to strike another hammer that drives a nail, bolt, screw, star drill, or pry bar.

(2) When striking metal or masonry with a hammer, wear safety glasses.

(3) If the handle of a hammer is loose or damaged, to not use the hammer. The head can come flying off the damaged handle, hitting you or a nearby observer.

(4) Use the proper hammer for the job. Drive spikes with a claw hammer or baby sledge hammer; drive tacks with a tack hammer.

Maintenance. Hammers need little care. However, they can become rusty and the faces pitted. For rust, clean the metal with steel wool and machine oil. It's a smart idea to wipe the metal parts with an oily rag before you store the hammers.

If the face of a hammer becomes pitted from hard use or rust, try filing or grinding the face smooth again. If you can't do this, throw the hammer in the junk and buy a new one. You'll be safer.

Use. To start a nail in almost any material, choke up on the hammer handle toward the head of the hammer. Then, when the nail has been started into the material, move your hand down toward the end of the hammer handle. As you become more and more skilled with this tool, you'll find that you don't have to choke the handle as much; your pounding accuracy will have improved.

A hammer is swung mainly with the forearm and wrist. The forearm supplies most of the power while the wrist sort of "snaps" the hammer head as it engages the nail. This snap generates speed, which in turn produces more driving power. The lighter the hammer, the less arm action required. For example, a tack hammer is mostly wrist operated. You don't need heavy blows to drive a tack. You do need accuracy, which the short, wristy movement produces.

Realistically, you need not bother about the body action required to drive a nail. However, when you have lots of nails to drive — such as on a paneling or re-roofing job — the arm/wrist action will enable you to drive nails faster, easier, and straighter for longer periods of time without tiring.

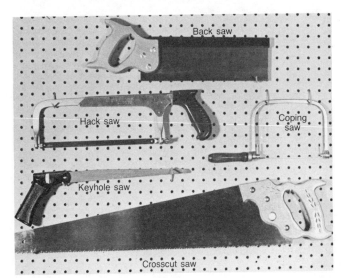

Your basic saw selection should include a backsaw for a miter box, hacksaw, coping saw, keyhole saw, and crosscut saw. You can use metal-working saws to cut wood, but don't use woodworking saws to cut metal.

Crosscut Saws and Their Use

A crosscut saw crosscuts — goes across the grain of the wood. Since the teeth of the saw are small and spaced fairly close together, a crosscut saw produces a smooth cut even when it is used for ripping wood. If your budget allows you to buy just one saw, buy a crosscut saw. You can use it effectively for most wood and light plastic sawing projects.

A crosscut saw has from 6 to 12 teeth per inch. The more teeth, the finer the cut. Each tooth is bent out from the saw blade in an alternating pattern: one tooth to one side, the adjoining tooth to the other side.

Maintenance. Crosscut saws should be racked up out of danger from other tools and materials that might smack and rub against the teeth. One way to protect the teeth is to split a length of garden hose and slip it over the teeth.

Pitch and tar from wood, hardened by the heat friction of the blade as it goes through wood, can cause the saw to bind. You can remove this crustlike debris with fine steel wool and mineral spirits. Do not use water.

To get the saw to slide easier, coat the blade often with paste wax or paraffin. If the wood you are cutting will be finished with paint, do not use light machine oil.

To remove surface rust from the blade, lightly rub the blade with fine steel wool dipped in machine oil. It's a good idea, too, to wipe the blade with an oily cloth after the saw has been used. This helps deter rust.

Most saws need an occasional sharpening. When your crosscut saw seems to be "chewing" the wood instead of slicing it, the saw probably needs sharpening. Sharpening is best left to a professional.

Use. Start the saw into the wood with a backward pull of the butt end of the saw along the cutoff line. Use the knuckle of your free hand to keep the saw blade on this line. This initial step will notch the wood to accept the saw blade.

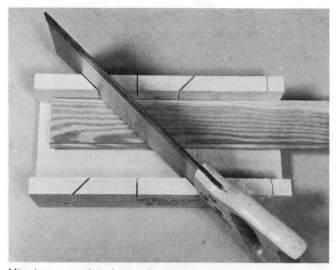

Miter boxes are slotted to cut these angles: 45-degree, as shown; 90-degree (center); reverse 45-degree (right), and 45-degree end angles (far right). Use a backsaw in a miter box. In a pinch, you can use a crosscut.

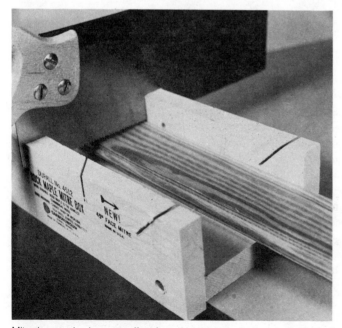

Miter boxes also have an offset face that rides against a bench top and keeps the box from sliding and slipping while you make the cut. Keep the material you are cutting pressed firmly against the back side of the box, as shown.

Hold the saw at about a 45-degree angle to the wood. Then, with an arclike rocking motion from the shoulder, push and pull the saw through the wood. Never try to force the saw into the wood. This might cause the saw blade to kink or buckle, and will at least cause the saw to bind and stick. Just let the weight of the saw make the cut; you supply the cutting power.

If you are cutting a long piece — such as across a piece of plywood — stick a 16d or 20d nail into the saw kerf as you make the cut. The nail will keep the saw kerf open so that the saw blade will not bind in the kerf.

The saw may wander off the cutting line. When it does, you can slightly twist the blade to bring the blade back on the cutoff line. But be careful. You don't want to cause the saw to bind in the kerf as you steer it back along the line.

Ripsaws and Their Use

Ripsaws do what their name implies: rip through wood *with* the grain. You can generate lots of speed with a ripsaw, because the chisel-like teeth are widely spaced, with 4 to 5½ teeth per inch. Like a crosscut saw, a ripsaw's teeth are alternately bent — one to one side of the blade, the adjoining tooth to the other side of the blade.

You can use a ripsaw to cut across the grain, although the finish cut will be rough and will have to be smoothed with a rasp, plane, or sandpaper, if smoothness is critical. Even cuts made with the grain are fairly rough.

Maintenance. Use the same procedures to keep a ripsaw in good working order as you would use for a crosscut saw.

Use. Start the cut by notching the wood with the tip of the saw. Use the thumb knuckle of your free hand as a guide. Push and pull the ripsaw through the material with a rocking arc from your shoulder, letting the weight of the saw make the cut. Do not force the saw into the material, which could make it bind. If the saw wanders off the cutoff line, stop sawing. Then reposition the saw back where it started drifting. The saw cuts so fast that it is almost impossible to twist the saw back onto the cutoff line without causing it to become out-of-square in the saw kerf.

When ripsawing long lengths of material, check the sawblade in the saw kerf often to make sure that you are keeping the saw square to the material. Use a try square or small combination square for this, letting the blade of the square rest against the blade of the saw and the tongue of the square rest against the material.

Ripsaws are basically wood saws. The teeth are so widely spaced on a ripsaw that the ripsaw usually is impractical for cutting aluminum or plastic. Use a hacksaw or crosscut saw to cut the softer metals.

Hacksaws and Their Use

Metal — and some plastics — should be cut with a hacksaw. Since metal has varying degrees of hardness, you can buy a variety of hacksaw blades to match the metal you need to cut with a hacksaw.

Teeth in a hacksaw blade are spaced from 18 to 32 points per inch. The more teeth, the smoother the cut. As a rule of thumb, use less teeth per inch for tough metals, and more teeth per inch for soft metals.

Maintenance. Although hacksaws are rugged, you still have

to baby them somewhat. Hang them away from other tools that can damage the blades. If a blade becomes damaged, it is best to replace the blade than attempt to repair it or sharpen it. Blades are fairly inexpensive to buy; a variety of sizes are sold.

Remove any surface rust from the hacksaw frame with fine steel wool dipped in machine oil. Also, wipe the frame with an oily cloth before you store the hacksaw. If the wooden hacksaw handle is damaged, you can buy a replacement handle at most hardware and home center stores.

Use. Hacksaws cut on the *forward* stroke only. Use the thumb knuckle of your free hand to start the saw on the cutoff line, lightly pushing the saw forward.

Hacksaw blades are under tension that you apply to the blade with a thumbscrew on the hacksaw frame. Hand tighten this thumbscrew. Then give the thumbscrew one quarter turn — no more — with pliers. This is enough tension. Too much tension will snap the blade. Too little tension will cause the blade to buckle, kink, and break.

When changing blades, loosen the thumbscrew, which in turn loosens the metal pins that hold the blade in position. Lift the blade off the pins and insert a new blade. Check that the teeth on the blade point forward.

A hacksaw is "stroked" across the material with a full arm arc motion. Since you want to keep as many teeth on the metal as possible for fast cutting, you do not want to "rock" the saw as you would a ripsaw or crosscut saw. Take small strokes, applying even pressure to the front and back of the saw frame with both hands. Press downward lightly on the forward stoke; lift up the sawblade slightly — or release the pressure — on the backstroke.

Coping Saws and Their Use

A coping saw by another name could be "fret" saw, "scroll" saw, "deep-throat" saw, and "hand jigsaw." Regardless of the name, the saws are designed to make very intricate and delicate cuts in wood, in some plastics and in light metals. Two pins, on which the coping saw blade is mounted, may be twisted in unison so that the blade can cut out curves and other ornamental features.

Coping saw blades have from 10 to 20 teeth per inch. The more teeth, the finer the cut. The blades may be flat, like a hacksaw blade, or round. The round blades are tagged "spiral" or "rounds."

The depth of the "throat" of the coping saw frame, which varies from about 4 in. to 12 in., determines how deep a cut can be made with the saw blade. A 6 in. frame is standard.

Maintenance. Rust is a problem with coping saws. Remove any light rust with fine steel wool dipped in machine oil. After each use and before storage, wipe the frame with an oily cloth. You can buy replacement handles if the handle becomes worn or broken.

Use. By reversing the blade, a coping saw can cut on the forward stroke or the backward stroke. If the work is held in a vise, the forward cutting stroke is best. If the work is delicate, mount the blade in the frame so it cuts on the backward stroke. You get more accuracy by pulling the saw toward you. To make some inside cuts, bore a small hole in the material; remove the blade from the saw frame and insert the blade into the hole. Reattach the blade to the frame.

Hacksaws are used for metal-working and cut on the forward stroke only. In a pinch, you can use a hacksaw to cut wood. The blade is especially suited to thin plastics, electrical conduit, thin sheet metals.

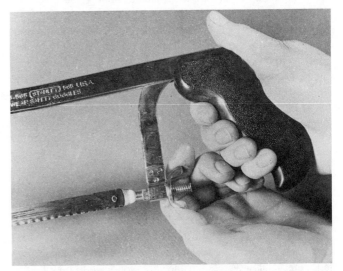

To change a worn or damaged hacksaw blade, loosen the thumbscrew at the back of the frame. This loosens a sliding pin so the blade can be removed. A drop or two of machine oil on the metal helps the saw cut faster.

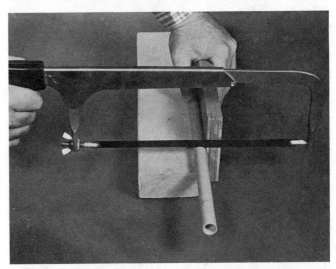

A wooden bench jig like this one is easy to fabricate from scrap materials. The jig holds round materials while you cut them. Offset the back of the jig slightly with the bottom piece to help guide the saw blade.

Use short cutting strokes since the saw blade is short. Apply some light downward pressure to the saw on the handle of the saw, and the same pressure to the front of the saw frame with your other hand.

Apply tension to the saw blade by twisting the handle onto a screw arrangement. Just turn the handle hand tight. Too much tension will snap the blade; too little tension will cause the blade to kink, buckle, and break. When a blade becomes encrusted with wood sap, dull, or breaks, replace the blade. It is less expensive than fixing or sharpening it.

Keyhole Saws and Their Use

Keyhole saws probably get their name because you have to drill a tiny hole in the work to insert the saw before it can be used. Inside cuts are easy with a keyhole saw. The tool can also be used for straight saw cuts, but only if a crosscut or ripsaw isn't handy. If you have a lot of sawing to do, don't use a keyhole saw.

Many keyhole saws have replaceable blades; you can remove the screws in the wooden handle holding the blade in position. Sawblades have from 8 to 10 teeth per inch. You buy blades for wood (usually standard on most keyhole saws), metal, or plastic, if the handle has an interchangable blade feature.

Maintenance. Keep the saw blade free from wood pitch using steel wool and mineral spirits. You can remove light rust with steel wool and machine oil. If handles or blades become damaged or worn, they can be replaced. From time to time, tighten the screws in the handle to prevent the sawblade from working loose.

Use. Start the saw on a vertical angle, using short strokes and your free hand to guide the blade along the cutoff line. As the saw kerf increases in depth, tip the saw downward at about a 45-degree angle to the work.

Depending on the width of the blade, you can saw out wide curves and circles with a keyhole saw by simply twisting the blade lightly. However, for inside cuts, you have to bore holes at opposite corners of the work and make straight cuts. Go halfway around the square or rectangle; remove the saw and insert it in the other hole; complete the cut. Keep the saw kerf toward the inside of the scrap piece. You will have to smooth the cut.

Screwdrivers and Their Use

Although there are many types and sizes, screwdrivers do just one job: drive and draw screws. Resist temptation to use them for paint paddles, backscratchers, icepicks, hole punches, and fingernail files.

The two basic screwdriver types are standard blade and Phillips head. You will need both.

Screwdrivers are manufactured with wooden handles, metal handles, and plastic handles. They have long blades, short blades, and offset blades for use in tight quarters. Some models even have attachments that convert them into socket wrenches.

A rule of thumb: the longer the screwdriver blade and the larger the handle, the more torque or twisting power you can apply to the screwdriver. Also, always fit the blade of the driver to the slot of the screw. Do not use over- or undersized blades, or the wrong blade in the wrong screw head; i.e., a standard

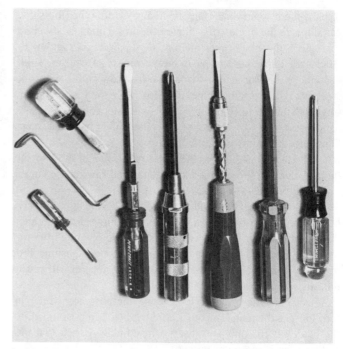

An ideal screwdriver selection includes (from rt.) Phillips head, standard blade; spiral ratchet; changeable blade; screw holding; stubby standard; offset; and small standard blade. The basic buy is Phillips and standard.

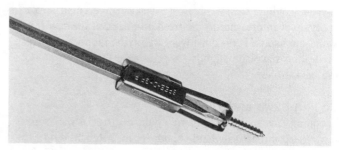

This screw-holding device on a standard screwdriver clamps the screw between two thin metal jaws. After the screw has been started, the screwdriver handle is flipped slightly to disengage the holder. The holder slides on the shank.

blade in a Phillips head or cross-head screw. If the blade is too big or small for the screw slot, you can damage the slot so the screw can't be either driven or drawn. If the blade is too wide, and it sticks out around the screw slot, the blade can damage the material surrounding the screw.

Safety. Do not strike screwdrivers with hammers or mallets. The blows can damage, even ruin, the screwdriver handle. Never use a screwdriver to probe around electrical connections such as junction boxes, light sockets, and outlets. Wooden and plastic handles are no guarantee against electrical shock.

When driving or drawing a screw, keep your free hand away from the tip of the screwdriver. The screwdriver blade could jump the slot and injure your hand.

Maintenance. Keep the metal blades rustfree with an occasional rubbing with steel wool and machine oil. Standard blade screwdrivers, after years of use, will wear and become rounded at the tip. Sometimes you can grind the tip square again — across the tip and up the sides of the blade. Use a file or a grinder for this. If the result is not satisfactory, toss the tool in the junk. The replacement will be less costly than damaged material or injury to your hands.

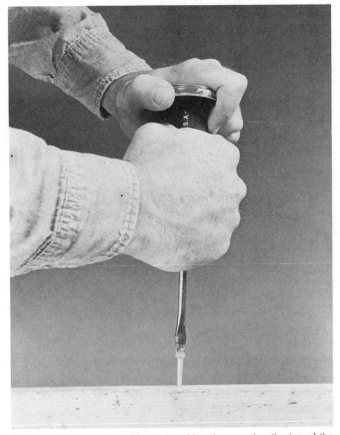

Get more driving power with a screwdriver by covering the top of the handle with a jar lid. The lid provides more "bearing" surface for your hand. For more leverage, use a screwdriver with a long shank or shaft.

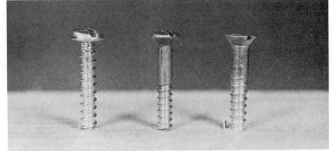

The difference in screw heads (from left): roundhead, ovalhead, and flat head. You can buy special washers for all three types of screws — flat, countersunk, and flush. Threads run about ⅔ of length or full length.

Use. The screwdriver turning force comes from your forearm, wrist, palm of your hand, and fingers. To drive a screw, you have to apply pressure with your hand to the handle of the screwdriver. To draw a screw, you have to apply light pressure with your fingers to the base or ferrule of the handle.

One of the biggest problems you will have with a screwdriver is drawing rusted screws.

STEPS, DRAWING RUSTED SCREWS

1. Coat the rusted screw with a rust penetrating oil such as WD-40. Give the solution time to work — 5 minutes or so. Don't begin right away.

2. Try drawing the screw. If it won't back out very far because the screw slot is damaged, recut the slot with a hacksaw blade once the screw is just a little distance out of the screw hole.

3. If the screw head breaks off, check whether the shank of the screw is above the surrounding material. If so, clamp locking pliers onto the shank and back out the screw. If you can't back out the screw, try using a screw extractor. This device is similar to a drill; it bores into the screw, then reverses to draw the screw.

Predrilling. To prevent splitting wood, screw holes should be predrilled or punched. Use a regular drill for this, or use a bradawl or nail if the screws are small. Also punch or drill holes in metal for metal screws. Pilot holes make driving a metal screw much easier.

Countersinking. If you want the screw to be flush with the surrounding surface of the material, you should first drill a pilot hole for the screw with a drill, and then countersink the hole with a wood countersink locked in the chuck of a hand brace or power drill.

To hide a screw in material, predrill a pilot hole for the screw head. The hole should be deep enough to support a wooden plug, which will hide the screw. Then, with a smaller drill, run the hole deeper into the wood for the screw threads. The plug hole should be the size of the screw head; the thread hole should be the size of the shank of the screw — the unthreaded part near the head.

Pliers and Their Use

Pliers, along with vises and clamps, squeeze materials and hold and twist them into the shapes you want. Pliers are extensions of your fingers, but in metal form. You will find a variety of them for sale in all different sizes and shapes. But at first you need only three models, all of which are inexpensive: locking pliers; slipjoint pliers; needlenose pliers with a small wire-cutter feature. Get the needlenose pliers with insulated handles so you can use them for electrical repairs.

Maintenance. Pliers require little or no maintenance. Keep the metal rustfree by wiping the metal occasionally with an oily cloth. If rust does appear, remove it with fine steel wool dipped in light machine oil.

If the pivot pin on pliers — the little bolt or rivet that holds the handles together — becomes loose or damaged, you may be able to tighten it with pliers. If not, toss the damaged tool in the garbage for safety's sake.

Use. Squeeze the handles together, and pliers become strong

Locking pliers can be used for lots of projects, including clamping materials while adhesive dries. The screw on the end of the handle adjusts the opening of the jaws; the opposite double handle unlocks the jaws.

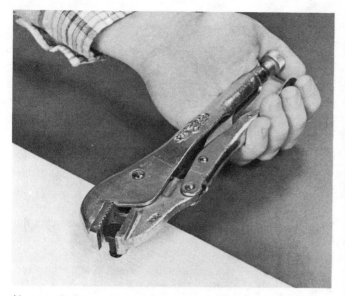

Always pull pliers and wrenches toward yourself, when possible. And always pull with the palm of your hand. If the work or tool slips you won't bark your knuckles against a nearby surface.

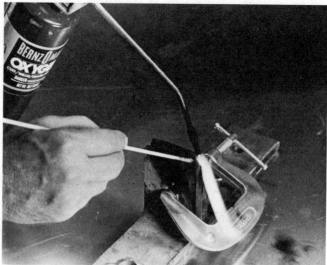

C-clamps are extremely useful tools for holding almost any material in any position. You can buy a wide variety of clamps in wood and metal and even cloth; most clamps are very inexpensive.

enough to crush metal. When using pliers, take it easy! Too much pressure can ruin expensive materials.

If you are using pliers to twist an object — continually in a series of open/close movements — hold the pliers so your ring finger operates the handle. And, when you're working with slipjoint pliers, be sure the slipjoint is engaged before applying pressure to the handles. Otherwise you may damage the pivot pin.

Vises and Their Use

Your best investment in a vise is a combination woodworking and metal vise. It attaches to a workbench or table top with a screw-type clamp. It may be removed quickly and easily so you can take it to another job location. You also can buy vises for just woodworking or metal working. Special pipe vises are available, too. A combination vise has removable jaw inserts that can be interchanged. Some combination types have pipe jaws, which ride along the threaded screw that activates the regular jaws when you turn the vise handle. This is an inexpensive but worthwhile aid for plumbing repair jobs.

Maintenance. Check from time to time to be sure the clamp, or bolts, that holds the vise to the bench top is tight. Keep the threaded screw that activates the jaws lightly lubricated. Graphite powder is best. The serrated jaws of a metal vise — or the jaw inserts — can become clogged with residue from wood and metal. Clean these little serrations with a wire brush.

Use. Operation of a vise is extremely simple. You simply position the wood or metal between the jaws of the vise and turn the handle to close (or open) the jaws. But be careful not to apply too much pressure to the handle. It is very easy to crush wood or metal between the vise jaws.

If you are working with delicate materials, or don't want to mar the surface of the material, pad the jaws of the vise with scrap wood metal, or pieces of cardboard.

Smooth-jawed vises are designed for woodworking. Serrated-jawed vises are for metal working. You may use either type for either job, but you should pad the serrated jaws for woodworking projects.

Clamps and Their Use

Clamps are basically designed for clamping glue jobs until the glue hardens, but they may be substituted as "holding" devices for almost anything. The workhorse is the C-clamp, which is available in a wide range of sizes, including the clamp opening and depth of throat. Bar clamps, which utilize metal bars or galvanized steel water pipe for length, are a must tool for woodworking. Spring clamps, which look like large metal clothespins, are ideal for furniture repairs and for gluing veneer to base or solid wood.

Maintenance. As with anything metal, rust is the big maintenance problem. Remove rust with steel wool and machine oil. If the clamp is aluminum, rust will not be a problem.

Use. Clamping action is activated by a turnscrew. The work is sandwiched between this screw and the clamp. As with a vise, you can generate lots of pressure from the turnscrew, so don't be heavyhanded.

To protect the work, pad the "jaws" of the clamp with scrap wood, cardboard, metal. These pads also help distribute the pressure from the clamp to the work. The actual bearing points of a clamp are small, so pads may be important for additional and even pressure.

Planes, Smoothing Tools and Their Use

With a sharp plane you can cut long thin ribbons of wood and make rough edges smooth, boards fit together snugly, doors open and close smoothly. You can buy a variety of them: block planes, jack planes, smoothing planes, rabbet planes, spokeshaves, cabinetmaker's planes, low-angle block planes. However, you need only two planes for most home repair jobs — a jack plane and a block plane — in that order.

Maintenance. Planes have a shaving action and cut like a jackknife. Therefore, the plane blade must be kept sharp. A dull blade can ruin expensive material, and is dangerous. Before each planing job, remove the plane blade and stroke the edge of the blade a couple of times on a whetstone. The whetstone will remove any metal burrs and renew the edge.

Keep blade-adjusting screws, blade assemblies and blades clean by wiping them occasionally with an oily cloth, or use a brush. Remove any surface rust with fine steel wool and machine oil. Beds (bottoms) of planes often become encrusted with wood pitch and tar. Remove this with fine steel wool and mineral spirits.

Always retract a plane blade, using the thumb-adjusting screw, when the plane is not in use (the blade is retracted by turning the thumbscrew). When working with a plane, never set the plane down on its bed or bottom. Instead, lay the plane on its side. This protects the blade and keeps it sharp. If the blade becomes nicked or pitted from use, you often can grind it smooth again. If not, you can buy replacement blades, which are fairly inexpensive.

Use, Jack Plane. Push the plane across the work at a slight angle to produce a slicing or shaving action. As you push the plane into the wood, apply downward pressure to the bed of the plane with both hands.

The pressure should be mainly on the front of the plane as the blade bites into whatever is being planed. During the stroke, the pressure should be distributed from the front of the plane back to the handle of the plane. As you complete the stroke, the pressure should shift toward the back or handle of the plane.

You need not apply a lot of pushing pressure on a plane to shave or cut wood. If you have to apply lots of push, the plane blade probably needs to be sharpened or squared with the bed of the plane. If the plane "chatters" as you stroke it across the work, the plane blade is dull or you are not applying even, equal pressure to the bed of the plane.

Always keep the blade of the plane parallel to the bed of the plane. Sight down the plane bed to determine this, like you would sight a rifle. If the blade is sticking out the bed at an angle, use the blade adjustment lever near the handle to straighten the blade. The thumbscrew that raises and lowers the blade is located near the handle of the plane. When in use, the blade should project about $\frac{1}{16}$-in., from the bed of the plane. However, this depth may be too much or too little; it is the average. The best way to determine the correct plane blade depth is to make an adjustment and then try the plane on a scrap piece of material. If the blade is set too deep, the material will come off in chunks and the plane will tend to stick in and

Keep plane blades square with the bed (bottom) of the plane. You can adjust the depth of the blade with a thumbscrew; adjust the angle of the blade with a lever. Both are located under the back handle of the plane.

chatter along the material. If the blade is set too shallow, the plane probably will not cut at all. Or the shavings will be tissue paper thin and sawdusty, instead of in tight ribbons.

Use, Block Plane. The primary purpose of this plane is to cut end grain. It also is made for delicate planing jobs where accuracy of cut is more important than removing material quickly. To use this tool, keep most of the pressure on the front of the plane bed and over the plane blade assembly. The blade must be square to the bottom of the bed; the depth of cut may be determined on scrap material.

The major point to know about planes is this: planes are made to *smooth* and *square* material. You first cut the material to approximate size and shape, then use a plane to finish the job.

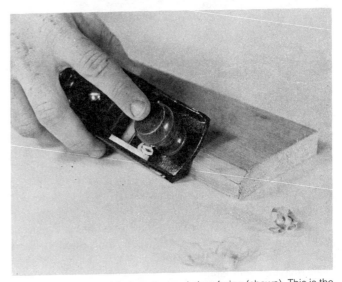
Block planes are used for beveling and chamfering (shown). This is the basic woodworking plane; for general use, buy a jack or block plane. Do not substitute a smoothing tool for a plane.

Multi-Blade Plane. A fairly new addition (and an inexpensive one) to the plane family is a multi-bladed forming tool, which is handled in the same way as a regular plane. The forming tool has a series of cross-hatched cutting edges along a blade that is attached to a handle. It looks something like a coarse file. You can buy these blades in flat, convex, and concave shapes to cut wood, plastic, and metal. The tools, however, should be used in addition to a jack and block plane, not as a substitute.

Chisels and Their Use

Wood and metal chisels are first cousins to planes. You can whittle, cut, smooth, and trim wood, metal, and plastic with them. And you can buy chisels to score and break stone, bricks, and concrete blocks.

A chisel set is a great bargain for most home repair chores. Most sets include four sizes of chisels: ¼-, ½-, ¾-, and 1-in., chisel widths. You can also buy wider and narrower chisels, along with cold and brick chisels for metal and masonry when the project calls for these specialty tools.

Maintenance. Chisels are knives. Therefore they must be kept sharp, with an occasional whetting on an oil- or whetstone. Or sharpen them by grinding, then whetting — especially if cutting edges become nicked. For surface rust, use

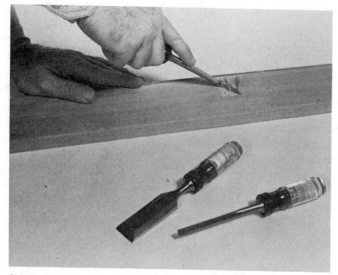

Chisels can do lots of jobs, but they cut mortises best. Keep your chisels razor sharp. For metal and masonry, use cold chisels and brick chisels. Never use a wood chisel for anything but wood.

Razor knives are good substitutes for chisels, and you need not be as careful with them as with chisels. Extra razor blades are stored in the handle, the halves of which are held together with a set screw.

fine steel wool and machine oil to restore the shine to the metal parts.

Never store chisels in a drawer or tool box unless the blades are protected. The best storage spot for a chisel is a tool board. Also, never strike a chisel with a metal hammer; use a rubber or wooden mallet, or the butt of your hand.

If a chisel handle becomes damaged, you may be able to buy a replacement handle to fit, especially if the handle is wooden.

Use. Chisels cut with the grain of the wood, never against it. Let the chisel slide into the material at a slight angle — like a plane — so that the chisel produces a "shearing" cut. You want shavings, not chunks.

Keep the chisel cuts shallow. Too much of a bite will split the wood. You supply the cutting power with one hand on the handle and the downward pressure with the fingers of your other hand on the blade of the chisel. The flat side of the chisel always goes downward, with the angled cutting edge of the chisel pointing upward.

To make mortise cuts (recesses) in wood (as for hinges), first outline the cut you want to make with a pencil or bradawl. Then with the chisel square to the outline, tap the chisel downward to about the depth of the cut you want. It should be short of the mark, not beyond it. Repeat this cut around the outline, overlapping each of the chisel cuts. Use a rubber hammer or wooden mallet to drive the chisel; slapping the chisel with the palm of your hand can hurt after a few blows.

Make a series of chisel cuts within the boundary of the outline. You should space these cuts about ⅛-in. apart. But be careful as you make these cuts; do not go beyond the depth cut should be.

Now clean out the mortise by holding the chisel flat to the work and shaving out the excess material. Use a narrow chisel for accuracy; use a wide chisel for removing lots of material.

Sometimes you may not be able to hold the chisel so that the bevel on the blade faces up. If so, hold the chisel so the flat side is up at about a.20 degree angle.

When working with chisels, check your work very often for depth of cut and squareness. Chisels cut fast. You can go beyond the point of accuracy before you realize it.

Files, Rasps and Their Use

These metal tools are similar to planes and chisels. Their contribution is to smooth wood, plastic, and metal; but usually after the material has been sawed, planed, or chiseled.

Some files have single rows of teeth. They are called single-cut files. Other files have two rows of teeth — one row crisscrossing the other row. They are called double-cut files. There are four basic types: (1) bastard, is used for rough cuts; (2) smooth-cut, for smoothing material after you use the bastard file — or initially on fairly rough material that doesn't require a bastard file; (3) finish, for final smoothing; and (4) rasp, for wood only. Although it looks like a file, with very coarse and widely set teeth, it really isn't a file as such, hence "rasp."

Your basic home repair kit should have an 8- or 12-in. smooth-cut file and a wood rasp. You can buy "shoe" rasps that have a combination of teeth — usually four types — two types to each side of the file. Or, you can buy rasps with two different sets of teeth — one set on one side, one set on the other side.

Maintenance. Keep files and rasps stored out of the way of other tools, which can damage the teeth of the files.

If the teeth become clogged with debris, clean the teeth with a file "card." The card is like a flat brush except that the bristles are metal instead of animal hair, or are manmade. File cards are inexpensive.

Use. Files cut on the forward stroke. Lift them off the work on the return stroke. Do not drag the file along the work in any direction. As you make the stroke, push the file across the work at a slight angle. This engages the teeth so they cut against the work. Keep the file square; do not tilt the ends up and down.

Downward pressure is applied to the work with both hands — one on the handle and one on the end of the file. Use about medium pressure. You will get the feel of correct pressure after several practice strokes. The idea is to apply even, equal pressure with both hands — pushing the file away from you on the forward stroke, then lifting the file up off the work and returning it toward you.

Abrasives and Their Use

Better known as "sandpaper," abrasives are cutting and smoothing tools, as are planes, chisels, and files. They remove a fair amount of material in first cuts, and smooth the work in final cuts.

As a benchmark, you need "open coat" abrasives for materials that are gummy (paint, sappy wood) and "closed coat" abrasives for fast cutting or smoothing on any material including metal and glass.

You can buy a wide variety of abrasive papers: emery paper for metal; aluminum oxide for wood and metal; garnet for wood; silicon carbide for glass; flint for gummy materials. Each type is clearly stamped on the back of the abrasive along with the abrasive qualities and grits.

Very fine abrasive is numbered from 220 (6/0) to 600. Fine abrasive runs from 180 (5/0) to 120 (3/0). Medium is 100 (2/0) to 60 (1/2). Coarse is from 50 (1) to 36 (2). Very coarse is 20 (3-1/2) to 12 (4-1/2). The higher the number, the finer the abrasive.

Abrasive paper also is graded. "A" is lightweight; "D" is heavy paper — usually sold for machine sanding. Cloth backing is noted as "J" for light and "X" for heavy. And some abrasives are termed "wet" or "dry." This simply means you can soak them in water or machine oil or you can use them without this liquid. Water and oil do supply some cutting advantages.

The best, all-around abrasive is aluminum oxide. It is fairly expensive, but it lasts a long time. The best paper for removing paint is flint abrasive. It is very inexpensive.

Steel wool also is considered an abrasive. It is usually sold in boxes or tubes marked "coarse," "medium," and "fine." You can buy special oil-free steel wool for furniture finishing.

Use. Use abrasive paper over a sanding block if at all possible. The block can be a scrap piece of wood or, if you want to be fancy, you can buy sanding blocks that are rubber or padded steel plate with handles. A sanding block keeps the abrasive square on the surface of the material you are sanding. This helps prevent dips and digs into the material and keeps sharp, square edges.

Some jobs will come along for which you cannot use a sanding block. In these cases, be careful. Abrasives cut fast and you should check the work often to make sure you are getting the results you want.

Pumice is an abrasive in powder form that is generally used in furniture refinishing. In appearance, pumice looks like fine sugar, but it cuts like the best of the sheet abrasives. Pumice usually is combined with linseed oil to make a paste that is applied with a soft cloth.

Hole-boring Tools and Their Use

To make a hole, you will need a brace/bit or a power drill with a drill. Bits are for wood; drills are for metal and wood. Initially, a ratchet hand brace and an assortment of bits is sufficient. If you will be working with metal, invest in a power drill and assortment of drills.

A hand brace is a crank that turns a bit which bores a hole. Hand braces are moderately priced, but be sure to buy one that has these features: an automatic chuck that perfectly centers bits and accepts square and round bits and drills; a ratchet to

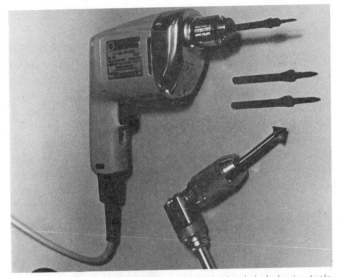

Portable electric drills and hand braces are the basic hole-boring tools. Shown with them are bits that drill pilot holes and countersink the pilot holes in one operation, and a countersink bit for wood and metal.

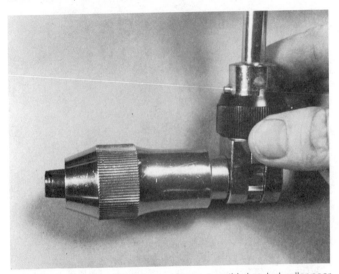

To set the turning direction of a hand brace, turn this knurled collar near the chuck of the brace. The setting also includes a ratchet. The jaws of a good hand brace automatically center the bits in the chuck.

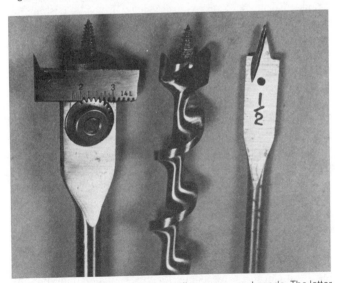

Types of bits (from left) include expanding, auger, and spade. The latter is used in electric drills. Twist drills may be used in power drills or hand braces; some twist drills have special shanks for chucks of braces.

reverse the cranking direction; handles with smooth-turning ball-bearings.

You also can buy a crank drill that accepts twist drills but usually not auger bits. This tool has a gear-type wheel activated with a handle.

Auger bits look like corkscrews. They are sized by numbers: 4 to 18. Each number represents 1/16 in. difference. You can buy different lengths of auger bits, ranging from 6 to 18 in. long. Longer bits, called "electrician's" bits, are available.

Expanding bits are expensive. They are made for hand braces and have an adjustable feature for large to very large holes. Beyond the large size — usually 3 in. — you will have to graduate to a hole saw, which is powered by an electric drill or drill press, or a keyhole or coping saw.

To change the cutting size of an expanding bit, you turn a screw. Note the cutting edge (right). Expanding bits can be expanded up to 3 in. Any hole larger than this has to be cut with a hole saw.

Drill bits, or twist drills, are for metal or wood — mostly metal. They usually have a round shank and can be locked in a combination chuck of a hand brace or the chuck of a power or "Yankee" drill. A "Yankee" drill is hand driven by pushing up and down on the handle. It looks like a big screwdriver; the handle contains the little drills inside.

In addition to bits and drills, invest in a countersink. You will need this specialty bit for countersinking (recessing) holes in wood so screws can be driven flush — or slightly below — the surrounding surface of the wood or other soft material. Other useful items are: a screwdriver bit, which can be used in a hand brace to drive and draw screws faster than with a screwdriver; masonry drills for concrete, brick, and stone. All these drills are best used in a power drill, because they need speed.

Star drills are for masonry, and they are the hand-driven counterparts of power-driven masonry drills. You drive star drills, which are available in assorted sizes and lengths, with a baby sledge hammer.

Maintenance. Bits and drills have sharp cutting edges; protect them during storage and give them an occasional sharpening. You can use a whetstone for this — maintaining the angles of the cutting edges — or a single-cut file or grinding wheel, if the cutters become nicked.

Rust is also a problem. Keep the metal lightly coated with machine oil after using the tools. You can remove surface rust with fine steel wool and machine oil.

If crank handles become worn or broken, you may be able to buy replacement parts. Some braces have an interchangeable feature; the cheap braces usually do not.

Use. One hand applies the pressure downward from the brace to the bit, while the other hand turns the crank that forces the bit into the wood or metal or plastic. The harder you push downward, the harder it is to turn the crank. So use moderate pressure and turn the crank slowly for best results.

If you need lots of push against the brace, press the top handle against your belt and lean your body into the brace. This way, you can have both hands free to turn the crank. Again, do not overdo the pressure. You can bend the bit, damage expensive material, and hurt yourself.

To reverse the direction of the crank, you turn a knurled knob located at the base of the chuck. You also can set the crank on "ratchet," which lets you use the brace next to objects where the crank cannot make a full, 360-degree turn. When the setting is on "ratchet," the crank "clicks" as it turns.

To operate a "Yankee" drill, simply match the drill to the spot where you want the hole and push up and down on the drill. The drill shaft works off a spiral thread.

To operate a crank drill, position the drill on the work and turn the crank at medium speed. Too little speed will chew the wood, too much speed will throw the drill out of alignment or out of square.

Taps, Dies and Their Use

To cut pipe threads, as for steel pipe repairs, a tap and die set is the equipment you need. This tool is really not necessary unless you are deeply involved in hobby work or have galvanized steel pipe to thread.

Taps and dies come in assorted sizes. The big sizes — those used for threading plumbing pipes — can be rented at "Rent-All" outlets, if you don't want to invest in the tools. Taps are for cutting the inside threads. Dies are for cutting the outside threads.

Use. To cut inside threads with taps, first drill a hole in the material one size smaller than the size of the tap. The taps are usually numbered to correspond with screw sizes. Twist the tap into the hole with a special tap wrench. Keep the hole lubricated with oil while you twist in the tap to make cutting easier.

There are three types of taps: taper, plug, and bottom. The tapered tap has the first few rows of threads tapered so the tap goes easily into the hole. A plug tap has about four threads tapered. A bottom tap is not tapered; it is used to cut threads right to the bottom of a predrilled hole — not through the hole as the other two tap types are designed to do.

You can buy three types of dies for outside threads: adjustable, solid, hexagonal. The dies are held by a die stock, which is a wrenchlike device with two handles.

You should bevel the edges of the rod or pipe to be threaded with a file before you start the die. Keep the die and metal lubricated as you cut the threads.

You will need a metal vise when you cut inside or outside threads to hold the work solidly. Pipe vises are available for rent, if you don't want to buy one.

Snips, Scissors and Their Use

Home maintenance projects can involve lots of metal working — mainly on ducts, vents, and metal roof flashing. None of this metal is very thick, which means that it can be cut to shape with tinsnips or, for thin aluminum sheet, heavy scissors. Snips and scissors also may be used for cutting carpeting, stair treads, sheet flooring, floor tile.

Maintenance. To keep snips and scissors sharp use a whetstone or a smoothing file, but for "touch-ups" only. Rust can also be a problem. Light rust may be removed with fine steel wool dipped in machine oil.

Use. Always scribe cut-off lines on materials before you make the cuts with tinsnips or scissors. Both tools have a habit of "wandering" during cutting; a cut-off mark helps you keep the tools on line.

In preformed duct work, and for some guttering, you will have to cut the metal with a hacksaw before you can use snips. Or predrill a pilot hole for the snips.

Measuring, Leveling Tools and Their Use

You will need a spirit level, rule, and square for almost any home repair or carpentry job. Don't skimp; buy quality tools. If the project is mismeasured, not level or plumb and not square, you will have wasted your time and a lot of your money.

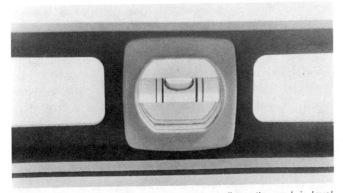

When the bubble in a level is between these lines, the work is level. Some levels have vials that turn for angle work. A 3-bubble level is your best investment; the frame can be wood or metal (metal is shown).

When the bubble in a level is between these lines, the work is plumb. Plumb is vertical level. You also can obtain horizontal and vertical level on flat surfaces such as walls; the level need not ride an edge.

Levels are sold in a wide range of lengths, from a small 2 in. up to 6 ft., and more. The frame may be wood or metal; the metal models usually are extruded aluminum and are lightweight. The vials inside that show level or plumb (vertical level) are generally plastic. The liquid in the vials is alcohol with a built-in bubble.

It is recommended that you buy a 3-vial level that is 3 ft. long. When your tool skills improve and your projects become more complicated, you probably will want to invest in another level. Even so, your first-bought level will be used a lifetime.

Rules are wooden, and they usually fold into 6-inch-long units. Tapes are thin strips of steel that roll into a metal housing automatically. Since they are fairly inexpensive, we suggest that you buy both for your basic kit. Folding rule features to look for include an extension end on the rule. This gimmick is a strip of brass that slides into the first 6 or 8 in. of the rule. Pulled out, you can make inside measurements accurately. Or, when measuring long distances, you can come within 6 in. or so of the total measurement, and then pull out the extension for accurate readings. You can use the extension as a straightedge for marking boards, lumber, plywood, and so on. Folded over once, the rule may be used as an approximate (rough) square.

A 25 ft. steel tape is a good length for a homeowner. The wider the tape, the better. A wide tape can be extended and won't buckle and twist as easily as a narrow tape. Since the tape is flexible, you can use it to measure rounds, half-rounds, contours, and other odd-shaped materials and projections.

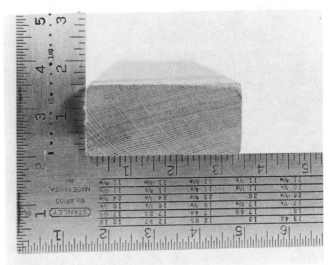

A carpenter's square or framing square has inch increments along both edges of the tongue and body of the square. Use the square to measure and mark angle cuts, as well as square almost any kind of building material.

There are two types of squares: combination and carpenter's squares. It is a toss-up which one you buy first. Hopefully, you can afford both at the outset. If not, you probably will be better off with the combination square since it is small, easy to handle, and will perform most squaring chores, plus some other operations.

Maintenance. Treat measuring and leveling tools carefully. Although they are made of metal, they are delicate and should not be handled roughly. Set them out of your traffic pattern when you are working with them. Hang them on a tool board when you are not working with them. Do not store them in tool

This is a combination square — so named because it can do a combination of jobs. Some of them include square, 45-degree angles, depth of cuts, and level. The blade slides out of the handle so you can use the blade as a ruler.

Use, Rules & Tapes. Rules and tapes, often called "inch machines," are usually marked in ⅟₁₆ or ⅛ in. graduations. Foot marks are clearly indicated every 12 in., and some models have a special mark at 16 in. — the standard width of studs, rafters, and other house framing members, which are 16 in. on center. There is no trick to using a rule or tape. Simply note the measurement and mark it down.

Use, Carpenter's Square. A carpenter's square has an L shape. The long part of the L is called the "body," and the short part is called the "tongue." Most squares have a 24-in.-long body and a 16-in.-long tongue. Squares are usually 1½ to 2 in. wide, although you can buy special widths.

Most squares also have special scales that can be used to figure out board feet of lumber, to scribe rafter cuts, and to figure the hypotenuse of a triangle of which two sides are already known.

The "outside" edge of the square is best used for "inside" measurements. The "inside" of the square is best used for "outside" measurements. For example, you square the edges of a 2x4 along the inside edge of the body and tongue of the square. You square the markings on a sheet of paneling with the outside edges of the body and tongue of the square, since the measurements can be from 1½ to 2 in. (or more) longer.

A combination square has a movable blade. The blade is grooved and rides on a pin which is activated by a thumbscrew in the handle of the square. The square also provides a 45-degree angle, and some models have a built-in level and marking scribe. The blade is graduated in ⅛, ⅟₁₆, and ⅟₃₂ in. measurements. It is 1 ft. long. The combination model is ideal for squaring and marking boards and dimension lumber up to 11½ in. wide. For larger jobs, such as squaring plywood, hardboard, and other sheet materials, you need a carpenter's square. The combination square also may be used for inside measurements and as a "depth" gauge.

Other measuring and marking tools you will want to add as you progress in home maintenance include a try square, marking gauge, plumb bob, and chalkline and chalk.

boxes, unless the entire level, square, or folding rule is protected from possible damage from other tools.

The edges of levels may develop light surface rust. You can remove this rust with very fine steel wool and machine oil. Vials on some levels are interchangeable so that if a vial breaks you may be able to replace it quickly and easily. If the level is wooden, coat the wood with paste wax about every six months. Then buff the wood with a soft cloth.

Folding rules need little maintenance — just a drop or two of light machine oil or graphite powder on the metal folding joints from time to time. After use, especially in wet weather or when you've been using the rule around water, wipe the length of the rule with a cloth.

Tapes should be extended every six months or so and wiped with an oily cloth. This keeps the metal lubricated and clean so the spring loading device works smoothly. Be careful when snapping the tape back into the housing. Most tapes have a little hook on the end of the tape. If you let this hook constantly bang against the housing when rewinding the tape, the hook will break off and the tape will disappear into the housing. The tape will then be useless.

Since squares are metal, they are subject to rust. Without fail, wipe the metal with an oily cloth before storing the squares. If you notice light rust forming, immediately remove the rust with very fine steel wool and machine oil. Do not rub the metal hard with the steel wool, just lightly buff it. Otherwise, you may remove the coloring in the indented markings and the markings will be hard to read.

Use, Levels. When the alcohol bubble in a spirit level is between the lines in the vial, the work is level. If the bubble is between the lines when the level is perpendicular, the work is plumb or vertically level. You also can lay the level flat on a surface, such as a wall, to level a line horizontally. The level need not set on an object for level.

A level may be used as a straightedge for marking materials, and you can use the level for rough squaring — horizontal and then perpendicular lines. The point where the lines cross should be fairly square.

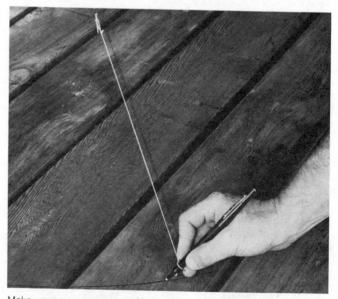

Make your own compass with a nail, string, and marking pencil. The trick is keeping the string taut while you draw a circle. You can buy small marking compass tools; one leg has a point, and the other leg holds a pencil.

Riveters and Their Use

Rivets look like fat bolts; they are made from aluminum and copper and other metals. You can rivet with a ball peen hammer, or you can buy a pop riveter or rivet set. A pop riveter looks somewhat like pliers and works by squeezing two handles together. A rivet set is used to align rivets, which are then driven with a ball peen hammer. Both tools are inexpensive. For joining thin materials rivets can be better than screws because rivets do not strip out as easily, nor do they leave sharp points.

You can fasten sheet materials together fast with a pop rivet gun. Just squeeze the handles and pop goes the rivet. You also can set rivets by hand with a ball-peen hammer.

Rivets are extremely strong (they are used to fabricate airplanes), so do not be afraid to use them for fastening almost any metal, leather, and some plastics. But do not mix metals; for example, use aluminum rivets in aluminum; copper rivets in copper; steel rivets in steel.

In selecting riveting tools look for models or styles with extended nose pieces. The nose piece should protrude about an inch from the tool base, at a 90° angle to the centerline between handles. In some models the nose piece will be in alignment with the hands, enabling the user to reach otherwise inaccessible areas.

Maintenance. Keep pivot pins lubricated with light machine oil or graphite powder. Wipe the tools from time to time with an oily cloth. The metal housing usually is of enamel or chrome steel and needs only an occasional cleaning.

Use. By hand, you set rivets with the rounded head of a ball peen hammer. But first align the material you want to fasten with rivets. Then drill holes for the rivets that are the same diameter as the rivets. Insert the rivets in the holes, and peen or flatten the rivets with the hammer.

You can buy split, roundhead, flathead, and countersunk rivets in many different types of metals including steel, brass, copper, and aluminum. Always use rivets that protrude about 1½ times their diameter beyond the surfaces that will be riveted together. For example: a rivet is ⅛-in. in diameter; it should protrude ⅜-in. from the work. This gives you ample metal for peening.

Pop rivets are set with a pop rivet tool. You can buy aluminum, copper, steel, and monel metal rivets for pop riveters. There also is a size selection.

Insert the rivet into the riveter (the rivet looks like a long nail). The shank of the rivet goes into the tool. Center the tool over the spot on the work where you want the rivet. Squeeze the riveter handles and pop — the rivet is set. With one action, the riveter drives the rivet into place, forms the heads, and discards the scrap from the shank of the rivet.

A rivet set is similar to a nail set. One end of the set has a hollow depression that is used to form the head of a rivet. The set also has a deep hole in it. You put the rivet into the hole, rap the handle of the set with a hammer, and the set flattens the work around the rivet and pulls the work tightly together.

Propane Torches and Their Use

With a propane torch you can weld and braze metal. Although propane torches really are not basic home maintenance tools, they come in handy for lots of repair jobs such as sweating copper pipe, and are fairly inexpensive.

Propane torches have a tank, which holds the propane fuel, and heads, which distribute the heat onto the work. There are several different types of heads: a flame spreader tip, which is ideal for removing paint and finishes; a soldering tip, which is used for small soldering jobs; a pencil burner tip, which is used for most general jobs such as copper pipe assembly.

Maintenance. Keep the burner tips clean with an occasional polishing using fine steel wool.

Use. You do not have to preheat a propane torch, as you do a pump-up blowtorch; just turn on the torch and light the flame.

Do not thrust the work into the flame. There is more heat at the tip of the flame than at the base of the flame. Also, match the head to the work, i.e., do not use the flame spreader head to sweat copper pipe joints. Separate heads are used for brazing

If you often work with metal, you will want to consider this new brazing and soldering torch. It puts out plenty of heat for such a small unit. A variety of fittings are available for the fuel tanks, even fittings to sweat copper pipe.

The hottest flame is at the tip of the flame, not at the base of it. When you work with propane torches, have plenty of ventilation and keep fire extinguishers handy. Lay the work to be heated on a concrete surface or asbestos board.

and welding, along with double tanks of propane. The different heads are interchangeable; just screw and unscrew them to the propane tanks. When the fuel tank is empty, throw it away. Tanks are not refillable.

Wrenches and Their Use

Your basic tool kit must contain two types of wrenches: an adjustable wrench and a hex wrench, also known as an Allen wrench. Allen wrenches usually come in a package with assorted sizes of wrenches.

Pipe wrenches (you will need two) should be your third buy, since you will need these tools for plumbing repair jobs. They are expensive. Open-end and socket wrenches should be purchased as you need them.

Maintenance. None.

Use. To use an adjustable wrench, tighten the wrench on the work. It must fit snug, or you will strip the bolt head. Position the wrench so that you are pulling against the fixed jaw of the wrench, not the moveable jaw.

When you turn an adjustable wrench, or any wrench, do not wrap your fingers around the handle. Instead, use the palm of your hand. This way, if the wrench slips, you won't bark your knuckles. Also, always turn the wrench toward yourself whenever you can. This protects your hand should the wrench slip.

Allen wrenches simply slip into the recessed holes of the screws and bolts they are supposed to drive and draw. Do not overtighten the fasteners by adding more pressure to the wrenches with pliers. Hand-tight is plenty. If you need more pressure, you may need a different type of fastener than a hex bolt or screw.

Steel pipe thread is tapered, rather than being straight as on a bolt. This taper creates a wedging action that produces tremendous pressure as the threads turn into a fitting. When working

with steel pipe, always use two wrenches. One wrench holds the fitting, while the other turns the pipe into it. Conversely, a wrench can hold pipe while a fitting is turned onto it. The use of two wrenches is especially important when working on pipe that is already installed. If you do not hold the existing pipe against turning pressure, you could turn a fitting somewhere inside a wall and cause a leak.

Whetstones and Their Use

Any cutting tool will become dull with use. You can delay a trip to a professional sharpening outlet by occasionally "touching up" cutting edges with a whetstone.

Whetstones, sometimes called "oilstones" or "sharpening stones," are usually laminated in two layers. One layer has a coarse abrasive surface; the other side has a smooth abrasive surface. First you use the coarse abrasive to remove any burrs from the cutting edges. Then you use the smooth abrasive to whet the edges sharp.

If cutting edges develop nicks along the surfaces, you sometimes can smooth out the nicks with a file or grinding wheel. Then give the cutting edges the whetstone treatment. However, if the cutting edges are badly damaged, the tool should be reformed and sharpened by a professional. Or throw out the tool and buy a new one. This may be less expensive than professional service.

Maintenance. Whetstones are easily broken, so they must be stored like lightbulbs. The stones need little maintenance; a drop or two of lubricating oil on the abrasive sufaces is all that's necessary.

Use. Always maintain the same cutting edge bevel on the tool when you whet the cutting edge. For example, hold the beveled edge of a chisel at the same angle while you sharpen it. Otherwise, you will dull the edge rather than sharpen the edge. In fact, you may damage the cutting edge so that it has to be reground and then resharpened.

STEPS

When you whet a cutting edge, press the edge lightly on the surface of the whetstone. Keep the pressure even so the entire cutting surface is against the sharpening surface. A drop or two of light machine oil is helpful during the whetting procedure.

Run the cutting edge around the stone in a figure 8. This configuration assures you that the entire cutting edge is receiving the same degree of whetting. Make the figure 8 four or five times. Then test the edge of the tool for sharpness by sliding the tool through a piece of newspaper. The tool should cut the paper as though it were a new razor blade.

Once the edge of the tool is sharp, check the edges of the tool for burrs caused by the whetting operation. If you find burrs, use the coarse surface of the whetstone to remove the burrs. Keep the edges perfectly flat on the coarse abrasive surface, and push the tool away from you. Go just one way; do not slide the tool back and forth.

Portable Electric Drills

Power drills are so beneficial to home repair jobs that they may be taken out of the luxury class and put into the necessity class. Their cost is not prohibitive; in fact, cost is often comparable to hand tool counterparts.

Three drill sizes are sold: ¼ inch; ⅜ inch; ½ inch. The ⅜-inch drill is our recommendation. It is powerful enough to handle almost all repair jobs, yet light and compact enough to be handled easily.

For your comparison, here are several buymanship suggestions for all three sizes of drills:

The ¼-inch drill. This is the lightest of the three drills, and is the least expensive. This drill will handle drill shanks up to ¼ in. for ¼ in. holes in metals and ½-in. holes in wood and other "soft" materials.

If possible, buy a drill with a variable speed feature. This feature lets you start the drill into the material slowly, then increase the speed once you have the drill started squarely into the work.

Some ¼-inch drills offer a reversing feature, but you will pay extra for it. Most of the drills do not have a low-torque feature, and the drills will not stand up to a lot of constant hard usage, as when drilling multiple holes in concrete, brick, and stone.

The ⅜-inch drill. This gives plenty of power, and will drill up to ⅜-in. holes in metal and ¾-in. holes in wood — without a hole saw attachment that increases the hole size.

Many models have the variable-speed feature, along with a hammer mode that lets you drill easily into concrete and other masonry materials. Buy the reversing feature if you can; it will let you draw screws as well as drive screws. This can be important when you have a lot of fastening work to be done — hinging, for example.

The drills offer a mid-range in speed, which permits clean hole drilling in wood. Motors are strong and will handle a great deal of constant hard work and abuse.

The ½-inch drill. This is the model the professional buys, and it is the most expensive of the drills. It can punch holes in almost any material.

The ½-inch drill will drill up to ½-in. holes in metal and 1-in. holes in wood. It has a hammer mode and different drill chucks for different materials. The quality drills have variable speed, along with low rpms and high torque. Most models have trigger locks.

Accessories. All three size drills offer many accessories: screwdriver attachments, paint paddles, wire brush attachments — even attachments to convert the drill into saws, lathes, and other woodworking tools. The list of helpful drill accessories includes: paint mixers, hole saws, an assortment of spade bits, drum sanders, right angle drives (to drill at right or acute angles), wire brushes, wood countersinks, metal working drills, grinding wheels, rotary rasps and files, drill stands (to make a drill press out of the portable drill), and drill stops for depth drilling. These accessories cost extra, so buy them as your work dictates.

Safety. Portable electric drills are as safe as any tool, but you must exercise caution.

Power drills should be grounded with the 3-wire device. Never stand in water or on wet or damp ground when using an electric drill.

Always keep the work locked in a vise or clamped to a table when drilling into the work. Do not hand-hold the work. If you try to hand-hold it, the drill can catch a knot or other imperfection in the material and cause the work to spin out of your hand.

Portable Electric Jigsaws

Like power drills, jigsaws almost are a necessity these days. They will handle most cutting jobs with dispatch, and their cost is not prohibitive.

Most jigsaws, sometimes called saber saws and electric handsaws, will cut 2-in. thick dimension lumber easily. They can even cut 2-in. thick dimension lumber at an angle, but not as easily.

The biggest feature of a jigsaw is that it will make inside cuts in materials without a starting hole. You just tip the saw into the material and go about your business. However, to assure accuracy you should first drill a pilot or starting hole for the jigsaw blade.

Other sawing tricks the jigsaw will do include cutting scrolls, curves, gingerbread, straight cuts, angles, etc. You also can buy an assortment of blades which will let you cut metal, plastic, and masonry.

Like drills, jigsaws have the variable speed feature. Or you can buy them with one or two speed settings. We recommend the variable speed, because different speeds make the saw easier to use in different types of materials.

Jigsaws cut on the upstroke. For ripping wood, you want to use blades with 5 to 7 teeth per inch. This produces a coarse cut. For fine cuts, use blades with 10 teeth per inch. The cut you will get will be similar to that produced by a crosscut handsaw.

Safety. Use the same precautions that you would use with a portable electric drill. Always keep the baseplate against the work. If you do not, the saw will chatter through the work, causing a rough cut and possibly damaging the material. Blades are easily broken when the saw chatters.

Power Tool Use

Using portable electric drills and jigsaws involves specialized needs, and thorough coverage requires another book. Some suggested sources are:

Drake, George. *Everyone's Book of Hand & Small Power Tools,* 1974 — Reston

Jackson, Albert & Day, David. *Tools and How to Use Them: An Illustrated Encyclopedia,* 1978 — Knopf

Poteet, G. Howard. *Complete Guide to the Use & Maintenance of Hand and Power Tools,* 1978 — P-H.

When you buy a power tool, the manufacturer of the tool usually furnishes you with a complete instruction manual for the tool. Be sure to ask the retailer for this manual if one is not packaged with the tool.

It is our belief that you should know about and be able to use hand tools before you graduate to most of their power cousins. The only exception would be the portable electric drill and jigsaw. Your skill with hand tools will provide you with the basic knowledge you need to operate power equipment. In addition, this knowledge will help you be a better shopper for power equipment, because you will avoid buying expensive tools that you don't need, because you will realize what you can handle with the tools you already own.

Many interior repairs are not repairs as such; they really could be put into the maintenance or improvement category, or the "nagging-little-breakdown" category. They include the dings-in-the-wallboard, the squeaks in the hinges, and the brown spots on the ceiling tile.

But if you let them go, they will grow into the big, costly repair category.

Here, as throughout the rest of the book, we have stuck with the basics. There are, of course, other repairs and improvements that have not been mentioned — for the most part "specialized" repairs that are different for each homeowner. However, if you learn how to handle the breakdowns listed here, you will have little trouble coming to grips with the more specialized ones you come across.

STRUCTURAL BASICS
Anatomy of a Gypsumboard Wall

Gypsumboard is a plasterlike material that comes in 4x8-ft. sheets (standard). The gypsum core is wrapped in thick paper. The paper protects the gypsum and provides a smooth surface that is resistant to cracks. Gypsumboard is easer than plaster to apply to the framing members of a house, which is probably why its use is so common.

Gypsumboard sheets are nailed to the studs and rafters with gypsumboard nails, and fastened every 16 in. on center (usually the spacing of the framing members), and the nails are spaced from 2 to 4 in. apart.

The edges of the gypsumboard are slightly tapered. The taper compensates for the thickness of gypsumboard joint tape

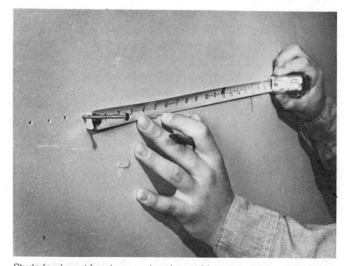

Studs (and most framing members) are 16 in. on center (o.c.). However, some framing may be 24 in. o.c. especially in garage, carport, and patio structures. Find the first stud, mark it on the wall and measure from this point.

that is applied over the joint and nails with joint compound. The compound is similar to spackling.

Inside and outside corners of gypsumboard walls often have a metal strip nailed to the gypsumboard, and the strips are embedded in joint compound. The strips add protection to the corners, especially the outside corners, and provide a straight and fairly square edge.

Gypsumboard varies in thickness: ⅜, ½, and ⅝ in. thicknesses are standard. When making a patch or replacing a

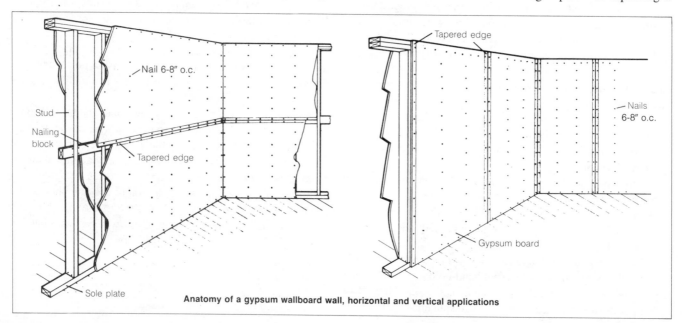

Anatomy of a gypsum wallboard wall, horizontal and vertical applications

panel, know its original thickness. If the replacement material does not match the original you will have a depression or projection.

Anatomy of a Plaster Wall

Plaster for walls and ceilings is applied over a wire mesh that has been nailed to the framing members. If your house is old, the plaster may cover narrow strips of wood called "lath."

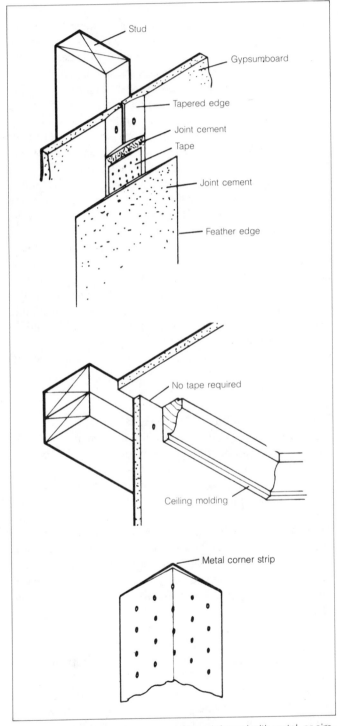

Inside gypsum wallboard corners can be reinforced with metal, or simply taped with joint tape. Have spackling or joint compound about the consistency of thick whipped cream so tape smooths easily. Outside gypsum wallboard corners should be reinforced with a metal strip for protection. Nail the strip to the corner, add joint compound, embed the tape into the compound, and smooth tape with a scraper.

Plaster is continuous in that it is not in sections as are gypsumboard panels. Nor is plaster covered with a paper wrapper, as is gypsumboard. When you dig into plaster, you are instantly into the wall.

You can patch plaster with plaster. Unless holes are huge, you also can patch plaster with spackling compound, which probably will be easier for you to buy than regular plaster.

Anatomy of a Concrete Block Wall

Concrete blocks are cored (hollow). Each block unit (8x8x16 in.) usually has two or three cores in it. Therefore, when you drill into the wall you will hit a hollow area before you hit the inside back of the block.

Exterior concrete block walls generally have insulation placed in the cores or hollows. The insulation is vermiculite — a mica product — or mineral wool, a fiberglass product. This type of insulation was installed at the time the wall was erected. Insulation may also be installed between the block wall and the back of the interior wall covering.

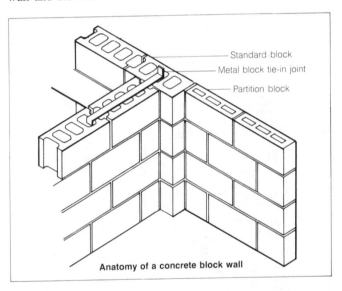

Anatomy of a concrete block wall

Some blocks are not concrete. They may be light aggregate blocks, made with cinders, slag, and shale. Their sizes are the same as concrete blocks, but they are lighter and have different insulation qualities and porosity.

Concrete blocks rest on a placed concrete foundation, just like regular wood framing. Similar construction techniques are also used around windows, doors, at top sills, and ridge lines. Over windows and doors blocks are placed on lintels (flat piece of iron or steel) for support.

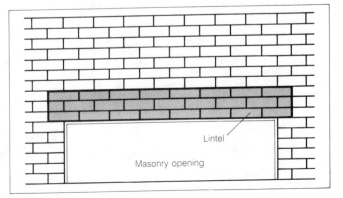

Most interior concrete blocks are covered with gypsumboard or paneling. The wall covering is installed on furring strips that are attached to the blocks with screws and lead anchors, toggle bolts, or building adhesive. The strips are mounted on 16 in. centers (usually) just like studs and rafters.

In repairing a wall covering mounted over a concrete block wall, you do not have to be concerned with the blocks. The repairs to the covering are made the same way as with standard framed walls.

Brick frame. If your home is constructed of brick, almost the same building methods were used as with concrete block.

Stucco frame. Stucco is similar to plaster. It is applied over a wire mesh to the exterior of a house and then finished with a stucco texture. The basic framing of a stucco house is the same as for a wood frame house, but the siding is stucco rather than wood, aluminum, brick, or concrete.

Anatomy of a Paneled Wall

Paneling offers two advantages: it covers the wall framing while decorating the room.

Paneling may be installed directly over the wall framing (studs) or to gypsumboard or plaster. Furring strips generally are not used when paneling is installed directly to the framing members. In wallboard and plaster applications, the paneling probably is attached to furring. It also can be cemented right to

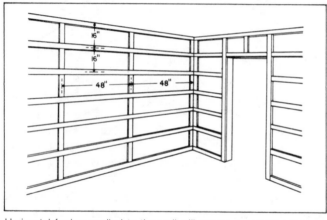

Horizontal furring applied to the wall will ensure a smooth and even surface over which to put your paneling. Since panels come in 4x8 ft. panels, and most ceilings are 8 ft. high, for vertical installation the panel seams will fall on 48-in. centers, over the furring strips.

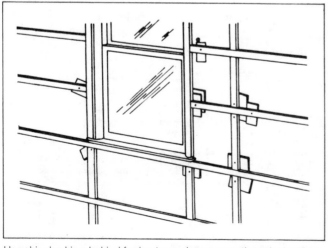

Use shingle shims behind furring to produce a smooth vertical surface.

the wallcovering with building adhesive. The adhesive method is fairly new. If your house is older than 1970 it probably will not use it.

To repair extensive damage to paneling, you almost always have to replace a complete panel. This is an easy job if the paneling is installed over furring strips or nailed to the framing, but a difficult job if the paneling has been glued.

How to Locate Studs

This job sounds difficult, but it should not be.

You can buy magnetic stud locators for not much money, and sometimes they work. You move them along a wall and when the magnetic finder goes over a metal nail a little needle in the finder wiggles. The wiggle indicates the stud location.

Another way is to pound on the wall with your fist. The thump will sound hollow until you hit a stud, then the thump will sound solid — hopefully.

Still another way is to measure from a corner out across the wall. The corner is framed with double studs and the next stud out will be 16 inches — or at least it ought to be.

One last quick try: Pry off the baseboard along the wall in which you want to locate the studs. The baseboard covers the vertical untaped joints of the gypsumboard. These joints are supposed to be spaced 48 in. apart.

The best way: Measure out from a corner 16 in. Drive a nail, such as a 10d finishing nail, into the wall at this point. If you hit something solid, it probably is the stud. If you do not hit something solid, keep trying until you do. Then mark this location on the wall. You can always patch the little nail holes with a daub of spackling compound, and you will be sure of the stud location.

All other stud locations can be measured from the first stud you found with the nail. The studs will be 16 in. on center across the wall.

SOLVING COMMON WALL PROBLEMS

Since they are so big and so accessible, walls are first in line for damage. The problems run from picture-hook holes to punched-out sections to hairline cracks.

Structural damage to walls is not common. Walls are ruggedly built and will withstand a high level of abuse. You may panic, however, when you see large cracks and gaps where the ceiling meets the walls, around doors and window headers, and in corners. Chances are these cracks are the result of the house settling on its foundation — a normal condition. If these cracks increase, you should call a professional builder to check out the structure just in case you have serious foundation troubles.

Repairing Dents and Dings

This is minor damage, usually caused from furniture being pushed hard against a wall.

Tools and materials: Razor knife, putty knife, touch-up paint, paintbrush, spackling compound, mixing container, medium-grit sandpaper, water.

STEPS

If the damage is not deep enough to hold even a small patch, you will have to enlarge the problem area.

For repairs in gypsum wallboard and plaster, use spackling compound. Small holes usually can be filled with one pass of the putty knife with spackling compound that has been mixed to the consistency of thick mud.

If the wall is of gypsum wallboard, use a razor knife to score the paper covering the gypsum core, making a square or rectangular cut. Just cut enough of the paper to surround the entire damaged area. Then, using the knife blade, peel the paper back to the scored lines. Again with the razor knife, remove a quarter inch or so of the gypsum core, making a little void in the core. This area need not be smooth and finely cut; it is better to leave it rough because the rough edges will hold the patch better.

After this point the procedure is the same for plaster and for wallboard repair.

Mix a small amount of spackling compound in the mixing container. Add spackling to the water and stir it with the putty knife until the mixture is about the consistency of putty. Balance the mixture on the putty knife and press the spackling into the hole.

Be sure the hole has been filled with spackling. You can probe into the patch with the tip of the putty knife to compact the mixture. When the hole is full, use the edge of the knife to smooth the fresh spackling. The putty knife serves as a trowel.

Leave the patch slightly higher than the surrounding surface of the patch. The spackling will shrink as it dries. Let the patch set for about two days.

Once the patch has dried, lightly sand it, working away the rough spackling and blending the patch in with the surrounding area. Check often; spackling sands quickly.

Spot prime the patch with paint. Let the paint dry. Sand the area lightly again, and then apply a second coat of paint. If the wall has not been painted for some time, you may have to repaint the entire wall to hide the patch, since the new paint will not blend in with the old paint.

Nail Hole Repair, Plaster or Gypsumboard

Tools and materials. Putty knife, spackling compound, mixing container, water, touch-up paint, paintbrush or cotton swab, sandpaper.

STEPS

Mix a small amount of spackling compound with water. The spackling should be a stiff mixture, about the consistency of putty or stiff whipped cream.

Press the spackling into the hole, using the tip of the putty knife. Then, with the putty knife, level the spackling in the hole. Let the spackling dry an hour or so. Then sand the area with medium or fine grit abrasive.

Touch up the spot with paint. Try to feather out the paint into the surrounding area. Sometimes just a daub of paint on the spot works best. You can try both and decide which looks better before the paint dries.

Patches for Plaster

Dents and cracks to plaster walls and ceilings are mended the same way as gypsum wallboard; check these techniques in this chapter. However, remember that plaster has several built-up layers which form the surface, while wallboard has a single core of gypsum covered with paper.

Tools and Materials. Razor knife, spackling compound or plaster patching material, wide wall scraper or joint tape knife, metal lath, water brush, paint, paintbrush, sandpaper, sanding block.

STEPS

Clean the break with the razor knife, cutting back to the hard plaster. The patching area should be free of loose debris; don't enlarge the damage more than necessary. Clean the area to be patched with water and a brush. Mix the spackling compound (or plaster patching material for a large, deep hole from which the metal lath is missing) to a fairly stiff consistency.

If the metal lath is still in place, you will follow these steps: Rewet the area to be patched; this prevents the plaster from absorbing water from the spackling mixture. Trowel in the spackling with a scraper. Level the patch and smooth it. After the patch has dried for several days, sand it smooth so it blends with the surrounding surface. Spot prime and paint the entire wall or ceiling.

For larger patches, substitute a mason's trowel for a wall scraper to apply and level the patch. Another possibility is to use a section of gypsum wallboard instead of spackling. The wallboard can usually be butted against the plaster and then taped and smoothed to match.

If the metal lath (a heavy mesh available in hardware stores) is missing, follow these steps. After cleaning the patch, as above, mix the plaster patch material according to instructions. Cut the mesh so it is a little larger than the hole — about 1 in. larger all around. Tie 5 or 6 in. of string through the center of the lath. Holding onto the string, bend the lath just enough to fit it through the hole, then flatten out the mesh. Tie a pencil to the string, and twist so that the pencil spans the hole and keeps the metal lath in place.

If the hole is fairly small, apply plaster patching to within ¼ in. of the surface and let it dry. Once the patch is dry and holds the mesh in place, cut the string and remove it and the pencil. Then put on another coat; allow it to dry, and sand smooth. If the hole is large, you will apply three layers rather than two. Fill the patch so that it will form a bond between the metal lath and the wall; let it dry; remove the pencil and string. Add another layer, up to within ¼ in. of the surface, and let dry. Then apply the last layer, let dry, and sand smooth.

Pinpoint Hole Repair, Gypsum Wallboard

Tools and materials. Putty knife.

STEPS

Often you can hide these tiny holes by pressing the tip of the putty knife around the hole and forcing the gypsum wallboard paper into the hole. You have to work very carefully in order not to gouge the paper as you press it into the hole.

Large Hole Repair, Gypsum Wallboard

Tools and materials. Razor knife, mineral wool insulation, spackling compound, mixing container, putty knife, sandpaper, touch-up paint, paintbrush.

STEPS

Clean out the break with the razor knife. Try not to enlarge the hole, just cut away the loose gypsum down to the firm inner core.

Mix up a large batch of spackling compound and make the mixture stiff. Then stuff the hole full of mineral wool insulation. The fibers of the insulation will catch on the gypsum board surface and hang in place.

Fill the hole with the spackling compound, being careful not to dislodge the insulation. You want to use the insulation as a backing material for the spackling. You may be able to tack the insulation to the back of the hole with small gobs of spackling.

When this initial job is finished, let the spackling dry a day or so. Then go back and fill the hole full of spackling. Level the spackling with the putty knife, but leave it a tad high for normal shrinkage.

When the spackling is dry, sand the area lightly so it is level with the surrounding surface. Then, touch up the patch with paint.

Very Large Hole Repair, Gypsumboard

You must now make a decision. Can you patch the hole with a piece of gypsumboard, or is it so large that you should remove the gypsumboard panel and replace it with a new panel? The latter may be easier than the former.

Tools and materials. For the patch: razor knife, pencil, square or straightedge, spackling compound, mixing container, a piece of scrap gypsumboard the same thickness as that of the

Run the wire through the patch, spread glue on it, and then angle it through the hole. You may have to pull the wires toward you several minutes until the glue sets enough to hold the patch on when you let go.

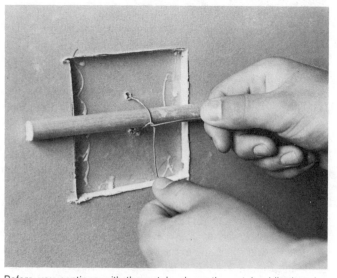

Before you continue with the patch, clamp the patch while the glue dries for a day or so. Apply lots of pressure to the clamp by twisting the wires with pliers. Don't overdo it, or you will damage the patch.

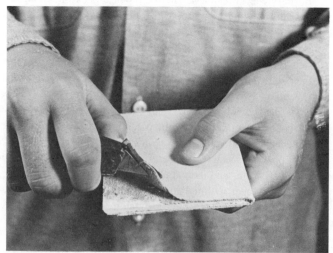

Cut another gypsumboard patch; this one will fit on top of the patch already placed in back of the wall. Remove the paper covering on one side of the gypsum core — the paper comes off more easily if you wet the surface with water.

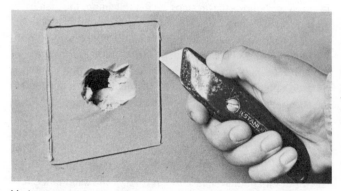

Mark a square or rectangle over home damage and score the marks with a razor knife. Make all needed cuts until the damaged area can be lifted out of the wall. Then slightly bevel the edges of the patch toward the back wall.

wall, a short length of 1x3 or dowel, wire, a nail, hammer, glue, pliers, putty knife, wall scraper, sandpaper, touch-up paint, paintbrush.

Using the straightedge or square, outline the damaged area with a pencil. Include all the damage within the lines, but no more than this area. The patch should be adequate, but as small as possible.

Score along the outline with the razor knife, bearing down hard on the knife. If you can, cut completely through the gypsumboard at this time. If you cannot cut completely through the material, repeat the scoring procedure with the knife until you remove this part of the wall. You now should have a nice square or rectangular hole where the damaged area once was.

Measure the hole and transfer these measurements to the scrap piece of gypsumboard, plus 2 in. on all four sides. The extra material will be used for gluing. When you are done, you will have the patch for the wall.

Since you need to be able to hold onto the patch while you fit it into the wall, punch two holes all the way through the patch with a nail. Aim for the center of the patch and space the holes about an inch apart. Thread the wire through these holes so the ends of the wire come through the front of the patch.

Now coat the face of the patch with glue; use a lot of glue. Place the patch inside the hole, seating the patch in the glue. Pull the patch toward you with the wire so that the glue makes a good bond with the back of the wall.

When you are sure the patch is seated, wrap the wire around the 1x3 or dowel, which should bridge the patch. Then twist the wire around the 1x3 or dowel and tighten the wire with pliers. This will anchor the patch on the wall so that the glue makes a good bond.

Remove the 1x3 or dowel from the wall when the glue dries, after at least a day, and test the patch. If it seems to be wobbly in the wall, very carefully "tack" the recessed edges of the patch with a stiff spackling compound. Let the spackling dry a day.

When the patch is securely in place, fill the recess between the patch and the surface of the wall with spackling compound. Use the wide wall scraper for this, troweling in the spackling mixture and smoothing it level. Use the surface of the surrounding wall to help guide the wall scraper so that the patch will be level with the wall. Or, cut another patch of gypsumboard the same size as the hole.

Check that the patch fits, then peel off the paper covering on the front side of the patch. Use the razor knife for this. Go right to the gypsum core on the surface of the patch that will face the room. You need not be too careful with the razor; the gypsum core should be a bit rough. Glue the patch in position. When the glue dries, fill the joints with spackling compound.

Once the spackling compound has dried — give it three days — sand the patch smooth, blending the patch into the surrounding wall surface.

Spot prime the patch with paint. Then paint the entire wall so the patch won't show.

Replacing a Gypsumboard Panel

When the hole is so large that you can't mend it with a spackling compound or a gypsumboard patch, you will have to

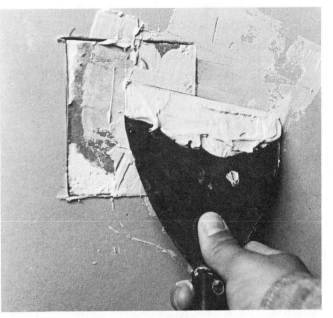

Glue the second surface patch over the first patch — paper to paper with the exposed gypsum core facing toward you. Wait one more day while the glue dries, then apply spackling compound to the joints and over the patch. A wide wall scraper serves as a good trowel.

Smooth the patch after the spackling compound has dried for several days. Try to "feather" the edges so they taper into the surrounding wallboard.

replace the panel. This is not especially difficult, but you need patience and must be careful not to damage the good surrounding panels.

Tools and materials. New sheet of gypsum wallboard the same thickness as the old material, pry bar, hammer, finishing nails, nail set, razor knife, wall scraper, putty knife, gypsumboard nails, joint tape for gypsumboard, spackling compound, mixing container, stain and/or paint, wood filler, paintbrush, dropcloths.

STEPS

Remove the base molding from the wall on which the damaged panel is located. Use a pry bar and hammer for this and take it easy when you pry; you want to save the trim and reinstall it after the repair has been made. When the molding has been removed, tap and pull out the nails and store the molding out of your way.

With a hammer, break out the damaged gypsumboard panel back to the studs to which the sides of the panel have been nailed. If you go very slowly, you can remove the entire damaged panel by removing chunks of the panel and pulling the nails as you go. Do it in small pieces rather than jerking off the whole panel at once.

When you come to the panel joints, you probably will have to cut the gypsumboard tape that spans the joints along the sides and at the ceiling line. Do this with the razor knife. Again, be careful not to rip into the adjoining panels or the ceiling.

With the panel removed, you should have a neat, clean hole in the wall with the studs exposed and the "good" gypsumboard panels overlapping the side studs by about half their width.

Insert the new panel over the framing members. You will need a helper to handle the new panel so that you can mark and fit it into position. Then remove the new panel and make any necessary cuts for correct fit using the razor knife.

Nail the new panel to the framing members with gypsumboard nails. Space the nails about three inches apart. When the nailheads are flush with the panel, hit them one more time with the hammer. This creates a "dimple" in the surface of the panel and countersinks the nailheads below the surface of the panel. These dimples will be filled later with spackling compound.

When the panel is in place, check the edges to make sure that they do not project above the surface of the surrounding wall. If the edges do project, you may be able to trim them down slightly with the razor knife. It is likely, however, that the panel will fit perfectly.

Mix a stiff batch of spackling compound. With a putty knife or wall scraper, trowel on a thin layer of the spackling at the joints and along the ceiling line. Then embed the joint tape into the spackling compound. Run the wall scraper over the top of the tape, pressing it into the spackling. Give the tape a downward swipe with the scraper.

With the tape embedded, fill all dimples with spackling

Apply even pressure while smoothing tape into wallboard seam.

compound, leveling the compound in these depressions using the wall scraper or putty knife.

Let the spackling dry one day. Apply a layer of spackling over the tape; let dry another 24 hours. Add a third coat. Once dry, sand the spackling lightly and prime the new panel with paint. Once the paint has dried, give the panel a light sanding and dust off the residue. Add a second coat of paint.

Replace the baseboard, nailing it to the studs with finishing nails. Countersink the nail heads using the nail set, fill the holes with wood putty or wood plastic, and touch up any spots with paint or stain.

Patching Gypsumboard or Plaster Cracks

The size of the cracks we are discussing here are hairline up to about ¼-inch wide. The repair technique for cracks in gypsumboard and for plaster walls is the same. If there are large cracks and lots of them, consult a professional; there could be structural damage to the house.

Tools and materials. Razor knife, putty knife or wall scraper, spackling compound, mixing container, sandpaper, touch-up paint, paintbrush, dropcloth.

STEPS

Clean out the crack with the razor knife. Undercut the crack with the knife to form an inverted V. This configuration will help hold in the patch.

Mix a fairly stiff batch of spackling compound. Trowel the compound into the crack, smoothing it with the tip end of the wall scraper or putty knife. Leave the patch a little high; spackling shrinks as it dries.

Let the patch set for two days. Then sand the area lightly and touch up the patch with paint. If the patch is large, you probably will have to repaint the entire wall, or room.

Mending Split Gypsumboard Tape

Tools and materials. Razor knife, carpenter's or white glue, straight pins, touch-up paint, paintbrush.

STEPS

Very carefully cut and open the split tape with the razor knife. What you want to do here is give yourself enough working room so you can force glue behind the tape.

When the split has opened, squirt glue in back of the tape. Press the tape down with your fingers. If the tape wrinkles at this point, cut it just slightly with the razor knife. The cut should let you position the tape flat against the wall.

Clamp the tape in position with the straight pins. Push the pins through the tape and into the wall surface. Let the glue dry for a couple of days, and then remove the straight pins.

Complete the project by touching up the area with paint, which will fill the pin holes and the razor cuts in the tape. You may have to repaint the entire wall to blend the repair in with the wall surface.

Nail Pops in Gypsum Wallboard

This is a common problem. The nails pop from normal settling of the house on its foundation and from materials drying out and shrinking slightly.

Tools and materials. Hammer, gypsumboard nails, putty

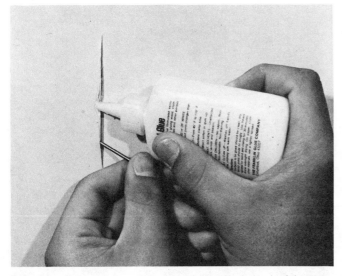

Open the split gypsumboard tape and force glue in back of the tape. Press the tape back against the wall, using your fingers to position the tape edges so that they butt perfectly.

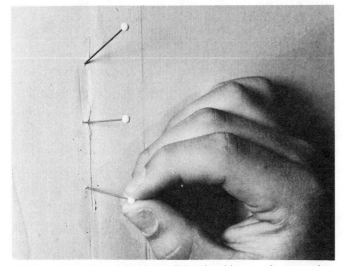

Clamp the joint with straight pins until the glue dries — at least one day. If you have been careful, you may not have to touch up the job with paint. However, if the break is bad, paint will hide the small patch you've made.

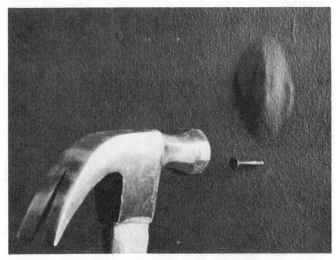

Looking straight on, nail pops are hard to see, so look at the surface from an angle. Drive a screw-nail under the pop and slightly counter-sink the nail. Then drive in the popped nail. Fill the "dimples" left by the hammer with spackling compound; sand and repaint.

knife, piece of scrap wood, spackling compound, mixing container, touch-up paint, paintbrush.

STEPS

Carefully try to drive the popped nail back into the framing. You may be able to do this by covering the nailhead with a piece of scrap wood and then tapping the wood with the hammer. The trick here is not to damage the paint with the hammer or wood while you reset the nail in the wall.

If this is not possible, then hit the nail so you dimple the wallboard. About one inch below the nail pop, drive in another gypsumboard nail. This will secure the joint to prevent the popping problem from recurring.

Fill the dimples with fairly stiff spackling compound. When the spackling dries, sand the patch smooth and touch it up with paint. If you have a lot of nail pops to repair, painting the room will look better than touching up the many patches.

Wallpaper cleaner — the dough-type stuff — can wipe away lots of grime — including plain dirt. Keep the dough *always* in motion as you apply it to the wallcovering, as it goes across the surface, and as it goes off it.

Regluing Wallpaper

Tools and materials. Razor knife, small brush, straight pins, regular white glue or contact adhesive.

STEPS

This repair is similar to repairing cracks in gypsum wallboard tape (this chapter). If possible, try to force glue behind the paper. Then press down on the paper and clamp it with straight pins until the glue dries. If the break is too small to force in glue, split the break, using a razor knife. Then follow the procedure outlined above.

If there is no bar to applying adhesive, use contact cement. Coat the wall and the back of the wallcovering with the adhesive, letting it set for about 10 minutes. Then press the paper against the wall. You may need straight pin clamps until the cement sets, which will be very fast.

"Clamp" the repair with straight pins. The pin holes won't show after the pins are removed, if you're careful when you stick them into the wall. Let the adhesive set for a couple of days before you remove the pins.

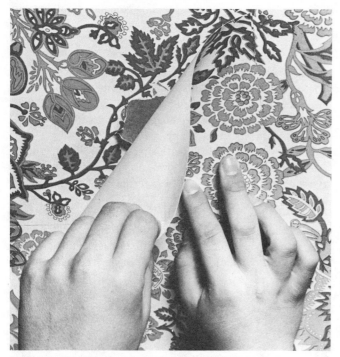

Cover the damaged wallcovering with a strip of the same pattern. Spend some time matching the pattern of the patch to the pattern of the material on the wall.

Tape the patching material over the damaged spot when the pattern matches perfectly. Then, with a sharp razor knife, cut through the patching material and the material over the wall.

Patching Wallcoverings

Tools and materials. Razor knife, masking tape, straight pins, wallpaper adhesive, water, sponge, strip of patching paper identical to that on the wall.

STEPS

You will need a fairly long strip of the same type and pattern of covering that is on the wall, especially if the wallcovering is patterned. The pattern must be matched, so you may need lots of new patching paper in order to find the match you need.

Unroll the patching paper and match its pattern to the pattern over the damaged wallcovering. When you match it perfectly, tape the patching paper to the wall with masking tape. Use plenty of tape; you do not want the overlay to slip and slide on the wall.

With the razor knife, cut through the overlayment paper and through the wallcovering. You need not be too careful with this; the cut will fit because it is identical on both layers of wallcovering. Remove the patching paper. Carefully remove the patch and lay it aside where it will not become damaged.

With a sponge and water, carefully soak the wallcovering where you scored it with the razor knife. Give the water time to soften the adhesive. Then carefully peel back the paper. You want to remove just the top layer of this area. You do not want to damage or tear the paper surrounding the patch.

Let the area dry. Then mix up a small amount of wallpaper adhesive. Coat the patch area on the wall and the back of the patch with the adhesive. Press the patch in position with your fingers, checking that the pattern is properly aligned. Then clamp the patch with straight pins until the adhesive hardens — about three days.

MOLDING, TRIM, AND PANELING

If trim or molding has been lightly damaged, you can probably repair it quickly and easily. If the material has been badly damaged, you may want to consider replacing it. This could be easier and no more costly than repair.

Repairing Molding and Trim

Tools and materials. Wood plastic or water putty, razor knife, putty knife, stain or paint, mixing container, sandpaper, paintbrush.

STEPS

If the damage to the material is shallow, enlarge it slightly so the wood filler will stick in the damaged area. Do this with a razor knife. If the damage is deep, scrape the area down to the firm wood using a razor knife. Leave no splinters or chewed wood areas. Dust the spot so it is clean; it should also be dry.

If the wood has not been painted, fill the area with plastic wood filler. You can buy wood filler to match — or almost match — the finish. If you cannot find an exact color match, buy a can of stain and restain the entire piece of molding. This may be easier than trying to blend in the patch.

If the wood has been painted, fill the damaged area with water putty, which is less expensive than plastic wood filler. Smooth this filler with a putty knife until it matches the surface of the surrounding molding or trim. Let the filler dry two days. Then sand the surface of the filler smooth so that it blends in with the surrounding molding or trim. Clean away the sanding residue and touch up the area with paint. You may have to paint the entire length of the molding or trim so the patch does not show. If so, sand the molding before painting it.

Replacing Molding and Trim

Tools and materials. Crosscut saw, pry bar, hammer, 8d finishing nails, razor knife, nail set, plastic wood filler or water putty, putty knife, stain or paint, paintbrush.

Remove the patch and the patching material you cut out. Then, with a razor blade, peel out the damaged area along the lines that you scored with the razor knife.

Paste the patch in the void left by the damaged area. The pattern and patch should match perfectly, because both cuts are the same on a matched pattern.

STEPS

Pry off the old molding. Saw off a short chunk of it and take it to a building materials outlet so you can match the pattern of the old molding with the new. Molding is sold by the lineal foot; you will need a measurement in order to purchase the footage you need.

If you are going to replace just one length of the molding, cut out the damaged section with a crosscut saw. Hold the saw teeth against the molding vertically and use short, even saw strokes to make the cuts. This will take time and care. You want to avoid damaging the wall with the saw while you are making the cut. Toward the end of the cut, you may need to score the wood in the saw kerf with a razor knife to complete the cut.

Pry off the damaged section, cut a sample of it, and buy the new molding; measure the gap for the amount of molding you need. Add a couple of inches to this length to allow for cutting, trimming, and fitting. Cut the new molding to fit, but make the cut just a hair longer than the length you need. This way, you can force the new molding between the old for a snug fit, tapping it in place with a hammer. Use a piece of scrap as a buffer block between the molding and the hammer head.

Nail the new molding to the studs or other framing members. Countersink the nails. Then fill the nail holes with wood plastic or water putty, depending on the finish. If the molding will be stained, use wood plastic. If the molding will be painted, use water putty.

Sand the filler lightly once it has dried. Then sand the entire strip of new molding. Dust. Apply the stain or paint to the new wood. Let the finish dry and then give the entire length of molding — old or new — a top coat of finish. Lightly sand the wood between finish coats.

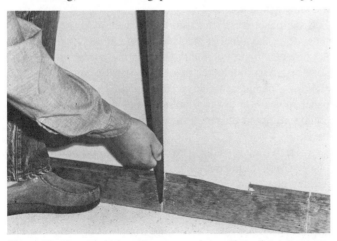

Cut out the damaged trim with a crosscut saw. Keep the cut square; marking cut-off lines on the surface will help. When cutting, keep the teeth of the saw away from the wall; masking the wall with tape is a good idea.

Use the damaged piece of trim you have cut out to mark and cut the replacement. You can make final fits with a razor knife. Fill the joint cracks with water putty and sand the wood.

Repairing Dents and Dings in Paneling

For all practical purposes, you cannot cut out a chunk of paneling and replace it with a patch. Therefore, for most little dents or scratches, you will just have to try to cover them so they do not show.

Tools and materials. Fine steel wool, matching wood stain, spray-on shellac or varnish, paste wax, paintbrush, soft cloth.

STEPS

As a precaution, it is best to test the paneling with steel wool in a spot where a mistake will not show. Some paneling is created with a thin plastic laminate that resembles wood; it is not real wood veneer. If the surface is plastic laminate, leave it alone. You simply cannot repair the damage. But if the paneling is wood veneer, you can go ahead.

Buff the spot very lightly with a fine abrasive. Clean off the spot. Then coat the wood with matching stain, blending the stain into the surrounding finished area. This is called "feathering."

Most "in-the-grain" blemishes in trim and moldings must be removed with abrasive (fine steel wool or sandpaper) — down to the bare wood. Cover a fairly large area, feathering the edges with the fine abrasive. Then wipe away the sanding residue.

Blemishes in plywood paneling can be repaired using stain applied with a cotton swab. Remove any blemish — pen marks, furniture nicks — with fine steel wool or fine grit sandpaper before you apply the new stain.

Let the stain dry. Lightly buff the area again with fine abrasive. Clean the spot with a soft cloth. Then lightly spray the spot with shellac or varnish. Sort of flick the finish onto the surface. You can buy shellac and varnish in spray-top containers. When the finish dries, lightly buff the area once again. Clean it. Then wax the entire panel and buff the panel with cloth.

You can also buy a paneling putty stick that matches the wood. The stick looks like a fat crayon, and it is about the consistency of a wax pencil. To use it, you stroke the stick over the hole and wipe away any excess on the surface surrounding the hole.

Replacing Damaged Paneling

In this case the entire 4x8-ft. panel must be removed. If the panel is applied to furring strips or the studs, the job will be easy. If the panel is glued to gypsumboard, the task becomes harder because you will have to remove the wallboard as well.

Tools and materials. Hammer, crosscut saw, nail set, screwdriver, razor knife, paneling nails, paneling putty stick, paste wax, soft cloth.

STEPS

Remove any trim pieces and switchplates and outlet covers. Since the panel is already ruined, pitch right in and rip it off the wall with a hammer. But be careful not to damage the wall, furring strips, or the surrounding paneling during removal. Be sure that all nails are driven into or pulled out of the furring strips, wall, or framing members.

Position the new panel in the void and check it for fit. You may need a helper for this. Mark any spots that need trimming and trim them with the razor knife or saw.

After fitting, slip the new panel into position and nail it along the top. Since the top of the old panel probably will be covered by a piece of crown molding or other trim, you do not have to be exact, just accurate enough to hide the nails under the trim.

Nail the panel to the furring or framing or wall, spacing the nails from 4 to 6 in. apart. If you countersink the nailheads, fill the holes with putty from a special paneling putty stick. Complete the job by paste waxing the entire wall and lightly buffing the wall with a soft cloth.

If the panel has been glued to the wallboard, run the razor knife down the joints of the paneling to ensure that the panel is not fastened to the adjoining panels. Remove any trim — baseshoe or crown molding. Remove electrical covers.

With a hammer, break out the paneling and the wallboard panel right down to the framing. Remove the debris in small chunks to avoid damaging the surrounding panels and wallboard.

Insert the new wallboard over the framing and nail it in place. Use gypsumboard nails and space the nails about 2 in. apart. Since the panel will cover the wallboard, you need not spackle the nail dimples or fill the joints. But be sure the panel is tightly fastened; use plenty of nails. Fit the new panel in the space. The panel may need some trimming or cutting with a razor knife or saw to fit tightly in the void.

After you are satisfied with the fit, spread building adhesive on back of the panel. Press the panel in position. Then pull the panel away from the wall from the top and press it down again. This distributes the adhesive evenly and provides a better glue bond.

Using a piece of scrap wood as a buffer block, lightly tap the paneling with a hammer to seat the panel in the adhesive. Then nail the panel with paneling nails in several spots. Countersink the nailheads, if you want, and fill the nail holes with paneling putty stick. Wax and buff the entire paneled wall.

Paneling maintenance. If the paneling is plastic laminate (simulated wood grain), no maintenance is required other than an occasional sponging with water and mild household detergent.

If the paneling is wood veneer, wash the surface once a year with water and mild household detergent. Wring out the cloth, and start at the bottom of the panel and work up. This way, the detergent won't streak dirty areas below. Thoroughly wipe the paneling with a dry soft cloth immediately after washing, making sure the wood is dry. Then give the paneling two coats of paste wax, buffing lightly between coats.

CERAMIC TILE

Ceramic tile replacement is far from impossible, but it may require special tools if the tile must be cut to fit. Most tile outlets will rent or lend such tools on deposit.

Replacement

Tools and materials. Hammer, glass cutter, scraper, sandpaper, putty knife, ceramic tile adhesive, ceramic tile grout, mixing container.

STEPS

Score an "X" on the face of the tile with the glass cutter. Bear down as hard as you can on the cutter, and then throw the glass cutter away; it will be ruined.

With a hammer, tap the "X'ed" spot lightly. This will break the tile into four sections. With a putty knife or scraper, pry out the broken pieces of tile. Clean the grout from the surrounding edges of tile and remove as much dried tile adhesive from the wall as you can. You can level it fairly well with a putty knife or scraper.

Score the face of the tile with a glass cutter. Tap the face with a hammer, and remove the broken tile. Use a cold chisel to remove the pieces. The same technique is used for floor and wall tiles.

Test the new tile for fit. Then put a walnut-sized amount of ceramic tile adhesive on all four corners of the tile. Press the tile in the void and align and space the joints to match the joints of the other tiles.

Let the job set a couple of days, and then mix up a fairly stiff batch of ceramic tile grout. Press the mixture into the joints around the tile. The best way to do this is with your index finger. When the joints are full, wash away any fresh grout on the tiles. Then, with a clean index finger, smooth the freshly grouted joints so they have a concave shape. Again, wipe away any excess grout or haze on the tiles. Let the job set for a week. Clean the area with regular ceramic tile cleaner, and spray with a silicone sealer.

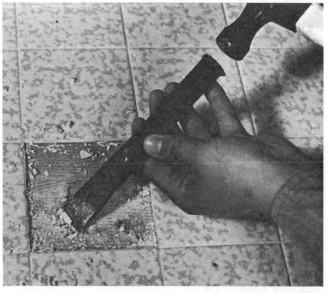

Chisel out dried adhesive and grout from the void left by the damaged tile. This area should be cleaned as best you can. The new tile has to fit flush with the surrounding tiles; debris can cause misalignment.

"Butter" the new tile with adhesive, or place daubs of adhesive at all four corners of the tile. You may also wish to put adhesive in the void to make sure the tile sticks. Then press the tile in place; space the joints evenly. Regrout.

Regrouting Ceramic Tile Joints

If you decide to regrout a whole counter, wall, or floor, note that the colored grout now on the market hides grime better than the white grout used in most homes.

Tools and materials: A short piece of 1x3, 10d finishing nails, ceramic tile grout, whisk broom, vacuum cleaner, sponge, mixing container, a supply of clean, soft cloths.

STEPS

Make a tool to dig the grout out of the joints by driving the 10d finishing nail through a piece of 1x3 near the end of the scrap. Remove the grout from the joints. This takes lots and lots of patience; the work goes very slowly. If the nail becomes bent, remove it and drive in another nail.

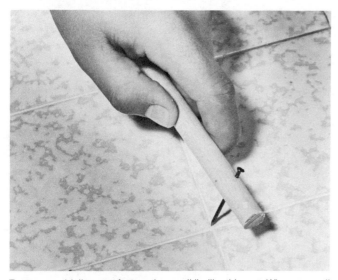

To remove old tile grout fast, make a nail jig like this one. When one nail wears out, replace it with another. After regrouting, use ceramic tile sealer to help protect grout from dirt and damage.

As you work, brush out the joints with the whisk broom and clean up this debris with a vacuum cleaner. It is important to keep the work clean. If you do not, you will track the grout all over the house, and then it is hard to remove.

When the joints are clean and you are satisfied with the job, mix up a small amount of grout. Spread this mixture over a small area of tile, using a damp sponge to distribute the grout and force the grout into the joints. When the joints are filled in this small area, wipe away any excess grout and move on to another small area. Repeat this process until the joints are filled.

Now go back to the first section you grouted. With a container of water, dip your index finger in the water and smooth the grout in the joints. Do not use too much water. "Damp" is good enough. Your finger will produce a concave joint, which is ideal.

Let the job set overnight. Go back with a damp sponge and wipe the haze off the tile. Keep using clean water as you go. This phase of the job will take lots of time, because tile haze is difficult to remove.

Give the grout time to harden — about a week — wetting the grout down twice a day to harden it. Then go over the tiles with tile cleaner and seal the tile with regular nonyellowing tile finish or a silicone spray.

Ceramic Tile Maintenance

The key to keeping the grout and tile clean is to scrub the area at least twice a month. You should use a regular ceramic tile/grout cleaner.

Once the tiles and grout are clean, seal them with ceramic tile sealer. The more often you clean the tile, the easier it will be to remove the dirt. If you let the job go for a long period of time, you may have to regrout the tiles.

SOUND CONDITIONING

Sound transmission may be structural or airborne. You cannot completely eliminate all sound, but you can put a damper on it with several of the techniques mentioned below.

Structural sound is generally created by a mechanical device and the sound is carried through the framing members of the house, ductwork, and even wiring. Part of the sound becomes airborne also. Structural sound can be transmitted by someone walking on a bare floor, doors and windows being slammed shut, water rushing through pipes, or air flowing through heating and air conditioning ducts.

Noise Control

Appliances. Install rubber pads under all appliances: dishwashers, refrigerators, washers, dryers, window air conditioner mountings.

Electrical. Change standard "click" toggle switches to mercury or "silent" switches.

Motors. Insert rubber pads under motor mountings — especially furnaces, attic fans, and ventilators.

Plumbing. Install pipe wrap around pipes. If water hammer is a problem, you can install an air chamber device (see Plumbing Repairs). Quiet-flush toilets and aerators eliminate splashing and rushing water sounds.

Floors. Repair any floor squeaks. Install carpeting, with carpet padding, over hardwood flooring.

Walls. Floor-to-ceiling draperies help block sound from windows. You may even wish to cover solid wall areas, if draperies can be used as a decorative effect.

Windows and doors. Double glazing (thermal glass and/or storm windows and doors) helps reduce sound through both of these openings. You can leave storm windows and doors on the windows all year long, especially if you have air conditioning. The insulation benefits are also good.

Ceilings. Acoustical ceiling tile absorbs about 60% of the sound that strikes it.

Insulation will help block some noise. Sound-deadening board, which looks like fiberboard sheathing, is the best way to sound condition walls. Unfortunately, it is best installed while the house is under construction. However, if the sound in your home is really bad, you may want to consider this treatment, which would cut down on the size of the rooms by about 2 feet. New wallboard or paneling must go over the fiberboard.

Airborne sound is created inside a room (as from a radio or stereo set), and it carries through the air more than through the structure or framing of the house.

CEILINGS

Unless a ceiling tile drops on the floor or there's a leak upstairs that comes downstairs through the ceiling, you almost have to

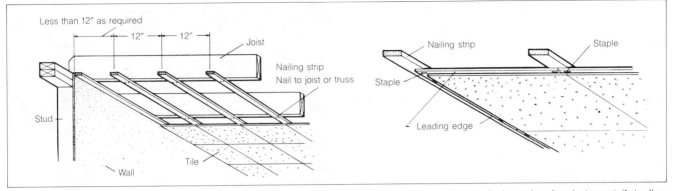

Here's how a ceiling-tile ceiling looks with some of the tiles removed. You can staple replacement tile to the furring strips. As a last resort, if stapling is too difficult, glue the tiles in position using building adhesive.

go looking for trouble on this part of your house. In this section, you will find some of the more common ceiling problems and how they can be solved.

Ceilings that Sag, Gypsumboard

Tools and materials. A stepladder, hammer, nails, tube of building adhesive, caulking gun shell.

Safety. Wear safety glasses. Be sure the stepladder is fully opened and locked before you climb the ladder. Do not climb the ladder above the third rung from the top.

STEPS, SAGGING GYPSUMBOARD

Impact from foot traffic on the floor above could have caused the nails in the gypsum wallboard on the ceiling to loosen. Loose nails, in turn, can cause the ceiling to sag or appear uneven.

Locate the ceiling joists, which probably are spaced 16 in. on center. (For how to find a stud, see earlier in this chapter.)

Renail the ceiling to the joists (or rafters), spacing the nails about 2 in. apart. To help hold the gypsum wallboard in place for renailing, build yourself a T brace from scrap 2x4, nailing the cross of the T on. Wedge this brace between the floor and the ceiling. You can kick it into position to apply needed pressure.

STEPS, SAGGING FROM WATER

First find and stop the leak. Let the ceiling dry. This will take weeks, even months sometimes, but the wait will save you money.

Once the ceiling has dried out, try renailing the gypsum wallboard back in position, as described above. If this works, you will have to spackle the nail holes and repaint the entire ceiling. But first coat the water spots with 4-lb.-cut shellac. Shellac will prevent any water spots from later bleeding through the paint job.

If renailing does not work, and the sag is not too large, you can try the same panel replacement technique previously described for walls. However, we would recommend that you replace the entire wallboard ceiling instead. It should not cost much more for the whole ceiling than for a large-area replacement, and will look much better. The panels can be nailed directly to ceiling joists once the old material has been removed. Slightly dimple the location of each nailhead using a hammerhead — being cautious lest you damage the surface of the paper. Finish the joints and nailheads as previously described under wall repairs.

Water Spots

Tools and materials. Sandpaper, shellac, throw-away brush, touch-up paint, paintbrush, dropcloth, ladder.

STEPS

Cover the water spot with 4-lb.-cut shellac. Use a throw-away brush, since the cost of brush cleaner is more than the brush is worth. You can buy spray-on shellac, which replaces the brush technique.

Let the shellac dry about an hour. Then touch up the spotted area. You may have to repaint the entire ceiling for best results.

Painting ceilings. Use flat paint especially made for ceilings. When should you repaint a ceiling? Paint the ceiling once for every three times you paint the walls of the room. Of course, this formula does not apply if you are changing color, or the ceiling is especially dirty from soot, or you have just made a repair and need to blend it in.

Replacing Damaged Ceiling Tile

Tools and materials. Stepladder, stapler/hammer and nails, razor knife, building adhesive, caulking gun shell, putty knife.

The tools and materials you will need depend on how the ceiling has been installed. We list here the tools and materials for all types of installations. Take your pick, according to your ceiling.

STEPS, SUSPENDED CEILING TILE

These tiles are supported by metal grids that hang from the ceiling or joists or rafters above. To replace a damaged tile, push up on the tile to dislodge it from the grid. Then remove it and replace the old tile with a new one.

STEPS, CEILING TILE ON FURRING

With a razor knife, cut an X from corner-to-corner across the face of the tile. Go completely through the thickness of the tile with the knife.

You can probably remove half of the tile after you finish cutting it. This will be the half that has a tongue that goes into a groove on the adjoining attached tile. Leave the old tongue in place, taking out only the rectangular half.

You will probably have to cut loose the other half of the tile. Use the razor knife and run it along the joint of the ceiling tile. Press down hard. If you hit a metal staple, let the knife slide over the staple and continue.

With the old tile removed, cut the tongue from the new replacement tile, using the razor knife. You will not be able to

Cross-score the damaged ceiling tile with a sharp razor knife. If you can, cut through the tile. You will be able to remove half the tile by pulling it carefully from the adjoining tile.

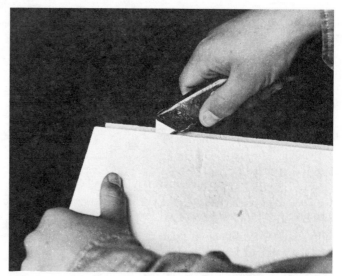

Trim the tongue off the replacement tile. You probably can fit it into the groove in the adjoining tile on the ceiling without damaging the tile already there. This new tile fits flat on the furring.

Cut along the "tongue" edge in the tile joint. If you strike staples, skip over them. Pull the tile out of the ceiling, taking care not to rip or damage the adjoining tile.

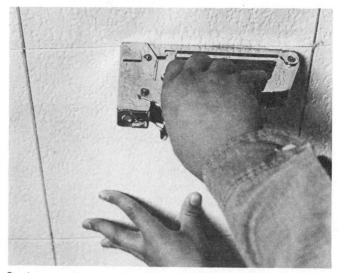

Staple across the joint, if there is no other way you can attach the new tile to the old tiles. The staples won't show unless you nick the tile with the stapler, or get it dirty with your hands or tools.

fit the tongue from the old tile into the groove and make the tile seat properly unless you remove this tongue. Match the tile in the void to determine where the cut is to be made.

Insert the tile in the void. Seat it so the surface of the tile matches the surrounding surface of the adjoining tiles. This may take more cutting with the razor knife. Go slowly to prevent damage to the tile.

When the tile fits, staple across one side of it into the adjoining tile along the joint. One tongue of the new tile will fit into a groove to hold one side of the tile; the staples hold the other side of the tile.

STEPS, CEILING TILE GLUED TO WALLBOARD

With a razor knife, cut out the damaged tile after scoring the joints of the tile with the knife. You may have to do this in strips, using a screwdriver or bradawl to remove all the cut pieces. When you have finished, scrape away any debris and old adhesive with a putty knife.

Cut off the tongue of the new tile so it will fit into the void.

You may have to do some razor trimming, too, so the new tile seats properly in the space.

Squirt a walnut-sized daub of building adhesive on each corner of the new tile and press the tile in place. Hold it in position for several minutes while the adhesive dries slightly. If you get adhesive on the face of the tile, remove it instantly with mineral spirits on a soft cloth. Do not rub; blot the area.

FIREPLACE REPAIRS

If your fireplace has been idle for some time, first make sure the fireplace will support the fire with safety. Check the chimney for obstructions. With the damper open, you should be able to see daylight through the chimney, even though there is a bend in the chimney structure. Be certain that none of the firebrick are broken, missing, or lacking mortar between joints.

Firebrick Maintenance

Tools and materials. New (matching) firebrick, firebrick

mortar, tuckpointing trowel, brick or cold chisel, baby sledge hammer, a container for debris. Wear safety glasses and gloves.

STEPS

Inspect the brick in the fire chamber for any damage. Broken and missing firebrick must be replaced. Also check the mortar between firebrick joints. If the mortar is loose and crumbling, the mortar lines should be tuckpointed (see Chapter 8).

Mortar for firebrick contains fire clay. The mixture (you will probably have to mix your own) is one part cement containing fire clay to three or four parts sand.

The same procedures for tuckpointing and replacing masonry units (see Chapter 8) are used for firebrick.

When a Fireplace Won't Draw

This can be a smoky situation, and it can be caused by several problems or a combination of problems.

Damper won't open. Soot or rust may be sticking the damper shut. With a hammer and a length of scrap wood, try tapping the damper along one edge while a helper moves the operating lever to the open position. Once open, open and close the damper several times to break away any residue. This usually solves the problem.

Fireplace won't draw. Make sure there are no obstructions in the chimney or at the top of the chimney. An overhanging tree limb can block the chimney, or animals could have built a nest in the opening.

The size of the opening or firebox may be too large. Short of rebuilding the fireplace, there is nothing much you can do about this problem. However, you can find out whether this is the problem.

With a piece of hardboard or asbestos board held across the top of the fireplace opening, lower the material slowly while there is a fire going in the fireplace. When the smoking stops, this is the height the top lintel of the fireplace should be.

Smoke will not go up the chimney, if the firebox is too big. You can check this by filling in extra courses of firebrick along the back, sides, and floor of the fireplace. If the extra bricks solve the problem, set the bricks in position with mortar made for fireplaces.

Fire won't burn. The wood could be wet. Or, the fire is not getting enough air to burn properly. Try opening a window slightly for the extra air you need.

Make sure the fire is in the center of the fireplace. If the fire is too near the opening of the fireplace, the back of the fireplace will not warm properly. This warmth creates the draft for the needed updraft for the fire to catch and burn properly.

When possible, leave a bed of ashes under the andirons. The ashes are warmed by the fire, and they prevent a down-and-out draft from the firebox.

Damper Maintenance

Tools and materials. Hammer, screwdriver, pliers, gloves.

STEPS

Dampers are operated by pull chains or levers. Sometimes the levers become bent and the chains broken.

You can try to straighten a bent lever with pliers. Go up under the firebox until you locate the damper and then trace the lever backward. You may be able to bend the lever enough so it slides fairly smoothly.

A chain pull is easier to repair. Simply hook a new chain to the damper and thread the chain through to the outside opening. You usually can separate the links for attachment with pliers. If not, try driving a screwdriver through a link to separate it. Protect the screwdriver handle with a piece of scrap wood, or use a rubber hammer instead of the screwdriver.

Cleaning Out the Chimney

Chimney linings sometimes need to be cleaned. Soot buildup can block the air (smoke) passage, usually after the fireplace has been in service for some time.

You can buy a chemical cleaner that you throw on the fire; the chemical activates the soot, which is burned away. Or you can load an old burlap bag with paper and a couple of bricks, tie a stout cord to the end of the bag, and then lower the bag down the chimney from the roof. Be sure to have the damper closed when you try this; it is also a good idea to seal off the face of the fireplace with heavy paper and masking tape. Soot is as insidious as dust; it will stain anything it touches.

FOUNDATION AND BASEMENT REPAIRS

Moisture is a foundation's biggest enemy. Water in the form of snow, rain, and humidity, can wreck mortar joints in brick and concrete block, rot wooden sills and other foundation-connected framing, and can cause other problems such as flooded basements.

Solving Drainage Problems

Tools and materials. Since the problem can involve gutters, downspouts, broken concrete joints, tools are related to each job as outlined below.

Gutters and downspouts. Look for trouble here if your basement is leaking water. Often, faulty gutters and downspouts are serving as funnels to carry the water down against the foundation wall. The result is a damp or wet basement. Repairs or a new rain-carrying system may be the answer. (See Chapter 8 for repair details.)

Press hydraulic cement into leaking foundation/basement floor joints, after you have cleaned the joint with a cold or brick chisel. You can use your fingers to make the patch; then smooth the patch with a trowel as shown.

STEPS, FOUNDATION SEEPAGE

First try patching any interior cracks with hydraulic cement.

Clean out the crack with a cold or brick chisel, driving these tools with a baby sledge hammer. Make the cut in the form of an inverted V, if you can. This will help hold the patch in place.

Press the hydraulic cement into the break and smooth it level with the surrounding surface of the foundation wall with a putty knife. You will have to work fast. Hydraulic cement sets very quickly. Wear gloves for this job, since hydraulic cement creates heat that could injure your skin.

Water Backup and Seepage

Water may be coming up through the floor, out of a drain, or from an open or dripping faucet outlet.

STEPS

Seeping water. Try filling the cracks in the floor and along the foundation with hydraulic cement. Clean the cracks with a cold or brick chisel and baby sledge. Press in the cement and trowel it smooth with a putty knife.

Flooding drains. Water backing up out of a floor drain can destroy a basement. If this is a common occurrence, try rodding out the drain with a plumber's snake. If this does not work, have a professional drain-cleaner cut through the debris. Then ask for root-inhibiting chips that you can add to your drain.

Overflowing water. Check all pipes and drains in the basement area. Sometimes a leaky pipe joint can drip itself into a flooded floor without your noticing the leak. Leaks usually have to be repaired by replacing a length of pipe. (See instructions in Chapter 5.)

Sump Pumps for Excessive Water

You can buy portable sump pumps and hook them up in your basement to remove excess water due to an unusual occurrence. But if excessive water is a constant problem, and a sump pump could be the answer, you should have a permanent pump installed. This involves digging a shallow well in the basement floor and lining the well with concrete. This, too, is a job for a professional. The sump pump goes into the well. When the water in the well reaches a predetermined level, the pump starts, removing the water before it seeps onto the surface of the basement floor.

To install a portable sump pump, set it on the floor, and connect a hose to the pump and to a drain. The pump will pump the water from the floor into the drain.

Water vacuums. For occasional flooding, a water vacuum may be the answer. It does what the name implies: vacuums up the water on the floor. The vacuums are fairly inexpensive; buy them at hardware stores or home centers.

Rotting Sills

Tools and materials. Penetrating wood sealer, paintbrush.

STEPS

First find where the water is coming from and stop it. Do not overlook damaged gutters and downspouts, back-flowing drains, leaky siding, leaking roofs.

Coat the sill with penetrating wood sealer. Try to work the sealer into all joints and along adjoining framing members. This will help prevent further damage, but it won't repair previous damage. If the sills are really badly rotted, you will have to have them replaced by a professional. Do not attempt this job yourself.

Basement Waterproofing

This treatment will help solve a slight moisture problem, but it is not a permanent cure for seeping water.

Tools and materials. Masonry paint, paintbrush, dropcloth, a brick, broom.

STEPS

Smooth any pieces of concrete stuck to the walls with a brick. The brick works as an abrasive and will make fast work of concrete blobs. Clean the walls, using a broom to sweep them.

Mix the concrete paint according to the manufacturer's instructions on the container. Some finishes require that the wall be wet before the mixture is applied. Others require an etching compound and scraping out of any recesses. Work from the upper left hand corner of the wall and then down and across the wall. Apply a heavy coat of paint to the wall — don't skimp.

To patch cracks, chips, and breaks in the masonry, use a stiff sand mix. Tuckpoint joints that are crumbling. You want the wall to be as smooth and watertight as possible before applying the masonry paint.

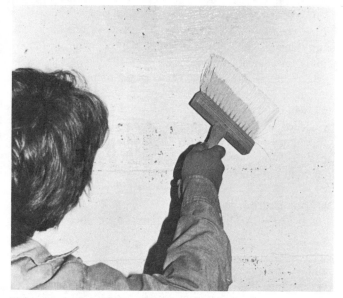

Masonry paint helps "dampproof" basement walls, but the paint can't stop water from penetrating the foundation from the outside.

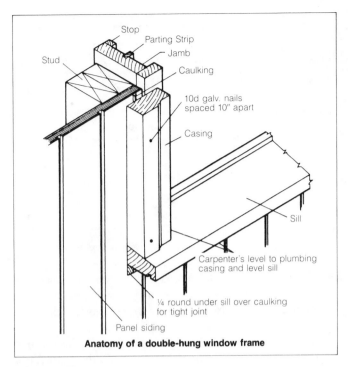

Anatomy of a double-hung window frame

(Labels: Stop, Parting Strip, Jamb, Caulking, Stud, 10d galv. nails spaced 10" apart, Casing, Sill, Carpenter's level to plumbing casing and level sill, ¼ round under sill over caulking for tight joint, Panel siding)

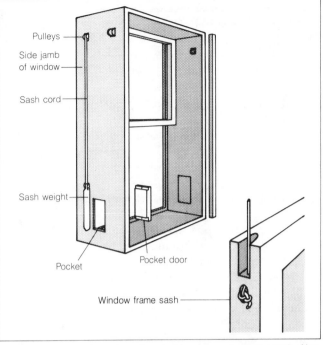

(Labels: Pulleys, Side jamb of window, Sash cord, Sash weight, Pocket, Pocket door, Window frame sash)

WINDOWS
Adjusting Window Spring Lifts
Tools and materials. A screwdriver.

STEPS
Most spring lifts are contained in a tube which is installed along the channel of the window.

Loosen the screw at the top of the tube just enough to allow you to pull the tube away from the window channel. As soon as the screw is free of the channel grasp it between your thumb and forefinger so that you do not lose the tension on the spring inside the tube. If the window has been creeping open, the spring is too tight: give the screw several turns to decrease the tension. If the window has been creeping shut, the spring is too loose: turn the screw in the opposite direction to increase the tension. Keep your finger on the screw to maintain the new tension while replacing it in the window channel. With a screwdriver, reseat the screw.

How to Replace Spring Lifts
Tools and materials. A new lift (remove the old one and take it to the store for a sample), hammer, screwdriver, thick-bladed putty knife, 6d finishing nails, nail set, wood putty, touch-up paint, paintbrush.

STEPS
Pry off the window stops that hold the window in position. The stops form a channel for the edges of the window. Use a putty knife for a prying tool, driving the knife with a hammer. Be careful not to damage the window stops, which are usually narrow. Remove the spring lift tube.

Now lift the window from the channel. You will see how the spring lift is fastened to the window — usually with a screw-like rod.

Replace the new lift the same way you removed the old lift, and adjust the tension as outlined above. Then replace the window in the channels and nail on the stops. You probably will have to countersink the nail heads, fill the holes with water putty, and touch up the paint.

To replace sash cords, remove the window stop and window sash. Also remove the door in the window channel to expose the sash weights. Cord goes over the weight pulleys. The sash cord is slipped through the window channel, knotted, and then pulled back into the recess. Spring lifts are screwed in position. Spring lifts also are made in removable "cartridges" that fit a slot in the window.

How to Replace Sash Cords
Tools and materials. New sash cord, hammer, screwdriver, razor knife, pry bar or butt chisel, nail set, 8d finishing nails, touch-up paint, paintbrush.

STEPS, DOUBLE-HUNG WINDOWS
Remove the window stop from the window casing. Use the pry bar or butt chisel for this. Be careful not to split or break the stop. Now remove the window. Don't pull it all the way out — just enough to expose the cord. The cord will lay in a channel along the edge of the window.

Have a helper hold the old cord while you unfasten it from the window. Tie the end of the new cord to the old cord and let the sash weight pull it over the sash pulley and down in the window framing. Then fasten the end of the new cord to the window.

In the channel of the window, you will find a little door. You can pry this door open to expose the sash weight. Pull out the sash weight and bring the old and new cord out with the weight. Then untie the knot and attach the new cord to the weight and replace the weight.

Replace the window, check the tension on the cord, and replace the window stop. You may have to countersink the nail heads, fill the nail holes with water putty, and touch up these spots with paint.

If the window doesn't have the sash weight door feature, you will have to remove the window casing to get at the cord and sash weight. Use a pry bar or butt chisel. Just do one side of the window; you need not disassemble the entire window.

Repairing Drapery Hardware
Tools and materials: Screwdriver, pliers, plastic wall an-

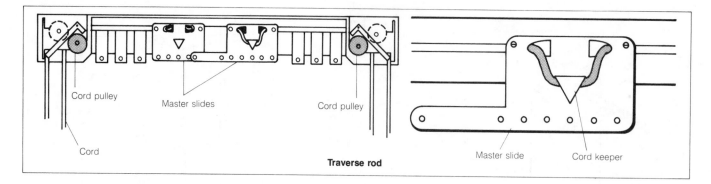

Cord pulley   Master slides   Cord pulley   Cord

Master slide   Cord keeper

Traverse rod

chors, screws, brace/drill, ¼-in. bit/drill, long nail.

STEPS

A loose and wobbly traverse rod is the No. 1 problem. First, check the mounting brackets to see if they are either screwed tightly to or snapped in place on the rod.

The mounting brackets may be loose on the wall or in window casings where they are fastened. If so, use a screwdriver to tighten the screws. If the screws won't tighten, the screws may be broken in the plastic or lead anchors in the wall, or stripped in the molding.

Try replacing any loose screws with screws one size larger. The larger screw trick will work in the molding but may not work in the wall anchors.

Remove the mounting bracket from the wall and the rod. With a long nail — 16d or 20d, punch the anchor through the wall so it drops between the framing. Insert new, larger anchors in the holes, remount the brackets, and align the rod.

Misadjusted Traverse Rod

Tools and materials. Screwdriver.

STEPS

Remove the traverse rod from the mounting brackets and the spring-loaded pulley, which is located near the baseboard. You may need either a standard or Phillips screwdriver.

Lay the rod flat on the floor, with the working parts facing you. Do not accidentally lengthen or shorten the rod. It should remain the same length.

On your left, you will see a little pulley where the cord runs. Or, you will see the double cord go into the rod. About halfway over on the rod, you will see a master slide. A bit farther to the right you will see another master slide. These two slides open and close the draperies. The problem is the cord and how it is attached to the slides.

First, pull the cord and let the slide on the left travel as far as it will go toward the center of the rod. Hold onto the cord. Now move the right slide toward the center as far as it will go. The two slides should meet about halfway in the rod. If not, loosen the cord on the slide at the right. Then move the slide to the left until it meets the left slide. Rehook the cord on the right slide.

Both slides should now work perfectly and meet at about the center of the traverse rod.

Installing a New Traverse Rod

Tools and materials. If mounted on a wood casing: bradawl, screwdriver, screws, tape measure. If mounted on a wall: plas-

tic or lead wall anchors, screws, screwdriver, brace/drill, bit/drill, tape measure.

STEPS

This is *very* important: Before you buy a traverse rod, note the exact measurements in inches that the rod will span. Incorrect measurements are the No. 1 reason why rods won't fit properly and cause time-consuming exchanges of rods. Most drapery hardware comes packaged with the manufacturer's instructions for installation. These instructions supersede the instructions below.

As a general rule, a rod should be placed about 4 in. above the top of the window. The rod should extend from 6 to 18 in. on each side of the window. If the rod will be attached to the window casing, these measurements will be shortened somewhat. However, try to maintain the measurements as best you can. If the rod goes next to the ceiling, align it with the level of the ceiling, not the window.

Lay out the rod on the floor, extending it to the length needed. Then adjust the pull cord, as previously outlined.

With a helper, position the rod over the window and mark the locations of the mounting bracket on the wall or window casing. Doublecheck these markings with a tape measure before you proceed.

If plastic anchors, lead anchors, or toggle bolts will be used to mount the brackets (these come with the rods), drill the holes for them in the wall. If the rod will be mounted to the wood casing, punch pilot holes for the screws with a bradawl. Or use an ice pick or a 10d nail.

Now fasten the brackets to the wall or casing. Then install the rod. If the cord has a spring-loaded pulley, mount this to the wall with lead or plastic anchors and screws. The cord should be taut between the rod and pulley.

Casement Operator Maintenance

Tools and materials. Screwdriver, paste wax, soft cloth or vacuum.

STEPS

Two screws hold the casement window operator (crank) to the window frame. Back out these screws and slip the crank up off the frame. This will expose the gears of the operator. On some models you may have to remove a plate that covers the gears; use a screwdriver for this.

Clean the gears as best as you can with a cloth. Then, puff graphite powder or light machine oil into the gear mechanism. Graphite powder is better than grease since graphite does not collect and hold dirt and grit, which makes the gears hard to turn. To complete the job, replace the metal plate — if there is one — and screw on the operator.

You may need to lubricate the arm where it goes through the window frame and where it hinges to the outside window. This will make the entire cranking unit easier to operate.

Sliding Window Maintenance

Tools and materials. Block of wood, rubber hammer, fine steel wool, graphite powder or light machine oil.

Sliding windows balk because the channel in which the window slides is bent, dirty, or corroded.

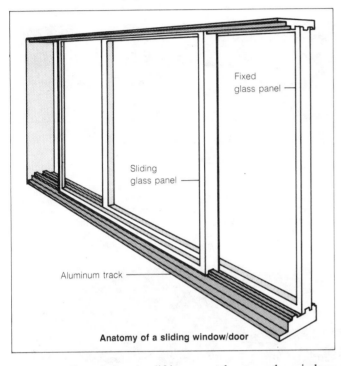

Anatomy of a sliding window/door

Remove the window by lifting up and out on the window. With a vacuum or brush, clean out the window channel. Coat the channel with paste wax and buff the wax with a cloth. If the channel is really dirty, first clean the area with a vacuum or cloth. Then buff the channel with fine steel wool. Clean away the residue; wax and buff the channel.

If the channel is bent, you sometimes can straighten it with a rubber hammer. Place a block of wood in the channel where the window slides. Then tap the metal lightly with the rubber hammer to straighten. (See also p. 53.)

If the weatherstripping on the window is shot, you can buy replacement weatherstripping and install it with a screwdriver, per the instructions.

Awning Window Maintenance

Tools and materials. Screwdriver, graphite powder or light machine oil, block plane, steel wool.

STEPS

Awning windows work almost the same way as casement windows (see above). The crank and hinges need some maintenance about every two years or so.

Remove the crank from the window with a screwdriver. This will expose the gears of the crank. Lubricate the gears with graphite powder or light machine oil. Also lubricate the hinge pins with graphite. If paint or rust is causing the linkage to stick, remove this obstruction with fine steel wool.

If you want to remove the window, unscrew the crank and then lift out the linkage in the mounting brackets on the sides of the window.

Awning windows can stick. You can stop this by planing off a small amount of the wood at the binding point. Use a block plane or sandpaper for this. Go slowly; if you take off too much, the swelling that now causes the window to bind may become a crack when the humidity drops.

Jalousie Window Maintenance

Tools and materials. Screwdriver, pliers, graphite powder or light machine oil.

STEPS

Like casement and awning windows, jalousie windows operate with a crank. The only maintenance needed is lubrication of the crank gears, pivot pins, and replacement of glass slats if the slats become cracked or broken.

Remove the crank assembly for lubrication by backing out the screws that hold the assembly to the frame. Puff graphite powder or light machine oil into the gear box and replace the assembly. The pivots need graphite lubrication annually. Open the window to expose the pivots.

To replace a glass slat, you have to bend little metal tabs on the frame that hold the glass in position. With pliers, bend the tabs out and down so the glass slips out. Install the new glass and bend over again the tabs to secure it.

How to Replace Window Glass

Tools and materials. Putty knife, razor knife, tape measure,

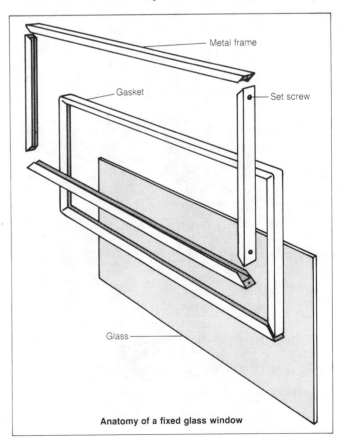

Anatomy of a fixed glass window

glazier's points, glazing compound, glass, gloves, paint, paintbrush.

Safety. Wear gloves when handling glass.

STEPS

With a putty knife and razor knife, remove the old glazing around the mullions (frame) of the broken glass. For replacement glass, measure the length and width between the mullions. The glass should be about ⅛ in. *smaller* than this measurement. The glass should "float" in the mullions to permit expansion and contraction of the wood.

Before you install the new glass, paint the mullions. This seals the wood against moisture and rot.

Install the new glass in the frame and secure it with glazier's points pressed into place in the wood with the tip end of the putty knife. Space the points about 2 to 3 in. apart; install the points on all four sides of the frame. Don't skimp.

Form a ball with the glazing compound. Then with your thumb and index finger, make a little string of the glazing compound and press this string into the mullions. Go completely around the frame with glazing.

When the glazing is packed into the mullions, press the flat side of the putty knife against the edge of the glass and the edge of a mullion. The angle should be about 45 degrees. Press down firmly on the putty knife and pull it along the glazing compound. This motion will cut, flatten, and smooth the glazing in the frame.

After the glazing is smoothed to your satisfaction, let the job set a day. This permits the glazing to "harden" so it is easier to paint. Give the glazing and frame two coats of paint, running the paint about ⅛ in. onto the glass. This trick seals the glazing.

Metal windows do not use glazier's points to hold the glass in place. Instead, small metal clips are snapped into holes in the frame or mullions of the window. To remove and replace these clips, use pliers in combination with a standard blade screwdriver. Glass measuring and glazing techniques are the same for metal windows as for wooden windows.

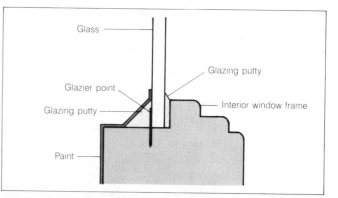

When inserting glazier points, tap in carefully so you won't break the glass. Place points first near the corners, and then every 2 to 3 in. along the glass — or where the old points were removed. Fill the groove with glazing compound. Leave ⅛ in. gap between the height of the compound, and the inside level of the mullion. Then paint over the glazing compound to match the height of the mullion and form a seal.

Remove the broken glass, old glazing, and glazier's points from the window mullions. Clean the mullions with a putty knife, or use the edge of a rasp. Then prime the mullions with paint or sealer and insert the glass panel.

Knead the glazing into a ball or string it out, as shown. Then press it in place in the mullions. Use plenty of glazing; you will trim off any excess with the putty knife. Glazing is better than putty, since glazing stays pliable.

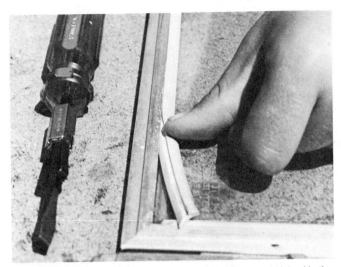

Glass in storm window insets fits into a gasket that is sandwiched in the metal frame of the window. Remove two set screws in the frame to "spread" the frame so you can remove and re-install the glass and gasket.

Screen wire in metal windows usually is held by a spline that runs in a channel around the edge of the frame. Some splines are metal; pry them out of the channel with a screwdriver. Be careful; do not bend or kink the spline.

How to Replace Screen Wire

Tools and materials. On wooden frames: chisel or thick-bladed putty knife, hammer, 4d finishing or box nails, staple gun, razor knife, screen wire, two lengths of 1x3, two C-clamps. On metal frames: putty knife, razor knife, screen wire, screwdriver, spline material (if needed).

STEPS

Remove the screen molding around the wire and frame with the chisel or putty knife. Be careful not to split or break the molding so you can use it again. Remove the screen wire, prying up the staples with the tip of the putty knife or hammer.

Cut the new screen wire to fit, using the edge of the screen frame as a straightedge to guide the knife. Use the old screen wire as a template (pattern).

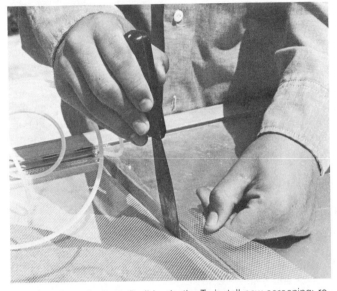

Some screen splines are flexible plastic. To install new screening: remove the spline, rough fit the screening, and then press the new screening in the spline channel that runs around the screen frame.

With the staple gun, fasten the screening to one end of the screen frame. Then lay the frame on a flat table surface.

Slip one length of 1x3 under one end of the frame and the other 1x3 under the other end of the frame. Clamp the center of the frame to the table. This will produce tension in the frame. Don't screw down too much on the clamps — only a little tension is necessary.

Now fasten the other end of the screening to the frame. Remove the clamps. When the clamps are removed, the frame will spring flat again, stretching the screening tight. Finish fastening the screening to the frame, and nail on the molding to complete the job.

If the screen frame is metal, the screening is probably held in place with a plastic or metal spline around the edge of the framing. You can remove this spline with the tip of a putty knife or a standard blade screwdriver. Once the spline is out, you can remove the screening. Cut the new screening to fit and replace the spline in the groove. If the spline is plastic, you may have to replace it with new material.

For this job, you may want to buy an inexpensive spline tool. The tool has a wheel on one end of a handle; the wheel fits the spline groove. You simply run the wheel along the screening to press the screening into the groove. The wheel also enables you to replace plastic splines more easily.

Pretrim the screening with a razor knife and fit the spline into the channel. You can cut the spline material with a razor knife or scissors to fit each side separately. Or you can insert it in a continuous piece with the ends meeting.

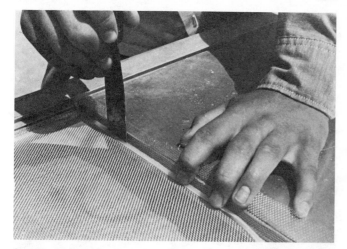

Screen panels in combination screen/storm doors and windows also utilize a spline to hold the screening in the metal frames. You may have to "miter" the screening (use a razor knife) so it fits smoothly in the grooves.

Patching Screen Wire

Tools and materials. For metal screening: tinsnips or a razor knife, block of wood. For plastic screening: scissors, upholstery needle, heavy thread the same color as the screening.

STEPS

Cut a patch of metal screening to fit over the tear in the screening, plus 2 in. Unravel the tiny strands of wire along the edge of the patch about ½ in. from each side. When you are finished, the patch will be surrounded by a series of tiny wires.

Carefully bend the wires over at right angles to the patch. You may want to use the block of wood for this so the wires are straight and bends are sharp.

Stick each wire though a hole in the screening until you've worked entirely around the patch. This takes a lot of patience, so plan to spend the time. When you're finished, press the wires against the screening with the block of wood. The patch will be obvious until the new wire changes color through corrosion.

If the screening is plastic, cut a patch to cover the tear in the screening. It should overlap the tear about ½ in. on all four sides. With the upholstery needle and heavy thread, "sew" the patch to the screening, using the holes in the screening to guide the needle and thread.

Screen patches are a stop-gap measure. Screening that has ripped or rusted out should be replaced.

Window Shade Malfunctions

The usual problem is spring tension in the roller.

STEPS

Roll the shade up to the very top of the window.

Remove the shade from the brackets and then unroll the shade about 10 to 12 in. Replace the shade on the brackets. Now roll the shade up and down five or six times. This action should restore the proper tension to the spring inside the roller.

Replacing Venetian Blind Cords and Tapes

Tools and materials. Screwdriver, razor knife, plastic tape, cord, tapes. Make sure the cord is the same size as the cord in

the blinds. Tapes should be the same width and have the same number of ladders (for slats) as the old tapes.

STEPS

To replace the cords, first untie the cord on the tilt side at the bottom slat. You probably will have to remove metal end caps in order to gain access to the cord. Use a screwdriver for this.

Tape the end of the new lift cord to the old cord, and then pull the new cord up through the slots in the slats. When the old/new cord appears out the opposite end, pull out enough cord to form a long loop. You will see how to do this from the adjustment of the old cord. At the top of the loop is a small clip which "locks" the cords together.

It is a good idea to also replace the tilt cord at this time. The only thing you have to do is loop the cord over the pulley at the top of the blind. Remove the handles on the old cord, slip them on the new cord. Tie knots in the new cord and pull the handles down over the knots.

To change tapes, remove the blind from the window with a screwdriver. Lay the unit on the floor. Now unhook the cords from the bottom slat and pull the cords up through the slats. This will free the slats. Replace the tapes, insert the slats, and rethread the cords through the slats.

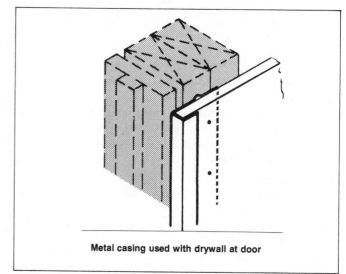

Metal casing used with drywall at door

DOORS

Hinge Repair and Replacement

Tools and materials. Steel wool, graphite powder, hammer, block of wood, nail, match sticks, screws one size larger than the screws already holding the hinges.

STEPS

If the door binds at the hinges, it is likely that the hinge pins are rusty or coated with paint.

The bottom of the hinge pins may be encased in metal. However, this covering will have a small hole in it. Insert a nail in this hole and hit the nail with a hammer. This will force the hinge pin up out of the hinge barrel. To remove the pin, tap the head of the pin upward with a hammer. Use a block of scrap wood to buffer the blows. If the hinge barrel doesn't have a hole, the pin will be exposed at the bottom. Use the nail/buffer-block technique to remove the pin.

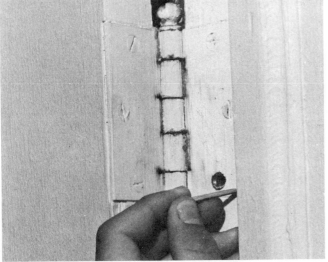

Loose hinges are quick to tighten by filling the screw holes with toothpicks or matchsticks — after removing the match heads. As an alternative, try longer screws in the holes.

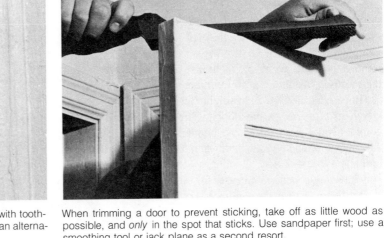

When trimming a door to prevent sticking, take off as little wood as possible, and *only* in the spot that sticks. Use sandpaper first; use a smoothing tool or jack plane as a second resort.

Storm door hinges sometimes fit in back of a metal covering that helps support the door. You may be able to remove the hinge by unscrewing it along the edge of the door, or you can unscrew the metal framing.

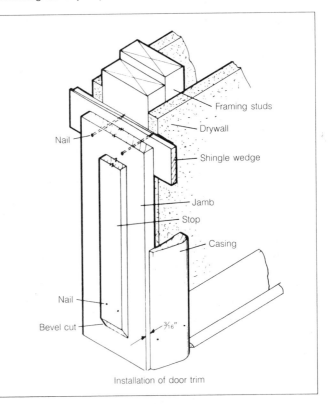

Installation of door trim

Labels in figure: Framing studs, Drywall, Nail, Shingle wedge, Jamb, Stop, Casing, Nail, Bevel cut, 3/16"

Remove bottom hinge pins first. Shine the pins with fine steel wool, rub graphite powder or light machine oil on the metal, and reinsert the pins. Do the same with top pins.

If the hinges are loose, try tightening the screws. If this does not work, remove the screws and replace them with screws that are one size larger and longer. If this does not work, fill in the screw holes with match sticks and re-insert the screws.

Replacing hinges usually calls for nothing more than removing the old hinges with a screwdriver and installing the new hinges. You may need longer screws than those provided with the new hinges.

If the new hinges do not fit the mortises in the door and door casing, you will have to enlarge the mortises. Use a chisel and rubber hammer for this job. For a chisel guide, scribe the outline of the new hinge onto the wood.

When Doors Stick

Tools and materials. Medium-grit abrasive, sanding block, jack plane, wide butt chisel, rubber hammer.

STEPS

First, make sure that the door hinges are not causing the binding problem. Hinge maintenance is outlined above.

Doors stick and bind for three reasons: the wood is swollen from excessive humidity; the hinges are not supporting the door, causing the door to sag; the door is too large for the opening.

If swollen wood is the problem, note the exact spot the door is sticking. Put a piece of abrasive on a sanding block and sand this spot with the grain of the wood. Keep the sanding block square to the edge of the door. Check the job often by closing the door in the frame. Just as soon as the door opens and closes freely, stop sanding or today's bind will be tomorrow's crack.

If the door is too high, plane along the top edge of the door until the door will fit properly. Run the plane from the edge of the door toward the center of the door. This way, you won't split the wood along the length of the door. If this does not solve the problem, you'll have to take the door off the hinges and plane the top edge from both directions.

If the door is too wide, remove the door from the hinges, remove the hinges, and plane the door from the hinge side. Do not plane the door from the latch side. Since planing will remove the mortise cuts for the hinges, you will have to recut the mortises, using a chisel and rubber hammer.

Hinges that are too lightweight can cause the door to sag, which in turn causes the door to stick and bind. This is a common problem these days; builders sometimes skimp on adequate door and window hardware. The solution to the problem is easy: just replace the hinges with stronger hinges. You may have to deepen the mortises for this. Use a butt chisel and rubber hammer to make the necessary cuts.

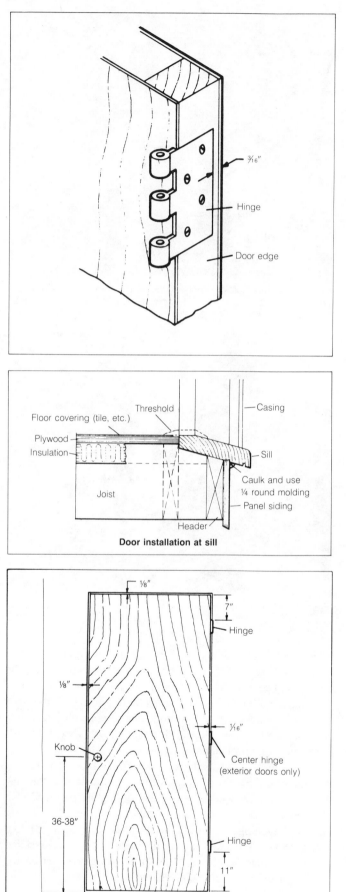

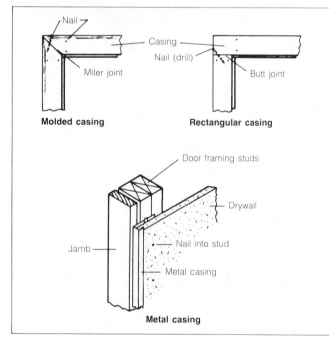

Metal casing

Door trim may be installed with casing or with finishing nails in pairs, nailed to both jamb and framing every 16 in.

Door installation at sill

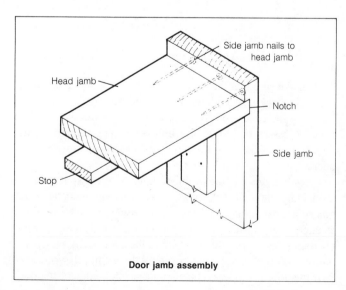

Door jamb assembly

Door clearances

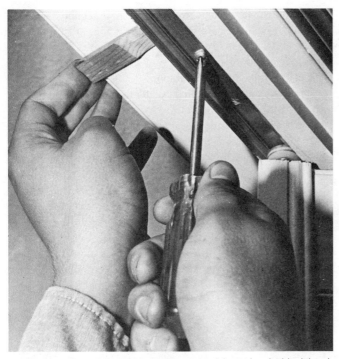

If doors on tracks stick and bind because track is not level, shim it level. Back out the holding screws and insert a shim between the casing and track. Keep the track clean and lubricated with graphite powder.

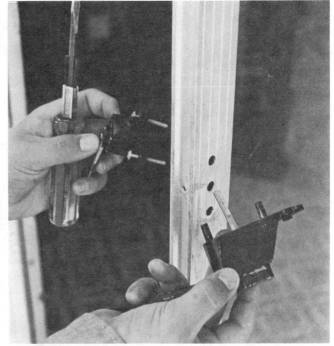

Storm door locks/latches can be in two pieces or a clamshell assembly. Both are held to the storm door with screws. You usually need to change the strike with the lock.

Sticking Track and Runners

Tools and materials. Screwdriver, pliers, vacuum cleaner, graphite powder.

STEPS

When sliding doors balk, look for dirt and grit on the tracks. Usually, a good vacuum cleaning will solve the problem.

If dirt isn't to blame try adjusting the wheels that run in the track. Use a screwdriver for this. There may be too much tension on the wheels or the wheel hangers.

The track may be bent. You can sometimes straighten the track with pliers. If not, replace the track. It is held in place with screws along the bottom of the track, or by mounting brackets fastened on with screws.

Warped Doors

Tools and materials. Screwdriver, hammer, nail, chisel, rubber hammer.

STEPS

Remove the old door, hinges and all. Buy a new door the same size. Transfer the lockset and hinges from the old door to the new door. You may need to cut mortises for the new hinges and latch. Do this with a butt chisel and rubber hammer, as outlined earlier in this chapter.

Replacing Screening in Storm Door Panels

See screen replacement for metal window frames.

Replacing Storm Door Locksets

Tools and materials. New lockset, screwdriver, hammer.

STEPS

This is a take-off-the-old, put-on-the-new procedure, since storm door locksets are usually in a single unit: knob, latch handle, latch.

Unscrew the old lockset which is held by screws at the edge and on the face of the door. The entire unit will pop right off. Then install the new unit by driving the screws in the same holes used by the old lockset.

You may have to adjust the strike plate/latch slightly so the door will stay latched and locked. You can do this by prying up on the wire in the strike. Or, tap this wire down with a hammer. Or, shim out the strike with a piece of cardboard. To insert the shim, remove the two screws that hold the strike to the casing.

Lockset Repair and Replacement

Tools and materials. Screwdriver, (Allen wrench), graphite powder, rubber hammer, chisel, touch-up paint, paintbrush.

STEPS

If you can't turn the handle to activate the latch, the problem could be a loose handle. You can tighten the handle by turning a lock or set screw on the hub of the handle. Use a screwdriver or Allen wrench to turn the screw.

If the latch is balky, the trouble could be rust or dirt inside the lockset. Try puffing a little powdered graphite or light machine oil into the lock through the tiny crack around the latch. Turn the handle a couple of times to work in the lubricant.

If the lock is balky, lack of lubricant usually is the problem. Puff graphite powder into the key hole of the lock, insert the key, and turn the lock.

If the lock is frozen, heat the key with a match and insert the hot key into the lock. You'll need gloves to protect your hands and be careful with the fire.

To replace a lockset, first buy a replacement lockset that fits the thickness of the door. This information will be on the package. Then remove the door knobs on the old lockset. The knobs are usually held by set screws at the base of the knob.

To replace a lockset, unscrew the escutcheon plate (shown) and the door knob. The screw for the knob is in the handle; sometimes the escutcheon plate holds the knob in place.

Remove the knob assembly by simply pulling it out of the hole in the door. Remove the latch. The latch assembly is one unit that slips into a pocket in the door.

Enlarge the mortise in the door for the lock, if necessary. If the mortise is too big, install the lock and fill the space with water putty. Sand and paint the edge of the door.

Next, remove the square rod on which the knobs were attached. The rod slips out of the locking device. Just push on it and slide it out. Finally, pull out the two screws that hold the lockset in the door on the edge of the door, and lift out the lockset from the edge of the door.

The new lockset is installed exactly the reverse from the way you removed the old lockset.

If you want to change the style of a lockset, almost the same procedures are used as outlined above. You must always buy a lockset that fits the thickness of the door, however. Differences in mortise sizes can be corrected by enlarging the mortises with a chisel. If the mortises are larger than the hardware, you can fill the void with wood plastic or water putty. Touch up any patched area with paint.

Door strikes are fastened on with screws. You just remove the screws to remove the strike. On new locksets, you may have to deepen the mortise to accept the latch. Do this with a chisel or brace and bit. The strike will cover the mortise.

The new lockset goes together like the old one came apart. The square rod goes through a hole in the latch assembly and into the other knob. Screws hold the lockset together.

FLOOR REPAIR AND REFINISHING

Wooden floors and stairsteps can squeak. The problem may be caused by the normal settling of the house on its foundation, or the sheathing under the floor may have worked loose from the sheathing nails. Repairs are quick, easy, and inexpensive.

Silencing Squeaks from below the Floor

Tools and materials. A helper, hammer, cedar shingles.

STEPS

Have a helper jump over the squeaky spot upstairs while you locate the squeak in the basement. When you find the spot, drive a wooden cedar shingle between the floor joist and the sheathing right at the squeaky spot.

Sometimes you can stop squeaks by renailing the bridging between the floor joists. The "Bridging" is the crisscrossed pieces of 1x4s or metal that help support the joists laterally. In some new homes, the bridging has not been fastened to the joists by the builder, since the house should settle a year or so before the bridging is final-nailed.

Another trick is to sandwich a block of 2x8-in. wood between the joists at the squeak point. The wood is then toenailed to the joists with 16d nails.

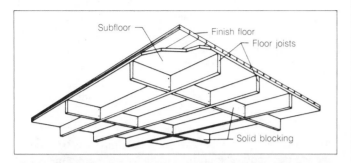

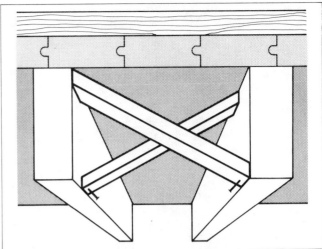

To add joist rigidity, nail loose diagonal bridging. If necessary, add diagonal bridging.

A cedar shingle shim driven with a hammer between subflooring and joists will stop most floor squeaks.

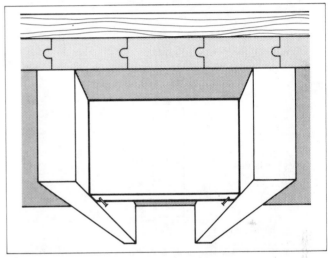

To add additional solid bridging for reinforcement, cut lengths of 2x6 or 2x8 bridging as needed for each span. Force new bridging into opening. Then toenail into adjoining joists at top and bottom of each end of solid bridging. Do not raise the floor; just support it.

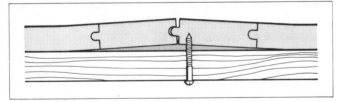

Alternate solution: drill pilot hole through subflooring at point of squeak. Be careful not to go through finish floor. Drive a wood screw up to pull loose flooring down to the subfloor.

In any of the above repairs, make sure that you don't raise the subflooring (sheathing) above the level of the surrounding floor. If you do, this area will have a noticeable "hump" that will show through the floor covering. The idea is to support the floor so it is level and won't compress on the joists when you walk on the floor — that is what causes the squeak.

Silencing Squeaks from above the Floor

Tools and materials. Hammer, 16d finishing nails, nail set, graphite powder, wood plastic, putty knife.

STEPS

If the finish flooring is strip or block, try puffing a little graphite powder between the cracks or joints of the flooring at the squeak point.

If graphite does not work, try nailing down through the flooring. Drill pilot holes, countersink the nails and fill the holes with wood plastic.

If the floor (subfloor) is carpeted, drive finishing nails at the squeak point, and countersink the nailheads slightly. The pile of the carpeting will cover the nails.

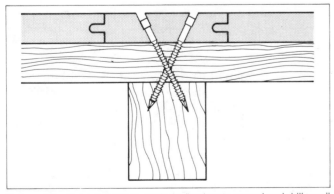

To toenail the finish flooring to subfloor, first locate squeal and drill small pilot holes. Use finishing nails; countersink the nailheads, and fill with matching wood plastic.

How to Boost Sagging Floors

Tools and materials. Metal jackpost, two pieces of 2x12x3-ft. long lumber.

STEPS

Metal jackposts are designed for sagging floors. They are simply a column of steel with a screwtype jack on one end of the column or post.

Sandwich the jackpost between the two pieces of 2x12 — one piece on the floor, the other spanning the joists. The 2x12s help distribute the pressure from the jack. Give the jack a quarter of a turn once a week, until the floor is level.

It may take many weeks to get the floor level, which you can determine by stretching a chalkline across the joists. Leave

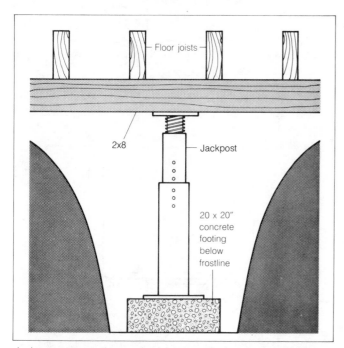

Jackpost supports the sagging joists in a crawl space. In mild climates, the footing may be above the frost line.

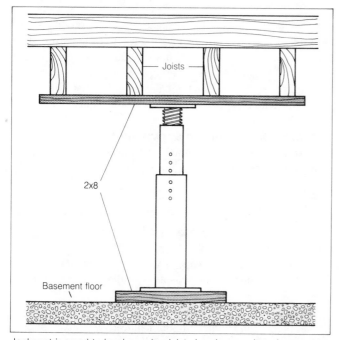

Jackpost is used to level sagging joists in a house with a basement.

the jackpost in place and check for level on an annual basis. If the floor goes out of level again, again give the jack quarter turns until the floor is level.

If the floor spans a wide area, you may have to install several jackposts to boost the sag. Jackposts are inexpensive.

Some codes require that the adjustable jackposts be set or buried in 6 to 8 in. of concrete as a permanent repair, or that you weld the screw of the jackpost at the point where the floor is level.

Another method is to replace the jackpost with metal Lally columns after the floor is level. Two Lally columns should be used to support a 4x8-in. beam, which in turn bridges and supports the sagging joists. If Lally columns will be used, a concrete pad should be positioned under each column. A pad 24 in. square by 12 in. thick usually is standard.

If this treatment does not work, consult a building professional. You may have serious damage to the house framing that only special equipment can remedy.

Replacing Damaged Underlayment (Sheathing)

Tools and materials. New underlayment plywood or particleboard, threaded nails, hammer, pry bar, level, cedar shingles, crosscut saw, square, tape measure.

STEPS

Remove all furniture from the room and take up any rugs or carpeting.

If the damaged underlayment is near a wall, you will have to pry off the base shoe on this wall; be careful not to damage the base shoe, so it may be used again. If the underlayment is not near a wall, you may be able to remove the underlayment from the joists without removing the base molding first.

Pry up the sheet of damaged underlayment. Since the material will be replaced, you don't have to be careful with it. Cut, saw, pry, and/or chisel it — anything you have to do to remove it quickly and easily. But be careful not to damage the underlayment panels around the piece you are taking up.

Examine the joists and the edges of the underlayment panels around the void. Any nails and damaged wood should be removed and smoothed.

Set in the new underlayment panel. Check the panel for level and alignment on the framing members and with the surrounding panels. You may need cedar shims under the panel to bring the panel to level. Tack the shingles to the joists when the panels are level.

Use threaded nails to fasten down the underlayment. Space the nails about three inches apart, countersinking (dimpling) the nails slightly with the hammer head.

Covering Damaged Underlayment (Sheathing)

Tools and materials. Hammer, pry bar, level, cedar shingles or thin wood strips, threaded nails, crosscut saw, square, tape measure, block plane, butt chisel, chalkline, tempered hardboard or particleboard.

STEPS

When flooring or underlayment (sheathing) is in bad repair, you may be able to cover it with new, thin underlayment. Tempered hardboard or particleboard may be used for the underlayment. If possible, buy this material in 4x4-ft. squares (instead of 4x8-ft. panels); the smaller panel dimension is easier to handle.

Remove the furniture, carpeting or rugs from the room. You may also want to consider prying off and replacing the base molding where the wall meets the floor.

Start at one corner of the room and very carefully inspect the old flooring or underlayment. If you find protruding nail heads, ridges or bumps, countersink the nail heads and smooth the ridges with a butt chisel. Fill any large holes with water putty and sand the patches smooth.

Before the underlayment is nailed down, you should lightly bevel (chamfer) the top edges of the material with a block

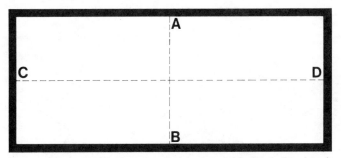

Use a long, metal tape measure to find the length of each wall and mark the centers (ABCD). Cut a length of string about a foot longer than the room width (AB) and rub the string with chalk. Drive a small nail into the floor at A and another at B; tie the chalked string tightly to each in turn, leaving no slack. Pluck the string smartly, snapping it against the floor. Repeat the process at points CD for the two short walls. The intersection of the two chalked lines marks the center of the floor.

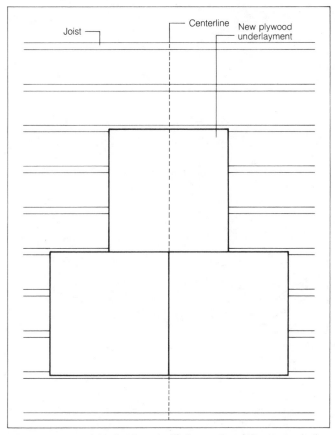

Align the center of the first board with the center of the room, placing one edge on the center of a joist. Stagger placement to avoid four corners meeting.

plane. This provides a better fit at the joints. Before installation, let the underlayment material set about 72 hours in the room in which it will be used. This adjusts the material to the humidity within the room.

Use a chalkline to locate the center of the floor.

Nail the first piece of underlayment at the center point, using the chalkline as a guide for the edges of the underlayment panel. Space the threaded nails about three inches apart around the edges of the panel. Set the next panel against the first,

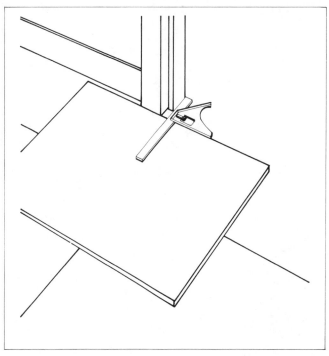

Use a combination square to mark out the profile at the doorway. Trim hardboard along this pattern.

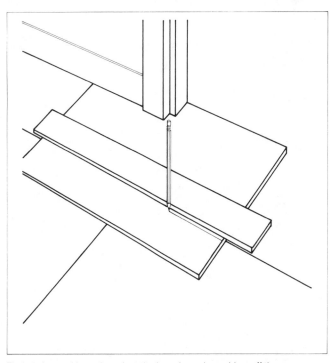

Fit the trimmed board against the baseboard, marking off the excess on the opposite side. Cut, and nail into place.

staggering the joint several inches or so. Nail this panel in position.

Continue setting and nailing each panel so each panel is "staggered" throughout the room. You do not want the joints to be in alignment or uniform. Four corners should not meet at the same spot.

Since base shoe and casing will cover the edges of the new underlayment, you don't have to worry about a tight fit at these joints. However, the joints should not be sloppy; cut them as neatly as you can.

After the job is completed, inspect the new underlayment. If

you find any high spots, you can sand them level. Make sure that nail heads are properly countersunk so they won't stick up through the new flooring.

Replacing Damaged Strip Flooring
See "Replacing Damaged Porch Floor Boards," Chapter 9.

Wood Floor Refinishing Basics
Removing an old finish and applying a new finish to strip wood flooring is a fairly easy job if:

  (1) the floor is not "cupped" or badly uneven between the strips;

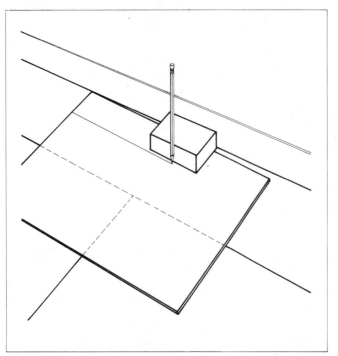

To fit a piece to the baseboard, pull a small piece of wood along the baseboard, marking with a pencil as you go. In this way, any irregularities will be transferred to the hardboard. Trim off along this line.

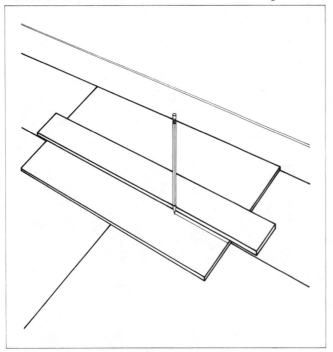

Cut off the excess on the side opposite and nail into place.

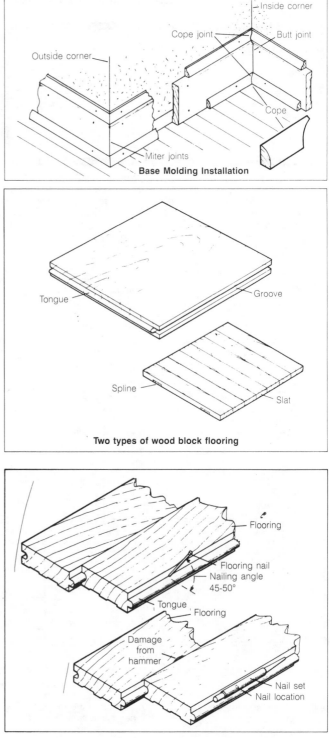

(2) you can rent professional sanding equipment.

Otherwise, the job will become a nightmare, since the humps and dips of uneven flooring must be leveled with the smaller sanding machine in order for the machine to give the proper finish. In some cases, this can involve many hours of sanding to remove the above-level wood.

Tools and materials. Hammer, nail set, pry bar, vacuum attachment, a disk sander or edger, a supply of sanding belts (or paper) depending on the design of the machines. Use Nos. 16 or 20 abrasive for rough sanding; No. 30 abrasive for second cuts; No. 60 abrasive for third cuts. Also, you will need a buffer and polishing machine, buffing and polishing pads, wood filler, putty knife, lamb's wool finish applicator; paintbrush, steel wool, sealer, wood filler, 10d finishing nails, burlap, No. 2 steel wool, penetrating wood finish, wax.

STEPS

Remove all furniture and rugs from the room. With a hammer and pry bar, carefully remove the quarter-round molding nailed to the baseboard and the floor. Then vacuum the floor.

With a hammer and nail set, go completely over the floor and countersink any nail heads that you find. During this inspection, renail any loose flooring, using 10d finishing nails. Countersink the nail heads. Vacuum the floor again.

Move the sanding equipment into the room. Then seal off the doorways into the room. Sanders make lots of fine dust, which can be tracked into other rooms. Turn off the heat or air conditioning to the room so the air circulation will not carry the fine dust into your heating/cooling system. If the weather permits, open the windows into the room for ventilation.

The sanding operation is done in three stages.

1. Use the coarse abrasive for the first sanding cut. Run the sander in the direction of the wood grain in the floor, if at all possible. Take it very easy with the sander. The machine cuts fast and should be in motion at the start and finish of each cut. Do not let the sander sit and run on the floor. If you do, you will cup the wood, making more sanding necessary.

Start at one end of the room with the sander and work toward the other end of the room. Make each pass across the flooring as continuous as possible. When you come to a wall, slowly push down on the handle of the sander, lifting the abrasive drum up off the floor.

The first cut should take the finish down to the raw wood flooring. Depending on the number of coats of finish on the floor, you may have to change the abrasive several times, since it can wear out fast or become clogged with sanding residue. Be sure to use an open-coat abrasive for this job. Do not use paint and varnish remover in conjunction with the sander.

Along the walls and in corners, use the hand-held disc sander to remove the finish. Start with coarse abrasive first. This is a delicate job because the disc sander must be moved over the flooring evenly to maintain the level of the floor and to match the sanding cut left by the larger drum sander.

Since the disc sander cuts fast, you may tend to cup the flooring or make circular ridges in the wood. These ridges are caused by the edge of the abrasive. The trick is to feather the sander into the finish, keeping the sander in motion at all times. Try to float the sander over the surface; let it do the work. You just steer the sander.

On your first sanding attempt with the disc sander, we suggest you work in an area that won't be too noticeable.

2. For the second cut, use the medium-grade abrasive. Work both sanders just as you did for the first cut. However, this cut should be made diagonally across the floor so all the old finish is removed and the wood becomes semi-smooth. Do not go at right angles across the first sanding cut.

3. Use the fine-grade abrasive for the third and final cut, running the sanders diagonally across the flooring. Make this third cut very lightly against the grain of the wood. The result should be a glass-smooth floor surface.

After each sanding operation, clean up any sanding residue with a vacuum cleaner.

If you can't use the disc sander in corners or under obstructions such as radiators or shelving, you will have to use a hand sanding block, teamed with paint and varnish remover and a stiff-bladed scraper or putty knife. Ventilate the room when using the chemical finish remover.

When the sanding job is completed, go over the floor once again with the vacuum cleaner, removing all sanding residue. Then, with a tack rag, go over the entire floor again. Change rags when the one you are using becomes filled with wood dust. This will happen often. Vacuum the floor again.

Finishing hardwood floors. If the floor is oak (which it probably is) or a similar hardwood, you will have to go over the floor with a wood filler made especially for this purpose.

Generally, you should thin the filler slightly with turpentine or mineral spirits so the filler has the consistency of thick paint. Apply the filler to the floor with burlap cloth. Rub the filler onto the floor across the grain of the wood. Work in a small confined area; don't go across the entire room.

When the filler begins to appear dull, wipe off the excess filler with clean burlap. Then complete the job by wiping the area again with a clean piece of burlap. Now you can move onto another section of the floor and repeat the process until the entire floor is filled.

Let the wood filler dry for two days. Then lightly buff the floor with No. 2 steel wool, working with the grain of the wood. You may be able to use the buffer/polisher you bought or rented with steel wool pads.

Vacuum the floor to remove all steel wool and filler residue. It is a good idea to again go over the floor with a tack rag.

With a lamb's wool applicator, apply penetrating wood finish to the floor. Don't use too much finish. Spread it fairly thin with the applicator, but do not miss any areas. Try to keep a light between you and the finishing operation; this way you can see the wet finish and can catch any dull spots that have been missed.

Let the finish set for about 20 minutes. This gives it time to penetrate into the wood grain. Again, go over the surface with the applicator to remove any finish that has not penetrated into the wood. Cover the entire floor with the sealer, and then let the job set for about 24 hours.

In a corner that will not show, test the finish with a knife blade to make certain that the material has dried completely. If not, the finish will curl and stick to the surface of the knife blade. Wait another day. Then try the test again. Drying times for finish will vary somewhat because of the humidity in the room.

If the finish is dry, go over the entire floor with No. 2 steel wool. Don't bear down on this abrasive; just lightly buff the finish, removing any gloss from it.

Vacuum the floor, removing all residue.

Apply the second coat of sealer with the lamb's wool applicator. Let the finish set for 20 minutes or so. Then remove any excess finish with the applicator.

Wait three days, or until the finish is hard. Vacuum.

With a polisher, apply a semi-soft wax to the floor. Be sure the wax product is made especially for hardwood floors. Do not use a water-based wax. Wax the floor with the grain of the wood and let the wax dry. Then go over the floor with the polisher to complete the job.

Finishing softwood floors. Softwoods such as pine do not need a wood filler, although any holes and cracks should be filled with a matching wood plastic following the final sanding of the floor. Press the plastic in the holes with a putty knife; let the plastic set for 30 minutes; sand the patch smooth.

Apply the first coat of finish to the floor with a lamb's wool applicator or brush made for oil-based finish. This coat of finish should be thinned slightly. Check the manufacturer's recommendations for thinning and proper application of the finish.

Let the finish dry for at least 48 hours. Check the finish with a knife blade to see if it has dried hard. If so, go over the floor with No. 2 steel wool just as you would for a hardwood floor (see instructions above).

Apply the second coat to the floor; let the finish dry; apply wax and buff and polish the wax. Do not use a water-based wax on the softwood floor.

Your finish may call for additional coats. If so, always lightly buff the finish between coats with No. 2 steel wool, and remove the residue with a vacuum cleaner and tack rag.

We recommend that you consult a paint or flooring dealer before you decide on any floor finish. There are several different types available — in a wide range of prices. The procedures outlined here for floor refinishing are for standard penetrating finishes. Techniques may vary slightly with different finishes.

To complete the job, replace the quarter-round molding and/or baseboard. If this trim should match the floor finish, you will have to remove the old finish by hand. Do not attempt to use a machine floor sander or disc sander on the trim.

Replacing Damaged Slate Flooring

Tools and materials. New slate, brick chisel, cold chisel, baby sledge hammer, building adhesive, grout, sponge, mixing bucket, water.

Safety. Wear safety glasses and gloves when chipping slate.

STEPS

Remove the damaged slate with a cold or brick chisel and sledge, being careful not to disturb the slate surrounding the damaged area. Remove the grout and all the adhesive that you can from the subflooring.

Fit the new slate into the void. If you must trim it, use the brick chisel and work very carefully. Just chisel off small bites at one time, testing to make sure the new slate fits properly.

When you're satisfied with the fit, coat the back of the slate with a lot of building adhesive, which you can buy in gallon containers. Press the slate in position and wipe away any excess building adhesive.

Let the job set for 24 hours. Then mix up some grout. It should be the consistency of thick mud. Sponge the grout in the joints around the slate, leveling the grout with the sponge. The joint probably won't be even, since the slate will vary in thickness. However, it should be level with the top of the floor.

Let the grout dry for several days. Then clean the slate with slate cleaner and finish the floor with a stone or slate sealer.

Chips and Cracks in Concrete Floors

Tools and materials. Cold chisel, baby sledge hammer, "top" bonding cement, trowel, mixing bucket, water.

STEPS

With the cold chisel, chip out any concrete debris. If you can, cut the hole or crack in an inverted V shape which will help hold the patch in position.

Mix up a batch of bonding cement. This cement is preformulated; you just add water. Press the patch into the hole or crack with a trowel, smooth the top of the patch.

STAIR REPAIRS
How to Stop Stair Tread Squeaks

Tools and materials. Hammer, 10d finishing nails, nail set, hand drill with a drill one size less than the diameter of the nails, wood filler, putty knife.

STEPS

Locate the squeak by hopping up and down on the tread.

Drive the finishing nails down through the tread into the riser. Space the nails about two inches apart. You may have to predrill pilot holes for the nails. Treads are usually oak and extremely difficult to nail without pilot holes for the nails. Countersink the nail heads and fill the nail holes with matching wood plastic.

If the stair is carpeted, you can nail down through the carpeting. The pile of the carpeting will hide the nail heads.

How to Stop Stair Riser Squeaks

Tools and materials. Hammer, 10d finishing nails, hand drill with a drill one size less than the diameter of the nails, graphite powder.

STEPS

Go under the steps and have a helper jump up and down on the step that squeaks so you can find where the squeak is below.

Drive finishing nails through the back of the riser into the tread, drilling pilot holes for the nails. Space the nails about two to three inches apart. If you can't get under the steps, try puffing the graphite powder between the tread and the riser.

If the graphite powder does not work, try to drive the nails at an angle through the tread into the riser. This will be at a very low angle, so you will have to first drill pilot holes for the nails, then finish driving the nails with a nail set. Go slowly and carefully.

If the stairsteps are "open" underneath, you can stop squeaks two ways:

1. Screw metal angle brackets (three to a step) where the *top*

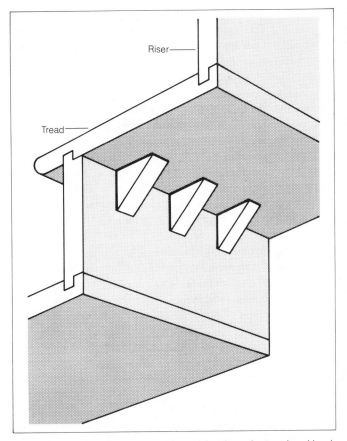

Glue and screw wooden blocks underneath, where the tread and back of riser meet.

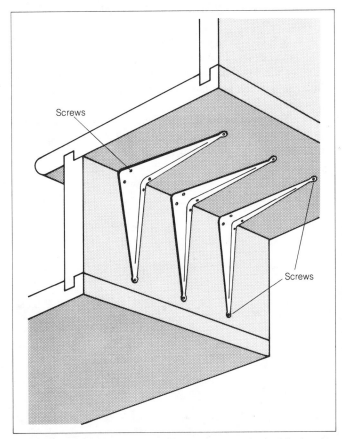

To eliminate tread creak, metal shelf brackets can be installed underneath the juncture of back of riser and tread.

of the riser meets the tread. Where the *bottom* edge of the riser meets the tread, use 10d finishing nails. Drive the nails up through the tread into the bottom edge of the riser.

2. From soft wood, cut several triangular bocks about three inches long. You can use a piece of 2x4 scrap for this; two right-angle sides will already be formed after each cut is made. Spread glue on the right angle sides and position the blocks between the tread and the riser — three to a step spaced evenly along the joint.

Replacing Treads and Risers

Tools and materials. New treads and risers, hammer, pry bar, crosscut saw, 16d finishing nails, hand drill, drill one size smaller than the diameter of the nails, nail set, chisel, wood plastic, varnish (paint or other finish), paintbrush.

STEPS

If there are balusters, remove them first. Pry off the end trim, and then pull the balusters out of the notches in the side of the treads. Then pry off the old treads and risers from the stringers, starting at the bottom of the stairs and working up. This should be easy once you have the first tread off. If you meet resistance, it is probably the nails at the top of the tread. Cut any nails that have been hammered through the riser into the tread, using a utility saw. After you have removed about three steps, install the new treads and risers. Then pry off more old ones and replace them until the job is done. Sometimes the riser and tread are dadoed. You will have to drill holes at the base of the riser so you can cut along the joint with a saw blade.

You can buy precut treads and risers in standard measurements. If you have to cut them to fit, use a crosscut saw and chisel for fine fitting. Predrill pilot holes for the nails, since the treads and risers probably will be oak or similar hardwood. Countersink the nail heads, fill the holes with plastic wood, and finish the steps. (See also "Stair Repairs" in Chapter 9.)

Stair Rail Maintenance and Repair

Tools and materials. New mounting brackets, new railing, screwdriver, screws, crosscut saw, finish, paintbrush.

Mounting brackets for stair rails are screwed to the framing or paneling, or to the studs in back of the wall covering. Tighten the brackets every year or so; always replace them immediately if they become broken.

STEPS

Loose stair rails are easy to tighten; just tighten the screws holding the mounting brackets in position. These brackets are fastened to framing members in the wall.

If the rail is damaged and you must replace it, remove the old rail from the brackets. Use a screwdriver for this. Fasten on the new rail with screws in the same mounting brackets. You can trim the new rail to fit with a crosscut saw.

When you replace the old rail, be sure to check the brackets for damage and wear. If you spot trouble, replace the brackets, using a screwdriver.

Finish the new rail with stain, varnish, paint, or any finish you want. Sand the rail before you apply the finish and between coats.

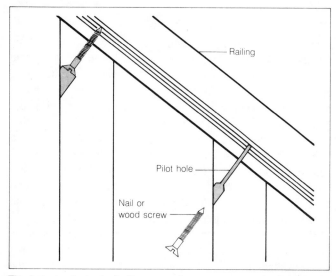

The baluster fastener (nail or screw) goes at an angle through the baluster into the railing. Drill a pilot hole for the fastener to avoid splitting the wood.

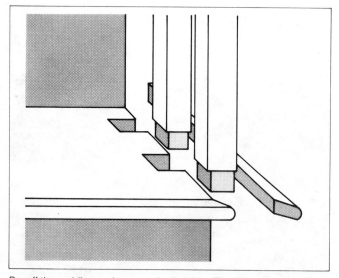

Pry off the molding and remove the baluster. The baluster may be held at the top with a nail or glue. In new construction, the baluster may be toenailed to the tread.

Tightening Loose Balusters

Tools and materials. Drill, 16d finishing nails, or long, thin wood screws, hammer or screwdriver, nail set, countersink, wood plastic.

STEPS

Drill a small hole at an angle up through the edge of the baluster into the railing. The size of the hole will depend on what type fastener you use: nails or screws.

Drive the nail or screw into this predrilled pilot hole. If you use a nail, countersink the nail head with a nail set. If you use a screw, you can countersink the hole for the screw head. Then fill the hole with wood plastic. You probably won't be able to see this repair, so you don't really need to spend the time and money adding wood plastic.

Replacing Broken Balusters

Tools and materials. Hammer, pry bar, butt chisel, glue, 10d finishing nails, new balusters, wood finishing materials (sandpaper, stain or paint, paintbrush, etc.).

STEPS

At the exposed edge of the stair tread you will see a small strip of molding. This molding is nailed to the edge of the tread and holds the balusters in position on the tread (in standard construction).

With a butt chisel, very carefully loosen this strip of molding. Then, insert a pry bar into the gap and remove the molding, prying it off evenly and slowly.

The balusters are nailed to the tread. Pry the damaged ones out from the tread and carefully pull out the top of the balusters from the railing. The balusters may be nailed or glued into the railing.

Once out, clean the slot in the railing where the damaged baluster was fastened. Also clean out the notch in which the bottom of the baluster was fastened. Insert and fasten the new baluster in position and nail on the molding. You can use glue and nails.

Finish the new wood to match the old wood with stain, varnish or paint. Sand lightly between the prime and finish coats, removing all sanding debris.

3 Kitchen Improvements and Emergencies

The only remodeling projects in this book have been organized and written to help you make repairs to your kitchen.

We will assume here that you will be attempting lower-cost alternatives rather than changing your kitchen structurally. You may wish to add new cabinets, a new floor or a new range hood or countertop. Therefore, we have started with basics.

REMODELING PROCEDURES
Here are the suggested steps you should take to make your kitchen remodeling flow smoothly.

1. Lay out your present kitchen to scale.

2. Choose and buy the cabinets and related materials and products. This will include flooring, appliances, plumbing and electrical items, ceiling materials, exhaust systems, paint and finishing materials, needed tools.

3. Obtain a building permit, if necessary.

4. Have the products and materials delivered to your home. If possible, schedule the delivery in the order you will do the remodeling: flooring, cabinets, ceiling, finishing materials. This will free your storage space.

5. Remove the old kitchen cabinets — wall cabinets first so you have a top on which to lay tools and materials.

6. Prepare the ceiling and walls for the new cabinets.

7. Save the old kitchen cabinets for storage elsewhere — in your attic, garage, basement.

8. Make any necessary adjustments in wiring and plumbing — such as extending plumbing, adding power. If you do not have the know-how, we suggest that you call in professionals to do these jobs since special building codes probably are involved, which include inspections.

9. Install the new ceiling.

10. Install the cabinets.

11. Install the countertops.

12. Hook up the plumbing and electrical power.

13. Finish the walls and ceiling.

14. Install the new floor.

If you follow this program you will find that your job will be easier and you will be more satisfied with the results.

KITCHEN REMODELING BASICS
Buy a pad of lined graph paper, a hard lead pencil, a 1-ft. ruler, and a 25-ft. measuring tape.

Determine how many spaces on the graph paper equal one foot of space. You can make it as big or small as you want. Just be consistent.

Draw a floor plan of your kitchen to this scale. Then draw in the kitchen cabinets, sink, range, dishwasher, and other appliances to exact scale. Include lights, wall switches, windows, doors, furniture. You now know how much space you have.

This is not an exercise in mechanical or architectural drawing. You *must* have these dimensions *before* you go shopping for building materials and kitchen components.

The kitchen components you will buy are manufactured in modules. The modules range from 2, 4, 8, 10, 12, and 16 feet. If you stick with these modules, which are standard building sizes, you can save plenty of money and time. You automatically eliminate special orders for off-size and odd-size components; you can work with standard size, lower-cost framing and finishing materials such as 2x4s, 1x2s, ceiling tile, floor tile, plumbing pipe, etc.

When you go to a store to shop for these products, take along the sketch of your kitchen with the 25-ft. measuring tape. Thus prepared, you will be able to match your selections to the available space.

Measuring for New Cabinets
Base and wall cabinet sizes either match or complement each other. That is, if a base cabinet is 36 in. wide, you will find a

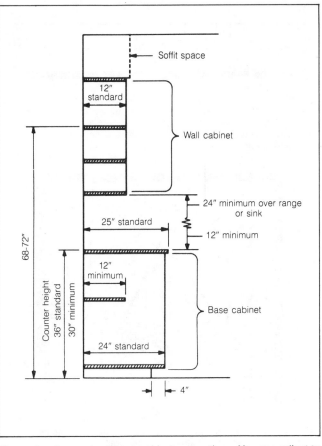

Shown are the most common cabinet proportions. You can adjust to suit your own height and needs.

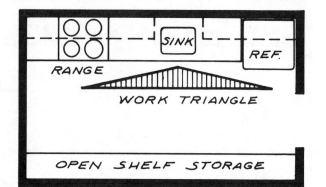

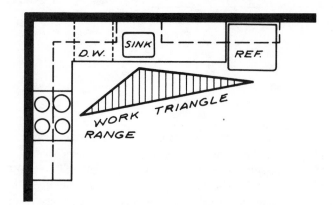

Single-Wall. The single-wall kitchen is ideal as a second kitchen, or as the main kitchen when space is a prime concern. Place the sink near the center of the cabinet wall and keep the range and refrigerator close together. Consider a shallow pantry or open storage shelves on the opposite wall.

"L" Shape. The "L" Shape is usually built into the corner of a room, especially when the kitchen includes a dining area. This design should not be broken by a door or passage.

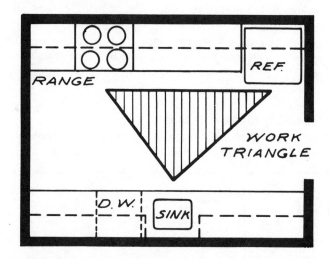

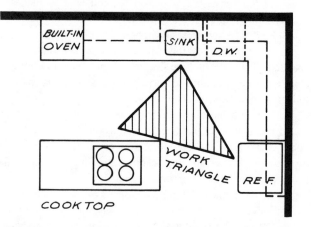

Parallel Wall or Galley. This design works well in narrow areas,   but not too narrow, or the work space becomes cramped. About 4 ft. between the cabinets will provide ample space. Be wary of doors at both ends of the galley, which can turn the kitchen into a hallway and break down good working conditions.

Island. The island is a variation of the "L" or "U" shape and helps make an extremely large kitchen more efficient. By building an overhang and placing stools at the island, it can also be used as an informal eating area.

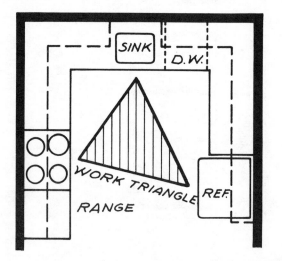

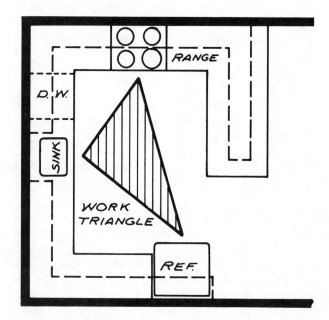

"U" Shape. This is an extremely efficient and convenient kitchen design when one leg of the work triangle is on each wall. Often, one leg forms a divider between the kitchen and a dining or family room. For the best use of a "U" shape kitchen, place the sink in the center leg.

Surround. The four-sided or surround kitchen usually has one leg, often an eating bar, as a divider between the kitchen and another room. It may be broken twice for doors and passageways, but be careful not to funnel general traffic through the area of the work triangle.

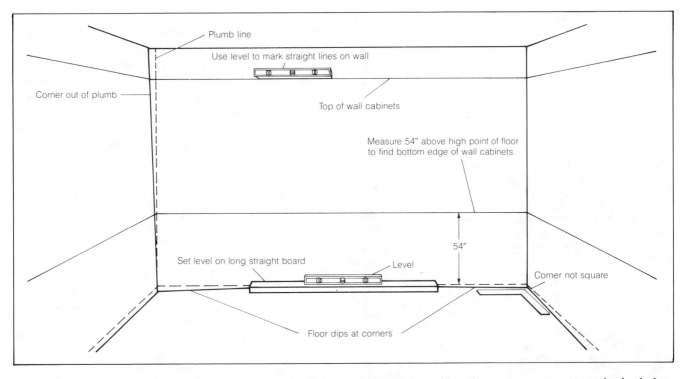

Plumb line

Use level to mark straight lines on wall

Corner out of plumb

Top of wall cabinets

Measure 54" above high point of floor
to find bottom edge of wall cabinets

54"

Set level on long straight board

Level

Corner not square

Floor dips at corners

wall cabinet, valance board, range hood, range, or sink light, that will correspond with the 36-in. base cabinet.

If your kitchen measurements are not in a module size, you often can use special filler strips to increase or decrease the size. Do not overlook filler strips as a way to fit new cabinets into existing space, especially if your old cabinets were custom-built for your kitchen.

Kitchen cabinets usually are sold by the specific cabinet, not as a group or package of cabinets. Some stores do sell kitchen packages, but make sure that the package includes all the cabinets you want in the kitchen.

Countertops generally are sold separately by the lineal foot. Laminate patterns usually are standard, although you can buy speciality tops at an additional cost. Or, you can buy the materials to fabricate your own top. We recommend that you buy a readymade countertop.

Base cabinets are 24 in. deep and 34½ in. high. The width will vary, depending on the type of cabinet. The standard height of base cabinets, after the countertop is installed, is 36 in. Wall cabinets range from 12 to 15 in. deep and from 12 to 34 in. high. The width will vary.

As you make your selection in the store, sketch the measurements of the new cabinets on spare sketch paper. You can arrange almost the entire kitchen this way and will get an idea of what you will need.

The dealer should be able to supply you with literature that specifies all sizes — height, width, and depth — of the cabinets the dealer has in stock. At the same time, you can match ranges, dishwashers, sinks, lighting, and countertops, with the cabinets.

Measuring for Countertops

After you have the base cabinets sketched on the graph paper, take another piece of graph paper and mark the width, depth, and length of the countertop.

The measurements should include: sink location — plus

width, depth, and length measurement; corners; backsplashes; overhangs. You must know these breaks and cut-outs in order to specify the countertop measurements and ensure that the top will fit.

If you will be fabricating your own countertop, these measurements are needed so you can buy high pressure laminate, underlayment, trim, backsplashes, and adhesive. Remember to buy the metal or plastic brackets that fasten the countertop to the base cabinets.

CLEARING OUT THE OLD KITCHEN
Removing the Old Cabinets

Tools and materials. Hammer, pry bar, crosscut saw, hacksaw, screwdriver, pipe wrenches, electrical tape, butt chisel, adjustable wrench, containers for junk.

STEPS

Look for the molding at the back bottom edge of wall cabinets and along the wall at end cabinets. Pry off this molding first, since it helps hold the cabinets in position.

Wall cabinets may be held by screws or nails to the studs. Sometimes cabinets are fastened to the wall with toggle bolts or Molly anchors. If the walls are masonry, the cabinets probably are held with lead anchors and screws.

Look for these fasteners along the top and bottom inside edges of the cabinets and remove them with a screwdriver. If held by nails, place a pry bar in back of the cabinet and against the wall and lift out.

The cabinets probably will be fastened together at the fronts, along the inside framing or at the top (and even along the bottom) with nails or screws. Remove these fasteners.

If the cabinet tops butt up against a soffit, the tops may be fastened to the soffit, which is a framework of 2x3s or 2x4s covered with gypsum wallboard.

Once you remove one cabinet, the rest will be easier since you will know where to find most of the fasteners. Enlist the aid of a helper to steady the cabinets while you remove the final few fasteners.

Base cabinet removal is next. First check for any electrical and plumbing connections that might be in the way. You will probably find these only at the sink unit and on the wall over the range. Plan to remove these cabinets last, since you want to maintain water and electric power as long as possible. If you will be making disconnections, *turn off both the water and electricity at the main service entry.*

Main water shut-off valves are near or next to the water meter, usually in the basement or a heated crawl space. For gas or electric water heater, water may be turned off instead at cold water inlet.

Remove countertops first. If they are laminate, they will be screwed to metal or plastic brackets located at the inside top of the base cabinets. If the counter is of tile, remove as described in the previous chapter, using a cold chisel and a sledge hammer.

Remove any molding or trim around the ends, kickspace, and back of the base cabinets. The base cabinets probably are fastened to each other with nails or screws along the front inside edge. Pull these fasteners out.

Begin with the end cabinets and work toward the sink cabinet. When you remove an end cabinet, the cabinet next to it will be easier to work with, and the job will start to quickly "unravel." Use a hammer and a pry block of wood for the nails, and a screwdriver and pry bar for the screws, toggles, Molly bolts, anchors, and large nails — 10d and up.

The range hood is fastened to a valance or soffit, usually with screws. But first disconnect the electricity that powers the exhaust fan and hood light. You probably will have to unscrew a metal pan covering that hides the junction box that houses the electrical connections.

Turn on the exhaust fan and/or light. Go to the main circuit breaker or fuse box and turn off the power on this circuit. You will know the power is off when the light goes out and the fan stops working. It is now safe to make the disconnections.

Use a screwdriver to back out the terminal screws so you can remove the wires. Separate and tape the ends of the wires with electrical tape. Use plenty of tape; the wires should be completely wrapped.

Now remove the hood unit by backing out the screws that hold it in place. Then remove the valance, which probably is fastened to the wall cabinets with screws or to the soffit with metal brackets, screws, or nails. The hood will have a vent duct. This duct will have to be unscrewed from the main vent hub above the exhaust fan. The duct may go directly through the outside wall, or through a soffit to the outside wall.

You may have several preliminary jobs at the sink cabinet. If the sink has a disposal unit, disconnect the power from it. The wires may be in a junction box on or near the unit. Or the wires may come from a wall outlet or both. Tape the ends of the main supply wires.

The disposal is connected to the sink with a mounting ring and two (usually) set screws. You can get at the screws from inside the cabinet at the top of the disposal unit. Also disconnect the disposal drain. You will need a pipe wrench or large adjustable wrench for this. The drain pipe fits a connection at the side (usually) of the disposal unit.

If you don't have a disposer, disconnect the kitchen sink drain using pipe wrenches at the first joint down from the sink drain opening. This will be a U or P trap fitting, and the fitting will slip down and off the drain tailpipe that is connected to the drain in the sink. Also disconnect the water supply pipes to the sink faucets. But first, turn off the water at the shut-off valves where the water supply comes through the wall. Or turn off the water at the main water entry. Do not disconnect the water supply pipes until the water is off. (See Chapter 5, Plumbing Repairs.)

If the supply pipes are copper, you will need an adjustable wrench to remove the pipes at the faucet connections. If the pipes are galvanized steel, you will need pipe wrenches to remove them — also at the faucet.

Disconnect water supply and drain pipes to your dishwasher at this time. Water supply for the dishwasher may be connected through the floor. You will have to go into the basement to shut off this valve and (perhaps) disconnect the pipe. Or the water supply may come from a tee fitting off the faucet supply pipe. A compression fitting, which may be turned with an adjustable wrench, is usually all you need to disconnect from the main supply line.

The dishwasher probably has separate electrical power, which comes up through the floor or through the wall in back of the unit. The dishwasher may be on a separate circuit. Make sure the power is off before you start working.

The dishwasher drains into the kitchen drain pipe or the air gap, which has an inlet/outlet tube. Simply trace the hose and you will find the connection.

Electric ranges are simply plugged into an outlet. You usually have to turn the plug slightly to disengage the prongs in the outlet. Gas ranges commonly have a gas supply shut-off valve where the gas supply comes through the wall or floor. Turn the handle of this valve at right angles to the pipe. Then check the burners. If they light, the gas has not been turned off. If you cannot seem to turn the gas off at this shut-off valve, call in a professional. Often your utility company will provide this service at a fairly reasonable cost. Gas pipes are similar to galvanized steel water pipes. You need pipe wrenches to disconnect them.

The range probably has electric power running to it for oven lighting. Trace the wiring to the junction box and disconnect the wires at this terminal, after you have turned off the electricity at the main electrical entrance.

If washers and dryers are in the kitchen and you will move them, simply unplug the appliances from the wall outlets and remove the hoses and vents. You will probably need only a screwdriver to unscrew the clamp that holds the dryer vent to the back of the dryer.

Now you are ready to remove the rest of the cabinets. They are fastened the same way to the wall as those previously described.

EXTENDING UTILITIES
Plumbing
This job sounds harder than it actually is. Since the supply and drain pipes are already in, you just have to add to the length of the pipes, if indeed you must extend them at all.

You have a choice: for supply pipes you can remove the pipe back to the shutoff valves and add new pipe to the length you need. Or, you can install a union fitting at the end of the old pipe and add new pipe to the union.

Drain pipes may be disconnected below the trap and then extended out to the length you need with no problem. However, the drains should have a trap, which is located near the sink outlet. Do not install the trap next to the floor. (See Chapter 5, Plumbing Repairs.)

Wiring
Most appliance wiring comes out of a junction box in the wall or floor. To extend the length of the wiring, you must go back to the junction box and disconnect the new wires at this point. Do not splice new wiring to old wiring.

Kitchen electrical systems do not utilize any wiring smaller than No. 14 wire. If your home has 115-volt housepower (standard), the No. 14 wire will handle 15 amp fuses and a 1750-watt capacity.

Wires with black insulation usually are power wires; these wires carry the juice. White wires usually are neutral wires. Green-covered wires are usually grounding wires. Do not connect black wires to white wires.

If you have to move junction boxes — or add junction boxes — for the remodeling, we recommend that you have a professional electrician make the hook-ups. You can do the roughing-in work, which will save you money. (See Chapter 7, Electrical Repairs.)

INSTALLATION METHODS
To keep the kitchen available for food preparation during the remodeling, you should immediately set the new base and wall cabinets in position and make the plumbing and electrical connections.

Floor Preparation
Before you move those cabinets into position, prepare the floor area under the base cabinets. If you are installing new flooring, you will want to remove the old flooring under the cabinets at this time. Remove carpeting by pulling it up and off the subflooring. It may be stapled to the subflooring, or it may be held in place by a tack strip which runs along the wall. A hammer and/or pry bar is all that you need to remove these fasteners. If

the floor is tile, you can remove the tile with a brick chisel and baby sledge, or a thick-bladed wall scraper and propane torch. The torch melts the adhesive holding the tile; the scraper lifts the tile. See the flooring section later in this chapter.

Cabinets
Locate and mark the positions of wall studs on which you will install cabinets. This may seem like a lot of unnecessary work, but later you will be happy that you did this.

Lay out and mark an outline of each cabinet to be hung on the wall. Mark down the sizes, any identification numbers or names for each individual wall or base unit. Also use your graph paper plan, mark the location of the refrigerator, range, and other major appliances on the wall.

Recheck all of these measurements and identifying codes. Use your floor plan for this check. When you are finished, you will have a very good idea how the kitchen will turn out. If you do not like the plan, now is the time to make necessary changes. Most changes can be made by simply switching cabinet positions. However, you must make sure the measurements correspond with the changes. Always leave an inch of extra space as a backup; do not try to fit 108 inches of cabinets into exactly 108 inches of wall space.

Tools and materials. A helper, hammer, rubber hammer, nails, screws, washers, cedar shingles, level, square, tape measure, marking pencil, chalkline and chalk, pipe wrenches, adjustable wrench, pipe for extensions, screwdrivers (standard and Phillips), brace and an assortment of bits or a power drill and assortment of drills, flooring materials, plumber's putty, butt chisel.

STEPS
Patch any holes or tears in the wall. Since the cabinets will hide most of the wall surface, you do not have to make minor patches behind cabinets. (See Chapter 2, Interior Repairs, for patching details, tools, and materials.)

New type of kitchen cabinet by Belwood is assembled with screws through a plastic mounting that aligns the cabinet front with the sides, top, bottom. Parts fit right-or-left-handed.

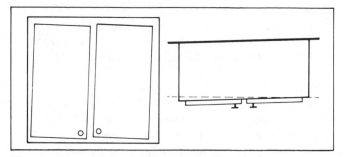

Where a cabinet pulls into low spot on wall, add a shim between cabinet and wall. Check for plumb on both sides. If cabinet is placed on high spot on wall, either sand high spot or shim other 3 corners.

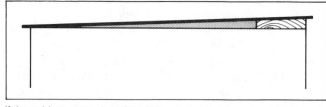

If the cabinet corner is pulling into a depression in the wall, you should add a shim between the cabinet and the wall to fill out the low spot.

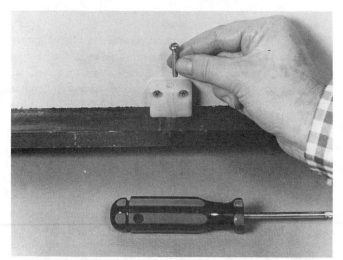

The mounting brackets in Belwood cabinets are preinstalled; you just screw the pieces together. All hardware is included in package.

Dowels create self-aligning cabinet fronts, which is the hardest part of hanging any cabinet. Once the first cabinet is set, the rest align on these dowel pins.

Hang the wall cabinets first. Start at a corner, if there is a corner. If not start at the end base line you drew on the wall.

If you do not have a helper, you will have to build a "T" support of 2x4s. Prop this against the wall to hold the cabinets up while you drill the holes and tighten the screws.

Set the first cabinet. Level and plumb it. Then drill pilot holes for the screws in the cabinet rails or stretchers and into the studs. Loosely fasten the cabinet with screws and washers to relieve your helper and to free both hands for the work to come.

Chances are very good that you will have to use cedar shingle shims to level and plumb the cabinet. Position the shims, then tighten the holding screws slightly so the shims are held in place. With a level, plumb and level the cabinet, adjusting the

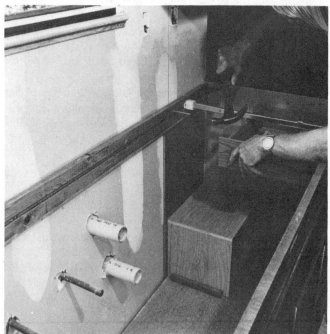

Wall and base cabinets are screwed (preferably) or nailed to the framing members of the wall. Or, you can use a combination of nails and screws. Plumb and level each cabinet as you set it.

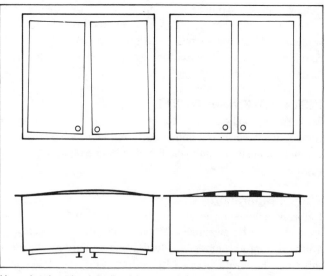

Use a level to check wall cabinets on front, sides, and bottom. It cabinets are out of plumb, use shims between cabinets, between wall and cabinets, or underneath cabinets, to level. Do not tighten screws until all cabinets and doors are correctly aligned.

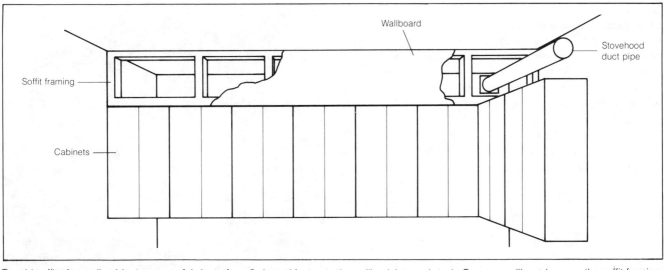

To add soffit after wall cabinets are up: fabricate from 2x4s and fasten to the ceiling joists and studs. Gypsum wallboard covers the soffit framing, so allow for its thickness in measurements.

shims to obtain level and plumb. Now, drive the screws all the way in and tighten them. At this point, double check your measurements, and level and plumb the cabinet again. If it is not perfect, loosen the screws, adjust the shims, and retighten the screws.

The shims probably will stick out along the edges of the cabinet and flat against the wall. Trim them with a butt chisel so the shims are flush with the edges of the cabinet. Use molding or trim pieces to hide the cracks.

Hang the adjoining cabinets as you come to them, using the same hanging techniques used to install the first cabinet. As you work, make sure the fronts of the cabinets align. You can buy self-aligning cabinets (see illustration for the details). When you come to a blind corner cabinet, match the filler strip to the cabinet and then hang the cabinet the same way as the rest of the cabinets.

Valance units are fastened to the front frames of the facing cabinets with screws through the frames into the ends of the valance piece.

When the wall cabinets are in position, and are level and plumb with the fronts aligned, fasten the cabinets together along the front framing of the cabinets with screws. Eyeball the cabinet fronts before you fasten them together. This way, you can see if the door fronts align. If not, you still have an opportunity to make small adjustments. Check the alignment using a level both horizontally and vertically. Look for high and low spots on the wall behind any incorrectly aligned cabinets.

Base cabinets are set almost the same way as wall cabinets.

Start at a corner and work across the cabinet run, setting each cabinet as you come to it. Fasten the cabinet back to the studs with screws and washers. Then level and plumb each cabinet, using cedar shingle shims at the back and under the cabinet.

A sink cabinet may not be a cabinet at all. It could be just a front with doors, a floor support rail, and hanger strips that hold it together. Or it may be a full cabinet. Either way, fasten the back rails to the studs, leveling and plumbing the front, or cabinet, with cedar shims.

Blind base cabinets are fastened to the wall, leveled and

plumbed, and fastened to the adjoining cabinet. See illustration for details.

Oven cabinets also are installed just like any other cabinet. However, you may have to cut out the opening to fit your oven. Manufacturer's instructions usually are furnished for this cabinet; follow them exactly.

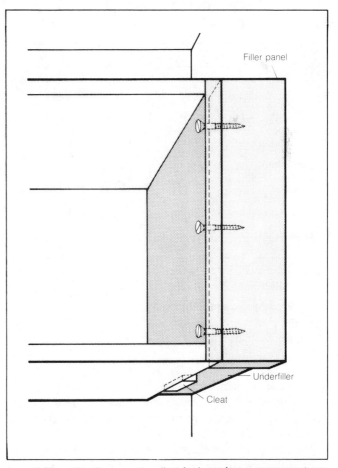

An end filler strip allows you to adjust for imperfect measurements on small leftover spaces, and can help center a sink under a window or along a wall. The strip fastens to the cabinet frame and is nailed on with a support block or cleat placed underneath the filler strip. Drill holes first into the cabinet and then into the filler strip. Match up the holes and then put in screws.

Soffits

If the kitchen needs a soffit, build it first, in sections. Fasten it to the ceiling before the cabinets are put up; skin with wallboard; sand and paint. By doing all this before putting up the cabinets, you avoid damage to them. It is also easier to tape, spackle, sand and paint before cabinets are up. Even if you will be wallpapering the soffit, give it a layer of paint to seal the wallboard.

The soffit can be built as an "L" shape or as three sides of a box, with the wall serving as the fourth side. If in an L, the soffit attaches to the cabinet and to the ceiling (see illustration); if it has a three-sided configuration, you will attach it to the wall in two places. Use screws, not nails, to attach the soffit to the wall and the cabinets.

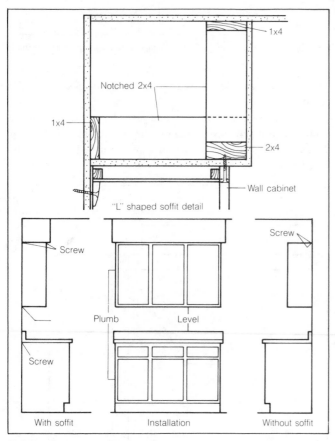

To frame and wallboard the soffit before putting up cabinets, here is an alternate pattern.

Readymade Countertops

Tools and materials. Screws, screwdriver, countertop mounting brackets .

STEPS

Readymade countertops are very easy to install since all the cuts, miters, end caps, backsplashes, and sink openings have been made. We suggest you buy a top cut to your specifications rather than attempt to build it yourself from scratch.

Set the top on the cabinets. Center it so you have an overhang at the front of the cabinets. You may or may not have a slight overhang at the ends of the cabinets, depending on the design. The backsplash, which is part of the top, usually will determine the overhang. The sink cut-out should be centered with the center of the sink cabinet.

Have a friend help you lift and position the countertop. The top is fastened from the bottom of the cabinets up through brackets. Space these brackets at least two to each cabinet — front and back side.

Many cabinets already have the top mounting brackets installed along the inside top edges of the cabinets. If so, you only have to drive screws up through the screw holes into the countertop.

If you do not have brackets on the cabinets, install them yourself by screwing them to the back edge at the top of the cabinet fronts and back rails or hanger strips. Then screw the top to the brackets.

Countertop Fabrication

Tools and materials. ⅜ in. particleboard, high pressure laminate, contact adhesive, slip sheets (paper), smooth cut file, razor knife, power router (if available), brace and bit assortment or power drill and drill assortment, keyhole saw, power jigsaw (if available), tape measure, square, countertop mounting brackets, screws, 1x3 lumber.

STEPS

Cut the particleboard to fit the top of the base cabinets. The top should overlap the cabinets at least 1½ in. At this time, cut any countertop miters (where you turn a corner to cover other cabinets), and the backsplash, which may be any height — 3¼ in. is standard.

Remove any metal or wooden trim from the old countertop before you rip off the old laminate to remodel it with new laminate. Throw away the trim; it won't be used again.

If the backsplash is molded plastic or rubber, pry it off. If it is strip of wood covered with laminate, it may be fastened to the wall. Remove the fasteners. Also remove fasteners holding the backsplash to the top from under the cabinets.

Clean the countertop right down to the bare wood, removing all adhesive and other debris. Then patch any holes, big nicks, and other damage to the top. Use water putty or wood filler. Sand the top smooth; clean away debris.

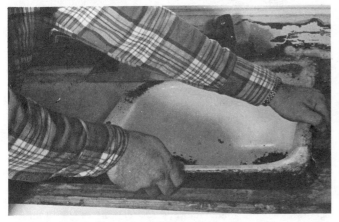

Remove the sink. The sink may be held by clips and/or mounting brackets from below. At this point, you will have to shut off the water, and then unhook the faucets and the kitchen drain. (See Chapter 5, Plumbing Repairs, for details on this procedure.)

Plastic laminate needs a good base. So you'll probably have to "thicken" the countertop with a false edge of 1x3 trim nailed to the edge of the top. Make sure this edge doesn't interfere with drawer or cabinet operation.

Remove the old countertop covering. For this, you'll need a hammer, pry bar, cold chisel, and any other equipment you can innovate.

To obtain the "thickness" at the overhang, nail on 1x3-in. strips of solid wood. You can make the top look as thick as you want, by adding 1x3s in a stack. Nail down through the particleboard into the 1x3s. Prefit the top and make any adjustment cuts at this time. When you are satisfied with the fit, begin lamination of the high-pressure plastic to the wood.

Clean the wood and slightly countersink any nail heads so the top surface is absolutely smooth. Sand any rough spots you find, and clean away the sanding residue.

Fit the laminate on the top and mark it so there is a ¼ in. lip projecting around the front edge of the top.

Cut the laminate from the back using a razor knife. The knife will score the material so it can be crimped and snapped off. You will need a straightedge to "fold" the cut over so the laminate will snap clean and will not crack.

An easier alternative is to use a fine-tooth blade in a power jigsaw. If you have lots of cutting to do, buy or rent this tool. Before you make any "final" cuts, test the blade on a scrap piece of laminate. The blade should not splinter the laminate. If it does, get another blade. Special blades are made for cutting laminate.

Cut the edge strips for the top. Then cut the strips for the backsplash. Again, leave a ¼ in. lip, which will be used later for trimming purposes.

Prefit the edges at each end. Apply contact adhesive to the wood and the back of the laminate. Set the laminate aside for 30 minutes or according to the manufacturer's instructions on

Cut and trim the new plastic laminate to fit. Then mark each piece so you can re-assemble the puzzle when you glue the laminate to the countertop. If the old countertop is badly damaged you can re-cover it, or replace it.

Trim the laminate with a file or a router (shown). The router throws lots of laminate chips, so wear safety glasses. You can buy special laminate cutting bits for portable routers.

Apply the adhesive to the back of the laminate and set it aside. Then apply adhesive to the countertop. Wait the recommended time and press laminate to top.

Tap the laminate. This gives the laminate a better glue bond. Use a wooden buffer block to absorb the blows from the hammer, and to help distribute pressure.

the contact adhesive container. Then stick the laminate to the wood and press it tight. Since the adhesive sticks on contact, you must be sure you have the laminate straight on the very first try. You can't move it once the two surfaces have met.

With the edges complete, you are ready to put on the laminate. This piece of laminate should sandwich between the lipped edges of the end pieces (except where a miter cut is made to turn a corner).

Apply the adhesive to the back of the laminate and the top, according to the manufacturer's instructions on the adhesive container. Then press the two surfaces together and tap the surface lightly with a hammer and wooden buffer block. Now apply the front edge strip to the top so it projects ¼ in.

Trim the edges. You can use a file for this, although a router with a plastic laminate bit is better. Run the file lengthwise of the strips and/or toward the top. When you are finished, you will have a smooth joint between the laminate with a long even joint line.

How to Replace Laminate

Here are instructions for removing the old countertop.

Tools and materials. Hammer, baby sledge hammer, cold chisel, butt chisel, rubber hammer, thick-bladed putty knife, coarse, medium, and fine grit abrasive, sanding block, pull scraper, adhesive spreader or paintbrush, water putty, screwdriver, mineral spirits, level, square, tape measure, high pressure laminate, contact adhesive, smooth-cut file or router with a laminate blade, building adhesive, caulking gun shell, keyhole saw or jigsaw with laminate-cutting blade, 1x4 for backsplash, tile and tub caulking.

STEPS

With a screwdriver, remove any metal trim from the countertop and backsplash. Also remove any metal cove molding between the backsplash and countertop, and take out the sink.

Find a loose spot in the old laminate and insert a cold chisel, thick-bladed putty knife, or the claws of a hammer under the spot. Pry up. This will break loose a chunk of the laminate so you can pry, chisel, and chip at it until all of the old material is off the countertop surface. As you work, it is a good idea to junk the debris in a garbage container.

Once the old laminate is off, remove any dried adhesive with a pull scraper. Then, with sandpaper — from coarse to fine — smooth the countertop and backsplash. Fill any holes, cracks, dents, or splits with wood putty and sand the patch smooth and level with the top.

For appearance, you may want to increase the "thickness" of the old countertop. You do this by nailing a piece of 1x3 along the edge of the top. This edge will be covered with new plastic laminate.

When you are satisfied that the top is smooth, free of old adhesive, patched with nailheads countersunk, you are ready to apply the laminate, which should be precut and fitted to the top. *(See how to apply pressure laminate to a new top, above, in this chapter.)*

Test the new laminate to make sure all measurements are correct. Time spent on a "dry run" now can save you plenty of grief later. Mark the pieces for lay-down order.

Apply the adhesive to the back of the laminate. Then apply the adhesive to the surface of the top. Let the adhesive set according to the manufacturer's instructions on the adhesive container, and then press the laminate in position.

Follow the same laminating procedures for the backsplash. If the old backsplash was of rubber molding, you will have to fabricate a new backsplash from a length of 1x4. Prelaminate the 1x4 and stick it to the wall with building adhesive. The bottom of the backsplash must butt against the top of the countertop *after* the countertop has been recovered. Fill this crack with tub and tile caulking to seal the joint.

With a regular hammer, or rubber hammer if you have one, tap across the surface of the top. Use a wooden buffer block to protect the new laminate and to help spread the blows of the hammer along the surface. The tapping helps the glue bond between the top and the laminate. Now apply the laminate to the edges. It should protrude about ¼-in. for trimming purposes.

With a smooth-cut file, trim the joints of the laminate — or use a router with a laminate bit for this job. Cutting techniques are discussed earlier in this chapter.

Sink Cut-Out

To make the sink cut-out:

(1) locate the center of the sink cabinet and mark this on the countertop with a wax pencil, or a pen that has easily removable ink;

(2) from this mark, measure to each side of the line half the width of the sink;

(3) measure 2 in. from the front of the top and connect the lines at the sides;

(4) measure 1 in. from the back of the top and connect the lines at the sides.

You now should have a rectangle drawn on the top. Most sink manufacturers include a cut-out template with the sink, or explain how to mark the countertop for the sink cut-out. Use this template for cutting instructions from this point on. The purpose of the lines is just to establish approximately where the sink cut-out will be. If the sink does not come with a template you can make one by tracing the sink on a piece of cardboard. Or, if the sink has a rim, trace the inside of the rim on cardboard and cut out the cardboard.

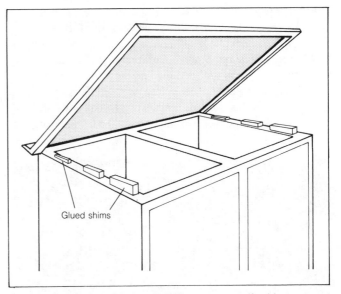

Glued shims

Use tapered wood shims when installing countertop if cabinets are not level. Or use uniform shim blocks to raise countertop for necessary clearance between front edge overhang and undercounter features.

Recheck all your measurements before making the cut-out. First drill a hole for the jigsaw or keyhole saw blade inside the cut-out line. Then cut and lift out the cut-out.

Cement the laminate to the backsplash. Trim the edges. Then attach the backsplash to the back edge of the top with screws driven up through the top into the edge of the backsplash. You should predrill pilot holes for the screws and countersink the holes for the screwheads.

Run a fat strip of tile-and-tub adhesive along the bottom edge of the backsplash before you screw it onto the top. This will provide a water seal between the two surfaces. You can hold the backsplash to the countertop with large C-clamps while you drive in the screws. No. 10 flathead wood screws are suggested; this size depends, however, on the type of material you are using. Ask the dealer.

Screw the countertop to the cabinets, using the mounting brackets, as indicated on p. 70 in "Readymade Countertops." On p. 72 you will find instructions and how to replace laminate. Read all of this material before you get started on a new countertop project. Also, many dealers that sell high-pressure laminate will be able to provide you with information about top lamination. Ask them for this important material and for any special instructions you might need for your particular project.

Cabinet Trim

Tools and materials. Miter box, backsaw, coping saw, nail set, finish nails, hammer, tape measure, chisel, sandpaper, wood plastic, wood finish, paintbrush.

STEPS

There probably will be little cracks and gaps around your new cabinet job. This cannot be helped since most walls are not level and plumb, but you can hide these little imperfections with molding and trim.

The type of molding or trim you use depends on what style you like. It probably will be either quarter-round molding or ½x1-in. batten strips. Before you make a choice, go shopping in a molding and trim department of a home center store. Lots of different patterns are offered for sale; pick the one that suits the job best. Application is fairly standard for all types.

Measure, recheck the measurements, and cut the trim to fit the cabinet application. Smooth the wood by lightly sanding it. Attach the strip to the wall, nailing it to the studs with finishing nails. Use 10d finishing nails, unless the molding is extra thick or thin. Countersink the nail heads with the nail set. Then fill the holes with plastic wood. Stain or paint the trim to match or complement the cabinets.

To "cope" quarter-round molding, first cut the molding at a 45-degree angle. Use a miter box; don't guess.

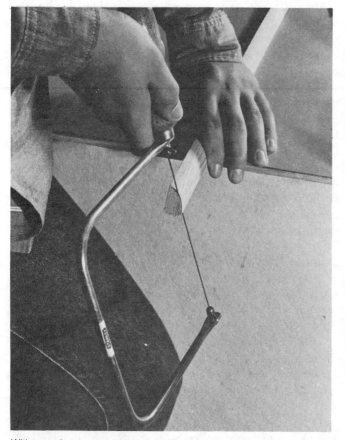

With a coping saw, cut around the shape of the molding, as shown. You can turn the pins in the saw frame to match any curves. It is easier to make the cuts "downward."

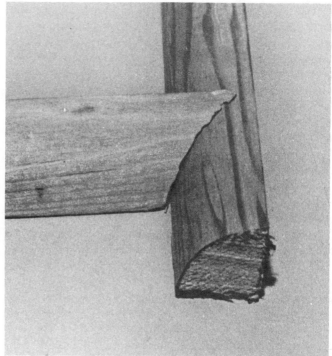

Here's how the molding fits together after it has been coped. You can match the joint first, then trim the other end of the piece to fit the space.

How to Install a Range Hood

The size of the hood is predetermined by the space between the cabinets. If you followed a building module when laying out the cabinet job, selection will be no problem. If you did not

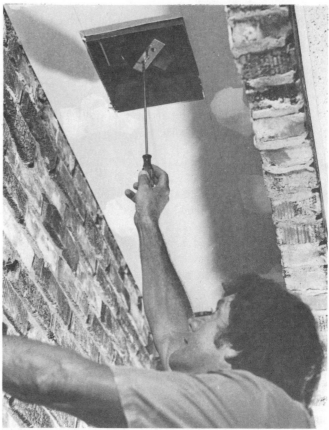

Mounting brackets for some range hood models are attached to ducting. The ducting should be installed first. Then match the range hood to the duct and assemble the unit.

follow the layout, you may have to use valance or cabinet fillers to make the hood fit.

Tools and materials. Hammer, screwdriver, roundhead screws (usually furnished with the hood), wire nuts for electrical connections, level, tape measure, sheet metal screws, duct tape, keyhole saw or power jigsaw.

STEPS

Install the ducting first. It can go through a soffit, up through the ceiling, attic, and out the soffit on the roof overhang, or through an outside wall.

The ducting is rectangular or round sheet metal pipe that you can buy prefabricated to length. You assemble it on the job with sheet metal screws and duct tape. Outlet holes for the ducting can be cut with a keyhole saw or jigsaw in the soffits or through the exterior wall of your house. Manufacturers of range hoods include detailed instructions with the product.

First, mark the location of the duct cut-out on the bottom of the cabinet under which the hood will be installed. You will

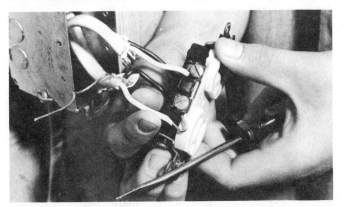

Power for the range hood — fan and lights — can come from a wall switch or outlet near the range. Turn off the power at the master switch, then make connections.

need a helper to hold the hood in place.

Saw out the opening in the cabinet bottom. Use a keyhole saw or power jigsaw. You may need to drill a starting hole for the saw.

Attach the duct connection to the hood. This part is usually supplied by the manufacturer. Determine the position for the mounting slots for the hood and drill holes in the cabinet bottom for the screws or bolts that will hold the hood in place. Install the hood, screwing or bolting it in place. At this point, you should connect the duct to the duct collar of the hood. Several metal screws hold it in position.

Hook up the power to the fan and light (see electrical section, this chapter). You do this by removing a metal pan covering inside the bottom of the hood. This panel should be marked. A wiring diagram is furnished with the hood; you may need wire nuts to make the power connection, which may not be furnished.

Maintenance. Range hoods become grease-covered very quickly. Remove any grease weekly with household detergent and water. Every two months, release the metal filter and wash it in household detergent and water. About every six months, remove the metal covering at the bottom of the hood and clean the motor housing, wiring and other exposed parts. Use a soft dry cloth.

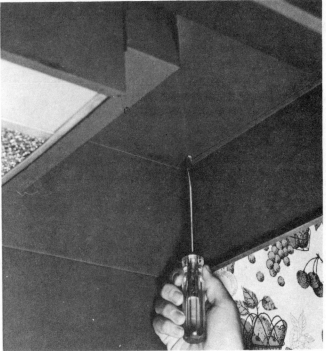

Assemble the range hood parts. They go together with sheet metal screws — usually furnished by the manufacturer.

Flooring

The world of floorcovering is a large one. It becomes somewhat smaller, however, when applied to kitchens. Since kitchen floors should be soil-proof and easy to keep clean, the choice narrows to resilient tile, sheet vinyl, hardwood block or parquet flooring, and indoor/outdoor carpeting.

If a new kitchen floor is not in your budget at this time, you probably will have to make repairs to your old floor before or after installing new cabinets and appliances.

This section is divided into these two projects: how to repair an existing floor; how to install a new floor. Products are limited to the most common flooring used in a kitchen area — wood block, asphalt and vinyl tile, and carpet tile.

Sheet vinyl flooring is a fairly new product and it is as easy to install as laying a blanket down on the floor. In fact, you can even fold the material like a blanket. It is held to the floor surface with double-faced tape; you can cut the sheet with heavy scissors.

Replacing One Tile

Tools and materials. Propane torch, or clothes iron, soft cloth for padding, scraper, putty knife, cold chisel, hammer, rubber hammer, razor knife, new tile, adhesive.

STEPS

Remove the damaged tile. If the tile is asphalt or vinyl you can sometimes heat the surface of the damaged tile with an iron or propane torch to soften the adhesive under it. This makes removal easier. If not, you will have to chip out the old tile, using a cold chisel or a putty knife driven with a rubber hammer. When the old tile is out, remove any adhesive residue from the subflooring.

Fit the new tile into the void. You may have to trim it slightly with the razor knife to get a tight fit at all four joints.

To replace a damaged floor tile, remove the damaged tile with a scraper or putty knife. You can soften stubborn adhesive with a propane torch, but be careful that you don't scorch the adjoining tile with the flame.

With a putty knife, smear a walnut-sized dab of adhesive near all four corners of the tile and press the tile in place. Or apply the adhesive directly to the subfloor. Then cover the tile with a soft cloth and stand on the tile to bond it solidly to the subfloor. Wipe away any excess adhesive to complete the job.

If the tile is a peel-and-stick product, you must prefit the tile in the void before removing the protective paper that covers the adhesive backing.

Installing a New Floor

Tools and materials. Hammer, nail set, propane torch, razor knife, ice scraper or tile spade, wood putty, putty knife, wall scraper, cold chisel, chalkline and chalk, tape measure, carpenters' square, tinsnips, cardboard for templates, adhesive spreader, adhesive.

STEPS

Check the old floor for damage. If the floor is in good repair, you may be able to install the new floor over the old floor. But if the old floor is damaged or uneven, you must remove the covering down to the subflooring.

First, remove the baseboard around the room. There is no easy way to remove old flooring. The best way is with an ice scraper or a flat tiling spade. You can get under the tiles with either of these tools and pry and chip until the flooring pops loose. For stubborn areas, try lifting the old tile by first heating it with a propane torch, being careful with the flame. Or, in small stubborn areas, you may be able to remove the old tile with a cold chisel. Work clean; put the old tile or flooring residue in a garbage sack or container as the job progresses.

Once the old tile is off, fill any splits, cracks, or holes with water putty. Then clean away the old adhesive. You can do this with a propane torch and scraper, or rent a floor sander with medium grit abrasive and go over the floor. You do not want to remove the wood, only the adhesive, so be careful. Sanders cut fast.

Make "sawdust" from a scrap piece of resilient tile. You can do this with a regular knife or razor knife. Then mix the residue with white glue. Press this mixture into any small holes in resilient tiles. The colors will match, if the scrap tile is the same as the floor tile.

Remove the old tile from the floor. You can do this with an ice scraper or a flat tiling spade. For stubborn tiles, heat the adhesive with a propane torch.

If the subfloor is badly damaged, it is best to re-cover the subflooring with hardboard or particleboard underlayment. This material is nailed to the subflooring with screw-nails spaced about 2 in. apart. The joints in the panels should be staggered, not aligned. Make any necessary cuts at the center of the room, if possible, to give you plenty of room to trim and nail.

When the subfloor is ready for the new tile, lay out the guidelines for the tile. Find the centers of facing walls and snap a chalkline between the walls. Then find the centers of the adjoining walls and snap a chalkline between these walls. When you have finished, the room will be divided into equal quarters. Check the squareness of the lines where they cross in the center of the room. If the room is badly off-center, you will have to square the room with a straightedge. See the illustrations for this technique.

Snap only one chalkline until you are sure of the tile spacing against the wall. You may need to move the next line slightly. When you are sure of the layout, snap the second line — stretch the chalkline taut, pull it up with your fingers, and release it, and chalk it onto the wall.

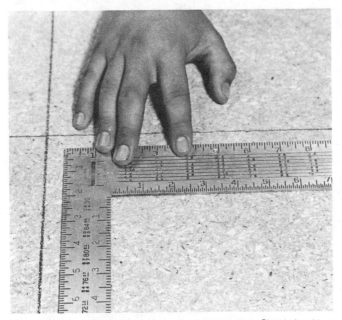

The point where the lines cross should be square. Check it with a framing square. If the lines are not square, re-snap the lines.

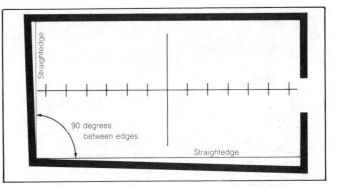

If the room is badly out of square, you can realign it with straightedges. This then will let you reposition the tile so you need not do so much cutting. As you can see by the tile layout — marks along a line — you will need more tile in some rows than in others.

As a test run, lay a row of tile along the chalklines across the room. This will let you adjust the tiles to fit and to change the pattern of the tile if necessary.

If the last tile in the row, next to the wall, is less than one half tile width from the wall, you will have to move the original chalkline over by one half tile width and snap a new chalkline. This takes time, but not as much time as cutting and fitting each tile at the wall.

Set the first tile at the center of the room where the chalklines cross. Double and triple check this measurement since all the tiles you set will stem from this key tile. Continue setting the tile in just one quarter of the room at a time. You should fit, trim, and cut the end tiles around the edge of the room once all the field tiles have been set.

Lay a row of tile along the lines — without adhesive. This will give you a chance to match patterns and make any tile adjustments before actually setting the tile.

Butt the edge of the peel-and-stick tile tightly against the edge of the tile already set. Then press the tile to the subfloor. Make sure the match is perfect before you set the tile down; you cannot move the tile afterward without breaking it.

To cut a tile to fit a space less than the full width of the tile, you must measure accurately. To do this simply, lay the tile you intend to cut (Tile #2) squarely on top of the last full time (Tile #1) you had set in place.

When Tile #2 is absolutely square with the one below it, position a third tile (Tile #2) so that one edge is flush with the wall and the other edge overlaps Tile #2. Our photo shows the overlap being marked on Tile #2; however, use a sharp pencil to make the mark so that you have a fine, clear line on which to cut. When you have cut Tile #2, you will find that the portion on the left (as seen in the photo) will exactly fit the space between the wall and Tile #1.

To cut the edge tile to fit, place a whole tile over the top of the last whole tile you set. Align the edges perfectly. Now place a second whole tile so it overlaps the previous tile and align the second tile with the wall. With a marking pencil, draw a line on the bottom tile along the edge of the overlapping tile. Remove all the loose tile. Cut the tile you marked along the cut-off line. This cut tile will fit perfectly on the subflooring next to the wall. (See the photos on this technique.)

Carpet Tiles

Carpet tiles are set almost the same way as resilient tile, except that you must match the pattern or pile in the carpeting. To help you do this, many carpet tile manufacturers have stamped an arrow on the back of the tile. Make sure that when you lay the tiles all the arrows point the same direction.

Carpet tiles usually need no adhesive. They are held in place by friction from the floor and pressure from the adjoining tiles. However, perimeter carpet tiles usually are secured to the floor with double-faced adhesive tape, which is sold in rolls of various widths and lengths. To use the tape, simply cut off a piece of it to fit the tile, tear off the paper backing, adhere the tape to the tile, and press the tile in position on the subfloor or old finished flooring.

To remove carpet tile, heat the tile with an iron. Then pry up the tile with the edge of a putty or case knife. Carpet tile usually is set without adhesive. You can use double-faced adhesive tape in problem areas.

Hardwood Tiles

Hardwood block flooring may have straight edges or tongue-and-grooved edges. The tile is laid out and set the same way as resilient and carpet tile. If the tile has tongues-and-grooves, you will have to align them as you set them so the tile fits properly. Make any necessary cuts with a crosscut saw, sawing the tile from the finished side.

Special Cuts

Measure and mark all tile to go around obstructions and curves. With a thin piece of cardboard, make a template of the shape. Then use the template to mark the cut-off lines on the tile.

You can cut resilient and carpet tile with a razor knife or heavy scissors; cut hardwood tiles with a power jigsaw or coping saw.

Hardwood block flooring usually is tongue and grooved. It also is pre-finished. Once set, just clean off any adhesive residue and polish the wood.

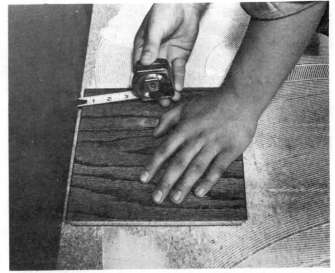

Space hardwood block tile about ⅛- to ¼-in. from the wall. This allows for any expansion and contraction of the wood. The crack will be hidden by molding.

Lay block flooring in a pyramid configuration. This way, you can match the grain of the wood — or alternate the grain — to any pattern. Set the tile without adhesive to establish design and spacing. Then mark each tile as you take it up so you can set it back again in the same spot with adhesive.

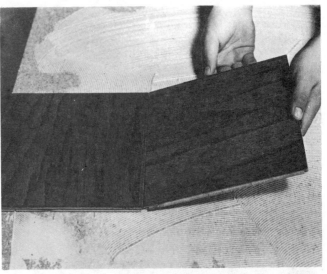

Align the tongue in the groove, and then lower the tile into the adhesive. Press the tile down. The tile may be adjusted *slightly* by sliding it in the adhesive. But don't overdo it, or you can make an adhesive mess.

Spread the adhesive for block flooring, or any flooring, in a small area. The adhesive should be applied with a notched trowel. Try to make the thickness of the adhesive even throughout; remove any lumps or debris as you go.

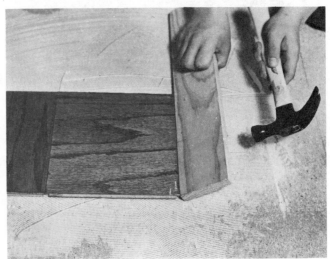

Tap stubborn tiles in position. Then press the tiles down into the adhesive. It is smart to "work clean"; remove any excess adhesive as you set the tile.

For special cuts, make a cardboard template the same size as the tile. This applies to any tile material. The cardboard must be a perfect size match or the real tile won't fit.

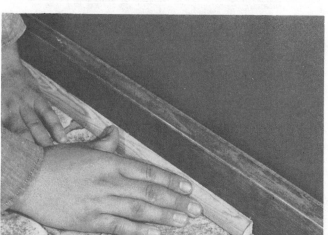

At joints, stick sheet vinyl flooring to double-faced tape. The tape assures a neater, stronger joint that does not peel or bunch as the flooring conforms to the sub-floor.

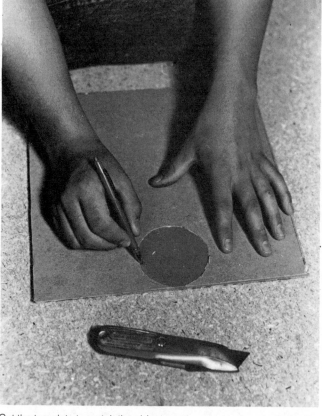

Cut the template to match the object you want to go around with the tile. Then transfer this shape to the tile and cut the tile to fit. This trick can save lots of tile material; experiment with different cuts.

Finish any flooring job with base molding. This trim makes the job neater and hides any cutting imperfections along the wall. Nail the molding and trim to the wall framing and the subflooring. Use 10d finishing nails; countersink the nail heads; fill the holes; stain or paint the wood.

4 Climate Control

Climate control offers both increased comfort and decreased energy costs. Since the "energy-crunch" is reportedly permanent, it is extremely important to make your home as energy efficient as you possibly can. These improvements can cost you money in the short run, but, over time they will save you money. To help your budget, the Federal Government is allowing a tax credit (since 1979) on your income tax return, if you add insulation, storm windows, or weatherstripping to your home. It isn't a lot of tax relief, but every little bit helps. Some states also offer an income tax credit. Be sure to save your cash register receipts when you buy these materials.

Some of the efficiencies cost very little. These include cleaning and/or washing filters, tightening connections, and leveling mechanical units. We have purposely stayed away from very technical projects in this chapter, preferring instead to offer cost-cutting endeavors that can be handled by anyone, and which are easy and fast.

When you buy the products mentioned here, be sure to ask the dealer for any manufacturer's recommendations, instruction booklets and literature concerning the products. Specifications for some products change; therefore, compare products before buying.

A Checklist of Climate Control Problems

Below is a list — from roof ridge to basement floor — of areas and building components that need attention. This checklist can save you time and money. The list points out the problems; the solutions can be found in this and other chapters of the book. (See index)

Broken chimney caps
Loose mortar between chimney masonry units
Damaged and loose shingles
Exposed roofing nails

Cracks and gaps around roof flashing
Damaged roof gutters and hangers
Non-functional downspouts
Cracks and breaks in siding

Cracks around windows and doors
Lack of storm windows and doors
Lack of weatherstripping around windows and doors
Cracks between exterior doors and thresholds

Broken windows
Ill-fitting storm windows and doors
Leaking basement sash
Poorly sloped grade level

Broken or tipped splash blocks
Cracks in foundation walls
Crumbling and loose mortar in foundation walls
No (or inadequate) insulation in walls and ceilings

Noninsulated crawl spaces
Uncovered crawl spaces
No insulation on hot water pipes
No insulation on heating/air conditioning ducts

Leaking duct joints
Dirty furnace filters — or no filters
Dirty air conditioning filters
Dirty range hood filters

Dirty or blocked heating/cooling registers
Poor basement ventilation and humidity control
Leaky pipes
Stopped drains

Dirty thermostats
Malfunctioning thermostats
Inefficient lighting fixtures
High thermostat setting (heat)

Low thermostat setting (cooling)
Malfunctioning water heater
No (or inadequate) clothes dryer vents
Misuse of dishwashers, ranges, or other major appliances

Leaking faucets
Leaking toilets
Heating, cooling, and lighting in never-or-seldom-used rooms.

INSULATION

There are nine types of insulation on the market. One type — insulation board sheathing — has to be installed while the house is being built, or when you put on an addition. It is nearly impossible for you to add any insulation to the side walls of your home. To do this, the siding or the gypsum wallboard has to be removed — a job that probably would cost more than the energy you would save over a very long period of time. Loose fill insulation may be installed, but this is a job for a professional.

Before you sign any contracts with a contractor, make sure that the contractor is bonded and reliable. Check out the firm with the Chamber of Commerce, Better Business Bureau, National Home Improvement Council, the local office of the U.S.

Department of Housing and Urban Development (HUD), or the local chapter of the National Association of Home Builders (NAHB). You can't be too careful. The energy crunch has produced a brand new legion of operators.

What can you undertake yourself? You can add insulation to attic and crawl spaces. Ideally, the attic should have about 8 to 9 in. of insulation for a factor of R-30 for the northern tier of states.

All house insulation is based on R (for resistance) factors. The higher the R factor, the more insulation quality of the product.

Before you buy any insulation, ask the dealer for the recommended R factors in your area. The factors will vary as to climate, i.e., northern state residents need more insulation in their homes than coastal residents. Southern state residents need insulation for air conditioning rather than heating.

Three and one-half in. of foil faced insulation has an R-factor of R-11. Six in. of unfaced insulation provides R-19. You can work a combination of these products to get the R-factor recommended for your area. You also have to take other materials into consideration when you figure out the R factor.

R RATINGS

Material	R Rating
Air space (per inch)	.94
Gypsum wallboard (½ in.)	.79
Hardboard (¼ in.)	.20
Plywood (¾ in.)	.93
Asphalt shingles	.44
Plastic vapor barrier	trace
Padded carpeting	2.09
Common brick (4 in.)	.85
Concrete block (8 in.)	1.10
Floor tile	.04
Sheet/sprayed plastic foam per in.	5.0
Polystyrene boards per in.	4.0
Polystyrene sheet per in.	4.0

Types of Insulation You Can Install:

Flange batts. One side has a moisture barrier, while the other side has a kraft "breather" paper wrap. Use this insulation for crawl spaces.

Foil-faced fiberglass insulation. One side has an aluminum foil type covering; the other side is exposed. This is a standard material for attics, sidewalls, crawlspaces, and other insulation installations.

Paper-faced fiberglass insulation. Similar to foil-faced insulation, but with a kraft paper vapor barrier.

Unfaced fiberglass rolls. No vapor barrier at all. If you want a vapor barrier, use polyethylene film, usually called sheet plastic or polyfilm.

Loose wool. Usually fiberglass, this material comes in bags and looks like chunks of pink cotton. It is spread or blown between studs and rafters.

Vermiculite. This is expanded mica; it looks like the stuff you use to pot plants. It is poured or blown between framing members.

Vapor barriers must always face the *warm side* of the room. On an attic floor, the barrier is *down* toward the heated rooms below. If the attic floor will be covered and the attic space heated, you can use unfaced insulation between the floors, or insulation between the rafters. On the rafters, the vapor barrier faces the room, NOT roof. In crawl spaces, the vapor barrier usually faces up toward the heated room area.

How To Insulate Walls

Tools and materials. Insulation with the recommended R factor, stapler, razor knife, straightedge (board), tape measure, foil-faced adhesive tape, step ladder.

Safety. Wear safety glasses, long-sleeved shirt with cuffs and collar buttoned, gloves, filter mask. Leave the room every 30 minutes or so for fresh air.

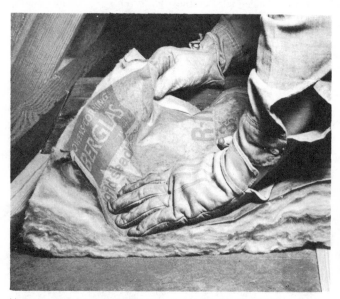

Hang insulation from the top down to get a better fit. Cut the insulation to length and press it between the framing members. Never wrap insulation around framing. Always wear gloves, safety glasses and a mask when working with this scratchy material.

You can set insulation batts over loose fill insulation, as long as the batts don't have a moisture vapor barrier. You can also add loose fill insulation over batt insulation if the loose fill is not covering the moisture vapor barrier.

To cut insulation, lay one board under and another on top of it. Then step on the board, squeezing the material together. Run the razor knife through the insulation, using the straightedge of the board as a guide.

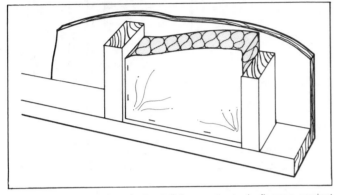

Staples should be spaced about 8 in. apart; staple flanges against insides of studs.

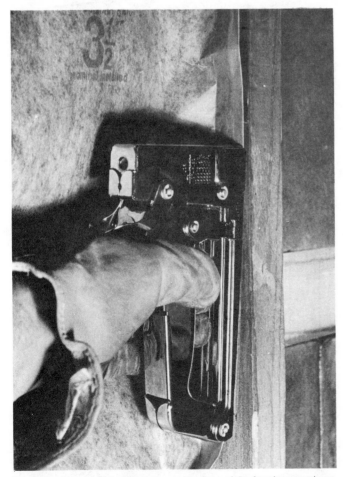

Staple the flanges of the insulation to the face of the framing members. Do not overlap the edges of the framing. Space the staples about 2 in. apart. Pull down as you fasten the insulation to remove gaps.

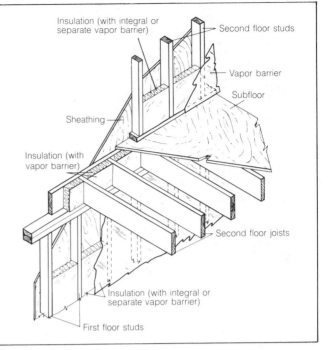

Vapor barriers and insulation in exposed second floor walls should be put up in the same way as for walls of one story houses. Alternatives include: standard blanket insulation with vapor barrier, friction-type insulation with separate vapor barrier, or reflective insulation with protective vapor barrier. The space between the joists along the stringer joists should take snugly fit insulation with a vapor barrier.

STEPS

Measure between the studs from the ceiling to the floor. Cut one piece of insulation to fit and try it for size. If it fits, use this piece as a template to cut the rest of the strips. Use a razor knife to cut insulation. Lay a board with a straightedge across the insulation; stand on it with one foot to compact the insulation. Then make the cut with the razor knife, using the edge of the board as a guide.

Staple the insulation to the inside faces, not edges, of the studs. Space the staples about 2 to 3 in. apart so there are no gaps between the framing members and the insulation. Most insulation comes with flanges for staples. The flanges measure ¾ in. wide, which automatically spaces the insulation on the framing members. The flanges should be flush with the edges of the framing members and flat against the face of the framing members. The face of the moisture barrier then should be about ¾ in. from the finish wall or ceiling to produce an air space.

If you tear the moisture vapor barrier, patch it with a strip of foil-faced tape. Also, tape around projections in the wall such as heating/cooling ducts.

When you come to pipes or wires in the wall:

(1) pull the insulation out from between the studs;

(2) approximate where the pipe or wiring will cross the insulation;

(3) cut the insulation (not vapor barrier) with the razor knife — just cut part way through the thickness of the insulation with a quick slicing movement of the knife;

(4) insert the pipe or wiring in the slash and continue with the stapler.

At the top and bottom of the strip, tuck the insulation back away from the vapor barrier. Staple the vapor barrier to the bottom face of the header and the top face of the sill.

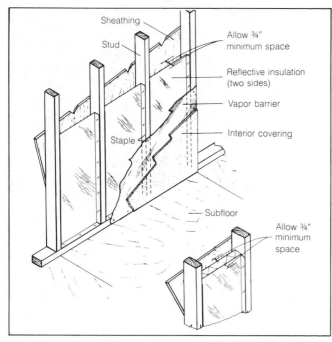

Reflective insulation comes in single sheets, reflective two sides, and as multiple reflective insulation for which you need to allow a ¾" space.

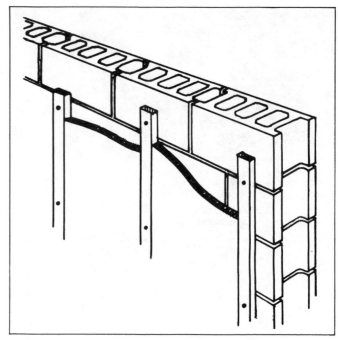

When insulating a masonry wall, first nail studs into place. Then fit insulation between studs and put up vapor barrier.

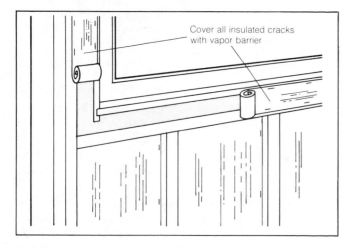

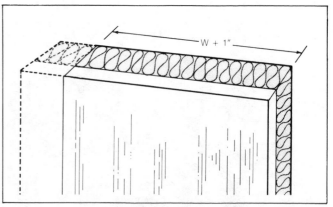

When insulating a nonstandard width, cut insulation about an inch wider than the space needed.

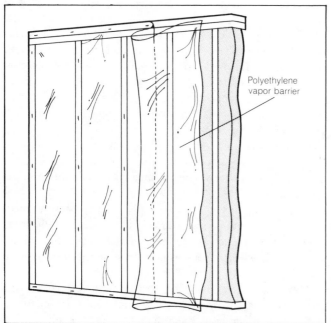

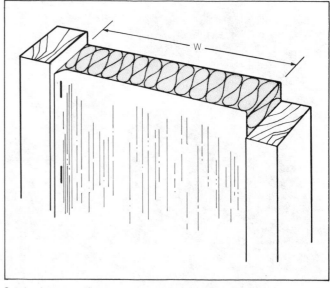

Staple the uncut flange to the stud, as before. Then pull the vapor barrier from the stapled side to the other stud. This will compress the insulation behind it. Staple through the vapor barrier.

How To Insulate Ceilings

Tools and materials. Same as for walls.
Safety. Same as for walls.

STEPS

Insulating ceilings involves the same techniques as insulating walls, but you need not fasten the insulation between the floor joists. If you are insulating between the rafters, you have to use staples.

If there is no insulation in the ceiling, place insulation with a foil or paper vapor barrier facing *down* between the joists. Then you will probably have to place unfaced insulation on top of the first layer of insulation to achieve the necessary R factor recommended for your area.

If there is insulation in the ceiling and the foil is incorrectly facing upward between the floor joists, try to remove this first layer of insulation and turn it over so the foil faces the heated rooms below. You shouldn't, of course, damage the vapor barrier. Otherwise, slit the foil with the razor knife. Then add unfaced insulation on top of this first layer of insulation.

For already-installed unfaced insulation, remove the insulation, install a polyfilm moisture vapor barrier over the top of the ceiling between the joists, and replace the insulation. If you need to increase the insulation in this application, simply lay unfaced insulation over the installed strips.

If the ceiling is insulated with loose fill or vermiculite insulation, you can increase the R-factor by pouring more of this material between the joists, on top of the old insulation.

If the ceiling is insulated with roll or batt insulation and has some loose fill or vermiculite insulation placed on top of it, you can either add unfaced insulation or more loose fill insulation on top of the existing insulation to increase the R factor. Because of a low roof pitch, it may be difficult to extend the insulation back to the eaves. Make this job easier by rolling or smoothing the insulation out with a broom. Be careful to get the material centered between the ceiling joists.

If you have to cut and splice insulation in the attic, use the long pieces from the eaves to the center of the attic space. This way, you can tape the joints with foil-faced tape more easily, since you have more room in which to work.

How To Insulate Between Rafters

Tools and materials. Same as for walls.
Safety. Same as for walls.

STEPS

The installations are very similar to those for walls and ceilings. You will be working off a step ladder in order to reach the ridge of the roof. Make sure the ladder is open, locked, and on a firm footing.

Insulation that goes between rafters should have a vapor barrier. This covering should point down toward the room.

To create the R factor you need, you'll probably have to install unfaced insulation between the rafters first and then install faced insulation over it. You can lightly tack the unfaced insulation to hold it in place while you cover it with the foil-faced material. A helper would come in handy for this job, too.

If the rafters are already insulated and you want to add to the R factor, you will have to remove the existing insulation and

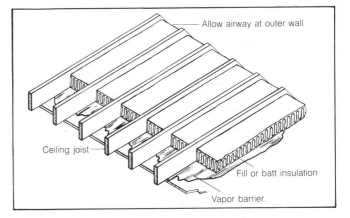

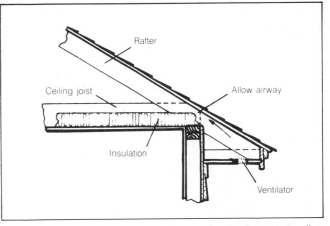

When installing ceiling insulation and vapor barrier, be sure to allow airway at the outer wall.

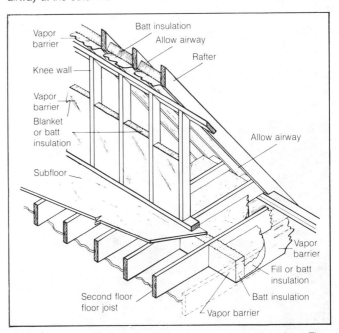

Knee walls are partial walls that extend from the floor to the rafters. They are commonly found in 1½ story homes and are most frequently used as bedrooms or bonus space. Height will vary from 4 to 6 ft.

install *unfaced* insulation. Then cover the unfaced material with the old insulation you carefully removed from between the rafters.

If the existing insulation has a vapor barrier that faced the roof, try to remove the insulation and reinstall it so the vapor barrier faces the room.

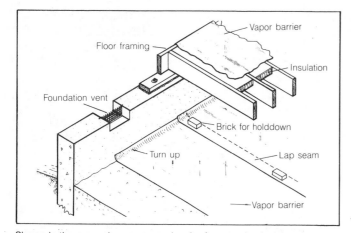

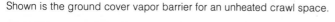

Shown is the ground cover vapor barrier for an unheated crawl space.

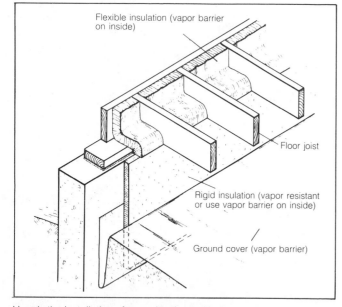

Here is the installation of vapor barrier and insulation for a heated crawl space.

Chicken wire holds insulation in position in crawl spaces where you can't use the vapor barrier flanges to staple the insulation. You can use wire insulation hangers that spring out between the joists and hold the insulation.

How To Insulate Crawl Spaces

Tools and materials. Foil-faced insulation, stapler, razor knife, wire insulation hangers or chicken wire, polyfilm, a cartridge of asphalt roofing cement, caulking gun shell, brickbats.

Safety. Same as for walls, ceilings, rafters.

STEPS

Measure and cut the insulation to fit. Use the long pieces in hard-to-get-at areas; patch the small pieces in the center of the space where it is easy to work.

Staple the insulation where you can. You can't use the insulation staple flanges because the vapor barrier will face the floor, so hold the insulation in position with insulation hanger wires or chicken wire that has been stapled over the insulation and onto the edges of the joists. The wire hangers are simply lengths of spring-type wire that have been cut to fit between joists. You just snap them into position between the joists, spaced about 12 to 15 in. apart.

When you have finished with the insulation job, cover the crawl space floor or bare earth with sheets of polyfilm. Use the 4 mil thickness, if possible, and overlap the joints 4 to 6 in. Weight these joints with brickbats, and place several brickbats on the main surface of the covering to hold it down. Position the polyfilm about 6 in. up sidewalls. Tack it in place with daubs of asphalt roofing cement.

The polyfilm keeps moisture from seeping up through the earth or floor, then through the insulation and into the living areas above. Besides providing more comfort and saving energy, the polyfilm installation also helps prevent rot.

How To Insulate Basement Walls

Tools and materials. If insulation is to be applied directly to the wall: styrofoam panels, building adhesive, razor knife, tape measure, straightedge. If insulation is to be built into a wall: moisture-treated 2x4 framing lumber, lead anchor bolts and lag screws, square, measuring tape, 16d common nails, polyfilm, building adhesives, caulking gun shell, stapler, razor knife, crosscut saw, star drill, baby sledge hammer or power drill and masonry bit, adjustable wrench, cedar shingles for shims.

Safety. Wear safety glasses, a long-sleeved shirt with cuffs and collar buttoned when working with fiberglass insulation, filter mask. Stop every 30 minutes or so for fresh air.

STEPS

If your basement walls are bone dry, you can insulate them with sheets of styrofoam. The job is very easy and offers strong insulation benefits.

Start in a corner. Apply the insulation panels to the wall with building adhesive. If you use the cartridge-type adhesive in a caulking gun shell, spread a ribbon down the edges of the panel and at a couple of points at the center of the panel, and stick the panel in place. You can cut the panels to fit with a razor knife. Make sure all joints are tight and all the wall surface is covered.

If you will panel the basement wall, attach furring strips to the wall first. Then stick the insulation panels between the furring. The panels are sized to go between framing 16-in.-on-center. The wall covering then may be attached to the furring

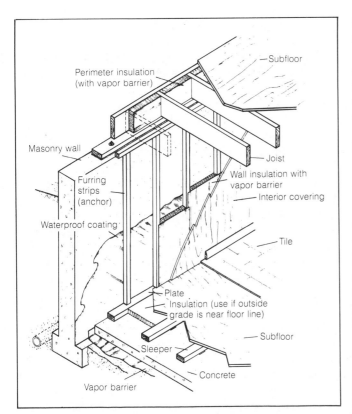

You may need to add furring strips when finishing off a basement. They will give a nailing surface for interior finishes, and provide space for blanket insulation with attached vapor barrier.

strips in the normal way. You should, however, give the back of the paneling a coat of penetrating wood sealer. This further protects the paneling against moisture damage.

For regular fiberglass insulation, the technique is different. You will have to build a false wall in order to hang the insulation between the framing. (First correct any basement water problems; see Chapter 2 for details.)

The false wall will butt against the foundation wall. It is a good idea to cover the foundation wall with polyfilm. Stick the polyfilm on the wall with ribbons of building adhesive applied from a caulking gun. Lap the joints about 4 in. and seal them with adhesive. Also lap the floor about 3 in., sealing the film with adhesive.

Nail the header of the false wall to the bottom edges of the floor joists. Fasten the sill of the wall to the floor with lead anchors and lag screws. Be careful to align the header and the sill so the studs will be plumb when you nail them into position.

You will need a star drill and baby sledge hammer to make the holes in the floor for the anchors — or use a power drill and masonry bits. Either way, space the anchors about 2 ft. apart, and predrill pilot holes in the sill for the lag bolts. Drive the bolts with an adjustable wrench.

As you attach the header and sill, check this framing for level. You may have to shim the 2x4s with cedar shingles. You can trim the excess shingles later with the crosscut saw or a sharp chisel.

Toenail the studs, 16-in.-on-center, across the wall between the sill and header. Due to odd measurements, you may not be able to get all these members spaced perfectly at 16 in. The wall is not load-bearing, so spacing is not that critical, except

for the width of the insulation. You can always trim the insulation with a razor knife to fit the wall.

Attach the insulation to the wall the same way you would to a regular wall. The vapor barrier always faces the room (see instructions, earlier this chapter). Finish the wall with gypsum wallboard or paneling in the same way you would any other wood-framed wall.

How To Insulate Floors in Unfinished Attic

Tools and Materials. Same as for walls.
Safety. Same as for walls.

STEPS

The steps are the same as for walls, keeping in mind that the vapor barrier will be beneath the insulation, facing toward the heated room below. If you are laying new insulation over old, and both the new and the old insulation have vapor barriers, slash the vapor barrier in the new insulation before laying it in place. Openings to attics are insulated by tacking a strip of insulation to the back of the lay-in panel or entry hatch to the attic. You may instead glue the insulation batt to the back of the panel.

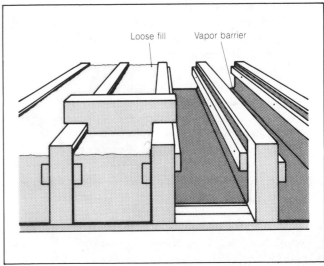

Loose fill insulation is placed between the joists and is leveled with a notched board to maintain the right height of the insulation between the joists. A moisture vapor barrier must be installed beneath the insulation, facing toward the room below.

Insulating Adjoining Structures

Tools and materials. Same as for walls and ceilings.
Safety. Same as for walls and ceilings.

STEPS

Garages, storage areas, and sheds that adjoin your home should be insulated. At least the wall that is attached to the house should be insulated. Usually, these walls are framed like any wall, so insulating them is not a problem. Just follow the same instructions as given earlier for a regular wall.

CAULKING AND WEATHERSTRIPPING

Of all the building products for sale, caulking and weatherstripping probably cost less and do more good than most other weather protection. As a bonus, both caulking and weatherstripping are easy to apply and install. Here's a check-

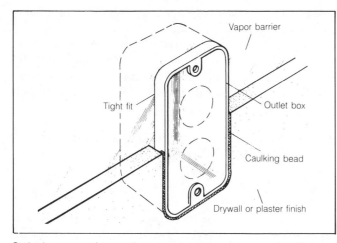

Outlet boxes need protection against moisture in exposed walls.

list of places to apply and install caulking and weatherstripping. Caulking:

(1) around windows and doors;
(2) around basement sash;
(3) in splits and cracks in siding;
(4) between joints in wood siding;
(5) cracks between door thresholds and stoops;
(6) between dissimilar materials such as wood and masonry, masonry and metal, wood and metal;
(7) along the bottom of siding where it meets the foundation;
(8) at dormers and roof flashing;
(9) around dryer and exhaust fan outlets;
(10) between soffits and siding;
(11) at power entrances and exits;
(12) around gable vents and roof vents.

Look in these places for weatherstripping protection: (1) around windows and doors; (2) along bottoms of doors; (3) around storm doors; (4) bottoms of garage doors.

How To Apply Caulking

To caulk, you need two products: a metal caulking gun shell and the caulking, which comes in a cardboard cartridge and fits a caulking gun shell. You also can buy caulking in bulk and fill a steel-tubed caulking gun with it, like you would a water pistol. The bulk savings probably wouldn't be worth the mess. For small jobs you can buy caulking in a plastic tube.

You have a variety of caulking from which to choose.

Oil-based caulking: This is the inexpensive spread, and you can use it almost anywhere.

Polyvinyl acetate: A very good buy for almost any surface. It is medium-priced.

Latex: Known as "painter's caulking." It is quick-drying, and may be thinned with water.

Silicone: It will last for years on most surfaces, but doesn't stick well to paint. Costly.

Butyl rubber: The best of them all, butyl will withstand the elements for years. It is tops for sealing masonry joints, and is fairly expensive.

You have to do a little probing to tell whether a joint needs caulking. Take a putty knife and press the blade into the caulking. If the caulking is still "gummy", the material doesn't have to be replaced. But if the caulking cracks and falls out of the

joint when you scratch it with the putty knife, remove the old and apply new caulking to the area.

Tools and materials. Caulking gun shell, caulking, razor knife, 20d nail, putty knife, wire brush, coffee can full of water, cloths.

STEPS

Insert the caulking cartridge in the caulking gun shell. Cut the nozzle of the cartridge at about a 45-degree angle with the razor knife.

The plastic nozzle is tapered — small at the tip and large at the base. You should cut the angle on the nozzle at about the point you think it will span the crack which you will fill with caulking. Step back and figure an average for the crack widths. This will help you make the cutting decision. Some manufacturers have stamped a graduated scale on the plastic nozzle to help you cut it properly. For example, if you are going to be filling cracks that average ¼-in. wide, cut the nozzle at "¼". These numbers are difficult to see; look closely.

Then with the 20d nail, puncture the seal between the nozzle and the cartridge. You'll have to poke the nail down the nozzle to do this. If you do not break this seal, the pressure generated by the gun on the cartridge can crush the cartridge, resulting in an awful mess.

With the putty knife and wire brush, clean the joint that you

Slice through the plastic nozzle of the caulking cartridge at about a 45-degree angle. Note how the nozzle is tapered. The closer you cut to the base, the wider the strip of caulking compound will be when it is forced out the nozzle.

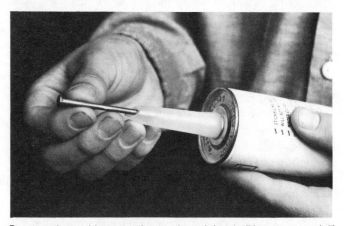

Puncture the seal between the nozzle and the caulking compound. If you don't break this seal, pressure from the caulking gun can split the paper cartridge.

Hold the caulking gun at about a 45-degree angle — the same angle you cut the nozzle. Always pull the caulking gun downward, applying pressure to the trigger as you go. Wet a finger to smooth caulking compound.

are going to caulk. Remove any old caulking, putty, dirt, grit, and so on. The wire brush helps rough-up the surface so the caulking can get a good bite on it. The brush serves as a broom to clean the area.

To operate the caulking gun, turn the plunger in back of the tube to engage the trigger mechanism. As you pull the trigger, the plunger is forced down into the caulking cartridge and the caulking is squeezed out of the nozzle into the crack you are filling.

Hold the caulking gun at about a 45-degree angle — the same angle as the cut on the nozzle of the cartridge — pull the trigger, and pull the caulking gun down the crack. After several runs, you will be able to judge the speed you should move the gun in relation to the amount of caulking coming out of the nozzle. If you pull the gun too slowly down the work, the crack will overfill and the caulking will bulge out of the crack. If you move too quickly, the caulking will be stringy and not fill the crack.

Always pull the caulking gun toward you. Never push it up along the crack or break you are trying to caulk.

Usually, the final caulking job will be smooth. But occasionally the surface of the caulking will look rough and uneven. You can smooth it with a wet finger. Dip your index finger in a coffee can filled with water. Then lightly run your finger down the caulking. Rewet your finger as needed. The caulk will clean off with a cloth.

Let the caulking set at least a day before you paint over it. Caulking develops a light seal after it sets for 24 hours or so. You then can run a paintbrush over the caulking without its sticking to the brush, or being damaged by the brush. Latex caulking, however, sets faster — 30 minutes or so. You can paint right over it after this time period.

When you have finished running a caulking line, *immediately* turn the plunger at the back of the caulking gun. This releases the pressure so the caulking doesn't run out the nozzle.

If there is any caulking left in the cartridge after you've finished the project (you'll know by how far down the plunger has gone into the cartridge) stick the 20d nail in the nozzle to keep the caulking fresh for the next project. Or you can stick a golf tee in the nozzle.

If the caulking is latex, you can clean up any caulking mess with water. If the caulking is silicone, oil-based, or butyl, you should immediately use mineral spirits for cleanup. Do not use water. Water will only smear the material, making everything worse.

All About Weatherstripping

Weatherstripping is available in most home-center, hardware, and building-material stores. Choosing what you need may be harder than installing the product.

Weatherstripping is usually classified by the area: door and window weatherstripping; garage door weatherstripping; threshold weatherstripping. It can be manufactured from brass, aluminum, plastic, felt, rubber, and fabric. Most of it will work well for the job it is designed to do; most of it is not expensive.

Tools and materials. Hammer, putty knife, razor knife, hacksaw, screwdriver, pry bar, wire brush, caulking, tape measure, cross-cut saw.

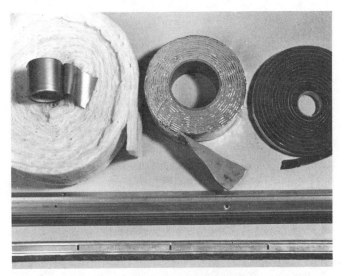

Weatherstripping variety includes (from left) fiberglass and tape wrap; pipe wrap with a foil face; sponge rubber door and window weatherstripping; rubber door sweep; felt door and window weatherstripping.

STEPS

Weatherstripping is nailed (sometimes glued) to windows and doors. The fasteners are usually supplied by the manufacturer, along with complete installation details.

Be careful not to tangle the weatherstripping as you unroll it to nail or glue it into position. As you install it, pull the material taut. It should not bunch or gap along the door or window frames.

If the metal kinks when you are installing the thin metal weatherstripping, try to straighten it by tapping it on a concrete or other hard, flat surface. If you can't remove the kink, throw the strip away.

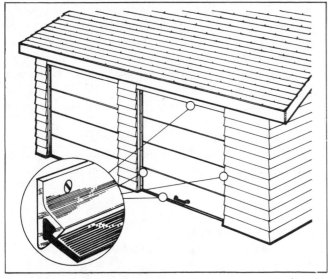

The weatherstrip for a garage door serves two purposes. The rubber flange held by the metal strip attached to the base of the door seals out the cold air in winter, and because it is flexible enough to conform to the drainage curve graded into the concrete of the driveway and garage floor, it will also keep out rain.

Install garage door weatherstripping along the bottom edge of the door. Galvanized shingle nails are the best fasteners to hold the weatherstripping in place. Space the nails about 2 to 3 inches apart.

Garage weatherstripping is "tubular" in cross-section. When the door is closed, the weatherstripping compresses, forming a seal between the bottom of the door and concrete. It is a good idea to weatherstrip your garage door even if the garage is not attached to the house or heated. The weatherstripping helps keep out insects and small reptiles and mice, and protects the wood from moisture and water damage.

ALTERNATIVE: THERMAL THRESHOLD

Thermal thresholds are great energy savers. The wide aluminum strips have a concave plastic strip running down the center of them. After installation, the bottom of the door sweeps across the plastic strip, compressing the strip. This forms an airtight seal between the bottom of the door and the threshold.

The thresholds are manufactured in standard sizes. Buy one that fits your doorway — measure from the inside jambs. You will have to cut out a small chunk of door stop to fit the ends of the threshold flush against the side jambs of the door. Take this measurement into consideration before you cut the threshold.

Trim the threshold with a hacksaw. You should remove the plastic strip before you make this cut. You can cut the strip to fit with a razor knife and reseat the strip into the metal channel when you're finished.

Remove the old threshold from the floor. You will need a screwdriver and pry bar for this. When the old unit is out, scrape away any debris and old caulking compound. The area should be clean.

Install the new threshold. It is screwed in position. You may want to predrill pilot holes for the screws since the door stoop probably is oak or another hard wood.

After the threshold is in place, run a small bead of caulking compound along the joint between the metal and the wood. The caulking keeps out moisture and insects.

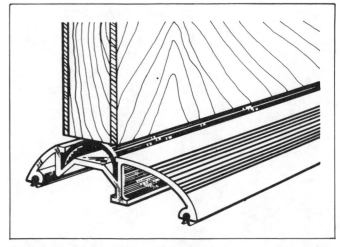

Thermal threshold is aluminum with a vinyl insert across the top of the aluminum plate. When the door closes, the door bottom compresses the insert forming a seal. You have to remove the old threshold to use this product, which can be screwed or glued to the floor.

STORMS AND SCREENS

You can keep heat in with storm doors and windows. You can save air conditioning costs with storm doors and windows. If you run the air conditioner in hot weather, leave the storm windows and doors on your home all year long. To save even more money, caulk the storm windows shut. If you open the windows in hot weather, you need screens.

Storm windows and doors are available in a wide range of sizes. Standard stock sizes are listed below. Other sizes may have to be ordered by the dealer; this takes from four to six weeks. Special order sizes are priced about 10% higher than stock sizes.

Width and height in inches

24x38	28x46	32x46	36x54
24x46	28x54	32x54	40x38
24x54	32x42	36x38	40x46
28x38	32x38	36x48	40x54

How To Install Storm Windows

Tools and materials. Measuring tape, rubber hammer, claw hammer, screwdriver, level, caulking compound, caulking gun shell, hand or power drill and drills, galvanized metal screws.

STEPS

Measure the windows for the storms. The best way is to measure any screens already on the windows. The storms will be the same size as the screens. If the windows do not have screens, measure from the top header of the window to the sill. Note this measurement. Measure from one side jamb of the window to the other side jamb of the window. Note this measurement. These measurements will be the size of storm windows you need. You can have a small tolerance in size — from about 1/8 to 1/4-in. If your windows are within this size range tolerance, stock windows will probably fit.

Be sure you measure each window. Do not guess at the sizes or assume that one window is the same size as its neighbor. If you are off as little as 1/2 in. the storm window won't fit.

After you buy the windows, test each one in the window opening for correct fit. If a storm window does not fit the opening, return and exchange it at the store. Dealers prefer that you do this immediately, since the windows can be damaged while lying around. Be sure to have your cash register receipt when exchanging windows. Different stores often stock windows produced by the same manufacturer.

If the window fits, drill three pilot holes for the screws at the top of the window. You can identify the top because the bottom has small weep holes or indentations in the frame. The weep holes provide air passage between the storm window and the prime window. This small amount of air keeps the windows from fogging.

Do not tighten these screws; just let the window "hang" from them. Now, fit the window against the prime window stops or frame. If it fits, remove the storm window. Run a bead of caulking around the inside surface of the storm window frame, set the window back in the opening, tap the frame lightly with your fist to seal the caulking between the frame and the prime window frame, and drive in one screw at the top of the storm.

With the level, level the storm window in the window opening. Set the level on the metal dividing strip in the storm window. If the window is not level in the opening and the storm is a combination window with screen and storm window inserts, you won't be able to open the storm. If the storm window does not have the combination feature, it still should be level for best appearance.

With the drill, punch holes around the metal frame, spacing them about 6 in. apart. Then drive in galvanized metal screws. The size depends on how much wood you have to work with along the sides of the window frame. Use fat screws for lots of wood, and thin screws with little wood.

Complete the job by running another bead of caulking compound around the metal window frame at its joint with the window casing.

Hang storm windows and screens from the top. Drill holes in the frames, then put in a couple of screws.

Level the window in the opening. Do not take for granted that the window frame is level and plumb. If the storm window is the combination type, it must be plumb and level to get the windows and screens to run smoothly on their tracks.

Caulk the storm window or screen where it meets the window frame. Also caulk the back of the storm/screen frame just before you insert it into the window frame and drive in the screws.

Most bay windows require custom-made storm windows. However, there is a storm window product available that fits inside the bay window. The storm window is a plastic sheet held in position by strips of plastic that are attached to the casing of the window. The plastic strips have an adhesive backing; the strips may be painted or stained. The plastic sheet is inserted into the strips. The sheet may be removed and stored by unsnapping the plastic strips.

How To Install Storm Doors

If you are replacing a storm door, measure the old door. The measurement will be the door size you should buy. Or measure the length of the storm door opening from the door header to the door threshold and from one side jamb to the other side jamb. On some storm doors, you can adjust the height slightly by unscrewing and moving a strip of metal. However, your measurements should be absolutely accurate.

You can buy plain or fancy storm doors — cross-bucks, combination screen/storms, or single-panel storms.

The dealer needs to know the size of the storm door and how the prime door is "handed." This is the technical term for the hinging of the prime door. Stand in front of the prime door from the outside. Note from what side the prime door is hinged — right or left. Tell the dealer this so he can sell you a storm door that is hinged properly to match the prime door.

Tools and materials. Hammer, rubber hammer, screwdriver, chisel, 10d finishing nails, pry bar, nail set, water putty, level, cardboard, razor knife, flathead screws, door stop, paint, paintbrush.

STEPS

With a replacement door, remove the old door and door closer and install the new door. You may have to slightly recut the mortises to fit the hinges of the new door and the strike plate. Make sure the new door is plumb in the opening. If not, shim out the top or bottom hinge with cardboard to plumb the door. If the door is not plumb, it will bind when opened and closed.

Make sure the new door fits tightly against the old door stop. If it doesn't, pry off the old stop, tap out the nails, and reposition the stop on the frame. Drive in new nails, countersink the nailheads, and fill the holes with water putty.

If you're hanging a new storm door, set the door in the opening and mark the door jamb for the hinge positions. You may have to prop the bottom of the door up slightly — about ½ in. so the opening will be even around the top, bottom and latch side of the door. You'll need a helper to handle the door while you mark it.

Cut the mortises for the hinges. The depth of the mortises should be the thickness of the hinges — no more, no less. If you cut too deep, you can shim the hinges out.

Hang the door on the hinges and test the swing. If you are satisfied with the job, tighten the screws in the hinges, then install the door closer and the strike plate.

If your test shows the door is not plumb, shim out one hinge or the other until the door is plumb.

Install the door stop next. Close the door and fit the stop flush against the face of the door on the inside of the door. Tack the stop to the side jamb and top header of the door. Then fasten the stop to this framing, after you make sure the door closes properly against the stop. Use 10d finishing nails; countersink the nails and fill the holes with water putty.

To complete the job, paint the new door stop (or the old door stop) and the door casing.

Window Screens and Inserts

Tools and materials. Hammer, plane or smoothing tool, screwdriver, screen hangers or clips.

STEPS

Measure for new window screens the same as you would for storm windows.

If the screen frames are wood, you will need two-piece hangers. One of the pair is screwed to the window header; the other piece is screwed to the window frame. The trick is to match up the two.

Install the frame hangers first; then mark the window headers for hangers. This way you can use the window frame to hold the screen frame in position while you do the marking. Install the header hangers and hang the screen. Small metal clips usually are installed around a wooden or metal window frame to hold aluminum window screens in position. The clips are mounted with a single screw driven into the frame. Use two clips at the top and bottom of the frame; three clips along the side jambs of the frame. Space the three clips evenly.

Screen (and storm window) inserts are held in the frame with a spring or spring-loaded clip. You just remove the clip, or depress the spring-loaded clip, to remove the window or screen insert.

Emergency Window/Door Cover-ups

Windows get broken; screens become ripped. Here are some suggestions when you can't get to a store for replacement.

Tools and materials. Polyfilm or plastic film from cleaning store bags, masking or duct tape, scissors.

STEPS

Cut the plastic with scissors to match the window or screen you want to temporarily cover. Run a strip of masking or duct tape around the plastic so it overlaps the frame. Then press the unit in position.

Don't consider this a permanent repair. You should replace the damaged glass or screening just as soon as possible.

Plumb storm doors so they will swing smoothly on their hinges. This is the most important thing you can do when installing storm doors. You can achieve plumb by shimming out the storm door hinges with cardboard.

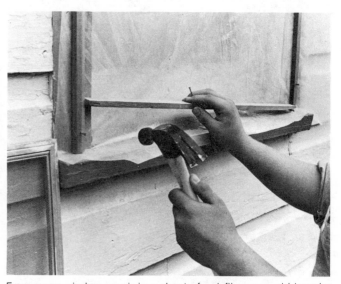

Emergency window repair is a sheet of polyfilm or an old laundry clothes bag held to the window frame with duct tape or strips of wood and nails — even a plastic garbage bag works. You can do the same thing for emergency roof leaks, but make repairs quickly.

FURNACE FIX-UPS

Furnaces are complicated pieces of equipment that become even more complicated when cooling is added to them. Therefore, other than the minor maintenance and fix-up jobs we list below, you should call in a professional when the furnace is not working properly.

Since a furnace is usually tucked away in a dark corner of your basement, a crawl space, or utility-type closet, you may tend to forget the unit until something goes wrong with it. You might be able to save some repair money by keeping the area surrounding the furnace clean, and giving the metal housing of the furnace an occasional dusting.

Furnaces need air to burn. Dust and dirt next to the furnace can be drawn into burners and filters, decreasing their efficiency. It is important that you keep louvers clean in a door that closes off the furnace room. Vacuum the louvers at least once a year.

Filters

Tools and materials. New furnace filters, cloths, pipe wrenches, adjustable wrenches, hammer, nails, duct tape, duct hangers.

STEPS

Change furnace filters once a month during the heating season. The cost of filters usually is less than $1. Don't try to clean the old filters.

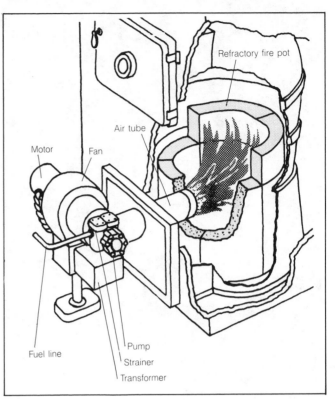

A gun or pressure-type of oil burner is popular for many home central heating systems.

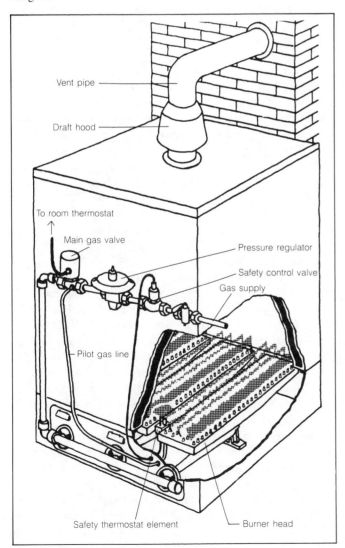

Although gas burners vary in design, they all operate on the same principle. The version shown indicates the controls essential for safe operation.

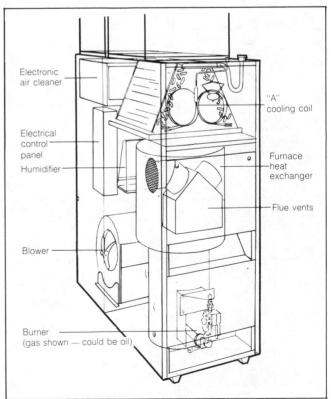

This modern furnace features a blower for forced-air heat, a humidifier to increase moisture in the home and an electronic air cleaner to remove the dust circulating in the heating system.

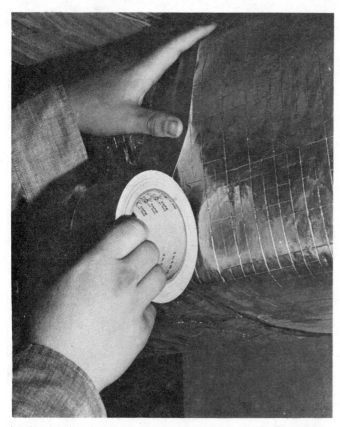

Insulate heating ducts that go through cold crawl spaces. Tape joints in ducts with duct tape, shown here being applied to insulation. You should insulate hot water pipes that go through crawl spaces and cold water pipes that run through hot rooms.

Replace damaged duct hangers. If you're getting lots of noise from the ducts, try padding the ducts with insulation sandwiched between the hanger and duct. Tighten any loose duct hangers to stop rattle.

On some furnaces, the filter slips into a channel. The filter is exposed so you can readily see it. You simply exchange a new filter for the old one.

Some furnaces have metal covers that hide the filters. Look for these covers around the base of the furnace. To remove the cover, back out the screws holding the cover in place. Then exchange filters.

Air flows through filters in one direction. This direction is stamped on the edge of the filter. Always position the filter in the channels or filter chamber so the arrow points in the direction of the air flow from the furnace blower.

Maintenance

Registers. Keep all heating and cooling registers and cold air returns clean, using a hose-type vacuum.

Radiators. These heating units need "bleeding" annually. You'll find the bleeder valve at one end of the radiator unit near the top of the unit. It looks like a metal cylinder with a screw running into one end. Loosen this screw. You will hear a hissing sound. Following the sound will be water. When the water has drained, tighten the screw. Give all the valves this treatment.

If a radiator valve is faulty, you may be able to disassemble it and repack the valve. If you can't, replace the old valve with a new one. You'll need a screwdriver and adjustable wrench for this.

Boilers. Call a serviceman.

Ducts. You can save heat by wrapping hot air ducts with insulation made especially for ducts. If the ducts run through an unheated crawl space, they absolutely must be insulated. The energy you save will be considerable. If you don't insulate the ducts, check the duct joints to make sure they are not leaking air. If they are, wrap the joints with duct tape. The biggest air loss comes from elbow joints where a duct makes a turn.

You should also fasten down, pad, and replace faulty duct hangers. This can stop lots of noise and vibration.

Furnace Checklist

Here's a checklist of furnace problems and quick solutions. Check these possibilities before you call the repairman.

Furnace won't run. Check the power at the fuse box or main circuit breaker. If the fuses keep blowing or the circuit breaker keeps tripping, you may have a short circuit in the furnace. Call the serviceman.

Motor won't run. Check the power source. Also push the reset button on the furnace motor, if the motor has one. If the motor won't start, emits an odor, sparks, or smokes, shut off the furnace and call the serviceman.

Pilot lights. Pilot lights in gas furnaces sometimes go out. You'll find relighting directions on the panel that you have to remove to get at the pilot.

If you detect a strong odor of gas in the house, turn off the gas immediately and call the utility company or a serviceman.

Oil furnace malfunctions. The same checklist applies to oil furnaces as to gas furnaces, except that oil furnaces have a switch on the stack control. Try flipping this switch if the furnace doesn't work. If this does not start it up, call the serviceman.

Furnace recycles. Set the furnace bonnet thermostat at a higher level. The only other problem you can fix would be a dirty or malfunctioning room thermostat (see Chapter 6, Heating Repairs).

Noisy blower. The motor or shafting may need oil. Or, the pulleys or belts are worn and need replacement. Also check the motor mounts; they may be loose.

Fireplaces. See Chapter 2, "Interior Repairs."

SPECIALTY INSULATIONS
How to Insulate A (Round) Water Heater

To cut energy costs on water heaters that feel hot to the touch, Owens Corning Fiberglas has an insulation jacket kit. For electric heaters, trim the kit to size. Trim to remove insulation from areas that cover the heating element controls and the power connection. If you do not, it could cause control wires to overheat, and deteriorate their insulation. The result would be a dangerous electric shock. For gas heaters, you must take care that the jacket does not interfere with proper venting across the top. You must also watch that the jacket bottom does not restrict air flow into the burner area. Do not use this kit on a gas heater which is equipped with a flue damper. Improper installation on a gas unit could cause an explosion. Be sure to wash off any insulation after handling, and wear loose clothing. Wash work clothes separately.

Tools and Materials. One 48″ wide insulated jacket, three 3″x12″ white vinyl tape for side seam — horizontal, one 6″x48″ white vinyl tape for side seam — vertical, two 3″x36″ white vinyl tape for top of heater, scissors or knife, pen, straightedge.

STEPS

Clean the top of the water heater using warm water and detergent. DO NOT USE SOLVENT BASE CLEANERS. Water heater top must be completely dry before installing jacket. Avoid contact with water piping and flue pipe as they may be hot.

Wrap the insulation jacket around the water heater with the vinyl side out and the 4″ collar at the top. Mark the vinyl jacket where the insulation begins to overlap itself. This mark will establish the final cut width of the jacket.

Lay the jacket on a flat surface vinyl face up and cut the jacket to the width established in step 2. If using a knife, draw along a straight edge while compressing insulation. See Figure A. Mark and cut the jacket height as follows:

For electric water heaters. For electric water heaters less than 50 inches high, wrap the jacket around the water heater as in step 2 with the insulation even with the water heater top. Mark and cut the bottom of the jacket at a level 2 inches above the floor. For electric water heaters greater than 50 inches high, no cutting is required.

For gas water heaters. For gas water heaters wrap the jacket around the water heater as in step 2 with the insulation even with the water heater top. Mark and cut bottom of the jacket 1 inch above the top of the burner access cover and provide cut out for burner controls. See Figure B.

Wrap the jacket around the water heater as in step 2 with the insulation even with the water heater top. Locate cut out over burner control on gas units or side seam over thermostats

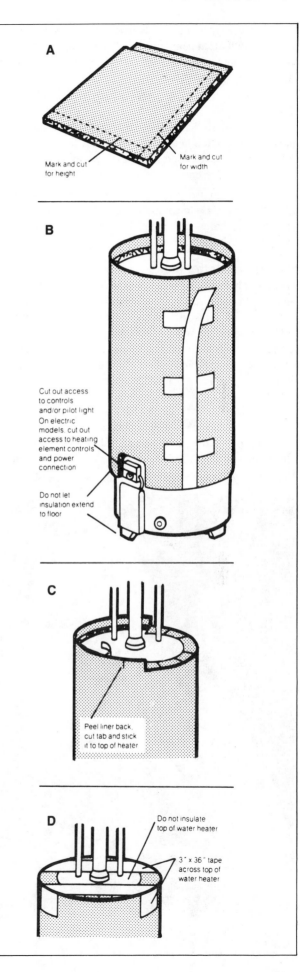

A
Mark and cut for height
Mark and cut for width

B
Cut out access to controls and/or pilot light On electric models. cut out access to heating element controls and power connection
Do not let insulation extend to floor

C
Peel liner back. cut tab and stick it to top of heater

D
Do not insulate top of water heater
3″ x 36″ tape across top of water heater

covers on electric units. Apply tape across the side seam at top, middle and bottom using the 3"x12" vinyl tape provided. Now center and apply the 6"x48" vinyl tape over the entire length of the side seam. See Figure B.

Note: Peel off release paper slowly while applying vinyl tapes.

Slowly peel off the release paper on the vinyl collar about 6 inches. Cut a notch in the collar 4 inches from the side seam, fold and secure to the water heater top. Continue this procedure around the entire collar. See Figure C.

Apply the two pieces of 3" x 36" vinyl tape across the top of the water heater as shown in Figure D. Extra insulation may be used to wrap hot water piping. Do not apply insulation on top of gas water heaters.

How To Insulate Pipes

Insulation not only prevents pipe freezes, but cuts heat loss in pipes and condensation dripping from cold-water lines.

There are several different types of insulation products sold, both of traditional and updated materials. Most of the traditional types spiral around the pipes and wrap around the fittings such as tees and elbows. Modern materials snap on, although they may not provide as much protection.

STEPS

Overlap the wrap about ½ inch and pull it fairly tight as you spiral it around the pipe. You probably will have to work in short runs—4 feet or so—since the wrap can become unwieldy in long lengths. Then spiral plastic tape around fiberglass.

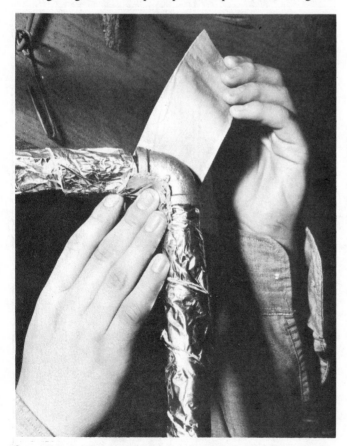

Some pipe wrap has a sticky backing that adheres directly to the pipe. The pipe must be clean and dry. All pipe wrap must be continuous—no gaps—for it to work efficiently.

Cut the insulation with scissors or a razor knife. If the insulation is fiberglass, you should wear gloves to protect your hands.

If commercial insulation is not readily available, you can insulate pipes with several layers of newspaper. Tape the newspaper to the pipes, or tie it firmly with a string. This is a stop-gap measure only and can be a fire hazard. Replace the newspapers with insulation as soon as possible.

If no insulation is available and a freeze is expected, leave the faucet open so water trickles out of the spout. This will help prevent freezing. It is not guaranteed, however, so use insulation whenever possible.

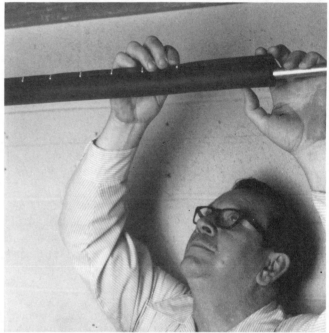

With this Armstrong pipe insulation, the flanged insulation is snapped over the pipe and held in place with clamps.

This insulation can be used on both hot and cold water pipes, and is particularly easy to apply and to remove (photo courtesy of Frelen).

AIR CONDITIONING FIX-UPS

Almost the same fix-up tips may be used for air conditioners as furnaces, especially if your home has central air conditioning. This air conditioning unit uses the same ducts and registers, and the unit generally is located next to the furnace. That big metal box out in the yard is the cooling coil of the air conditioner.

Filters

Tools and materials. Same as furnaces, plus a level.

STEPS

Replace the filters once a month during the cooling season. Window air conditioners often have washable filters instead of metal replaceable filters. Remove the filter, soak it in warm water and mild household detergent. Let the filter dry and apply several drops of light machine oil to the filter. Then replace it. You should clean this filter at least once a month during the cooling season.

Outdoor cooling coils. These have rubber hoses as well as metal pipe running in and out of them. Each cooling season, tighten the pipe connections with an adjustable wrench, and rewrap the hose connections with duct tape. Also make sure exterior units are level and plumb. If the unit is out of level and plumb, raise the concrete pad with dirt. The technique is similar to raising tipped and sunken walkways (see Chapter 9).

Keep air conditioners level. Check this level annually and have a professional check the working parts every two years. A little preventive maintenance can save a lot in repair costs.

Raise the concrete pad on which the air conditioner sets and pound dirt and gravel under the pad. When the air conditioner is level, check the other sides of the pad for any erosion around the pad.

Registers. Clean them before each cooling season. Use a hose-type vacuum.

Ducts. Wrap loose joints with duct tape. Also pad, tighten, or replace duct hangers that are damaged.

Dehumidifiers. These units need little or no maintenance. Make sure the drain is open so that the water is being channeled away. This is the first thing to check if it overflows.

Humidifiers. If the humidifier doesn't have an automatic water filler, keep the tank filled daily. Floats and moving parts inside the unit should be cleaned twice annually, particularly if the water in your area is loaded with lime salt. This mineral sticks to moving parts, slowing them down or stopping them completely.

Wrap air conditioning hoses with duct tape and tighten any loose connections with an adjustable wrench. If you notice any bad wiring connections that you can repair, turn off the power before making the repairs.

Thermostat Maintenance

Once every year, you should remove the cover on the heating/cooling thermostat and clean the parts. A dirty thermostat can cause malfunctioning of the heating/cooling unit and add to your fuel costs.

Tools and materials. Fine artist brush or soft-bristled paintbrush, piece of bond paper, small screwdriver.

Clean thermostats with a soft brush. Also check connections and points to make sure they are clean and tight. Thermostats seldom wear out. But if you do have a malfunction, a new thermostat is easily installed. It involves loosening a couple of holding screws and replacing wires.

STEPS

Remove the thermostat cover. Most models simply snap off the mounting rim. Some have a set screw. If your thermostat has small metal contacts in the working parts, very carefully insert a scrap of bond paper between these points and "sand" them. The paper is rough enough to do the job; *do not* use abrasive paper. With a small, soft brush, clean away any dirt and dust from the working parts, and clean the back of the cover. Then replace the cover.

Supplemental Heat

You can buy so-called radiant heating panels, fans, and base-board units as supplemental heat for basement rooms, at patio doors, large windows, and attic rooms. These units simply plug into a wall outlet. They may be mounted to the wall permanently, as in the case of a wall heater next to a patio door, or you can just set them into position when you need the heat.

Although radiant heating units are moderately priced, they utilize lots of electric power. This is why they should be used as supplemental heat rather than as the prime heat source in your home.

HOW TO INSTALL AN ATTIC FAN

The cooling power from an attic fan is more than you might think, and an attic fan can lower air conditioning bills considerably during the summer months when the night air is mild (not hot). An attic fan pulls outside air in through open windows and exhausts the hot air in the attic. This air then filters out attic gable and soffit vents. An attic fan does not cool your home as an air conditioner does. The fan circulates the air, and this air movement cools you via evaporation of perspiration from your skin.

Attic fans can move lots of air fast. Each model has a selection of capacities. Figure the amount of floor space in your home, and buy a fan to move air through this space. The fans are marked to indicate the cubic feet of space they can handle.

The fans come in two basic models. One unit is made for installation in the gable end of the house. The other model sits between ceiling joists. You must cut a hole in the ceiling, house siding, or roof and cover it with screening or louvers for the fan to work efficiently.

The ceiling-mounted attic fan probably is the easiest for you to install, although the wall-and-roof model is not difficult. Manufacturers of both types of fans offer complete installation instruction; you'll find guidelines here, although you should follow the instructions packaged with the fan. The details given are for a ceiling-mounted fan.

Tools and materials. Hammer, square, tape measure, 2x8 or 2x10 headers (one piece 4 ft. long), screwdriver, 16d common nails, armored cable and wire, junction box, razor knife, pliers, power jigsaw and crosscut blades or keyhole saw, brace and ½ in. bit.

STEPS

Locate a spot for the fan in the ceiling which separates the attic and the room below. Hallways are the most popular because they usually are central to the rest of the house and pull air through all the rooms. You can control air flow by opening and closing windows and doors.

In the attic or crawl space, measure the opening between the ceiling joists and mark this opening as a guide for the saw. The opening's size will depend on the size of the fan; this information will be packaged with the unit.

Make the cut in the attic floor (and room ceiling) with a power jigsaw — or use a keyhole saw to bore a hole in the ceiling to accept the saw blade. Clean up the mess from the gypsum wallboard on the floor below immediately. Check the louver panel against the hole to see if it fits properly. If not, trim the ceiling material with a saw or razor knife to obtain the proper fit.

Tie off the ceiling joists with headers the same size as the ceiling joists — usually 2x8s or 2x10s. Square the headers in the space and spike them to the joists.

Position the fan between the joists and headers. It should slip easily into the space. You may have to build a square or rectangle of 1x3 or 1x4 strips on which the fan can rest. This depends on the model; consult the directions.

Assemble the fan unit; place it over the ceiling cut-out and fasten the fan in position using the nuts and bolts and screws furnished with the fan.

Go into the room below and intall the louver vent or grill in the ceiling. It probably fastens to the fan housing. If not, you can screw it to the 1x3 or 1x4 frame that you made, up through the ceiling at the edge of the cut-out. Or tack it to the joists and headers through the ceiling.

To finish the job, connect the fan to electric power. Before you start work, turn off the power at the main fuse box or circuit breaker. Run BX cable from a nearby wall switch to a junction box fastened to a ceiling joist near the attic fan. A prewired junction box is usually furnished with the fan unit.

Connect the wires from the wall switch to the wires in the junction box, using wire nuts, or according to the wiring diagram and information supplied with the fan (see Chapter 7).

On a flat roof, mount the unit as close to the center of the ventilated area as possible. For other roofs, install power vent close to the center of the length of the roof. Be careful not to cut into the roof rafters.

5 Plumbing Repairs and Maintenance

BASIC RULES

Any plumbing repair is messy; most plumbing repairs are wet. All plumbing repairs are relatively easy, contrary to popular belief. Your home has just three sets of pipes that can cause trouble: (1) hot water pipes; (2) cold water pipes; (3) drains. These pipes can: (1) leak, or (2) clog.

Plumbing has just *one* cardinal rule: Turn off the water at the main shutoff valve or fixture before you make any plumbing repair.

Most of the repairs in this chapter are permanent. A few are "temporary"; i.e., they are emergency repairs that will solve the problem until you have time to make a correct, permanent repair or can call in a professional.

Where To Turn Off the Water

Tools and materials. Pipe wrench.

STEPS

Look below the fixture (sink, lavatory, flush tank) for shutoff valve that looks like a faucet. You can turn off the water supply to the fixture at this valve.

If the fixture does not have a shutoff valve, you will have to turn off the water at the main water entrance to your home.

Turn off the water to fixtures at shut-off valves below the fixture — shown here under a lavatory. If the fixture doesn't have a shut-off valve, turn off the water at the main meter.

This valve will be located next to or near the water meter. It's smart to locate the main shutoff valve right now, so that you can go immediately to the water source to stop the flow if an emergency arises.

As a last resort, you may be able to turn off the water at the street main. This main is usually located under a metal plate in your front yard or near the street. Most mains, however, take a special wrench to turn the valve, although in an emergency you may be able to innovate a tool for the job.

If all else fails and you can't shut the water off, call the city water department or a plumber immediately. Either usually responds quickly to an emergency situation.

Generally you can close a shutoff valve by hand. You may need a pipe wrench to apply some light turning pressure to the handle, but do not put too much pressure on the valve or you will break it.

REPAIRING FAUCETS, DIVERTERS

Faucets are plumbing *valves* and leaks are their most common problem. Leaks usually are caused by worn washers, worn cartridges, bad valve seats, and corrosion.

There are four basic types of faucets: stem, disc, ball, and cartridge. Stem faucets probably are the most common. They also need repair more frequently than the other faucets, because the washers wear from normal use, causing leaks. The other faucets often are advertised as "leak-proof". When they start to leak, you may be able to change washers in them, or exchange the "cartridge," which contains the working parts. Take the old part to the store so you can match it.

Replacing Stem Washers

Tools and materials. Adjustable wrench, channel lock smooth-jawed pliers, screwdriver, washer assortment, fine steel wool.

STEPS

Turn off the water. Remove the handle with a screwdriver — Phillips head or standard blade. The handle lifts straight up and off. You may need to give the handle some encouragement by prying up lightly on the handle.

When the handle is off, you will see a hex nut. This nut holds the stem assembly in place. Loosen and remove the nut, using an adjustable wrench or channel lock pliers. If you don't have channel locks, cover the jaws of regular pliers with adhesive bandages. This will protect the metal valve from the serrations of the regular pliers.

Now slip the handle back on the stem and turn the handle. You don't need to screw the handle in position; the handle will loosen the stem in its assembly. Then back out the stem —

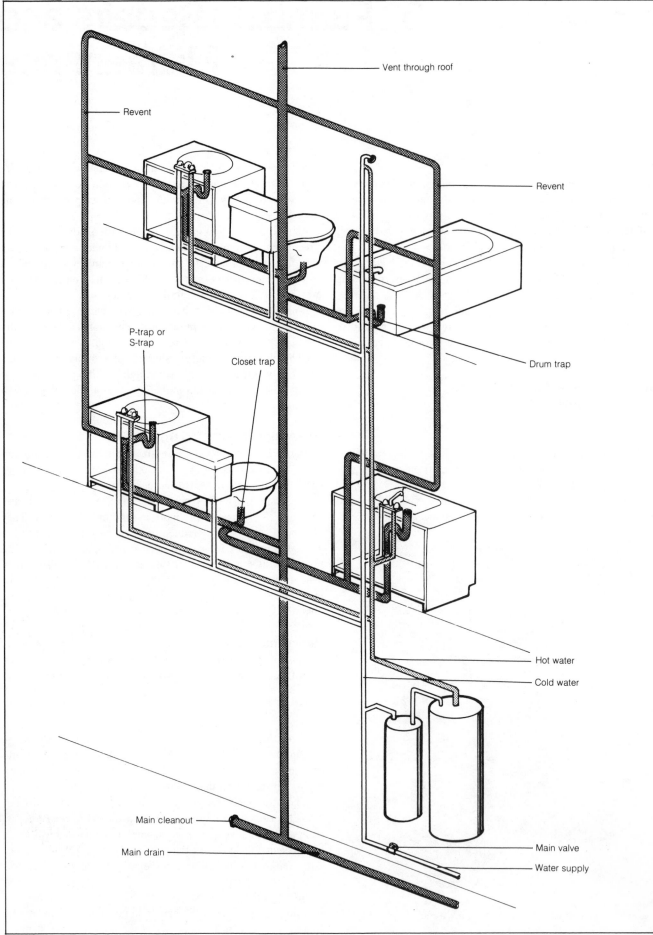

Vent through roof

Revent

Revent

P-trap or
S-trap

Closet trap

Drum trap

Hot water

Cold water

Main cleanout

Main drain

Main valve

Water supply

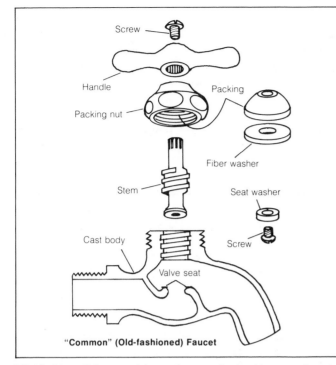

"Common" (Old-fashioned) Faucet

"Old-fashioned" (common) faucet has cast body with coarse internal threads into which threaded stem is screwed. Rubber washer at bottom of stem bears against the metal valve seat to shut off water. Packing at the upper end of faucet is squeezed around the stem to create a watertight seal.

The stem here is removed from a common faucet to show its configuration. The washer at right is fixed in place with screw; the one at left is snapped in place and held by friction.

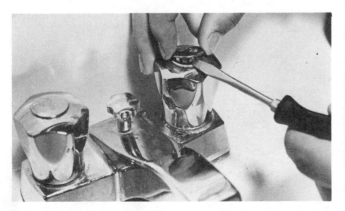

To disassemble most faucets, first remove the decorative cap that hides the screw of the faucet handle. Just pry the cap up and off the handle. Use a screwdriver or pick.

Remove the faucet handle, held by a standard or Phillips head screw. If the screw is stubborn, coat it with WD-40 penetrating oil. Let it set an hour; then remove it.

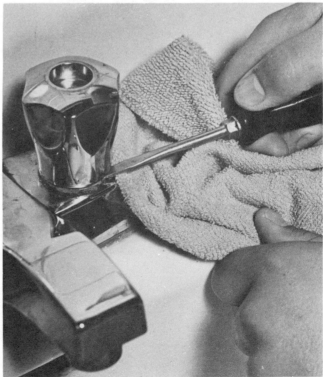

Pry off the faucet handle. Pad the chrome and china parts with an old towel, which also serves as a leverage "block." Some handles don't have screws; you just pry them off.

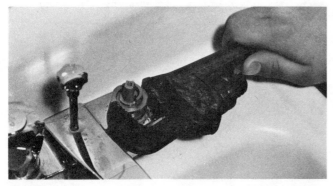

Remove the packing or cap nut. Then loosen the stem of the faucet, shown, with a wrench. Or place the handle back on the stem, without the screw, and loosen it.

Remove the stem, using your fingers. The stem is threaded, with a packing washer at the top and the faucet washer at the bottom of the stem.

Use caution and pieces of rubber on tools (or tape) to prevent scratching chrome plating or damaging delicate parts when disassembling faucets. Remember to close the drain (which this homeowner forgot to do); a dropped part could disappear forever.

which is threaded — with your fingers, or with the pliers or adjustable wrench.

At the bottom of the stem is the washer. It is held in place with a screw. Remove the screw and remove the old washer. Be careful not to damage the thin-walled housing that some washers set in.

Fit a new washer on the stem and fasten it in place with the screw. If the screw is damaged, replace it. Most washer assortments contain extra screws in the package. If there is any corrosion on the stem, clean off the corrosion with fine steel wool. Just buff the metal; don't try to remove any metal.

Re-assemble the faucet — stem, cap, handle. Be careful when you tighten the assembly with the wrench or pliers; too much pressure can strip the threads and cause the faucet to leak.

How To Replace Cap Washers

Tools and materials. Screwdriver, adjustable wrench or channel lock pliers, washers or string packing.

STEPS

Turn off the water. With a screwdriver, remove the faucet handle, exposing the cap that holds the faucet stem in place. Remove this cap. Under the cap, you will find a flat washer or the remains of a stringlike material.

The string is packing and serves as a washer between the stem and the cap. With the screwdriver, pry out the washer or packing, replace it with new, and reassemble the faucet. The string is simply wound around the stem so it forms a seal between the stem and the cap.

Replace the worn washer at the bottom of the stem. It is held by a brass screw. Since washer assortments are usually packaged with screws, replace the old screw as well.

String packing is wrapped around the stem of the faucet just below the packing nut. Or the faucet may have a rubber washer or gasket in place of the string packing.

Replacing O-Rings

Tools and materials. Screwdriver, adjustable wrench or channel lock pliers, new O-ring assortment.

STEPS

Turn off the water. First, remove the handle from the faucet with a screwdriver, then the cap nut with an adjustable wrench or channel lock pliers. Twist or pull out the stem of the faucet to expose the entire assembly.

O-ring washers look like tiny rings of rubberlike material. They can be found almost anywhere in a faucet assembly: on the stem, around the cap nut, under the handle, where two different parts are screwed together.

To replace the washer, remove the old one and slip on the new one, making sure it is properly seated. Reassemble the faucet.

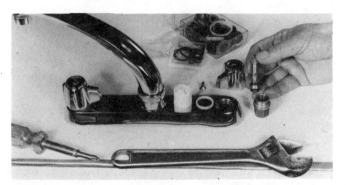

Newer types of faucets with washers may have some plastic parts; an O-ring is used instead of packing to seal the stem.

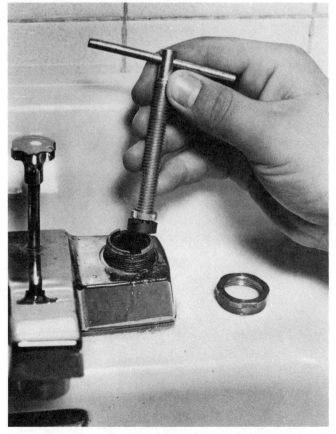

Insert the faucet seat dressing tool into the faucet housing and turn the handle to smooth the washer seat. Assorted size tools are available.

Regrinding Valve Seats

When a washer becomes worn, you probably try to turn the handle of the faucet tighter to shut off the water. This causes the stem of the faucet to grind into the washer seat at the bottom of the stem.

Sometimes a new washer will seal the resulting damage. If not, the valve seat must be "reground" so the washer seats properly when the faucet handle is closed.

Tools and materials. Adjustable wrench or channel lock pliers, screwdriver, valve seat grinding tool, new washer.

STEPS

Turn off the water. Remove the faucet handle, cap nut, and stem assembly.

Insert the grinding tool into the faucet housing and adjust the guide nut (it moves up and down) of the grinding tool to match the depth of the opening of the faucet housing. This aligns the grinding tool in the faucet housing and provides a turning base. Now turn the grinding tool with its handle or pliers. Take it easy; the metal is soft. You don't need much grinding to smooth the seat in the faucet.

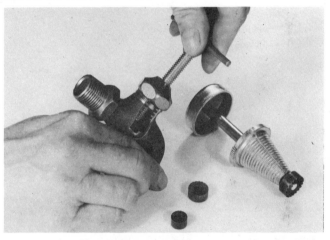

Worn or damaged valve seats that are not the replaceable type can be renewed with a tool that cuts a new face onto seats. The valve shown is cut away to show how tool is used.

Repairing Tipping Valve Faucets

Tools and materials. Screwdriver, adjustable wrench, O-rings, gasket, strainer.

STEPS

Turn off the water. Remove the handle, the faucet spout, and the metal escutcheon covering. This will expose the diverter assembly, bottom cage of the faucet, and the valve stem assembly.

You will see a plug at one side of this assembly. Remove this plug with the screwdriver. Inside will be a gasket and a water strainer. If these parts are clogged with sediment or damaged either clean or replace them.

Leaking can be caused by a worn O-ring that fits between the faucet spout and the diverter assembly. Replace the O-ring with a new one. Also replace any worn gaskets or O-rings in the cam valve assembly. The handle attaches to this unit. If the unit goes bad, which is unlikely, you may be able to buy a replacement. Take the old unit to the store for matching purposes.

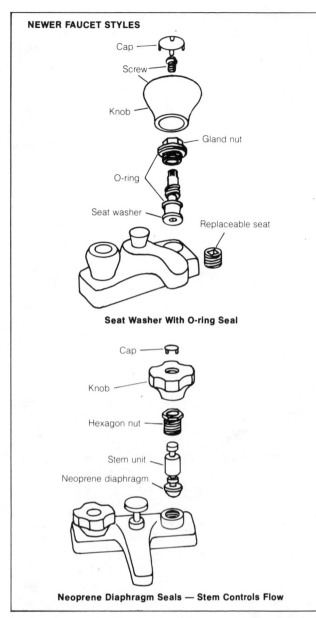

NEWER FAUCET STYLES

Cap
Screw
Knob
Gland nut
O-ring
Seat washer
Replaceable seat

Seat Washer With O-ring Seal

Cap
Knob
Hexagon nut
Stem unit
Neoprene diaphragm

Neoprene Diaphragm Seals — Stem Controls Flow

Common faucets come in a variety of shapes and sizes, but all work on the same principle of washer bearing against valve seat.

Unscrew the faucet cap and pull out the handle assembly parts, which are usually manufactured from plastic. If these parts appear worn or broken, replace them.

Gaskets and seals are positioned in a waferlike part at the bottom of the faucet. If worn or damaged, replace these seals and then reassemble the faucet.

To remove the handle of a tipping valve or handle faucet, back out to a set screw under the handle. You may have to remove the decorative cap to expose another holding screw.

Repairing Disc Faucets

Tools and materials. Screwdriver, inlet/outlet seals, adjustable wrench, O-rings.

STEPS

Some disc faucets have O-ring seals at the top of the stem; others don't. Turn off the water. Remove the handle and the escutcheon covering, which will expose the faucet assembly. The assembly is held together with two screws. Remove these. Below will be the O-ring (if there is one), a top disc, a bottom disc, and inlet and outlet seals.

O-rings and the inlet and outlet seals do need maintenance and, sometimes, replacement. Clean the assembly, make any

replacements necessary, and reassemble the faucet. If the discs are worn, you may be able to replace them. Take the worn parts to the store to match them. If not, you will have to install a new faucet.

Repairing Cartridge Faucets

Tools and materials. Screwdriver, pliers, O-rings, a new cartridge.

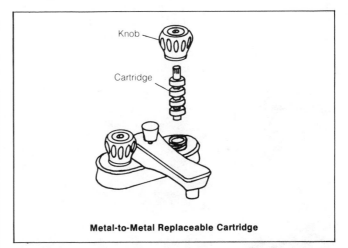

Metal-to-Metal Replaceable Cartridge

One of the modern "metal to metal" faucets offers an alloy valve cartridge that can be replaced if the faucet begins to leak. The cartridge cannot be repaired, but is inexpensive to replace.

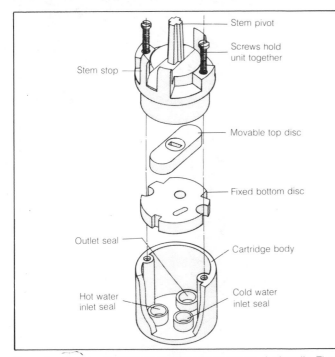

For a disc faucet, pry off the decorative cap to remove the handle. Then loosen the two screws to open the faucet housing. The seals snap out for replacement.

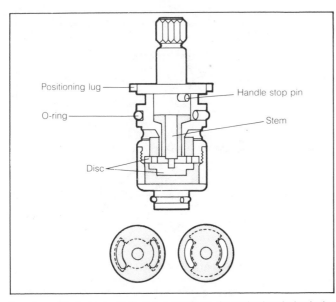

In a disc valve faucet with O-ring, water flows through when holes in the disc align as at left. Water flow stops when the discs align as shown at right.

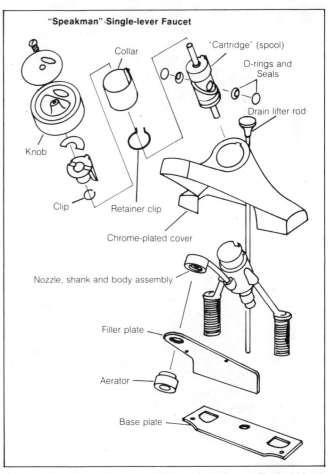

Cartridge is replaced for repair of this one-lever faucet. The lock ring is removed to allow lifting cup-shape retainer that holds cartridge. This "pull-apart" drawing shows the relationship of the various components of the cartridge-type faucet.

STEPS

Turn off the water. Remove the screw on top of the faucet assembly. This screw may be hidden by a decorative cap; pry it up and off. Push the tip of the screwdriver in the screw hole and press down on the screwdriver. At the same time, lift off the faucet handle and housing or sleeve. The screwdriver holds the cartridge in position while you lift off the handle and housing (sleeve).

If the faucet is dripping, the problem may be the faucet lever. Check that it is properly seated under the lip of the sleeve, so it fully engages the stem of the faucet and the handle that turns off the water. If you suspect this is the trouble, reseat the handle or lever, reassemble the faucet, and test it.

This faucet from "Speakman" has a spool (cartridge) that rotates and also moves laterally to control the flow and temperature of water. For quick repair, this faucet takes cartridge replacement.

One kind of single-lever faucet has ball that swivels in cup-shape (or cap) seat. The seals are in a dome that is covered by cup, which is moved by the handle. The unit shown is from "Peerless."

To remove the cartridge, pull out a little metal clip that holds the cartridge in the faucet stem. You may be able to slip the tip of the screwdriver into the slot in the clip. Pry out the clip, but keep it square to the assembly. If the screwdriver doesn't work, use pliers. You now can lift out — and replace — the cartridge.

Take the old cartridge to the store so you can match it with a replacement cartridge; not all are alike.

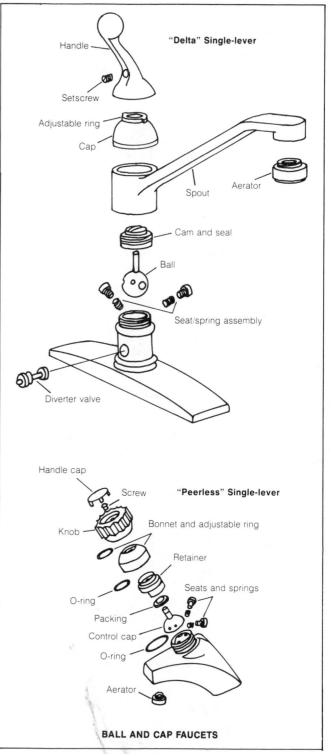

A "ball-and-cap" type faucet can be operated by the lever, as shown in top kitchen faucet; or the handle can be rotated and rocked to control flow and mix of hot and cold as shown in lower faucet that is fitted on vanity basin.

Another style of single-handle kitchen faucet operates by having the cam moved by a lever, to contact spring-loaded valves. Valves can be replaced by unscrewing caps that cover them (sold by Sears, Roebuck).

Repairing Rotating Ball Faucets

Tools and materials. Screwdriver, pliers, long-nosed pliers, washer/O-ring assortment, steel wool.

STEPS

Turn off the water. Turn the knurled cap assembly with your fingers, or pliers padded with adhesive bandages. With the cap assembly removed, you will see a valve seat in the center of the faucet housing.

Remove the valve seat to expose a spring and, probably, two rubber valve seats at the bottom of the faucet housing. Replace these parts; take the old parts to the store with you for matching purposes.

Reassemble the faucet. When you get to the ball and cap assembly, check the ball for any corrosion. You may be able to remove the corrosion with steel wool. If not, replace the ball.

Ball faucets have a tipping turn-on/turn-off feature and work on a disc faucet principle. Pry off the decorative cap to expose the screw that holds the handle in place.

With a Phillips head screwdriver, remove the handle screw, then pry up on the bottom of the handle to remove the handle. Pad when prying to avoid scratching the faucet.

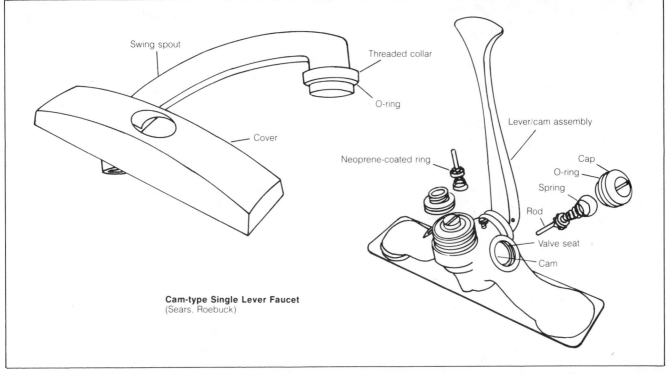

Swing spout

Threaded collar

O-ring

Cover

Neoprene-coated ring

Lever/cam assembly

Cap

O-ring

Spring

Rod

Valve seat

Cam

Cam-type Single Lever Faucet
(Sears. Roebuck)

To repair a faucet, the spout first is removed by unscrewing the holding collar, then the shell is lifted off to expose the casting.

Knurled retaining cap covers the "ball" of the faucet. Pad the jaws of the wrench to prevent marring the chrome cap, which turns counterclockwise.

The ball lifts out of the faucet housing after the retaining cap is removed. The water seals are located below the ball. Remove any corrosion from the faucet with fine steel wool. Buff the metal lightly; don't rub hard.

The ball fits into the housing with a tiny metal pin that projects from the ball. This pin must be aligned with the slot in the housing.

The cam assembly, which fits over the ball, also has a metal pin that fits a slot in the faucet housing. Be sure this pin is aligned and seated.

At this point, set the adjusting ring with the tip of a screwdriver. Just move it clockwise. Turn on the water and check for leaks. If water comes up through the stem, try turning the adjusting ring just a little tighter.

If the leak persists, turn off the water and replace the rubberlike parts in the cam assembly. To complete the job, reinstall the handle, which is held to the cam assembly with a set screw (usually under the handle).

As with all minor plumbing repairs, the most time consuming aspect will be getting the new parts. You would be wise to buy extra parts to have on hand for the next repair.

Water Diverter Repairs

Tools and materials. Screwdriver, channel lock pliers, steel wool, washer/O-ring assortment.

STEPS

Turn off the water. The diverter operates like a faucet. Remove the decorative cap and handle to expose the stem. Then, with pliers, back out the stem, which will expose the working parts of the diverter.

Replace any O-rings, packing, and worn washers in this assembly, and then replace it in the diverter housing. Also, remove any corrosion from the assembly with fine steel wool; just buff the metal with the steel wool (also see faucet repairs, this chapter).

Replacing Bathtub Spout Diverters

Tools and materials. Pipe wrench, new diverter spout, plumbing joint tape.

STEPS

Remove the old spout with a pipe wrench; one way is to stick the handle of the wrench in the opening of the spout and turn the spout counterclockwise.

Replace the old spout with the new spout, applying plumbing joint tape to the threads of the pipe to prevent leaking between the pipe and spout connection.

AERATORS, SPRAY HOSES, POP-UP STOPPERS
Solving Aerator Problems

Tools and materials. Pliers, washer/gasket assortment.

STEPS

Aerators have a screen which sometimes becomes clogged with sediment. Unscrew the aerator at the end of the faucet. You can loosen it with pliers and then use your fingers to remove it. Clean the screen piece and replace any worn gaskets or washers as needed.

Repairing Spray Hoses

Tools and materials. Screwdriver, pliers, adjustable or basin wrench, washer/gasket assortment.

STEPS

A small retaining screw holds the spray assembly together in the nozzle of the hose, which is connected to a diverter valve under the faucet on the sink.

By removing this screw, the entire assembly comes apart. Replace any worn gaskets and washers you find, and reassemble the nozzle.

If the nozzle or hose is damaged, replace the entire unit. You will have to disconnect the hose at the connection under the faucet. Use an adjustable or basin wrench for this. Then simply reconnect the new hose.

If the diverter valve is causing a no-water or little-water problem, turn off the water and remove the nozzle of the faucet. Under this, you will see a screw. Back out this screw, which will let you pull out the diverter valve. Around the valve will be a series of tiny holes. These holes might be plugged. If so, clean the holes with wire and replace the valve and nozzle.

Frequent cleaning of aerators is called for at some times of the year, when there is a lot of sediment in the water. They also can become so encrusted with minerals that the complete unit must be replaced.

Aerator screen on faucets often becomes filled with sediment, causing the water to flow slowly. Unscrew the aerator and clean the screen with a brush and water.

Do not use a matchstick or toothpick to clean the holes.

If the valve is beyond cleaning, buy a new one. The cost is not prohibitive. Take the old valve to the store for matching purposes.

Lavatory Pop-up Stoppers

Tools and materials. Pliers, screwdriver.

STEPS

To remove and clean a pop-up stopper in a lavatory (or in some bathtub designs), try turning the stopper to disengage it from the opening/closing lever. You may have to loosen or disengage the lever rod on the tailpipe of the drain under the lavatory in order to remove the stopper.

If the stopper doesn't fit tightly in the lavatory or tub, try adjusting the rod that goes from the opening/closing lever to the tailpipe. A spring clip usually holds these two parts together. You simply raise or lower the clip for more leverage on the stopper.

TOILET REPAIR AND MAINTENANCE

A flush tank breakdown is extremely easy to repair, and any repair in a flush tank is clean to make. The water is pure enough to drink, so don't concern yourself with unsanitary working conditions.

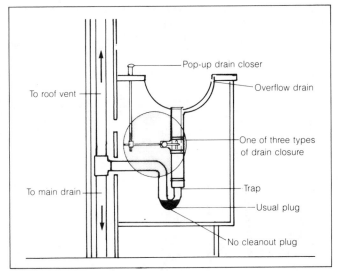

The typical vanity drain has a trap with one of three types of closer. Note that the overflow drain is cast into the sink basin; on rare occasions the overflow drain can plug and cause slow drainage.

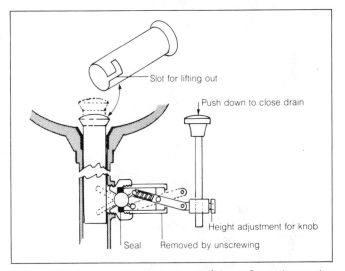

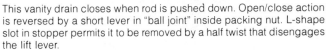

This vanity drain closes when rod is pushed down. Open/close action is reversed by a short lever in "ball joint" inside packing nut. L-shape slot in stopper permits it to be removed by a half twist that disengages the lift lever.

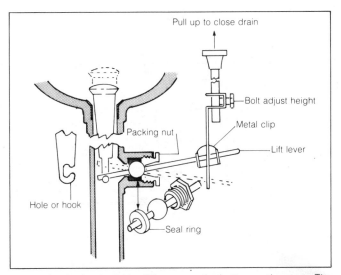

This drain also is closed by lifting up on the button on the stem. The stopper will have a hole or hook through which the lift lever fits. If it is a hook, the stopper can be twisted a half turn and removed.

A toilet has two parts: (1) the flush tank; (2) the bowl. Water in the tank flows through the bowl to flush the toilet; the "flush" goes down the drain at the bottom of the bowl and into the sewer system.

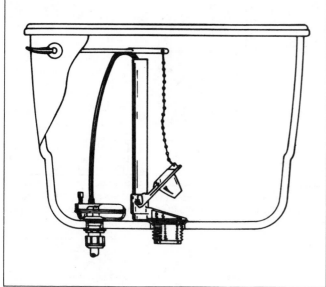

The fill valve has no float ball, shaft-mounted float, external levers, lift rods or tubes for the homeowner to worry about aligning. Instead, the compact unit actually measures water level from its position totally *underwater* at the bottom of a toilet tank (photo and line art courtesy of JH Industries).

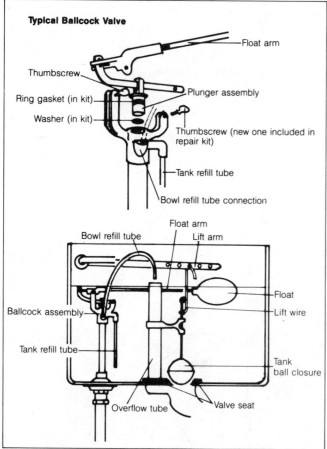

The old-fashioned ballcock assembly in your toilet tank has not changed much since the Englishman, Thomas Crapper, invented it in 1860.

There are many flush tank parts on the market, so your toughest job in making repairs probably will be selecting a product. High-profile inlet valves work just about as well as their low-profile cousins; parts manufactured from plastic are as trustworthy as parts manufactured from metal; you will have to choose.

What is important, however, is that you replace a part with a part of the same pipe size. Most parts are "standard" and interchangeable. But double-check the sizes to save yourself a trip back to the store for exchanges.

TROUBLESHOOTING TOILETS

Problem	Cause/Possible Solution
Water runs constantly in the tank.	(a) Tank ball is faulty or out of alignment. Replace it; align it. (b) Toilet ball seat is corroded. Buff it with steel wool. Also adjust rod that guides the toilet ball.
Valve sticks	Gently bend float rod arm *down* near the inlet valve. Check float for buoyancy. If it is filled or partly filled with water, replace it.
Water level is too high; low.	Maintain the water level about 1 in. below top of the overflow tube. If water is low, gently bend the float arm up. If water is high, gently bend the float arm downward.
Poor flushing action.	(a) Not enough water flow. Adjust tank ball by bending lift wire so it raises tank ball higher. (b) Check the flush handle and lift wires to make sure they are lifting the ball (see "Water level").
Splashing in flush tank.	The refill tube is not discharging into the overflow tube. The refill tube is held with a clip; re-adjust. Check inlet valve for leaks; if faulty, replace it.
Flush tank leaks.	Try tightening the connection between the water supply line and the inlet valve. Do not overtighten this nut, or you will crack the flush tank. Check the tank for cracks; washers for leaks.

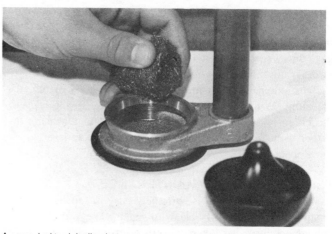

A corroded tank ball valve seat can cause the flush tank to leak. Remove this corrosion with steel wool after you disassemble the lift wires and ball.

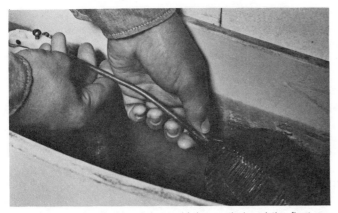

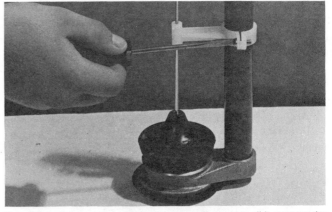

If the water in the flush tank is too high, gently bend the float arm downward. You may also be able to adjust the float with a screw located on top of the inlet valve.

The tank ball rides the water level down to the seat until it rests on the valve seat. The guide for the tank ball lift wires must be in exact alignment to prevent leaks.

Replacing a Float Ball

Tools and materials. New float ball.

STEPS

Turn off the water. Flush the tank. Unscrew the old float ball on the float arm. Screw on the new float ball. Do not try to repair a leaky float ball. The repair will be only temporary; a new ball is inexpensive.

Replacing a Tank Ball

Tools and materials. New tank ball.

STEPS

Turn off the water. Flush the tank. Unscrew the old tank ball from the lift wire that connects it to the tank ball from the lift wire that connects it to the flush handle. Then screw on the new tank ball. Also check lift wires to make sure they are in good working order. If not, make replacements.

Replacing a Guide Arm

Tools and materials. Screwdriver, new guide arm.

STEPS

Turn off the water; flush the tank. Remove the lift wires from the tank ball and unclip the bowl refill tube. Then unscrew the old guide arm, which is connected to the overflow tube.

Slip the old guide arm up and off the overflow tube. Insert the new arm down over the overflow tube and tighten the set screw, after the lift wires have been re-linked and aligned in the new guide arm. Attach the lift wire to the tank ball; hook up the refill tube.

Aligning a Guide Arm

Tools and materials. Screwdriver.

STEPS

Turn off the water; flush the tank. Loosen the set screw in the guide arm and twist the guide arm so it is in alignment with the lift wires and tank ball. Retighten the set screw.

Repairing Flush Handle Assemblies

Tools and materials. Screwdriver, pliers, adjustable wrench, steel wool.

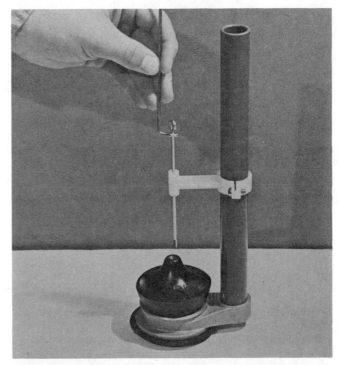

Lift wires should align with the valve seat, tank ball, and guide arm. Do not bend them for alignment; move the guide arm on the overflow pipe.

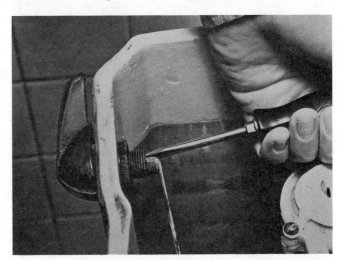

Corrosion can make the flush handle difficult to operate. Remove the assembly and buff it with steel wool, or try loosening the assembly slightly to free it.

STEPS

The collar connection between the outside flush handle and the inside trip lever often becomes corroded from the water in the flush tank, which makes the handle difficult to work.

First, try loosening the nut that holds the handle in place. If this doesn't work, remove the nut and the handle assembly, after you disconnect the lift wires.

Buff this assembly with steel wool and reconnect the assembly. If this doesn't solve the problem, replace the entire handle assembly; the parts are inexpensive.

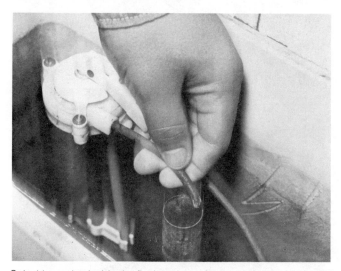

Splashing noise inside the flush tank can be caused by a misaligned refill tube. Make sure the refill tube is connected to the overflow tube, as shown here.

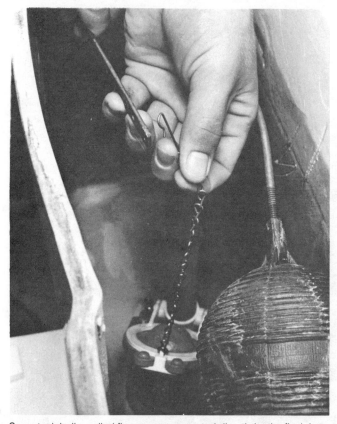

Some tank balls, called flappers are operated directly by the flush handle, not lift wires. The connection between the handle and the flapper chain often corrodes, causing problems. A brass link is the best connection.

How to Replace an Inlet Valve

Tools and materials. Adjustable wrench, screwdriver, new inlet valve kit, sponge.

STEPS

Turn off the water; flush the tank. When the tank is empty, sponge out any remaining water. The tank must be dry, or the water will leak onto the floor when the inlet valve is removed from the flush tank.

With an adjustable wrench, loosen the cap nut under the tank. This nut connects the water supply pipe to the inlet valve. Then, loosen the retaining nut that holds the inlet valve to the flush tank. Be very careful when you remove these parts. You do not want to crack the flush tank with the wrench. If the valve nuts are difficult to turn, try using two pipe wrenches. Hold the inlet valve inside the tank with one wrench while you loosen the retaining nut below the flush tank with the other pipe wrench — or with an adjustable wrench.

When the inlet valve has loosened, remove the float and float arm from the valve, along with the overflow tube. Now, unscrew the inlet valve and replace it in the same order with the new valve. The new kit should contain all the necessary washers and nuts.

Reconnect the water supply pipe to the inlet valve and turn on the water. If the connections leak, turn off the water and turn the connections tighter. Do not overtighten the connections.

Replace the float arm and float and the overflow tube, turn on the water, and flush the toilet several times to make sure all the parts are properly aligned and seated.

An inlet valve has washers that wear and leak. These washers—and O-rings—can be replaced. Remove the top of the valve with a screwdriver to expose the parts.

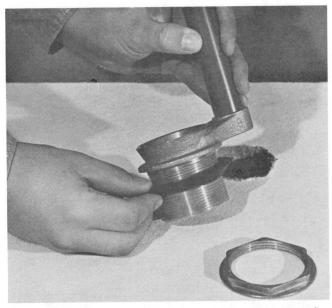

When water seals start leaking around the inlet valve and overflow tube, turn off the water, remove the retaining screws at the bottom of the flush tank, and replace the seals.

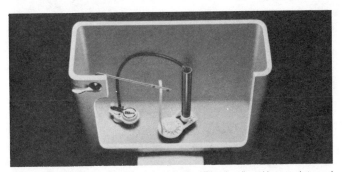

One replacement for a ballcock is called a "fill valve," and has an internal diaphragm that senses the weight of water above it to control water level in the tank. A screw on device is turned to adjust water level. Installation does require shutting off the water and removing the supply line and existing ballcock (photo courtesy of JH Industries).

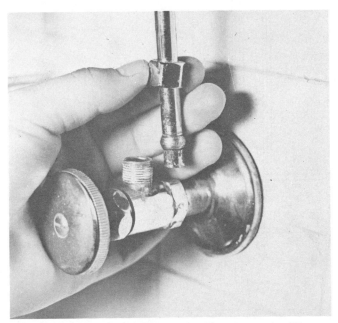

Water supply lines to flush tanks are joined by compression fitting, as shown. Thread on the nut and compression fitting before you cut the pipe to fit.

Water Supply Pipe Leaks
Tools and materials. Adjustable wrench.

STEPS
Connections between water shutoff valves (faucet) and inlet valves sometimes become loose or corroded from water, causing a leak. Try to stop the leak by tightening the connections with an adjustable wrench. If this does not work, you will have to replace the water supply pipe.

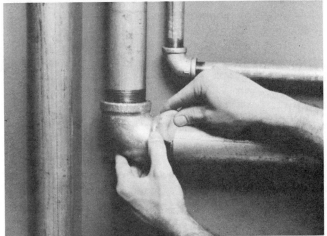

Two-part epoxy materials can be used to stop small leaks in water supply lines, including those around a threaded joint in a steel pipe. The line must be drained, the area cleaned of grease and dirt and wire-brushed to remove rust when necessary. Read instructions to find out how long the epoxy must set up before water can be turned on again (photo courtesy Borden Chemical).

Valves often will leak at the packing nut when turned off and then on again. Small valves such as the saddle type used to supply water to ice makers and humidifiers have small packing nuts, and should be tightened very gently until the leak stops.

Replacing Leaky Seals

Tools and materials. Adjustable wrench or pipe wrenches, new seals.

STEPS

Turn off the water, flush the tank. The seals that will leak are located between the inlet valve and the water supply line. Disconnect the water supply line.

With a wrench, remove the retaining nuts that hold the inlet valve in place in the bottom of the tank. Lift it up and out of the tank hole. You may have to remove the float and float arm and overflow pipe to do this. Replace the old seals at the bottom of the inlet valve and reconnect the water supply line.

If the tank is leaking where it is fastened to the toilet bowl, try tightening the bolts that hold the tank to the bowl. Be careful; too much pressure can crack the tank or the bowl. If this doesn't work, you will have to remove the bolts — after you turn off the water — and replace the gaskets and/or washers.

Pipe connections between the flush tank and the bowl should be tightened with a pipe wrench or channel lock pliers. Or, unscrew the connections and wrap the threads with pipe joint tape and reassemble the connections.

If the toilet bowl leaks around the floor, you may be able to tighten the hold-down bolts to stop the leak. On most toilet bowls, you will have to pry up the decorative covers that hide these bolts. If tightening doesn't stop the leak, call in a professional. The toilet will have to be "reseated" over the waste pipe.

HOW TO UNSTOP A CLOGGED TOILET

Of all plumbing troubles, a clogged waste pipe or toilet bowl usually is fairly simple to free, although unpleasant. The techniques are described and illustrated here.

A word of caution: do not pour or place liquid drain cleaner into a toilet that is clogged. The chemicals can't get to the clog to be effective.

Suction Cleaning

Tools and materials. Suction cup on a stick (plumber's friend).

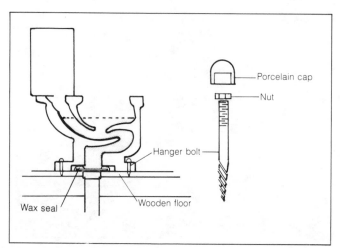

Try tightening the hanger (hold-down) bolts to stop floor leaks around toilet bowl. If tightening does not work, try inserting a new wax seal (two, if necessary) beneath the toilet.

STEPS

Insert the suction cup over the hole in the bowl. Then work the tool up and down with lots of force. Don't give up too quickly. Keep working until the obstruction is free. If this doesn't work, try the next step below.

Auger Cleaning

Tools and materials. Plastic garbage bag, coat hanger or toilet auger, wire cutters, pliers.

An auger has a corkscrew end that snags toilet obstructions. You turn a handle and pull a trigger to release the cable from the drum into the toilet opening.

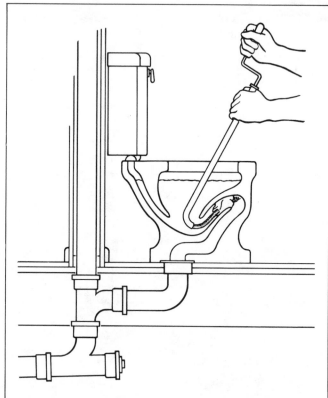

The drain auger can be used for vanity drains, but is specifically designed for cleaning toilets. The flexible, springlike end portion will bend around the sharp trap in a toilet.

STEPS

Cut and bend a coat hanger at one end like a large fishhook. Then, with a plastic garbage bag to protect your hand and arm, thread the end of the hanger into the drain of the toilet. The hook will snag the obstruction so you can pull it out.

More effective than a coat hanger is a toilet auger, made especially for this job. The technique is the same. You twist one end of the auger to activate a corkscrew end, which snags the obstruction.

If these techniques do not work, the obstruction is down in the sewer pipe.

WHEN DRAINS SLOW OR STOP

If the drain is slow or stopped completely, hair, grease, old soap, and/or other debris is clogging the drain. A chemical drain cleaner may be the answer if the drain is only partially blocked. But if the drain is stopped shut, the obstruction may be down in the waste or sewer pipe, not next to the drain opening or in the trap below the drain. Solve the problem in this order: (1) try to open the drain with a chemical; (2) try to open the drain with a plumber's friend; (3) try to open the drain with an auger or plumber's snake; (4) call a professional.

Blockage at Drain Openings

Tools and materials. Screwdriver, pry bar, stiff brush.

STEPS

When sink and floor drain strainers and lavatory and bathtub stoppers become clogged, remove the strainer or stopper and clean it.

Most strainers can be pried up and out with the tip of a screwdriver or a pry bar (floor strainers). Some strainers are held by screws. Remove the screws; then the strainer.

Stoppers may be removed by turning them or unscrewing a pivot rod connected to the opener/closer. If this is a recurring problem, use a chemical drain cleaner about every two or three weeks to prevent debris buildup.

Opening Clogged Traps

Tools and materials. Pipe wrenches or channel lock pliers, auger or plumber's snake, plumber's friend, screwdriver, pliers, chemical drain cleaner.

STEPS

Try the plumber's friend (suction cup on a stick) first. With a wet wash cloth, plug the overflow drain of a bathtub or lavatory. Then place the suction cup over the drain opening and work the tool up-and-down with force. Don't quit too soon. It sometimes takes lots of action to unblock the trap.

If the sink, tub, or lavatory does not have water in it, fill the basin or tub with about an inch or so of water. This will help produce more suction on the plumber's friend.

The next step, if the above method fails, is to remove the trap below the sink or lavatory. Use channel lock pliers or pipe wrenches to unscrew the connections, and have a bucket placed below the trap to catch any water.

About 90% of the time, the clogging problem is in the trap. Once removed, you can run hot water through the trap to clean it. Then replace the trap.

If the trap is clean and the blockage is beyond the trap, use a

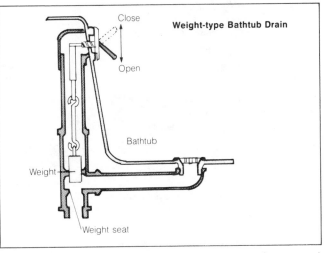

The drain in a bathtub with weight-type stopper cannot be removed. The weight can be removed for cleaning by taking off the overflow plate in which the open/close lever is located.

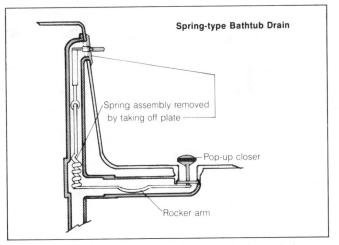

Spring-type bathtub drain has a rocker arm that is actuated when you flip the lever in the overflow plate. Rocker arm and stopper can be pulled out of the drain for cleaning.

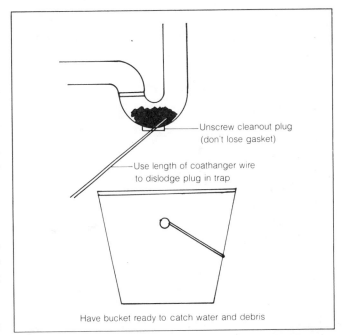

If the trap has a cleanout plug it can be removed and a wire or snake slipped into the drain to unplug the clog.

To reach a bathtub trap, you may have to remove the tub stopper handle by loosening two screws. You also can adjust the stopper lift rod by removing this escutcheon.

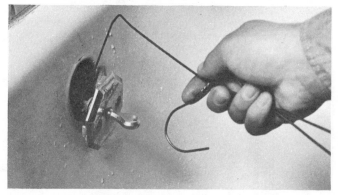

Run a wire or auger down the lift rod channel to reach the tub trap to snag the obstruction. The trouble may be a dirty stopper, not blockage in the trap.

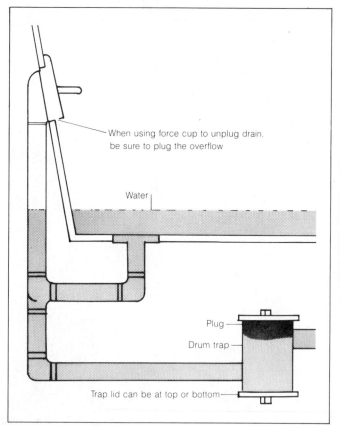

When using force cup to unplug drain, be sure to plug the overflow

Water

Plug

Drum trap

Trap lid can be at top or bottom

The drum trap for the bathtub can be located by its cap flush with the bathroom floor — or it may be under the floor in basement or crawl space.

plumber's snake or auger to ream out the pipe. You must remove the trap in order to get a straight shot at the pipe with the snake or an auger.

A bathtub drain trap is more difficult to clean, since you usually can't remove it or even see it. Here, remove the tub stopper and the stopper lever, which is held to the front of the tub with two screws.

Thread the snake or auger down the overflow drain pipe and into the trap. Once in position, you can either turn the auger or ram the snake back-and-forth to clean the trap. Flood the pipe with water and chemical cleaner after the blockage has been removed.

Bathtubs in older houses may have a "drum" trap instead of a "p" trap. This trap has a metal plate set into the floor near the bathtub; it may be in a nearby closet or next to the toilet.

Remove the trap cover with a pipe wrench or channel lock pliers. Then force the plumber's snake or auger into the pipe and clean the pipe. Go both directions in the pipe (toward and away from the tub) to make sure you penetrate the obstruction. When you finish this job, replace the trap cover and put chemical cleaner in the tub and let it work into the pipe. Then thoroughly flush the system with hot water.

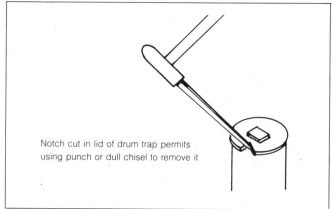

Notch cut in lid of drum trap permits using punch or dull chisel to remove it

If the cap of a drum trap cannot be removed with a wrench on hexagon projection, try notching the cap's opposite sides and using a hammer and chisel to loosen it.

Drum traps have a metal cover plate. You remove the cover to gain access to the trap for cleaning and to thread augers and plumber's snakes into the connecting pipes.

Opening Clogged Pipes

Tools and materials. Pipe wrench, channel lock pliers, plumber's snake or auger, garden hose.

STEPS

Open the blocked pipe at a clean-out plug or in back of a trap, as explained above. Use a pipe wrench or channel lock pliers to remove the cover.

First, try pushing a plumber's snake or auger into the pipe to remove the obstruction. Twist and ram hard; you will feel the obstruction breaking up as you work. If this doesn't work, try a garden hose in the pipe. The hose serves as a hydraulic ram.

Thread the hose into the pipe, after adjusting the nozzle on the hose to its heaviest setting. Turn on the water full blast. Then move the hose back and forth in the pipe, pushing the hose forward as you work.

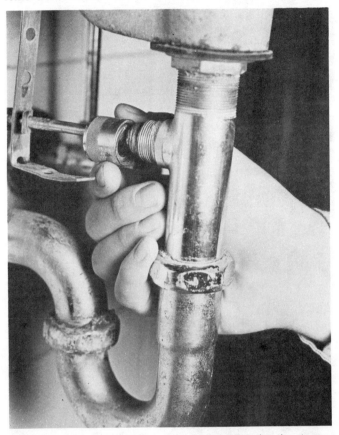

To remove a stopper in a sink or lavatory, first try turning the stopper counterclockwise. If this doesn't work, remove the pivot rod on the tailpipe of the sink or lavatory. It simply unscrews; pull out on the rod.

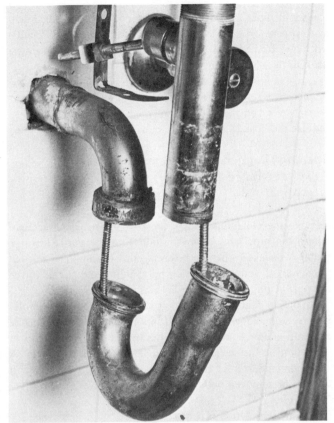

This simulated setup shows how an auger goes down and through a sink trap to remove debris blocking the trap. Most sink and lavatory stoppage is in the trap area.

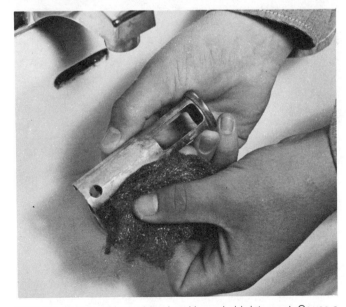

Clean the stopper with steel wool and household detergent. Or use a stiff brush. Stoppers should be cleaned every six weeks or so to remove grease, hair, and debris.

To remove a trap, unscrew the retaining nuts at the top and bottom of the drain pipe. Place a bucket under the trap to catch any water in the pipe and the sink above.

The water from the hose, teamed with the auger effect of twisting and pushing, should remove any obstruction. If it doesn't, you'll have to call a professional. Renting a power snake to clean the sewer lines will cost almost as much.

Vent Stack Cleaning

Tools and materials. Garden hose, ladder.

STEPS

The sewer pipes in your home are connected to the vent stack which opens on the roof. Sometimes it is possible to remove blockages from the sewer by running a garden hose down the stack to the obstruction.

Take the hose onto the roof. Turn the nozzle of the hose to the heaviest setting. Then thread the hose down the stack. When you reach the obstruction, open the faucet completely and use the hose as a hydraulic ram.

Opening Clogged Sewer Lines

Tools and materials. Plumber's snake, garden hose, pipe wrench.

STEPS

Remove the clean-out plug nearest to the main sewer line, where the pipe runs from the house to the yard. Insert a plumber's snake or garden hose into this opening and rod out the sewer. If you use a garden hose, adjust the nozzle to the heaviest setting, and use the hose as a hydraulic ram.

If you are continuously having sewer line blockage trouble, it is recommended that you call in a professional with special cleaning equipment to rod out the line. Often, especially in older homes, the sewer lines become filled with tree roots. A snake or garden hose ram will be ineffective; the roots will have to be removed with a special cutting tool.

Cleaning Septic Systems

Other than periodic chemical treatment, we recommend that you call in a professional to handle any septic system trouble.

EMERGENCY REPAIRS FOR LEAKING PIPES

Any leaking pipe or pipe connection must be repaired just as soon as possible. You can, however, temporarily stop a leak — or at least slow it — with the products and techniques listed below.

Tools and materials. Pipe wrenches, screwdriver, plastic electrician's tape.

STEPS, PINHOLE LEAKS

Mark the leak spot; turn off the water. With a sharpened lead pencil, force the tip of the lead in the hole and break off the lead. Turn on the water. The lead will conform with the size of the hole in the pipe, and may stop the leak.

Electrician's tape also can be used to stop pinhole leaks.

STEPS, LARGE LEAKS

If you own a C-clamp, pad the stationary jaw of the clamp with a rubber strip. Then position the strip and clamp over the leak and turn the clamp tight.

You may also use a pipe sleeve to stop the leak. The metal sleeve, designed especially for leaking pipes, is lined with a

An emergency leak stopper is a C-clamp and rubber pad over the leak in the pipe. The clamp has to be perfectly aligned on the pipe so it can be tightened without slipping.

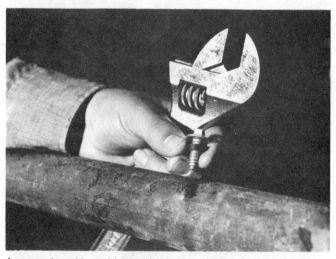

A screw plug with a rubber gasket is a good temporary repair for large pipes with holes in them. You may have to enlarge the hole slightly so the screw plug fits.

rubberlike pad. The sleeve goes around the pipe at the leak point and is bolted together to form a "clamp" over the leak.

If you have auto radiator hose clamps available, split a piece of garden hose, or radiator hose, and wrap it around the pipe at the leak point. Then clamp the hose with the auto radiator hose clamps to stop the leak.

You can buy tubes and cans of stop-leak products at many home center and drug stores. However, these products are intended for very short-term emergency use only. Follow the manufacturer's directions on the container.

A hose clamp with a rubber insert may be used to stop leaks in pipes. Any leaking pipe or pipe connection should be replaced quickly; "bandage" treatments are only temporary.

Special pipe clamp is a semi-permanent repair for a leaky pipe, although the pipe should be replaced eventually. The pipe clamp is screwed together over the leak. Before you make this repair, turn off the water to lower the pressure in the pipe. This clamp is best used on metal piping.

PIPE AND CONNECTION REPAIRS

There are three types of plumbing pipe: galvanized steel, copper, and plastic. Usually, each type requires a different set of tools to make a repair. Plumbing codes in your area may prohibit the use of some plumbing products such as plastic pipe and fittings. Before you make any repairs, be sure to check out the codes with local building authorities. Often, the home center store or plumbing retailer where you purchase plumbing

Union allows replacement of a section of pipe. Mating faces of union are left clean, but each end of the union, and the large nut that joins the halves, are coated with pipe joint compound.   (Photo Courtesy Genova, Inc.)

products will know local codes, if city officials are not conveniently available to answer questions.

Replacing Galvanized Steel Pipe and Fittings

The key to replacing galvanized steel pipe and fittings is *union fittings*. Union fittings turn in both directions. Therefore, you can assemble almost any pipe run where you add a pipe or replace a pipe.

You can buy galvanized steel pipe in a wide range of sizes and lengths. Pipes are available in ½, ¾, and 1 in. diameters; lengths usually run in multiples of 2 ft. up to 20 ft. in length. The pipe you buy in most home center stores is already threaded, although you can buy unthreaded pipe and thread it yourself. This takes threading dies, which are not expensive.

Always use two wrenches when working with steel pipe. One wrench holds pipe while fitting is turned onto it, or vice versa. Pipe vise takes the place of one wrench when it is used for making up pipe and fittings.

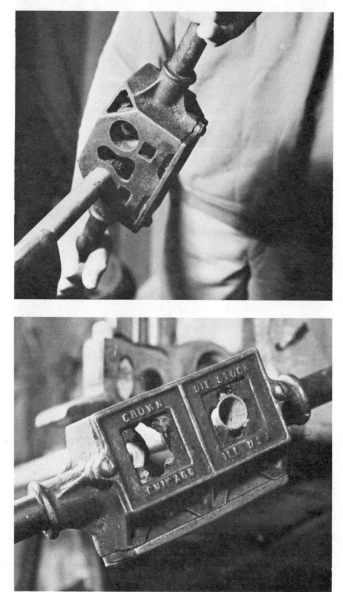

Die is used to cut threads on steel pipe. The tool can have a fixed die, or can have ratchet handle that makes it usable in restricted locations.

Tools and materials. Hacksaw, pipe wrenches; adjustable wrench, channel lock pliers, pipe joint compound or tape, pipe, fittings, union fittings.

STEPS, REPLACE A PIPE SECTION

Turn off the water. With a hacksaw, cut through the damaged pipe or the pipe you want to replace. Cut it at a slight angle so you can remove it from the fitting(s) with a pipe wrench without damaging the fitting(s).

Measure the distance between the two fittings, allowing for a union fitting within this distance or "run". For ½-in. pipe, the threads should go ½ in. into the fittings; for ¾-in. pipe, the threads should also go ½ in. into the fittings. If the pipe is 1 in., the threads should go $\frac{9}{16}$ in. into the fittings.

Apply pipe compound or joint tape to the male threads and screw the pipe into one fitting. Then apply the compound or tape to the other end of the pipe and screw on the union fitting. Do the same thing at the other end of the run, coming together at the union fitting. Then assemble both pipes at the union fitting.

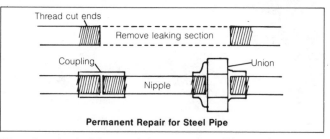

Where there is a leak in a steel pipe, a section will have to be removed and the cut ends threaded. Then a union, nipple and coupling are installed (described in Chapter 2).

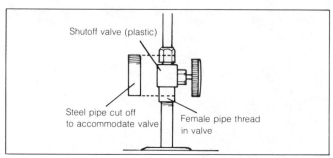

If you do not want to use plastic valves and fittings in steel piping, you must cut out a section and fit in a shutoff valve. No union is required, as pipe-to-tubing adapter provides the same action as a union. A short pipe nipple in the valve allows use of existing pipe-to-tubing adapter, with female threads.

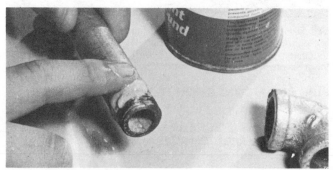

Pipe compound is always applied to the male threads of the pipe — never to internal threads. A plastic tape for pipe threads also can be used, and is less messy.

STEPS, REPLACE A FITTING

Turn off the water. Remove the old fitting, using one pipe wrench on the fitting and another pipe wrench on the pipe.

Coat the male threads with joint compound or tape and reassemble the pipe run with the new fitting. If the plumbing run is an old one, you should consider replacing the pipes that go into the fitting as well as the fitting. An entirely new assembly often works best.

Adding a New Pipe Run to an Existing Run

Tools and materials. Power drill, drill bit, saddle tee, joint compound or tape, new pipe and fittings, adjustable wrench, pipe wrenches.

STEPS

Turn off the water. Attach the saddle tee to the pipe you want to tap. Turn the tee clamp tight with an adjustable wrench. Match the drill bit with the hole in the saddle tee, using the saddle tee as a guide for the drill bit. Then drill the hole, and remove all metal debris.

Apply joint compound or tape to the male threads of the new

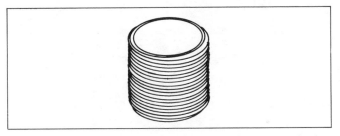

A close nipple is used to join two fittings that have female threads when space is at a minimum—it adds only ½ inch or less to the length of pipe and fittings.

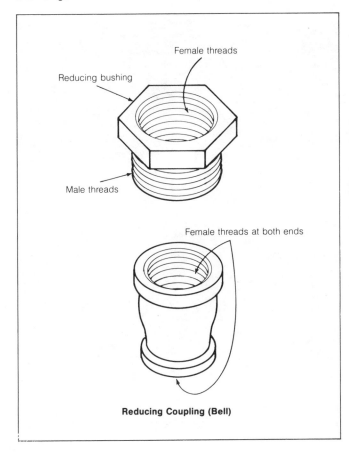

Reducing Coupling (Bell)

pipe and screw the new pipe into the saddle tee. The tee has a rubber type of gasket that seals the new pipe into the fitting.

Replacing Copper Pipe and Tubing

There are three types of copper pipe: Type K has a thick wall; type L has a medium thick wall; type M has a thin wall. You'll probably be working with type K and L most of the time, since it is used for both water and drain runs.

Copper pipe and tubing can be soldered together, assembled with compression fittings, or flare joined. If you go the flare-joint route, you will have to buy or rent a flaring block to make the joints. Soldered and compression joints utilize a propane torch and wrenches.

Tools and materials. Hacksaw or tube cutter, propane torch, new pipe and tubing, fittings, compression fittings, solder, steel wool, noncorrosive flux, round or triangular file, pliers.

STEPS

Turn off the water. Cut the tubing or pipe in half, using a hacksaw or regular copper pipe tube cutter. Let the pipe or

A saddle tee lets you tap a pipe to start a new run of pipe. Clamp the tee to the pipe, and drill a hole through the opening into the pipe. Then screw the new pipe into the tee.

You can add a sink, vanity, bathroom and not even cut a pipe. Saddle valves require only drilling a hole in a supply line (hot or cold as required), then clamping on the valve and piping from it to the fixture. Be sure the water is shut off before you drill the pipe (photo courtesy Chicago Specialty Mfg. Co.).

tubing drain. Then, with a propane torch, heat the joint at the fitting to melt the solder at the joint. Remove the pipe while heated with pliers. It should slide off the fitting.

Cut the new pipe or tubing to fit. Make sure that the cuts are square so the ends fit tightly against the metal shoulders of the fittings. If you peer down the inside of the fittings, you can see this tiny shoulder.

With a file, smooth the end of the cut and remove any metal burrs along the cut or on the inside of the pipe or tubing. Don't remove any solid metal with the file.

Shine the ends of the pipe or tubing that will go into the fittings with steel wool. The steel wool removes grease from the copper so the flux and solder adheres properly. Then prefit the pipe or tubing into the fittings, making sure the parts are snug and tight.

Coat the end of the pipe or tubing with noncorrosive soldering flux. Then assemble the pipe or tubing into the fittings. With solid-core wire solder (50-50 wire solder works best) and a propane torch, solder the joints together. Use just the tip of the flame of the torch to heat the metal.

Touch the solder to the joint. The solder will then run into the joint and form a tiny bead around the edge of the fitting.

Tubing is cut quickly, cleanly and square with tubing cutter. This compact unit can be carried in a pocket or even in a small tool box. Reamer is in back and pivots out for use.

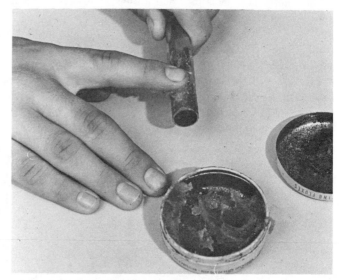

Professionals use their fingers to apply flux to the metal. You may want to use a cotton swab, which assures a grease-free application. Use plenty of flux on the metal.

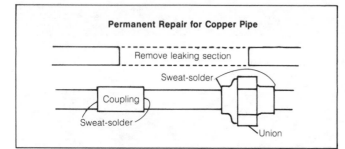

Permanent Repair for Copper Pipe

Remove leaking section

Sweat-solder

Coupling

Sweat-solder

Union

A permanent repair for a leaking section of copper tubing requires cutting out the section and replacing it with a sweat-soldered coupling and a union.

Heat the metal, then apply the solder to the metal. Do not heat the solder and drip it onto the metal. Back up the job with a heat-resistant brick, block, or asbestos board.

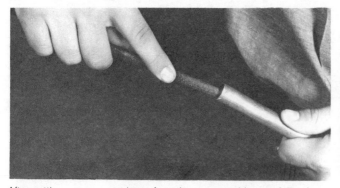

After cutting, remove any burrs from the copper tubing or pipe using a metal file. Do not dig into the metal. If cuts are not square, and smooth, the ends of the pipe will not meet in a tight fit.

The joint between the pipe or tube and the fitting should be full of solder. If you have made a mistake, reheat the fitting, remove it, clean it, and resolder it.

When finished, the joint should be "full" of solder — no gaps or breaks.

There are several tricks to using solder. (1) Never try to solder a pipe that has water in it. (2) Do not overheat the metal when soldering. You apply the solder to the metal. If the solder melts, the metal is the right temperature. (3) Be careful with the propane torch at all times. Back up the work with a thick concrete patio block or asbestos board. (4) Make any bends in copper pipe and tubing "gentle." Do not kink the pipe; use a fitting instead (45-degree, ¼ or ⅛ bend fitting). (5) Use copper plumbing only where specified by codes.

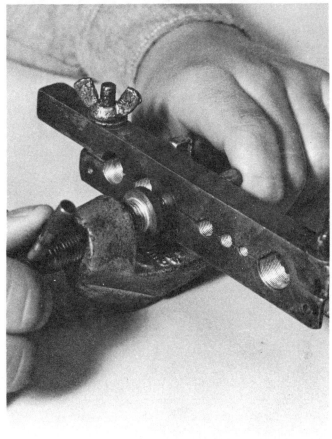

A flaring tool is clamped to the flaring block and the tool is inserted into the end of the tubing. You then turn the handle of the tool into the tubing and block.

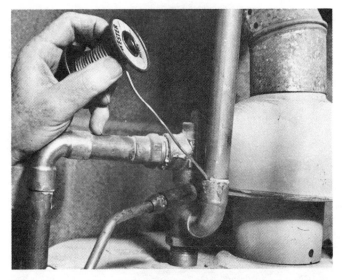

Wire solder must be added to a joint made with solder/flux in paste form. This assures a band of solder completely around the edge of the fitting.

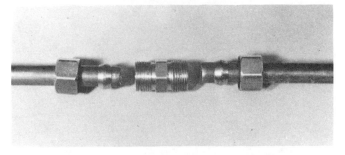

Compression fittings on copper tubing are little rings that slip into special fittings and retaining nuts. Always assemble the job before you cut the tubing to size.

The flare looks like this when it is completed. If the job is not satisfactory, cut the tubing square again and reflare the tubing. Don't try to rework the same flare.

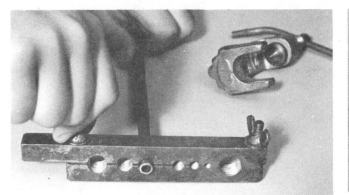

Flared fittings require a flaring block. The block can be expensive; it may pay to rent a flaring outfit if you have to assemble only a few pipes.

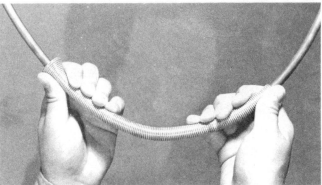

You can bend copper pipe and tubing with this spring-like bending tool, made especially for the job. You also can bend tubing over your knee, but do not kink the pipe.

Most brands of PB and CPVC plastic pipe can be flared to accept standard flare fittings as used for copper tubing. Don't forget to slip on the flare nut *before* making the flare (photo courtesy Genova).

Replacing Plastic Pipe

Because plastic pipe is a relative newcomer on the building and remodeling scene, check the codes regarding its use. Plastic pipe is restricted in many areas.

You can buy four types of plastic pipe: PB (polybutelene); PVC (polyvinyl chloride); CPVC (chlorinated polyvinyl chloride) ; ABS (acrylonitrile butadiene-styrene) .

You can use all four for cold water supply; however, in many areas, codes may restrict your use of plastic pipe to CPVC for hot water and drainage lines only.

Most plastic used for hot and cold water supply is ½-in. The ¾-in. size is used for main supply lines; the larger sizes are used for drainage and stacks.

Plastic pipe is rated as to pounds-per-sq.-in. (psi). This information usually is printed on the pipe. The psi figure should match the water pressure in your area. Do not use pipe that doesn't match the rating.

Flexible plastic pipe — sold in rolls — must not be used for hot water. You can use it for underground sprinkling systems or to move water from an outside silcock to a garden area, as drainage pipe. This pipe, which usually is black in color, is pressure rated to 125 pounds. The higher the rating, the better.

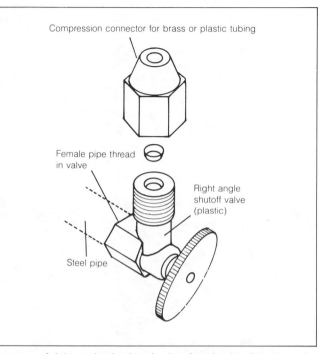

One type of right-angle plastic valve has female pipe threads on the inlet, and a plastic compression fitting on the outlet side that goes to the fixture. In effect, the valve is a steel-to-plastic adapter.

Cut the ends of plastic pipe square. A bench jig like this one helps. It is two pieces of scrap wood nailed at right angles. The jig will also work on steel and copper pipe.

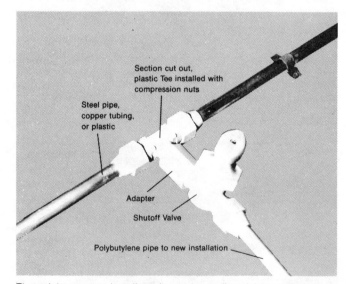

The quickest way to install a valve under a toilet, sink or vanity is to cut out a section of the existing line and install a plastic valve with compression fittings on the end. Compression fittings will make a watertight connection on steel pipe, copper tubing or rigid or flexible plastic piping. This means you can change the existing line from the valve to the fixture by replacing it with flexible plastic, which simplifies connecting up to the fixture.

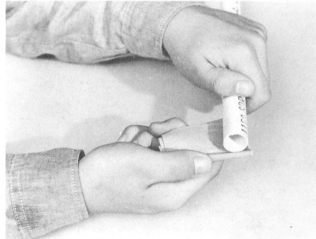

Lightly sand the cut ends of plastic pipe where the ends go into fittings. Pressure ratings of plastic pipe are stamped on the walls of the pipe, as shown.

Tools and materials. Hacksaw, emery cloth abrasive, pocketknife, artist's brush, plastic pipe cement, new pipe, new fittings.

STEPS

Turn off the water. Cut the damaged pipe at the fittings, or at each side of the damage, whichever takes less material or is easiest.

Measure and cut the new run of pipe to fit. You may be able to use the old pipe as a template. Make all the cuts as square as possible so the ends of the pipe slide into the fittings properly.

Remove any burrs from the end of the pipe and around the inside edges of the ends. A pocketknife is the best tool for this, although you can use a regular paring knife. Do not remove any "solid" plastic; just burrs.

Lightly sand the plastic at the ends of the pipe. This gives the smooth plastic some "tooth" so the plastic cement holds better when it is dry.

Assemble the fittings on the pipe and then assemble the entire job — without cement. Make any adjustments in the system at this time.

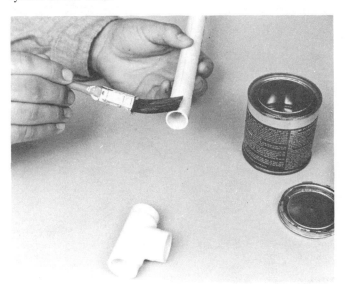

Apply plastic pipe cement to the pipe, not to the fitting. But before you cement the run, assemble the pipe in a "dry" run so you can make any adjustments before applying the cement.

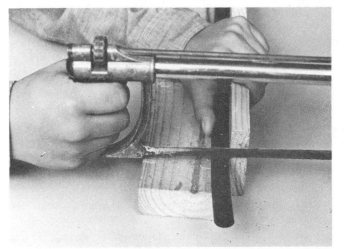

Flexible plastic pipe is also known as PB. It can be cut in the same manner and using the same tools as for rigid pipe. Remove any burrs with a knife.

With an artist's brush, apply the cement to the ends of the pipe and push the pipe into the fittings. The cement should form a small bead around the fitting where the pipe goes into the fitting. Work fast during this assembly. The cement sets up fairly quickly.

PB/Flexible Pipe

Tools and materials. Hacksaw, knife, hose clamp.

STEPS

Flexible plastic pipe is clamped, not cemented. Cut the end of the pipe using a hacksaw. Remove any burrs from the material with a knife. Place the clamp, which looks like an auto hose clamp, over the hose. Push the fitting into the hose and clamp the hose to the fitting.

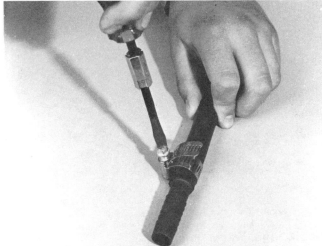

Assemble flexible plastic pipe with hose clamps. Screw the clamps tight, but don't overtighten them. Slotted clamps are best for connecting flexible plastic pipe.

We have found the added cost of PB to be worthwhile when plumbing in hard-to-reach locations, and when replacing other types of pipe inside a wall where your visibility and space are limited.

PB pipe can be worked very easily; we have pulled a length of it up through a wall with the aid of a "fish wire," much as you would pull a length of electric wire through a wall. The pipe can be used for hot water, as it is rated well above any temperature that will be encountered with an ordinary hot

PB plastic pipe is joined with compression fittings; it cannot be solvent-welded. One method (Qest products) utilizes nut, stainless steel lock ring, sealing ring and fitting. These components also can be used on CPVC plastic tube or pipe, and also on copper tubing to make watertight connections.

water tank. It also offers a safety factor of several times the pressure that will ever be produced in a normal water supply system, whether from a municipal line or a private pump.

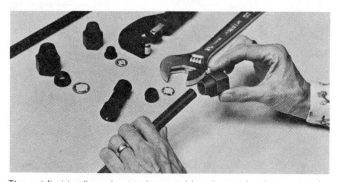

The nut first is slipped onto pipe or tubing; it must be the proper size (photo courtesy Qest Products).

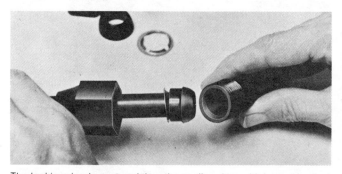

The locking ring is next and then the sealing ring, which must be flush with the end of pipe or tubing. This requires a square cut on pipe or tubing (photo courtesy Qest Products).

Replacing a Water Supply Pipe

Tools and materials. Adjustable wrench, hacksaw, new water pipe and connections.

STEPS, STEEL PIPE

Turn off the water; flush the toilet. Since the pipe will be replaced, you can hacksaw right through it at any spot; then loosen and remove the connections. This sometimes is easier than trying to remove the connections and then the pipe.

Cut the new pipe to match the length of the old pipe, using the old pipe as a guide. Before you make the cut, slip on the connections and compression fittings to allow for their lengths. Then screw the new pipe length to the connections.

STEPS, COPPER AND PLASTIC

If the old pipe is soldered in place, you may have to remove the shutoff valve, pipe, and the inlet valve. Turn off the water at the main. Cut the supply pipe in half with a hacksaw, and then unscrew the shutoff valve with a pipe wrench. You now can remove the old pipe from the inlet valve with a wrench. At this time, it's a good idea to replace the inlet valve.

Connect the new shutoff valve and water supply pipe to the inlet valve, using compression fittings instead of solder. Or, use a new plastic product that snaps in place; no wrenches are required (the Grabber System). The water supply pipe is plastic and flexible, so it may be bent around any obstructions. Hand-tighten the connections.

Turn on the water and check the connections for leaks. If you spot trouble, turn the connections a little tighter.

Special fittings let you adapt flexible plastic pipe to galvanized steel and copper pipe. The fittings slip into the end of the plastic pipe and are held with a clamp.

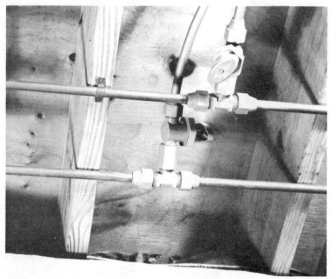

Plastic valves at top are attached to rigid copper pipe by compression nuts on T-fittings.

Noisy Pipes

For water hammer you will have to install air chamber pipes in the system. These pipes operate off a tee fitting and stop the chattering noise (see illustration). Air chambers should be installed at the high point of the plumbing run.

Faucet chatter usually is caused by a worn washer in the faucet. Turn off the water, disassemble the faucet, and install a new washer on the bottom of the stem of the faucet.

Angle bang is caused by water flowing against a 90-degree elbow. Sometimes you can stop this by adding pipe hangers to the pipe run. Or, nail little blocks of wood against the pipe at the fittings.

Pipe squeaks occur only on hot water pipes. The heat expands the metal, causing the pipe to move in the metal support brackets. Loosen the brackets and wrap the pipe at this point with fiberglass insulation or rubber padding. Then reset the brackets. Adding new brackets sometimes helps prevent the squeaking noise.

Tools and materials. Pipe insulation, pliers, hammer, nails, pipe hangers, pipe wrenches, plumbing tee to fit plumbing pipes, rubber padding, screwdriver, washers, wood blocks (depending on which cause).

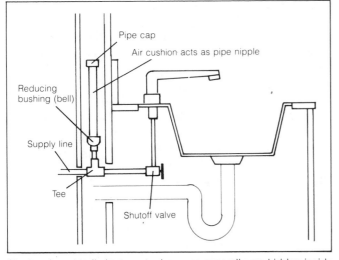

Air chambers to eliminate water hammer generally are hidden inside walls when the plumbing is installed. The air chamber is a vertical length of pipe larger than the line to the fixture, which traps air to provide a shock-absorbing cushion.

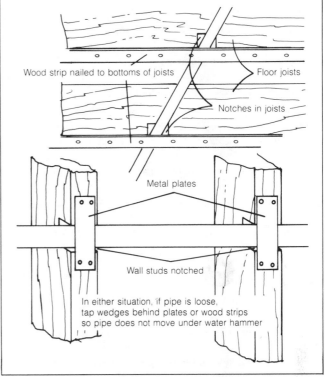

Pipes that are not securely fastened to the wall or (in basement or crawl space) to floor joists can bang when faucets are suddenly shut off.

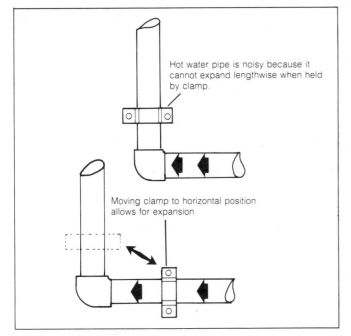

A clamp that is improperly located may keep the pipe from expanding due to hot water, which results in clinking and clanking.

PREVENTING FREEZE-UP AND CONDENSATION
How to Thaw Frozen Pipes

Tools and materials. (Depends on technique; see below.) Heat lamp, electric heating tape, propane torch, cloth wrapping, hot water, insulation.

STEPS

First, determine why the pipe has frozen. You may have to insulate the pipe or, if the pipe runs through an unheated space or terminates outdoors, turn off the water.

If the pipe is exposed, try these methods.

(1) Wrap the pipe with electric heating tape. Spiral the tape loosely around the pipe and then plug into an electrical outlet. Open the faucet for drainage so the heat will not create steam and break the pipe.

(2) Thaw the pipe with a heat lamp; open a faucet.

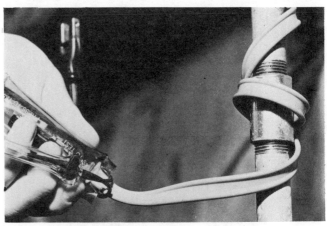

Electric heating tape is the best way to thaw a frozen pipe. It also is the best way to keep pipes from freezing in the first place. Some tapes come with automatic thermostats.

(3) Soak cloth strips in hot water; wrap cloth strips around the pipe until the pipe has thawed.

(4) Heat the pipe with a propane torch, but be very careful with the fire. Open a faucet and work from the faucet up the pipe to the frozen section.

If the pipe is behind a wall, ceiling, or under a floor, first try a heat lamp. The heat will penetrate the wall, ceiling or floor covering, thawing the pipe. This is a very slow technique, so be patient. Don't get the heat lamp too close to the covering or the lamp will scorch it. The other course is to open the faucets and allow the pipes to thaw through normal hot-water flow.

If a pipe breaks due to freezing, immediately shut off the water to this line and replace the pipe as soon as conditions permit. Do not leave the pipe as is, since breaks in the pipe may cause water damage.

PRESSURE PROBLEMS
Low Water Pressure
This problem can be caused by several things, none of which you can do much about yourself.

Limed pipes. Lime deposits in pipes are caused by lime in the water supply. The pipes probably will have to be replaced by a professional. DO NOT attempt to pour chemicals through the water system to remove the lime deposits.

Open faucets. Too many open faucets can cause a drop in water pressure, especially if normal water pressure is low in your area. Check the faucets in your home to make sure they are all closed — if, of course, they are not being used.

Meter pressure. Sometimes, but not often, the water meter can go on the fritz, causing low water pressure problems. Or a buried supply pipe in the yard breaks, resulting in low pressure. Both of these problems should be handled by the city water department.

Excess Pressure
If, on the other hand, your problem is excess pressure — which is indicated by water hammer even with all pipe securely fastened and all air chambers functioning — you can install a pressure-reducing valve with little hardship.

Most such valves are factory-preset at about 50 pounds, but you can adjust yours up or down to suit. Excess pressure is a problem that should not be ignored. Just as with constant water hammer, it can break joints, rupture pipes and cause faucets and fixtures to wear out prematurely.

This type of pressure-reducing valve in water supply line is in the author's home. Even in summer there is ample pressure to fixtures on second floor, which means that the unregulated pressure is much too high and could damage pipes and fittings.

Leaky Drains and Drain Connections
Tools and materials. Pipe wrenches, channel lock pliers, screwdriver, rubber hammer, putty knife, plumber's putty, medium steel wool (possibly new metal or rubber gaskets, depending on the design of the sink).

STEPS

Worn parts usually cause this problem. From underneath the sink, remove the trap, using pipe wrenches or channel lock pliers. Have a bucket handy to catch the water from the bottom of the trap. Remove the nut that holds the drain assembly in the sink basin. The nut looks something like the connecting nuts on the trap and trap tailpiece. Above this holding nut is a metal flange that has small slots around its edge. You'll have to position the tip of the screwdriver into the little slots and tap the screwdriver with the rubber hammer to loosen the flange. *Note:* Older sinks may have a large nut, not flange, holding the drain assembly. Use a pipe wrench to remove this nut.

Under the flange may be a metal or rubber washer. If so, it will be sandwiched between the flange nut and the bottom of the sink. Inspect this washer for wear and damage and replace the washer if necessary. The washer provides a watertight seal between the metal parts.

Now remove the drain assembly in the bottom of the sink. Lift out the assembly, clean it and around the opening in the bottom of the sink. Use a putty knife and steel wool for this job.

Spread a thin layer of plumber's putty around the hole in the sink and around the bottom of the drain assembly. Now reseat the drain assembly in the putty in the sink. Then reconnect the drain: flange nut, holding nut, and trap. Let the plumber's putty set for about five days. Remove any excess putty around the drain in the sink with a putty knife and/or steel wool.

HOW TO READ A WATER METER
Normally, reading a water meter is a job for the utility company. However, if you suspect a leaking pipe or hear running water that you can't locate, reading the water meter can be important. There are three types of meters; each reads differently.

Digital meters have a row of moving numbers like the odometer in your car. As you use the water, the numbers change. To check water usage, note the reading one day; wait two days; note the reading the third day. Then subtract the lower number from the higher number. The answer will be the number of cubic feet of water that has been used.

Six-dial meters look like a series of small clocks. The dials, clockwise around the face of the meter, are calibrated in cu. ft.: 100,000 cu. ft.; 10,000 cu. ft.; 1,000 cu. ft.; 100 cu. ft.; 10 cu. ft.; 1 cu ft.

Read each dial, starting at the 100,000 unit, and go around the meter face. Mark down the smaller of the two digits where the pointer points. This will give you, in cubic feet, the meter reading. Wait two days. Then read the dials again. Subtract the smaller number from the larger number. The figure will be the amount of water used in cubic feet.

6 Mechanical Repairs

For many repairs to your furnace, air conditioner, and major appliances, you will have to bite the bullet and pay a professional serviceman. Breakdowns often require special equipment — too expensive for a one-time fix-up — and the technical knowhow required transcends this book. But don't be discouraged. There are other repairs you can make, as well as lots of maintenance you can do to prevent costly repairs.

When trouble occurs, the best advice we can pass along is for you to first read the manufacturer's service manual provided with the equipment. Then use the material in this chapter to supplement the service manual. If you cannot find the answers in either place, call a professional.

A systematic approach is always the best way to root out mechanical problems and solve them. Start first with the power: Is the power on? Is the power getting to the equipment? From this point, check the switches, reset buttons, drive belts; look for burned-out motors, and so on. Coal, gas, electric and oil furnaces function similarly. Oversimplified, fuel (coal, gas, electricity, or oil) is fed into the furnace where a flame or spark ignites the fuel. The resulting heat is blown through a network of ducts to registers installed in individual rooms.

Another type of heat "furnace" uses radiant heating panels in individual rooms. The panels are installed in the ceiling and interior walls.

GAS HEATING UNIT REPAIRS
Anatomy of a Gas Furnace and Ducting

If the fuel is gas, it is piped from a distant hole in the ground to a distribution center in your area. Here, the gas is metered out to customers of the gas utility. The gas comes into your home through a pipe and meter — similar to a water pipe and meter, and you pay for the gas according to the amount of gas used. At the meter in your home, there is a shutoff valve. Locate and mark this valve right now so you will know where to turn off the gas when an emergency arises or you need to make furnace repairs. (See p. 98 for diagram of gas furnace.)

The gas fuel is fed into gas burners within the furnace. The furnace may have just one burner, or it may have several burners — similar to the burners on a gas range. The gas going into the burners is ignited by a pilot flame. The flame heats a little metal part called a "thermocouple." The thermocouple, when heated by the pilot flame, converts the heat into a small electric charge. This charge, in turn, ignites the gas.

When your furnace does not go on, the chances are that the pilot flame has gone out, cooling the thermocouple. The thermocouple then closes a gas valve so the burners do not get gas. This is a safety device. The gas will not go back into the burners until the pilot flame is lighted and the thermocouple is once again heated.

The gas shut-off valve will be located next to or in the furnace. Trace it by following the black gas pipe. Oil furnaces have a similar shut-off valve at the furnace and supply tank.

A toggle switch near or on the furnace turns the furnace on or off. In some cases the furnace power instead may be controlled through the main fuse box or circuit breaker power entrance.

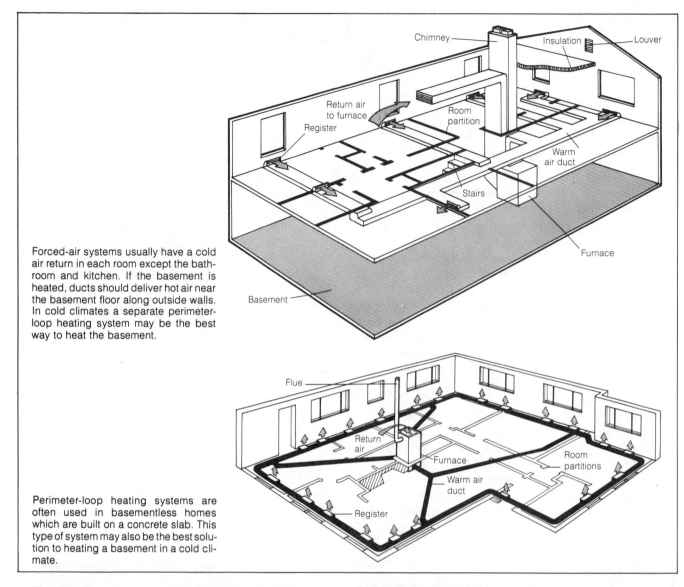

Forced-air systems usually have a cold air return in each room except the bathroom and kitchen. If the basement is heated, ducts should deliver hot air near the basement floor along outside walls. In cold climates a separate perimeter-loop heating system may be the best way to heat the basement.

Perimeter-loop heating systems are often used in basementless homes which are built on a concrete slab. This type of system may also be the best solution to heating a basement in a cold climate.

The pilot flame is protected by a "draft diverter." This device is located in the furnace or at the opening of the vent pipe that leads to the chimney.

Air is drawn into the furnace by a blower system. The gas burners heat the air; the air is then blown through ducts to the registers in individual rooms in your home. Once used, this not-so-hot air returns to the furnace through a cold air register and duct.

You need be concerned with the maintenance of only a half-dozen or so components of a gas furnace. Many utility companies that supply the gas will check your furnace every two or three years for any needed service. In the event of an emergency, immediately call the utility service department. Usually a repair person will respond quickly to your call — regardless of the time of day.

When You Smell Gas

If you are in the house and smell gas, immediately shut off the main gas supply valve near the gas meter.

If you are returning home and smell gas when you open the door, DO NOT turn on any lights or light any matches. Leave the door open and call the utility service department from a neighbor's home or pay telephone booth.

Relighting Pilot Lights

Safety. Do not attempt to relight a pilot flame until all smells of gas leave the furnace area.

STEPS

Look for a metal tag attached to the furnace. It usually is located near the burners of the furnace. Printed on this tag will be the instructions for relighting the pilot flame. Follow these directions to the letter. The procedure usually involves turning down the room thermostat that controls the furnace, pressing a gas restarting valve (for several minutes), and holding a lighted match next to the pilot jet.

If you cannot relight the pilot light according to the directions on the furnace tag, call the utility. The problem may be a malfunctioning thermocouple or a downward draft from the chimney vent.

Adjusting Air Shutters

Tools and materials. Screwdriver, pliers.

STEPS

Some furnaces have air shutters located near the burners. The device looks like a disc with triangular slots in its metal cover-

Diagnosing Heating Problems

Problem	Possible Solution
Furnace won't start	Set thermostat. Check fuses or circuit breaker for power. Flip furnace motor switches. Adjust furnace bonnet thermostat. Push motor re-sets.
Flame won't ignite (gas furnace)	Pilot light is out. Thermocouple is malfunctioning; draft diverter is malfunctioning; gas supply is off.
Flame won't ignite (oil furnace)	Tripped emergency switch; no fuel; stuck thermostat; malfunctioning ignition; motor overloaded (press re-set); low electric power.
Furnace won't heat (electric)	Check fuse box or circuit breaker; push re-set button on blower motor; element burned out.
Gas smell	Pilot light out; leaking pipe connections. Ventilate house; relight pilot. Tighten connections and test.
Low heat (forced air system)	Blower fan set too low; fan not working (push re-set button); blockage in ducts.
Low heat (steam system)	Lack of water in boiler; blocked pipe; pipe leakage; malfunctioning valve; radiator not sloped properly; pump not working properly (hot water system).
Radiators won't heat	Malfunctioning air release valve; malfunctioning valve in main stem; blocked pipe.
Noise in radiator	Improper radiator slope.
Noise in pipes	Improper pipe slope.
Blower noise	Loose or worn V belt; loose pulley; dirty fan blades; motor loose on mountings; cover plates not attached.
Rushing air sound	Filter not properly installed; air leak in ducting; fan set to run too fast.
Furnace goes on/off rapidly	This is called rapid cycling. Faulty room thermostat; try setting bonnet thermostat on furnace at higher temperature.

ing. You turn this disc to open and close the slots and regulate the air flow to the burners. You may be able to turn the air shutters by hand. If not, force them slightly (gently) with pliers or a screwdriver.

If the burners are not getting enough air, the flames on the burners will appear blue. If the burners are getting too much air, the flames on the burners will appear yellow. When the burners are functioning correctly, the flames will be blue with a light yellow tip at the end of the flame.

Furnaces must have air to function properly. Make sure vents to the furnace are clean and free from dust, which is usually pulled into vents by the furnace's blower system. Also make sure that louvers on louvered doors leading to furnace rooms are open.

Gas Line Checks for Leaks

Tools and materials. Water, household detergent, small mixing container, brush, pipe wrenches.

STEPS

Mix the household detergent with water so the solution will form bubbles when stirred.

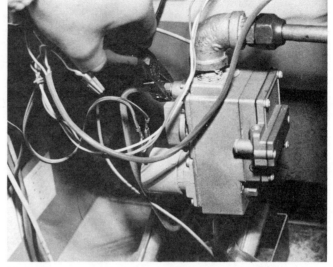

All gas furnace pipe connections should be inspected annually for tightness. Some utility companies provide this service for customers. Otherwise, if you suspect a leak call in a professional.

Apply the mixture with a brush to gas line connections. If you spot tiny bubbles emerging from the connection, the connection probably is leaking.

Try tightening the connection with pipe wrenches. Then test the connection again with the soapy water. If the connection is still leaking turn off the gas at the main entrance valve and call a service person.

Changing Filters

Tools and materials. Screwdriver, new filters.

STEPS

Filters should be replaced, never cleaned, every six weeks during the heating and cooling season. Most filters are located near the furnace's blowing fan that circulates heat/cold air throughout the house. If the filters are covered by a metal plate, unscrew the plate and replace the filters.

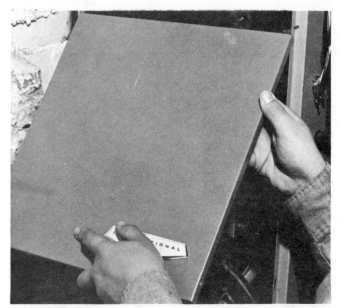

To open the furnace, you may have to unscrew and/or slide a metal panel off the furnace housing. Fan and blower parts may be within this housing or adjacent to the furnace.

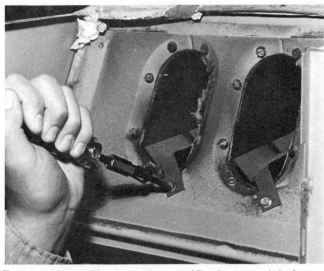

Tighten any burner, blower or motor parts. Vibration can work the fasteners loose, causing squeaks and rattles. Replace any damaged asbestos tape on the furnace and ducts.

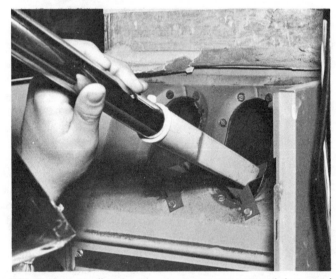

With the furnace off and cool, you can vacuum soot and dust out of burner chambers, blower housing, and around motors, valves, and thermostats. Clean the furnace yearly.

Furnace air vents should be cleaned annually. If the furnace is in a room with a louvered door, vacuum the louvers to remove lint and dust. A furnace must have air.

Some filters slide in a metal channel next to the blower. Here, slide the old filter up and out and the new filter in and down. One side of the filter must face the air flow of the furnace. This is marked on the edge of the filter.

Motors, Pulleys, and Belts

Tools and materials. Light-weight machine oil, Allen wrenches, an adjustable wrench, new V-belt.

Safety. Turn off the furnace.

STEPS

Most electric motors today are self-lubricating and sealed at the factory. However, some motors do have to be oiled.

Oil a fan motor at the start of each heating season (or cooling season) with just a few drops of light machine oil. Holes or spouts for the oil will be located at one or both ends of the motor housing.

Check the metal pulleys on the fan motor and the blower drive wheel. If the pulleys are loose, you often can tighten them with Allen wrenches. A set screw will be located in the hub of the pulley or inside the V part of the pulley. Or, the pulley may be fastened to the drive shafts with a square-headed set screw. Use an adjustable wrench to tighten this set screw.

Check V belts for wear annually. If the belt must be replaced, loosen the motor on its mountings with an adjustable wrench and force the motor toward the blower. Then remove the old belt, replace it with the new belt, reposition the motor, and tighten the mounting screws.

Manual Controls and Reset Buttons

STEPS

Some gas furnaces have special shutoff switches and reset buttons on motors. These switches can be accidentally flipped to an off-position, or an overloaded circuit may cause the fuse system in the motors to trip.

The switch to the furnace probably will be in a metal junction box attached to the side of the furnace near the burner unit. If the furnace won't run, try flipping this switch several times. If the furnace still won't run, check the main fuse box or circuit breaker box.

Most electric motors have re-set buttons on the housing of the motor. The top of the button usually is colored red or yellow. The button activates a type of fuse that trips when the motor becomes overloaded. This protects the motor from overheating and burning out.

If the motor doesn't run, try pressing this re-set button. Punch it several times. If the motor doesn't start, check the fuse box or circuit breaker at the main power entrance to make sure the furnace is getting power.

Registers and Ducts

Tools and materials. Vacuum with hose attachment, dust cloth, plumbing auger.

STEPS

Before each heating and cooling season, vacuum all heating and cooling registers. Remove the registers and vacuum the ducts below. Make sure the cold air register is clean. If the ducts are plugged with a foreign object, you probably can snag it with the corkscrew end of an auger. Or, disassemble the duct to reach the object.

Cleaning Blowers
Tools and materials. Vacuum with a hose attachment, screwdriver, adjustable wrench.

STEPS
If you can get into the furnace blower housing, vacuum the blades and inside the housing annually.

The housing may be screwed or bolted together near the base of the blower. Often you can remove a metal panel to gain access to the blower blades.

OIL FURNACE REPAIRS AND MAINTENANCE
Put the furnace on an annual inspection tour and follow this checklist: fuel tank and supply lines; connections; lubrication points; filters; registers and ducts.

Anatomy of an Oil Furnace and Ducting
Delivery trucks bring the oil to your home and pump the oil into your tank. Near this tank is a main shutoff valve. Locate and mark this valve right now so you will know where to turn off the oil flow in the event of a leak or other emergency, or when you want to make repairs to the oil furnace.

The oil furnace has an oil "gun" burner. Through this device air and fuel oil travel to a combustion chamber. At this point, the air and oil are forced into a spray nozzle which makes a mist that an electric spark ignites (see p. 93).

Should this spark fail to work, the furnace automatically shuts off. Bimetallic strips are the shutoff device. The strips simply expand and contract when they are heated and cooled. This movement operates a thermostat or switch.

Air circulated by a blower system is drawn into the oil furnace, heated, and forced through ducts. The ducts end at registers in the rooms of your home. When the warm air cools, the air is returned via cold air ducts to the furnace.

Maintaining Fuel Tanks and Supply Lines
Tools and materials. Wire brush, adjustable wrenches, metal paint, paintbrush.
STEPS
Exposed fuel oil tanks often are subjected to dampness, which causes rust. If the tank is starting to rust, clean the metal with a wire brush and give the tank a coat or two of metal paint.

Tighten connections between the tank and the furnace with an adjustable wrench. If you spot a leak, tightening a connection may stop the leak. If not, the line may need a new connection or new gaskets.

Furnace Motor Lubrication
Tools and materials. Machine oil (30 SAE).

STEPS
Most electric motors are self-lubricating; you can tell instantly by checking for oil cups at the ends of the motors. The cups are little spouts with a spring-activated cap on the opening of the spout.

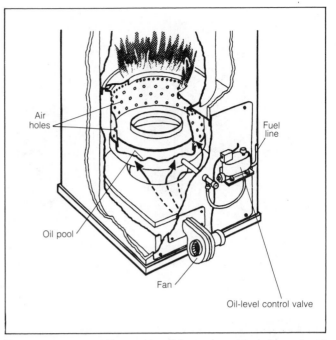

There are two types of burners for oil furnaces: pot-type (shown) and gun-type (pg. 93). The fuel oil is injected into the burner chamber; the air is heated and is then distributed through ducts.

Open the cap and oil the motor at least once yearly — more often if the heating season is extended. Remove any excess oil from the motor housing with a cloth. Oil attracts dirt, which can act as insulation on the motor and cause the motor to overheat.

Cleaning and Replacing Filters
Tools and materials. Adjustable wrench, screwdriver, kerosene, wiping cloths, bucket.

STEPS
The oil filters are usually located at the end of the furnace motor. You will have to remove a metal plate held by a series of bolts to reach the filters.

Turn off the furnace. Remove the bolts with an adjustable wrench or wrench socket set. Then lift off the metal covering that seals the filters.

Carefully lift out the filters and clean them with kerosene, working in a well-ventilated area. Replace the filters and the metal covering, and tighten the bolts. Then clean the motor and filter housing with a cloth.

COAL FURNACES AND DUCTING
Your coal furnace probably has a "stoker" system of fuel injection into the furnace. The coal is dumped into a bin or hopper. From here the coal is transported to the furnace by a corkscrew type shaft.

You may have to start the fire with kindling, or the furnace may have an automatic starting device. Once lighted, the stoker is controlled by a room thermostat.

Coal creates ashes when burned. Most coal furnaces have an automatic device that removes the ashes, or they have to be shoveled into buckets by hand.

A blower system circulates air through the furnace's fire box; the air is heated and ducted to registers in individual rooms.

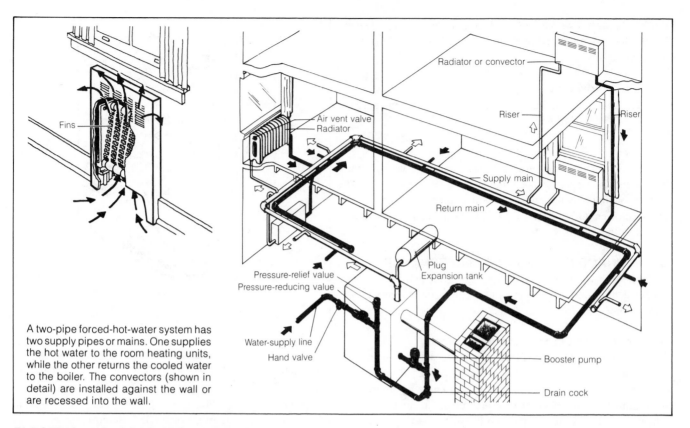

A two-pipe forced-hot-water system has two supply pipes or mains. One supplies the hot water to the room heating units, while the other returns the cooled water to the boiler. The convectors (shown in detail) are installed against the wall or are recessed into the wall.

ELECTRIC FURNACES AND DUCTING

If the fuel is electricity, it is generated from coal, oil, or nuclear energy by a utility company. The electricity comes into your home via wire through a meter and fuse box or circuit breaker. You pay for this electricity according to the meter reading. Locate this main fuse box or circuit breaker so you will know where to turn off the electricity in the event of an emergency, or when making any repairs to the furnace.

An electric furnace has several panels or elements that get hot when electricity is supplied to the panels. The heat from the panels is then distributed by a blower system through ducts to registers in individual rooms. The "used" warm air is returned via ducts to the furnace.

Electric furnaces need no chimney structures, since the electricity produces no smoke or fumes to be vented.

HEAT PUMPS AND DUCTING

Electricity powers heat pumps. Heat pumps, to oversimplify, remove the heat from the air outside, or heat from water, and transfer this heat to inside your home. In the summer, the heat pump removes the heat indoors and transfers it outside. This cools your home. When the temperature drops to zero or below zero temperatures during the winter months, an electric coil heater takes over to supply the needed heat.

The heating and air conditioning is distributed from the heat pump via ducts to individual room registers.

HOT WATER HEATING

Water to a boiler tank is heated by a furnace. When the water is hot, the water expands from the tank into and through piping to radiators or heating panels. This is called a gravity hot-water heating system.

A hydronic or forced hot-water system is similar to a gravity system, except that a pump is used to pump the hot water to radiators or heating panels. Usually, a hydronic system supplies hot water to plumbing fixtures as well as to the heating units.

In a steam system, water is heated by a furnace. When the water turns to steam, the steam travels through pipes to the radiators. At the radiators, the steam cools, creating water. The water is then returned, via pipes, to the boiler and is reheated to go through the heating/cooling cycle again.

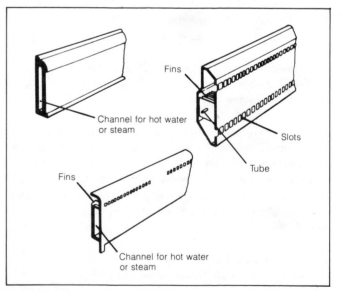

Baseboard radiator units can be used to replace the old-fashioned wood baseboard. In the drawings at left and center, water or steam flows behind the baseboard face. Heat from that surface is transmitted to the room. In the finned-tube version shown at right, the water or steam flows through the tube and heats the tube and the fins. Air passing over the tube and fins is heated and passed out to the room through the slots.

Steam systems may have one or two sets of pipes. In a one-pipe system, the steam travels to the radiator, cools into water, and is returned to the boiler. In a two-pipe system, the steam travels to the radiators in one pipe and the water from the steam is returned to the boiler in the second pipe.

How to Bleed a Radiator

Tools and materials. Adjustable wrench, screwdriver.

STEPS

Air can become trapped in radiator lines and the radiator won't heat. The radiator must be bled.

With a screwdriver (or pliers) open the little vent screw in the radiator valve. This screw usually is located on the underside of the valve.

First, you will hear a sort of hissing noise, then hot water will flow out of the valve. At this point, replace and tighten the vent screw in the valve. You will have to bleed all the radiators in the house.

Radiator Steam Flow

Tools and materials. Level, hammer, cedar shingles.

STEPS

Position a level on top of the radiator. The pitch should be toward the outflow of the radiator, toward the system's boiler. If the radiator is not on a slight slant, try driving cedar shingle shims under the base or "feet" of the radiator to obtain the slant, or use wooden blocks.

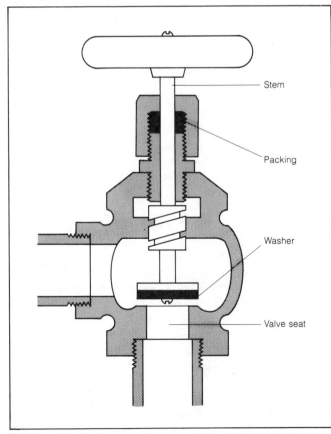

Radiator shut-off valves sometimes need to be repacked. This is done with regular plumbing packing string, applied to the valve stem next to the valve cap.

Steam Valve Leaks

Tools and materials. Adjustable wrench, washers, packing string.

STEPS

First, try tightening the valve cap with an adjustable wrench. This may stop the leak in the radiator steam valve. Don't overtighten the cap or you will strip threads.

Shut off the system. Remove the cap with an adjustable wrench. Under the cap you will find a flat washer or packing string — or both. Replace the washer or packing string and reassemble the valve.

Steam Pipe Maintenance

Tools and materials. Hammer, nails, pipe hangers.

STEPS

Steam pipe chatter usually is caused by sagging steam pipes, or the radiators are not set on a slope (see "Radiator Steam Flow," this chapter). Wherever possible, trace the steam pipes from the boiler to the radiators. If you see any pipe sagging, support the pipe by adding new pipe hangers.

Steam pipe chatter also can be caused by faulty steam valves at radiators. Make sure the valves are opened as far as the valves will turn.

Humidifier Repair and Maintenance

Tools and materials. Screwdriver, pliers, household detergent, fine wire, stiff brush, light machine oil.

STEPS

Turn off the furnace. Turn off the water supply to the humidifier. The valve should be located near the unit on the furnace; if the valve is not highly visible you may be able to trace the water pipe to the valve.

Clean the corrosion or hardened calcium deposits from the water pan. Use a stiff brush and a mixture of household detergent and water for this. Rinse thoroughly.

Clean deposits from drum or evaporator plate units with a stiff brush and household detergent. However, upon inspection, these parts may have to be replaced, especially if they are encrusted with calcium deposits or corrosion. The cost is not prohibitive.

Inspect and clean the water nozzle, using a stiff brush to clean the metal. If the water nozzle is clogged or encrusted with calcium, rod the nozzle with fine wire. Do not use toothpicks or sharpened match sticks. The wood can break off in the nozzle opening.

Lubricate any parts marked "oil" with light machine oil, after the parts are thoroughly cleaned with a brush and household detergents. A drop or two of oil is plenty; don't overdo it.

AIR CONDITIONER MAINTENANCE

There are two basic types of air conditioners: the window variety that cools one or two rooms, and the central units that cool the entire house. The central units usually are hooked to the furnace and use the same ducts and registers that are used for forced-air heating.

Like heating units, there are few repairs you can make to air conditioners, since special and costly equipment is involved.

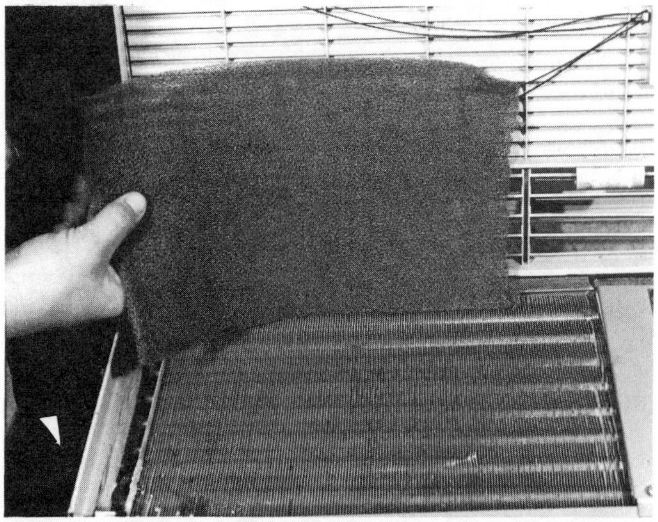

Most room air conditioner filters are washable in mild household detergent and water. Squeeze dry and replace when clean. Replaceable filters should be changed yearly.

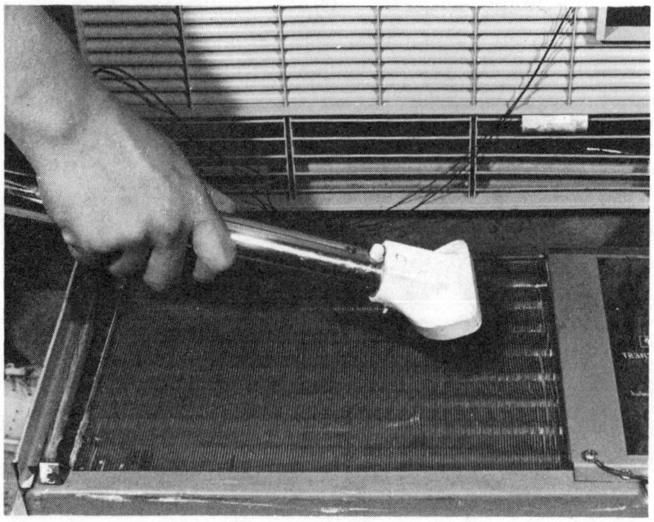

Vacuum air conditioning coils and fins before and halfway through the cooling system. Keep the inner parts clean with a vacuum and by wiping with a cloth moistened with light oil.

Air conditioners are complicated pieces of machinery; they take a specialist to doctor when inner parts fail to function properly.

There are some maintenance checks and minor repairs that you can make, however. These are listed below in a problem/solution format. Also refer to the air conditioning listings in Chapter 4, Climate Control.

Air Conditioner Won't Go On

Tools and materials. None.

STEPS

Check the power source first. If the air conditioner is a window unit, start at the plug in the wall outlet. Move from this point back to the main fuse box or circuit breaker. Some air conditioners are powered by a separate circuit and are not supplied with electricity through the main power entrance.

If the unit is a central air conditioner, go directly to the main fuse box or circuit breaker to make sure the unit is getting power. You may have blown a fuse.

Air Conditioner Blows Hot and Cold

Tools and materials. Level, pry bar, adjustable wrench, mounting brackets, cedar shingles, shovel.

STEPS

The window unit or outside compressor of a central unit may be out of level. At the start of each cooling season, level the units. You may have to add cedar shingle shims under the window sill to level window units; dig and place dirt and gravel under the slabs of outside compressors to level them.

Check the mounting brackets of a window unit. You may have to replace these brackets if the old ones are bent or broken, causing the air conditioner to tip.

Hot/cold problems may signal that the air conditioner is low on refrigerant; call a professional.

Noisy Compressor

Tools and materials. Screwdriver, pliers, adjustable wrench.

STEPS

Turn off the power. Remove the wire grill from the top of the compressor. It usually is held by four or six screws along the top frame of the compressor unit.

By hand, turn the fan blades in the compressor to make sure thay are not hitting against the housing. If they are, you may be able to bend them slightly with pliers to stop the noise. Check the hub of the fan also and make sure the set screw that holds the fan to the motor shaft is tight.

Turn on the power. If the noise still exists, chances are good that the motor is faulty or loose on its mountings; call a service person.

Air Conditioner Emits Smoke

STEPS

Turn off the power. Call a service person. The motor could be burning out or the insulation on wiring could be faulty. Further use of the unit could cause a fire.

Air Conditioner Won't Cool

Tools and materials. New filters.

STEPS

Check the power source to make sure the unit is getting electricity. Then check the thermostat. It must be below room temperature to trip the air conditioner controls.

Check the filters. Dirty filters can cause poor air flow resulting in low cooling efficiency. Filters must be changed at the start of each cooling season and about every six weeks during the season.

Window air conditioners often have washable filters. Remove these filters, load them with household detergent, and wash them clean with water. Then lightly coat the filter with household oil and replace the filter in the unit.

Oily Leaks around Air Conditioner

This probably is not oil but refrigerant — especially if you notice it on tubing in the air conditioner. Call a service person to make repairs.

Noisy Window Unit

Tools and materials. Adjustable wrench, screwdriver, foam rubber padding, length of 2x4, level, cedar shingles.

STEPS

Turn off the power. Slightly loosen the bolts in the mounting brackets after you prop up the air conditioner with a piece of 2x4 to support the weight of the unit.

Press foam rubber underneath and around the brackets so the foam rubber will absorb vibration from the unit. Use the tip of a screwdriver for this.

Now, tighten the mounting bracket bolts. Use a level to make sure the unit is level in the window. If it is not level, use cedar shingle shims to level the unit.

If the noise is coming from within the air conditioner, remove the panel that exposes the fan. Check the fan blades by turning them with your fingers. If the blades are striking the housing, you may be able to tighten the fan on the motor shaft with a screwdriver or bend the blades to stop the noise. A set screw for the fan is located on the hub of the fan.

Inside mountings are usually preset at the factory. They are spring-loaded. Sometimes these mountings work loose through vibration. You may be able to tighten them with a screwdriver. However, do not tighten them too much. The mountings should be fairly loose so the unit "floats" on the mountings.

WATER HEATER MAINTENANCE

Water heaters are wonderfully efficient. They need little maintenance and seldom need repairs.

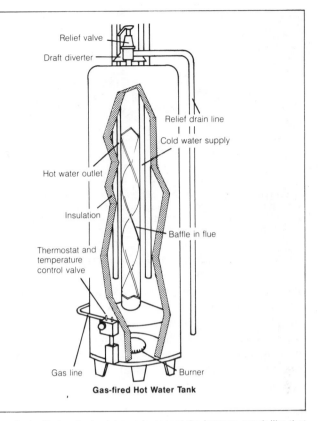

Gas-fired Hot Water Tank

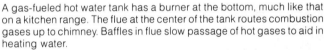

A gas-fueled hot water tank has a burner at the bottom, much like that on a kitchen range. The flue at the center of the tank routes combustion gases up to chimney. Baffles in flue slow passage of hot gases to aid in heating water.

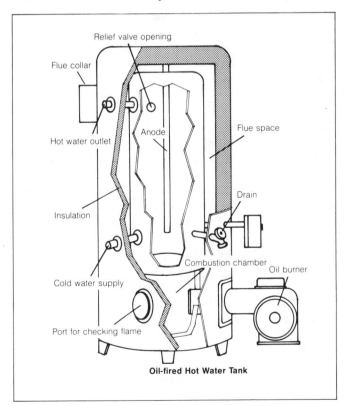

Oil-fired Hot Water Tank

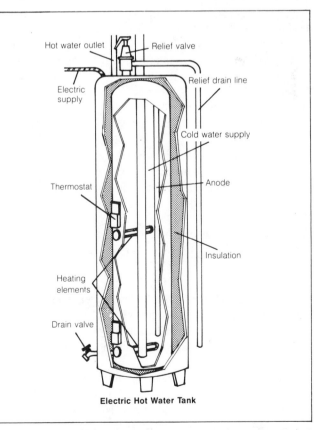

Electric Hot Water Tank

Oil-fired hot water tanks are not very common and will be even more of a rarity as heating oil becomes more expensive and difficult to obtain. In Northeast many users of fuel oil are converting to gas because of lack of availability of oil. The configuration of the tank inside the shell is somewhat different than gas or electric tanks due to the need for a combustion chamber for the oil burner.

Electric hot-water tanks used to be the most expensive to operate, but increased costs of other fuels make them somewhat more economical today. They also are a favorite with solar-assisted homes, where much of the hot water is supplied by the sun.

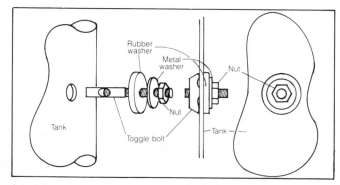

A leak in hot water tank can be temporarily fixed with toggle bolt, flat washer and rubber washer. In a real emergency you can cut the washer from a piece of inner tube, but a large faucet washer is better. Devices for stopping tank leaks are sold in some hardware stores.

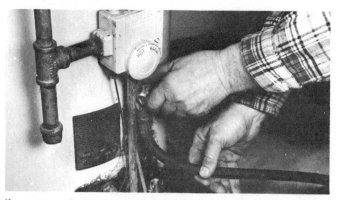

If you cannot fit a bucket under the drain valve of a water heater, you may be able to connect a hose to the valve so the water can be channeled away to another spot.

Water heaters can gobble up a lot of energy, however, so they should be properly set to conserve gas or electricity. The right setting is 140 degrees, if you have a dishwasher and washing machine. If you don't have these two appliances, turn the setting to 110 degrees. This heats the water to the right degree for average bathroom, kitchen, and laundry needs.

If your water heater springs a leak in its tank, immediately turn off the water and power and replace the water heater with a new one. It doesn't pay to attempt to repair a leaking hot water tank.

Water Won't Heat

STEPS

Check the power source from the heater to the main fuse box and circuit breaker, if the heater is electric.

If the heater is gas-fueled, make sure the pilot light is burning. If the pilot light is not burning, relight it according to the directions on a metal tag fastened to the front of the water heater.

If the pilot light won't light, the heater may not be getting gas. Check the gas supply line and make sure all valves are turned on.

Make sure the thermostat is properly set.

If all of these checkpoints prove positive and the heater still won't heat, chances are the element or burner is malfunctioning. Call a service person.

Hot Water Is Discolored

Tools and materials. Large bucket, pliers.

STEPS

Open the valve near the bottom of the heater. You may need pliers to turn the handle; don't force it.

Catch about two or three gallons of water in a bucket. Close the valve. This procedure removes sediment from the bottom of the tank.

If you have a new water heater, drain the heater about every two months.

If the water heater is an old one, it is best not to drain it. Draining can cause leaking that can't be stopped.

Leveling Water Heaters

Tools and materials. Hammer, cedar shingle shims, level.

STEPS

To function properly, a water heater must be level. Check the unit for level every three to four years. Floors can go out of level with time — a normal condition — but it causes the water heater to tip.

Set the level on top of the water heater. Drive cedar shingle shims under the base of the heater until the heater is level. Cedar wood works best, since water and dampness will not cause the wood to rot.

Water Is Too Hot

STEPS

This is a thermostat problem; the thermostat probably is set too high. If lowering the thermostat doesn't work, chances are the thermostat is faulty and needs replacing.

Most water heaters have a "relief" valve. This valve which is connected to a drain, usually opens when there is too much pressure in the water tank. If this valve continually activates itself, check the thermostat to make sure the setting is not too hot.

CLOTHES DRYERS

Lint is the ever-present enemy of clothes dryers. This fuzzy stuff can slow dryer drums, reduce heating output and cause all sorts of noises within the dryer. The remedy is to properly vent the clothes dryer to the outside, and clean the lint traps between each load of washing to be dried.

Mechanically, a clothes dryer is very simply constructed. The unit has a control panel, heating element, exhaust system, and a drying drum powered by an electric motor. By removing the back panel of a dryer, you can gain easy access to the parts and make lots of repairs yourself. The control panel, however, is a different story; most repairs and parts replacement should be made by a service person.

Venting A Dryer

Tools and materials. Hammer, pliers, screwdriver, putty knife, rigid or flexible dryer vent kit.

STEPS

Turn off the power. Assemble the vent pipe to the dryer exhaust pipe, usually located at the back of the dryer near the base of the unit. (Check the owner's service manual.) The pipe is held to the exhaust (usually) with a clamp; or, the venting may be a

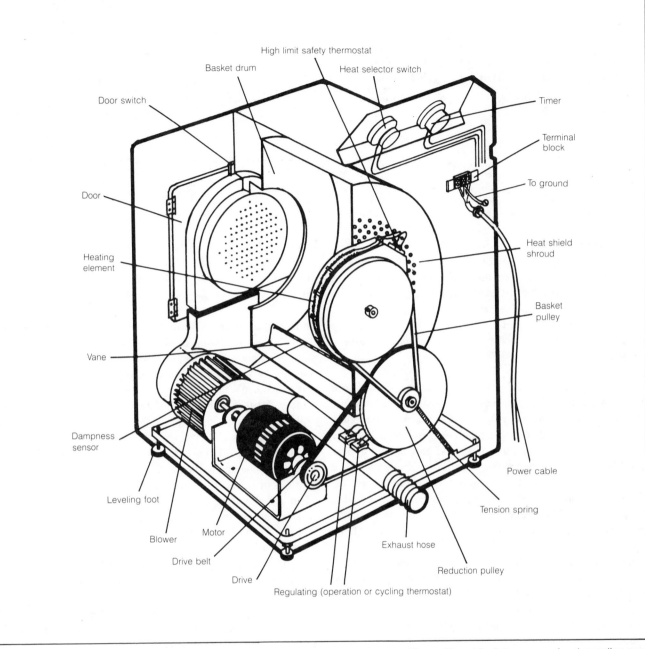

Keep the dryer level and properly vented, and clean away lint often to prevent breakdowns. The position of the lint screen varies depending upon the type, model, and age of the machine.

slip fit on the exhaust. Run the vent pipe to a window, assembling the pipe as you go. It is best to keep joints at a minimum. Preplan the run before pipe assembly.

If the room doesn't have a window, the vent can be installed through an outside wall. Here, you will have to cut a hole in the wall with a power jigsaw or keyhole saw (see Chapter 1 and 3) and flash the opening. Usually, instructions for this are provided in vent kits.

For window installation, you can remove a pane of glass from the window, insert the vent into a hole cut into a piece of *tempered* hardboard that matches the size of the window pane you removed. Insert the hardboard in the window mullions (like you would glass), and glaze the hardboard like glass (see Chapter 2).

Another window technique utilizes a board panel insert

sandwiched between the window sill and bottom sash. The vent is fitted into this panel.

Although vent pipe is extremely lightweight, it should be supported with hanger wires where possible. This keeps the pipe from sagging and kinking, which would lower the efficiency of the exhaust system.

Dryer Won't Start

STEPS

Make sure the dryer is plugged into the wall outlet. Then check the main fuse box or circuit breaker to see if the dryer is getting electric power.

If power isn't the problem, make sure the door is closed tightly; check the control panel to make sure the dryer is "on"; push the re-set button on the control panel, if there is a re-set.

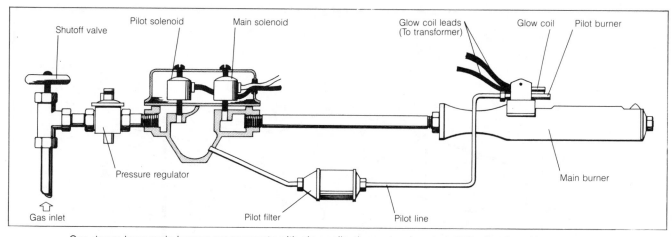

Gas dryers have main burner arrangements with glow coils; the system is not at all like that found in a gas stove.

Dryer Won't Heat

STEPS

First, make sure the dryer is turned on at the control panel to the "heat" position. Check that the thermostat and timer are properly set on the control panel.

If the dryer is gas-fueled, check that the valve behind the toe panel is turned to the "on" setting and the main gas line valve is turned on.

Improperly adjusted gas burners can result in a slow or poor heating of the dryer. The burner can usually be found near the bottom of the dryer. Remove the lower access panel and view the burner flame while experimentally running the dryer. The flame, which burns a mixture of air and gas, should appear light blue and should not make a roaring noise. If there is a roaring noise, it means there is too much air in the gas/air mixture. If the flame has yellow tips, it is receiving too little air. Correct to the best mixture by adjusting the air shutter in the burner (with the dryer OFF), retesting until the flame appears light blue when you run it but does not make a roaring sound. In some models it may be necessary to unplug the dryer, lift off the top, and then remove both the front panel and the drum before you can reach the air shutter and view the burner flame.

Electric dryers sometimes are controlled by two fuse plugs at the main fuse box or circuit breaker panel. Make sure that both of these fuses are operating properly.

Clothes Dry Slowly

Tools and materials. Screwdriver.

STEPS

First, check the fuse box or circuit breaker. The dryer may not be getting "full" power (see repair above).

Clean the lint trap and make sure there are no obstructions in the exhaust system and vent pipe. If this does not solve the problem, turn off the power. Remove the back panel of the dryer, after you remove the vent pipe, with a screwdriver. **Then clean out all lint possible, check the drive belts and the pulleys for slippage, as well as for wear and correct tightness.** The deflection on the belt should be about ¾-in. from normal when you press down on the belt. You can tighten the belt by loosening the motor mounts, repositioning the motor to take up excess belt slack, and retightening the mounts.

Dryer Is Noisy

Tools and materials. Depending on the problem: screwdriver, new V belt, adjustable wrench, pliers, level, cedar shims.

STEPS

Turn off the power. The trouble probably is lint buildup around the bands on the drum or in the fan unit. Remove the back panel with a screwdriver to expose the working parts.

Clean away the lint, using your fingers or a tip of the screwdriver. You may be able to turn the dryer drum by hand to remove lint that is under the drum bands.

Remove the housing from the fan and clean the fan blades, if this is necessary.

Some drums ride on bearings at the back of the drum and around the opening to the dryer. Lint can build up around these bearings or in tracks in which the drum bearings or rollers ride. Clean out this lint.

A frayed or cracked V-belt can cause lots of noise. Check this belt for wear and replace it, if it is needed, by loosening the bolts that hold the motor to its mounting bracket. Then move the motor forward to remove the belt. Another method is to cut the belt in half. Replace the new belt on the pulleys, reposition the motor, and tighten the bolts.

Keep the dryer level. If the feet are not adjustable for leveling, place the level on top of the dryer and hammer cedar shingle shims under the "feet".

CLOTHES WASHERS

Where there's water, there are leaks and corrosion. And most problems with clothes washers are water problems.

It's a smart idea to check washer hoses every month or so to make sure that they are not cracked or leaking — especially around connections and where the hoses are bent to fit against a laundry room wall. Also, periodically turn off the water at the faucets, unscrew the hoses, and check the screens in the hoses for sediment.

Sediment from the water supply can cause all kinds of trouble, mostly blockage of supply lines. You can clean the screens with a stiff brush, or replace the screens if they are broken, badly worn or bent.

A washing machine is a big investment. Here is advice on handling common problems yourself, but also on when to call in help.

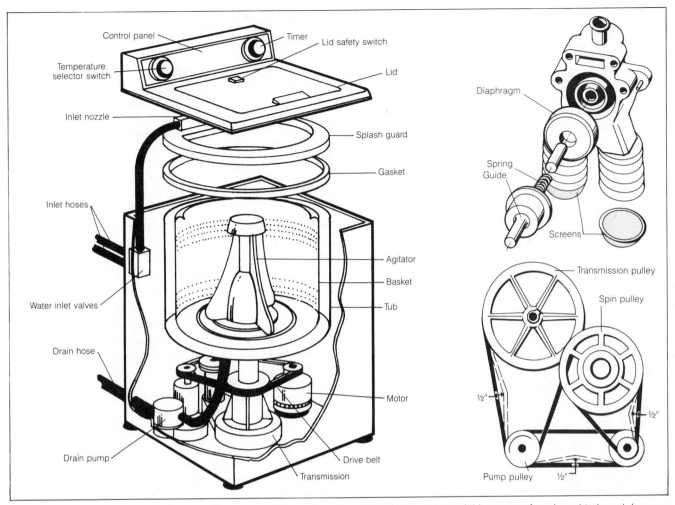

Shown here are the basic components of a washing machine, although configurations and special items vary from brand to brand. In some models a one-piece tubing replaces the gasket and splash guard. The water valve lets the water into the tub. It usually has two inlets: one connects to hotwater faucet via a hose; the other runs to a coldwater faucet. The usual problem with the water valves is clogged screens, which are easily taken out and replaced. Belts connect the motor and transmittion. The latter drives the agitator, whose oscillational rate depends upon the gears, the pulley size, and the motor speed.

Washer Won't Fill with Water

Tools and materials. Pliers, screwdriver, brush.

STEPS

The trouble can be one or a series of malfunctions. Follow the procedures below, in order.

1. Open the water valves fully.

2. Turn off the valves. Remove the hoses from the valves; you may need pliers to break the connections. Clean any sediment from the water supply screens with a brush.

3. Remove the back from the washer. It is held by four, six, or more screws. Now check the inlet hoses to make sure they are not kinked.

4. If the washer is getting water as far as the inlet hose connections, the problem probably is in the water valve or water valve solenoid. This is a job for a service person.

Water Won't Discharge from Washer

Tools and materials. Screwdriver, pliers.

STEPS

Make sure the timer on the control panel is properly set and that the timer has gone through the complete cycle.

Inspect the discharge hose for any blockage within the hose or kinks or severe bends in the hose.

Turn off the power and water. Remove the back panel of the washer. Check the wires leading to the impeller and the water pump motor. These wires could have vibrated loose from connections, or the wires could be burned out.

The trouble could also be a worn impeller, stuck wash and spin timers, or a malfunctioning motor — all problems for a professional.

Water Leaks

Tools and materials. Screwdriver, pliers, new hoses and gaskets.

STEPS

Find the leak. It probably will be in a hose connection, around the tub seals, at the drain valve, pump assembly, or water supply valves.

With pliers, tighten all clamps to stop leaks. If a leaking gasket is the problem, try tightening the connection with a screwdriver or pliers to stop the leak. If you can't, you'll have to replace the gasket.

Tub seals may be replaced by removing a retaining ring held by screws. Or, the seals may be held with adhesive. Leaking

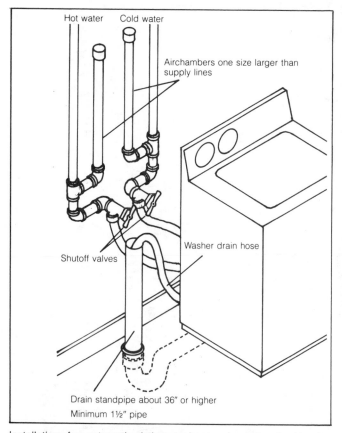

Hot water   Cold water

Airchambers one size larger than supply lines

Shutoff valves

Washer drain hose

Drain standpipe about 36" or higher
Minimum 1½" pipe

Installation of an automatic clothes washer requires hot and cold water supply lines at least ½ in. in size, along with a standpipe that should be a minimum of 1½ in. Air chambers should be on both hot and cold water lines because solenoid valves in washer shut off water so quickly that water hammer is a problem.

parts, such as impellers, pumps, and drains, should be replaced — not repaired — as a general rule.

Agitator Doesn't Agitate

Tools and materials. Screwdriver, adjustable wrench, pliers.

STEPS

The problem here probably is a defective timer or water level pressure switch. Replacement is a job for a professional. But, before you make a phone call, check these points: (1) turn off the power and water; (2) remove the back from the washer; (3) check the drive belt from the motor to the agitator to see if the belt is loose. Tighten it by loosening the mounting brackets on the motor, moving the motor backward until the belt is tight, and retightening the bolts in the brackets. If the drive belt is broken, you will have to replace it.

Check the transmission. First, set the washer in the "Wash" mode on the control panel. Then remove the drive belt from the motor. By hand, turn the agitator pulley clockwise. If the agitator is not moved by this action, the transmission probably has to be replaced.

Washer Drains between Cycles

STEPS

Reposition the drainage hose from the washer so the hose is higher than the water level in the washer.

No-Spin Problems

Tools and materials. Screwdriver, pliers, adjustable wrench, new V belt.

STEPS

A defective timer probably is to blame if the washer doesn't spin properly. But check out these possibilities, too, before you call a repair person.

1. Are you using too much detergent? The buildup of detergent can cause the machine to balk.

2. Are the controls set to "spin"?

3. Is the lid of the machine tightly closed?

4. Turn off the power and water. Remove the back panel of the washer.

Check the drive belt for wear or slippage. If worn, replace the belt. If slipping, tighten the belt. Procedures for both are outlined above.

5. The machine may have a worn clutch. Set the control knob in the "Spin" mode. Now remove the drive belt and turn the clutch unit by hand. The unit should turn fairly freely. If not, the clutch may have to be replaced by a professional. Some clutches (disc type) can be adjusted if loose. Try turning a nut located on the clutch plate, or a nut on the clutch shaft, after you determine from a dealer or service manual whether the clutch is adjustable.

DISHWASHERS

Dishwashers are of two basic types: built-in and portable, although the latter may be designed to be built-in if the situation warrants it at a later date.

No plumbing is required for a portable, as the hot water supply is provided by snapping a flexible line onto a special fitting that replaces the aerator, and the drain is simply dropped into the sink. A built-in dishwasher requires a drain and a hot water supply line; no cold water is used. An electric connection also is required, which powers the motor that rotates the spray impellers, the water pump (if one is used) and the solenoid valves that open and close the drain and turn the hot water on and off. The circuit must be a grounded one, as we again are dealing with an appliance that uses water and presents a hazard if there were to be any kind of an electrical short circuit.

If a dishwasher does not seem to be washing properly, the first thing to do is to check for any clogged filters, such as the one around the drain. If there is a water leak around the door, this indicates the need for a new gasket. Get the model number of the machine and purchase a new one from a dealer who handles that brand, or from one of the supply houses that sell appliance parts to do-it-yourselfers.

If the machine will not run at all, check the fuse or circuit breaker. If you install a new fuse and it blows immediately, or the circuit breaker immediately kicks out, call a serviceman; you have a real problem.

Timer switches often cause a dishwasher to malfunction. This switch turns the water on and off for the various cycles, tells the impellers when to turn, and the drain when to open and close. If the dishwasher stays in one cycle, or goes through just a couple and then stops, it is probably the timer that is causing the problem. Replacement of this part is fairly easy. First check the make and model and buy a replacement. Next, remove the front panel and find the switch. Because the timer has a number

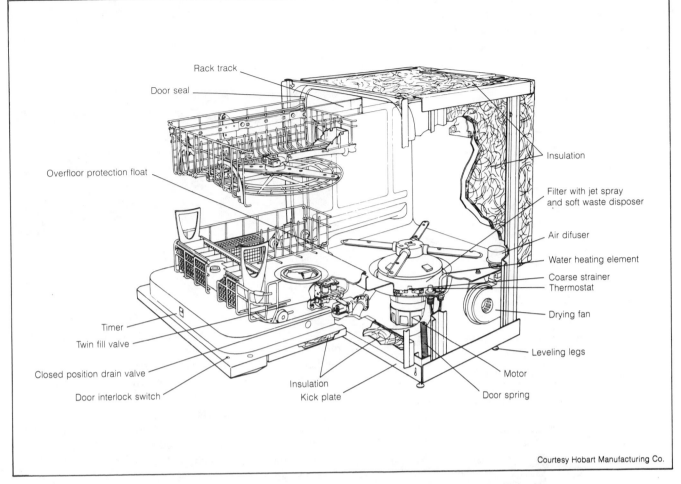

Rack track
Door seal
Overfloor protection float
Timer
Twin fill valve
Closed position drain valve
Door interlock switch
Insulation
Kick plate
Door spring
Motor
Leveling legs
Drying fan
Thermostat
Coarse strainer
Water heating element
Air difuser
Filter with jet spray and soft waste disposer
Insulation

Courtesy Hobart Manufacturing Co.

of wires connected to it, tag each one and make a sketch of the switch so you can be sure of making the proper connections on the new one.

If the timer switch does not solve the problem, or if there is more than one problem, it is best to call a serviceman. This is especially true if the water does not seem hot enough, or if the dishes will not dry properly. There is a heater in some dishwashers that heats the water to 160 degrees or so, and also

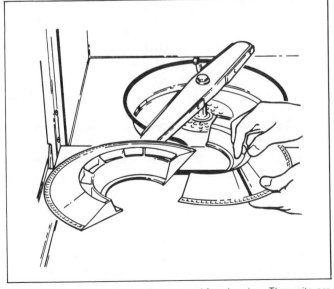

Clogged strainers can be easily removed for cleaning. The units are usually plastic or metal; to clean, just run under the tap and rinse well.

Diagnosing Dishwasher Problems

Problem	Possible Cause/Solution
Won't start	Close door tightly; engage door lock, which is the power switch; check for a blown fuse or tripped circuit breaker; check for bad contact between latch points (solution: replace the switch — there are only a few screws holding it in position).
Noise	Check motor for vibration (tighten mounting bolts); machine needs rubber pad mounting under base; check to see if impeller is rubbing against screen (adjust).
Leaks	Door isn't closed properly; seal around door is damaged (replace) or needs reseating (adjust screws).
Won't fill	Inlet valve is clogged or faulty; water pressure is low (test sink or lavatory faucets for pressure). If the problem persists, call the city water department for help.
Water drains too fast from the tank	The drain valve may be leaking. Tighten the flange on the valve. Inlet valve is faulty (replace).
Slow drain	Check filter; check hoses if a portable (replace); bad drain valve. Call a professional.
Dirty dishes	Preclean dishes; poor loading; wrong detergent; water not hot enough; clogged strainer; faulty timer; low water pressure; bad solenoid coil; (call a professional).
Dishes won't dry	Adjust water temperature to 150 degrees; bad inlet valve; heating unit is not functioning (call a professional).

provides heat for drying. A serviceman can quickly tell if this heater is not working. Replacing it requires a rather complete disassembly of the dishwasher, and is a project not recommended for the do-it-yourself homeowner.

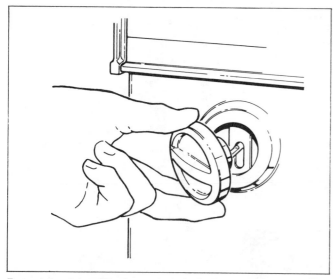

To reach the dishwasher timer switch, the front panel must be removed. The first step is to pull off the control knob. Make sure it does not have a setscrew that must be loosened.

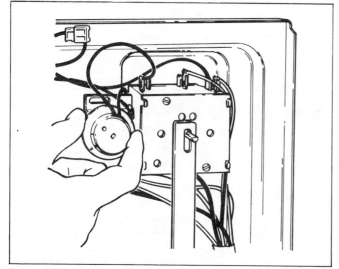

Before you touch the timer, unplug the dishwasher. Place the wires from the old switch, one by one, onto the new one to avoid making wrong connections.

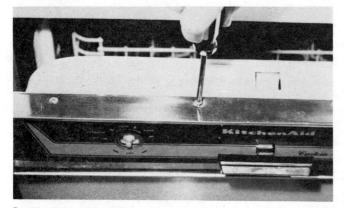

On this dishwasher the door is opened and the screws are removed from upper edge to remove the front panel. There are also screws on the edges of the door that must be removed.

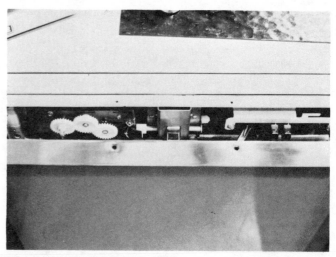

The panel is shown tipped back (but not removed) to reveal switches and components that can be removed and replaced.

GARBAGE DISPOSALS

At one time garbage disposals were a very popular kitchen plumbing item. In recent years they have somewhat fallen out of favor and, in some localities, are even forbidden by local plumbing codes or laws. The problem is that the disposals discharge garbage into the sewer system, overloading it if it happens to be marginal—and many are.

Disposals work on the principle that any garbage from the kitchen that can be pulverized by a whirling set of steel blades and mixed with water can be flushed down the drain. There have been disposals that claimed to be able to even grind bones. Perhaps they could, but the resulting heavy slurry certainly did not help the sewer system.

If your city or locality has an up-to-date sewer system, disposals are probably allowed. Installing one is not too difficult. Most disposals come with a special drain fitting to replace the existing one. The disposal is suspended from the fitting by bolts that hold it up under the sink against a shock-absorbing collar of some kind that minimizes the vibration and noise of the disposal.

Some types of disposal are fastened with a large rubber sleeve that provides the shock absorbing action. Stainless steel clamps on the sleeve hold the disposal at one end, the sink drain at the other.

Water should always be run into a disposal when it is being used. The water lubricates the blades that pulverize the garbage, flushes the garbage down the drain and cools the electric motor. The water should be allowed to run even after all the garbage has passed through the disposal, to assure that it will be flushed through the drains of the house and out into the street drain. A disposal should be fitted with a heavy cord and plug and fitted into a grounded receptacle. Any appliance that uses water should be grounded, because of the very real possibility of a short circuit.

Also, because the drain line from a disposal carries a heavy slurry of pulverized garbage, it is a good idea to have a separate drain from it to the main vertical drain, rather than running into the sink drain. Because the slurry of garbage tends to stick to the inside of the drain line and hold moisture, the drain from the disposal to the main drain tends to rust or corrode much more quickly than the drain from the sink. It is a good idea to remove the drain line of a disposal every couple of years and clean it out. It is a messy job, but it will assure a longer life for the drain line. It will be necessary to replace the gaskets in the slip joints when you disassemble the drain, and some of the slip nuts may have deteriorated and also require replacement.

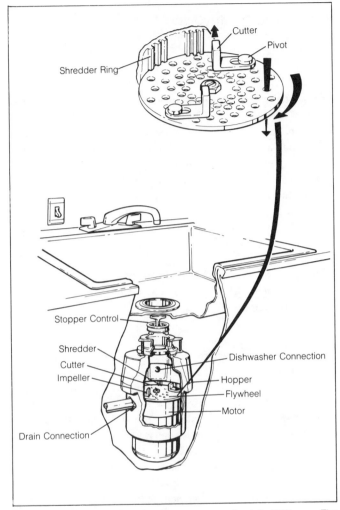

The garbage disposal flywheel spins at approximately 1725 rmp. The centrifugal force created by the disc forces the food against the walls of the disposal, where it hits the shredder ring.

Diagnosing Disposer Problems

Problem	Possible Cause/Solution
Stuck grinding wheel	Use a clothespin or broom handle to pry it free (do not throw bones in disposer); lots of water to flush food debris down the drain. Flick switch quickly to try to jolt it out.
Water leaks	Remove top flange and reset it in plumber's putty. Check drain hose connection for tightness.
Slow drainage	Keep grinder operating longer to flush food waste; drain line is clogged (use plumber's snake to clear it); increase slope of drain hose to kitchen drain pipe.
Vibration	Loosen mounting bolts slightly.
Noise	Loosen mounting bolts slightly.
Won't start	Press reset button on housing; check fuses, circuit breaker to make sure power is on.
Humming noise	Stuck grinding wheel; motor may be burned out (call professional). Loose terminal connections (tighten with a screwdriver after you turn off power).

DOORBELL MAINTENANCE AND REPAIR

A doorbell looks like a complicated mechanical/electrical device, but it isn't. The power to a door bell is usually 24 volts; the power comes through a transformer that is connected to a regular housepower circuit.

Ring Button Repair

Tools and materials. Screwdriver, knife.

STEPS

If the bell won't ring, remove the ring button escutcheon plate. It is held by two screws, or it may be a push fit to the button housing. You'll have to pry up on the corners of the plate to remove it. If the joint is painted over, try to break the paint seal with a knife or razor knife.

Carefully disconnect the wires to the ring button. Chances are the wires are corroded and simply need the corrosion removed with a knife blade in order to work.

Reconnect the wires to the button and push the button. If the bell doesn't ring, disconnect the wires again and touch the wires together. If the bell rings, the button is faulty and should be replaced. If the bell doesn't ring, the problem is somewhere else in the system.

Chime and Buzzer Repair/Replacement

Tools and materials. Knife, pliers, screwdriver.

STEPS

If the push button is working properly (see above) and the buzzer or chimes won't work, try cleaning the wires and terminal posts that connect to the buzzer or chimes. Disconnect one

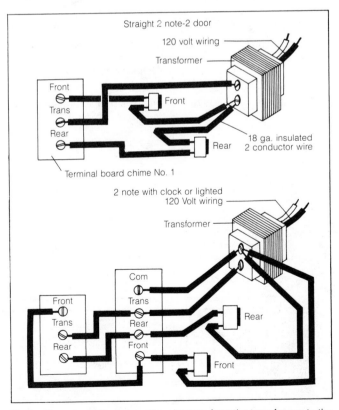

These diagrams indicate how the wires run from the transformer to the bell, chime, or buzzer, and how they then connect to several configurations or numbers of entryways.

wire at a time, clean it, and replace it — or turn off the power and disconnect and clean the wires and terminals at the same time.

Now try the system. If it still doesn't work, make sure that the clapper for the chimes is positioned properly. You can adjust it with a screwdriver and/or pliers. Also clean the clapper and clapper rods.

If the system utilizes a buzzer and the buzzer doesn't work after testing the buttons and transformer, replace the buzzer.

Transformer Replacement/Repair

Tools and materials. Screwdriver, knife, pliers.

STEPS

Turn off the power at the main power entrance.

Remove the wires from the transformer box and clean the wires and the terminals. Reconnect the wires to the transformer and turn on the power. Test the bell.

If the bell doesn't work, the transformer probably has to be replaced. Turn off the power. Disconnect the wires. Remove the transformer from its mounting, and take the transformer to the store for a replacement part. Then hook up the new transformer.

If the bell still doesn't work, the problem is in the wiring between the transformer and the bell or buzzer. You'll have to trace this wiring and replace it.

Diagnosing Garage Door-Opener Problems

Problem	Possible cause/solution
Door won't open	No power to automatic opener; weak batteries in remote control; burned-out switch; drive belt broken or slipping; clutch plate not tight; door connector broken or disconnected.
Door opens slowly	Clutch plate is slipping; pulley on motor is slipping; belt is slipping; door rollers need lubrication or realignment; loose connecting arm.
Door binds	Adjust opening/closing screw; tighten the automatic reverse so spring has ½-in. gap between coils; track assembly out of alignment; header bracket loose or out of adjustment; door out of balance.
Power off; door closed	Remove the connecting arm on the door and open the door. Or pull emergency release chain near front end of track.

LAWNMOWER REPAIR

When a gasoline-powered lawnmower will not run, or run properly, the owner will do one of two things: kick the lawnmower, or junk the lawnmower and buy a new one. The problem, however, may be easy to correct.

How to Clean a Dirty Filter

Tools and materials. Screwdriver, water, household detergent, bucket, light machine oil.

STEPS

Remove the metal plate that covers the filter. It is located near the spin-starter handle and is held by a single bolt that is slotted for a screwdriver.

Pull out the filter. It will look like a rectangle of sponge rubber. Cover the filter with household detergent and wash it clean in the water. Rinse and squeeze the filter dry.

Give the filter a couple of drops of light machine oil and replace it in the metal filter housing. Replace the cover. Filters should be cleaned at least twice during the lawnmowing season.

Changing Points and Condensers

Tools and materials. New point and condenser kit, fly wheel puller, screwdriver, pliers, adjustable wrench.

STEPS

If the lawnmower spark from the plug wire to the sparkplug is "hot" enough, you won't have to monkey with the points and condensers in the lawnmower. Test this by holding the sparkplug wire a short distance from the top of the sparkplug. Then pull the starter cord very slowly. You will see a spark jump from the sparkplug wire to the sparkplug.

If you don't see this spark (or feel it), you probably need to change the points and condenser.

Remove the wire from the sparkplug.

With a screwdriver and wrench, remove the pull cord assembly and the wire cage unit that covers the flywheel on top of the engine.

Remove the nut that holds the flywheel to the crankshaft of the engine. You may need a wheel puller for this, if you can't pry up the wheel with a pry bar or heavy-bladed screwdriver. Don't force the flywheel or you will crack it. It should be removed straight up from the shaft.

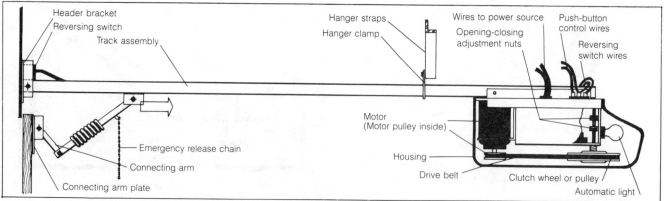

This is a simplified anatomy of an electric garage door opener. Check the track for level annually, and make sure the track assembly is kept lubricated according to your manufacturer's directions.

Once the flywheel is removed, you will see the tiny condenser and points. Remove these with a screwdriver and/or pliers, and replace the parts with new ones. (Instructions for replacement are printed on the points/condenser package. They may vary a little from brand to brand; follow these instructions.) Replace the parts in order: flywheel, retaining nut, wire cage; pull cord assembly.

Replacing A Sparkplug

Tools and materials. Lawnmower sparkplug wrench, new sparkplug, pliers, steel wool.

STEPS

Don't try to clean the sparkplug in your lawnmower; replace it annually. The cost is not high.

Disconnect the sparkplug wire. You usually just pull it off the end of the plug, or you may have to unscrew a tiny retaining nut that holds the plug wire to the sparkplug. Clean the end of the wire with steel wool.

Remove the sparkplug. Throw it out. Use a matchbook to set the gap in the new plug — there is a wire that reaches from the side of the plug to its center. The edge of the matchbook cover should slide between this wire and the plug. Use the pliers to make any adjustments.

With the wrench, screw in the new sparkplug and connnect the sparkplug wire to the plug.

Replacing Throttle Controls

Tools and materials. Pliers, screwdriver, adjustable wrench, electrician's or duct tape.

STEPS

Unhook the throttle wire from the speed lever. Then unhook the throttle wire from the retaining plate on the housing of the engine. Loosen a screw to remove this plate. Finally, remove the throttle handle, which is usually bolted to the handle of the lawnmower.

Bend the end of the throttle wire in a slight L-shape. Use the pliers for this, and follow the old wire as a template. Connect this wire to the speed lever and fasten the wire in the engine retaining plate, screwing the plate tight. Connect the throttle handle to the handle of the lawnmower.

Start the engine. Loosen the throttle wire in the retaining plate until the engine performs on command from the throttle (slow, fast, off, start). Then tighten the plate again.

You can secure excess throttle wire to the lawnmower handle with electrician's or duct tape.

Changing Lawnmower Oil

Tools and materials. Pliers, screwdriver, adjustable wrench, 30 SAE motor oil.

STEPS

Tip the lawnmower over. Near the hub where the blade attaches to the engine crankshaft you will see a square-headed plug. Remove this plug with an adjustable wrench. Let the oil drain out of the engine crankcase. You may want to remove the oil filler cap for better air circulation.

When the oil is out, replace the square-headed plug in the bottom of the mower. Then fill the crankcase with new oil through the filler tube. Use 30 SAE motor oil, or oil recommended by the manufacturer of the lawnmower.

Lawnmower oil should be changed before each mowing season. If your lawn is especially dusty during the mowing season, be sure to change oil frequently and to keep the air filter cleaned.

Engine Problems

Tools and materials. Adjustable wrench, new blade.

STEPS

Loss of power, poor idle, engine misses, and other engine problems often can be corrected by turning a small set screw near the engine carburetor.

Turn this screw counterclockwise until the screw is tight. Then turn the screw clockwise about one full turn. Crank up the lawnmower. Keep turning the screw a little more clockwise until the engine runs smoothly and evenly.

To remove the lawnmower air filter, loosen a screw holding a lid on the housing. The housing has a small gasket at the bottom of it. Re-install this gasket when you re-assemble the filter after cleaning the filter.

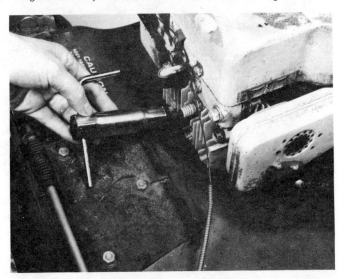

An inexpensive sparkplug wrench is the best way to remove sparkplugs without cracking the engine housing. Or use a regular socket set for this if you own these wrenches.

Tighten engine mounting bolts. Mower vibration usually is great so these bolts loosen frequently. Also make sure that the bolt holding the cutting blade is tight.

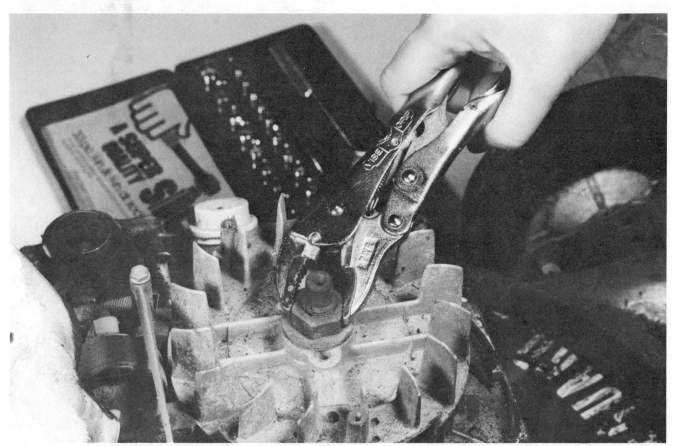

The condensor and points are under the flywheel of most lawnmowers. You may need a wheel puller to get at these parts. Don't pry off the wheel; you can break the metal.

7 Electrical Updates and Repairs

CHECK THE CODES FIRST

Your community undoubtedly has some kind of electrical code that must be followed when repairing, replacing, remodeling, or adding new wiring to your home. At first you may think that these codes are still another governmental restriction on your rights as a homeowner or even a tenant. Not so. Electrical codes are your protection for safe electrical performance and installation of the electrical components you now have, and will be using in your home.

Before you become involved in any electrical project other than a minor repair, be sure you check the codes for your area and follow them to the letter. If a professional is doing the work, make sure he has the permits or license necessary to do the work. You usually will find the electrical codes for your community at the Building Department of your local city or town hall. Otherwise, check with the manager of the store where you buy your electrical supplies.

You should respect electricity, not fear it. With a flick of a finger, you can turn off the electric power in your home, thereby neutralizing the wiring so that it may be repaired, added to, or replaced. There is only one electric rule that you do not break:

Turn off the electricity before you make any repairs to the electrical components of your home.

It is not the purpose of this chapter to teach you how to become a skilled electrical repair person. Instead, the projects detailed here are classified into two categories — minor fix-ups and remodeling — that can save you money without putting you or your home in any danger.

How the Electrical System Works

Electricity comes into your home through a service entrance called a circuit breaker or fuse box. At this point, the power is split into circuits — usually a separate circuit for your washer, dryer, water heater, lights, and so on.

The system is set up so you can turn off the power on individual circuits, or you may turn off the power to all circuits through one or two breakers or fuses. We recommend that you find this electric service entrance right now and test and label the various circuits. You will need a helper to tell you where the power goes off, as you turn off, then on, the various circuits at the main service entrance.

Multiple entrances are sometimes found in older homes and larger homes. Don't overlook these entrances in your identification project.

Turning Off Power; Replacing Fuses

If the floor is wet or damp, there's always an element of danger when you trip a circuit breaker or change a fuse. And since most main electrical service entrances are located in the basement, chances are good that the floor is damp.

You can insulate yourself from any danger by standing on a *dry* length of 1x2-inch board. Have this material handy to the service entrance in the event of emergency. Store it up off the floor in a dry spot.

When you change a fuse, use one hand only to unscrew the old burned-out fuse and screw in the new one. Keep your free hand in a pocket or hold the hand behind you.

Never replace a large amp fuse with a smaller amp fuse.

A circuit breaker has toggle switches that can activate or deactivate circuits throughout the house. When a breaker switch snaps from a power overload, the toggle will indicate the break.

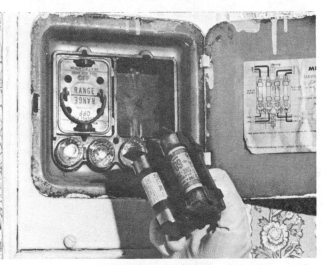

A fuse service entry utilizes plug and cartridge fuses that must be replaced if they blow out. Never put a penny coin behind a fuse to reactivate the fuse; do not use a 20 amp fuse for a 15 amp circuit.

Example: If the correct fuse to use is 20 amps, do not plug in a 15-amp or 30-amp fuse. A fuse protects the circuit against overloads of electricity. Too much power in the circuit can cause continual fuse failure and, in the case of overload, electrical fires. The amp size of the fuse is plainly marked on the face of the fuse. The metal tip on the bottom of the fuse also is stamped with the size of that fuse.

Never place a penny coin in the fuse socket in order to reactivate a blown-out fuse. Always use a new fuse of the proper amperage in the fuse socket. To reactivate a circuit breaker you simply flip a toggle-type switch. One flip usually reactivates a tripped circuit. However, you may have to slip the toggle several times to get it to work. If this is the case, you should have a professional check out the circuit breaker.

Fuse Selection

There are four basic types of fuses.

Plug fuses. These are the glass-collared models and most common type fuses. They simply screw into fuse sockets like light bulbs screw into light sockets. Hold onto the glass collar when you replace this fuse. Do not stick your hand or fingers against or into the socket. When this fuse blows, you will see a dark spot on the face of the fuse.

Time-delay fuses. These fuses look similar to the standard

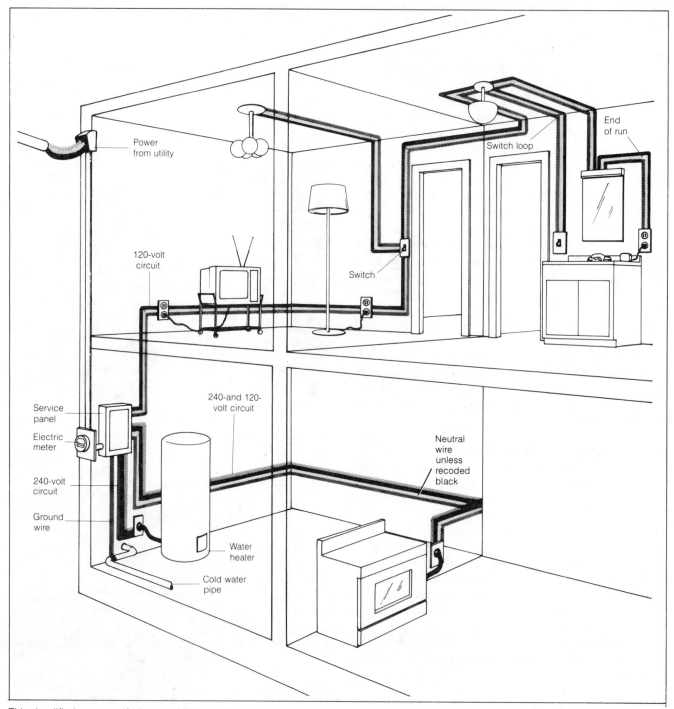

This simplified anatomy of a house wiring system shows how power comes from the utility company into a service panel where it is split into 240- and 120-volt circuits. The service panel is grounded to a cold water pipe; all switches and outlets are grounded to junction boxes. In the box, black wire is "hot"; white wire is "neutral"; the ground wire is either bare, insulated in green, or paper-wrapped.

fuse. The difference is that the fuse strip (inside the fuse) slowly melts when a circuit becomes overloaded. If the overload persists, the strip breaks, which causes the fuse to blow. The face of the fuse will appear burned when the fuse is blown-out. This time delay means that the fuse can handle short-term, sudden overloads without blowing.

Type S fuses. Type S's have an adapter base, so that you can't screw in a larger fuse. Also, the threads are different for different amps to prevent you from accidentally putting a 20-amp fuse in a 30-amp socket. The fuses are also time-delayed. The face of the fuse appears burned when the fuse burns out.

Cartridge fuses. These look like rolls of pennies with fins or copper strips on each end. The fuses are the time-delay type, and are usually used in main circuit panels. You should own special pliers to change these fuses; the pliers are insulated for protection. Since there is no obvious change when the fuse blows, to test which fuse gave out you will have to replace it with a new one.

Wiring Color Codes

Electrical circuits have either a 2-wire or 3-wire system. As a general rule, the black wire is the power wire, the white wire is the neutral wire, and the colored wire (usually green, but it can be another color) is the ground wire.

Wire terminals in switches also are "colored" for connections. The brass-colored screw is for the black or power wire ("black to brass") and the white-colored screw is for the neutral wire. The ground wire may be connected to a junction box or cold water pipe, in the case of an appliance.

Electrical Name-Dropping

When you go to the store to buy electrical components — even light bulbs — you should know the names of the components in order to get what you need. The names are standard and apply to any manufacturer's product.

Voltage. This often is referred to as "volt". The electrical service coming into your home probably is 240 volts. At the main power entrance, this power is split into 120 volt circuits, as well as remaining 240 volt circuits. For example: your water heater and clothes dryer may be on a 240 volt circuit. The circuit may be singular, i.e., one circuit supplies the water heater; another separate circuit supplies the dryer. The switches and wall outlets in your living room probably are on a 120 volt circuit. This splitting distributes power properly. A water heater or clothes dryer takes more power to operate properly than the lights in your living room. Therefore, they have separate circuits.

Watt. This is a measurement of electric power. The best example is the light bulb. A light bulb is marked in watts: 100, 75, 60 watts, and so forth. Therefore, the higher the watts (100 as opposed to 60) the more light (or power). One thousand watts make one kilowatt. The electric company charges you per kilowatt hour of power.

Amp. This is the shortened version of "ampere". An ampere or amp is a unit of electrical current. The more amps an appliance has, the more power the appliance will use.

Current. There are two types of electrical current: *direct current* (DC) and *alternating current* (AC). Your home probably has alternating current, especially if you buy electricity from a utility company. Direct current is power directly from the power source. A good example is a flashlight battery. It provides direct current to the flashlight bulb. If your home is on direct current, it probably is receiving electrical power from a generator/battery source. Alternating current is so named because it alternates in cycles. The cycles usually are preset at 60 cycles per second.

Use a voltage tester to check for power before you start a job. The tester has two metal probes: touch one probe to the hot wire, the other probe to the neutral wire. If power is on, the light will go on. To test for proper grounding, attach one probe to the hot wire and the other to the ground wire. If grounded, the light will come on.

UL. These letters on electrical products stand for *"Underwriters' Laboratory."* The UL organization is not a government agency. UL is a private company whose business is certification. UL certifies that an electrical component performs the job it was designed to do. Some electrical codes specify that electrical products be "UL approved".

New Shockproof Electrical Code: GFCI's

The grounding wires on tools, appliances, and other standard household equipment are *almost* shockproof. At some time, however, the equipment or wires may leak a tiny amount of electrical current. This current could cause injury — especially if the person using the equipment were standing on damp earth or touching a plumbing pipe at the time of contact with the electrical leak.

To prevent this problem, the National Electrical Code now requires that new 15- and 20-amp outdoor receptacles, as well as wiring in bathrooms, have a ground-fault circuit interrupter (GFCI) hookup. With this system, even the smallest current leak will trip a circuit breaker which will instantly shut off the electricity.

The devices are fairly inexpensive. They may be added to a regular entrance service panel, plugged into a receptacle, or substituted for a regular receptacle. The service panel model should be installed by a professional. The other two require little skill for proper installation. GFCI's are available at electrical stores and many home center and hardware outlets. Installation instructions usually are provided with the product.

Switches and Outlets

Wall switches — the type you flip to turn on the lights — and wall outlets — the type you plug a lamp cord or vacuum cleaner into — can wear or burn out over a period of years.

All switches and outlets are fastened with screws to metal junction boxes. The boxes and switches and outlets are covered with a "plate", which is also fastened with screws to the switch, outlet, or junction box. The change or replacement procedure is simply a matter of unscrewing the old and screwing in the new.

There are two types of terminals on switches and outlets. One type has screw terminals to which the power wires are connected. The other type has small holes in the switch or outlet housing. Here, you strip the insulation from the ends of the wire about ½-inch and push the bare wires into the holes so the bare wire is covered.

There are four basic types of toggle switches: single pole; 3-

way; 4-way; double-pole. If the packages are not marked, here's how you can tell the difference in switches. Single-pole switches have terminals on one side of the switch housing. The toggle is marked "on" and "off". Three-way switches have two terminals on one side and one terminal on the other side of the switch housing. The toggle is not marked. Four-way switches have two terminals on each side of the switch housing. The toggle is not marked. Double-pole switches have two terminals on each side of the switch housing. The toggle is marked "on" and "off".

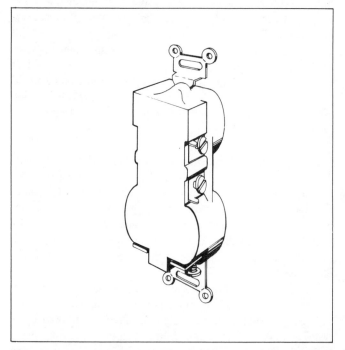

With a screw terminal, attach black or red wires to the 2 brass-colored terminals screws, and white wires to the 2 silver-colored terminals. The ground will attach to the green screw at the bottom.

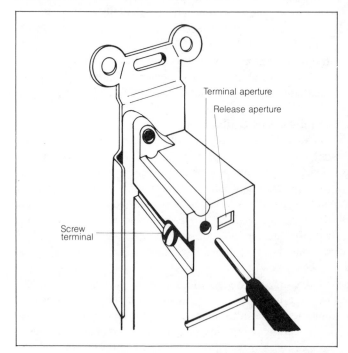

A push-in, back-wired receptacle has push-button release for disconnecting wires. A green terminal screw will be found at the bottom. Some of these receptacles also have screw terminals on the side.

Some switches are specially engineered to make wiring easier. The terminals may be on the side, end, front, or back of the switch housing.

Most switches are marked for power capacity. Volt and amp readings, type of current, type of wire, and the UL approval will usually be stamped on the front of the switch on the metal mounting bracket. The information may instead be stamped on the housing. A typical reading will be: "UL' or "UND LAB.INC. LIST"; "15 A-120V" means the switch may be used for 15 amp circuits up to 120 volts; "AC ONLY" means the switch may be used only for alternating current; "CO" means the switch may be connected with copper wire.

The same types of terminals and information are included on outlets or receptacles.

HOW TO CHOOSE AND HANDLE WIRE

Although you will seldom need electrical wire for repair projects, it's good to know some wire terminology for the sake of discussion in home center and electrical store outlets. Today, most wire is sold in boxes and packages, so the information you need to know for each specific product will be stamped on the package.

Some lamp and extension cord wire is sold by the lineal foot; it is stocked in stores on large metal spools. You measure out the amount you need and cut it off. There are two types of extension cord and appliance wire: heavy- and light-duty. As a rule of thumb, you should use the light-duty type for lamps and heavier wire for appliances, especially for motor-driven appliances.

There are different sizes of electrical wires and the sizes are numbered. The larger the wire is in diameter, the smaller will be the number designating the wire.

Most standard house wiring is No. 14 or No. 12 wire. You should never use any wire smaller than No. 14 for your repair project. For heavier power demands, use No. 12, 10, or 8 wire. This wire usually requires a 30-amp fuse, while No. 14 wire requires a 15-amp fuse. You can sometimes use fuse size to determine wire size.

Always use rubber- or plastic-insulated wire for repairs or wire replacement in damp areas, always use asbestos-insulated wire (or its equivalent) for heater wiring, such as replacement cords for irons.

Most wire information is stamped on the wire insulation. This data includes wire capacity and use. For example, the stamp may read "14 Type TW 600 volts UL." Translated, this means that the wire is No. 14 size wire; the wire is suitable for use (TW) outdoors or in a damp basement; it will handle an electrical load up to 600 volts, and it is certified by Underwriter's Laboratories to be everything the stamp says it is. If the stamp includes a "T" it means the wire may be used under a wide range of temperature variations. "TW" means that the wire may be used in damp conditions. Type "NM" wire is for indoor use where dampness is not present. Type "NMC" wire may be used in indoor locations that are damp and outdoors where the wire will be above ground. Type UF wire may be used underground.

On packages of wiring, two names will appear frequently: "BX" and "Romex". BX is wire that is sheathed in a metal casing. The casing is linked together in a series of "rings",

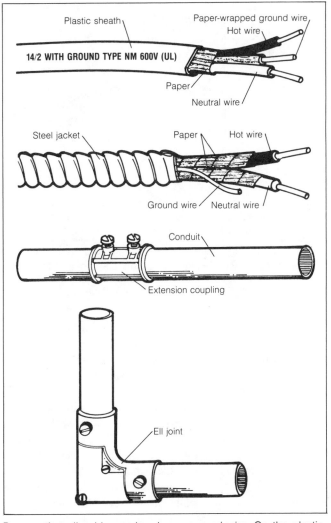

Be sure that all cable you buy has a ground wire. On the plastic-sheathed cable, markings (from right to left) indicate whether or not the cable has a ground wire, wire size, no. of conductors, and the type of cable. The steel-encased cable is recommended for areas where wires need more protection — such as within a wall where nails may penetrate. Conduit found within a home is usually thin-walled; lengths are joined with connectors.

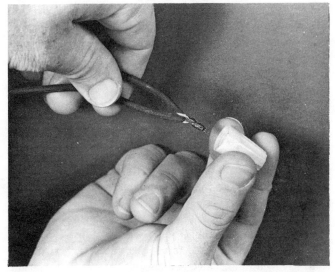

Wire nut connectors are plastic caps lined with threaded metal. Twist the splice tightly together, install the wire nut over the wires and twist the nut.

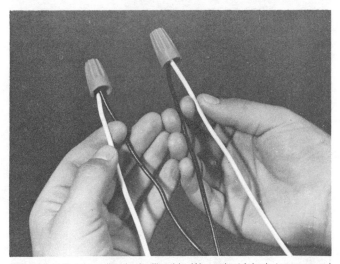

A finished wire nut splice looks like this. Wrap electrician's tape around the nut/cable juncture to prevent the nut from jarring loose. Recode white wires black with tape because this splice makes it "hot".

permitting the wire to flex so it can go around corners and in back of wall coverings with a minimum of effort on your part. You can use BX wire inside where there is no moisture problem (codes permitting).

Romex does not have a metal jacket. The sheath in which the wires are encased is a plastic material. Romex is extremely flexible so you may install it up, over, under or around nearly any obstruction. The type of sheathing (stamped on the insulation) determines where and for what temperatures the wire may be used: underground, interior, or exterior.

Splicing and Cutting Wire

Tools and materials. Wire cutters, long nose pliers, wire strippers, wire nuts, electrician's tape.

STEPS

Wire should never be spliced between junction boxes. You can splice wire inside a junction box, but the splice must be made with wire nuts and electrician's tape. The old way of splicing wire — wrapping one wire around another wire and covering

the splice with just electrician's tape — is no longer permitted by many codes, because this type of splice is very dangerous. It can cause an electrical fire.

Here is how to splice wire.

1. Cut the wire to length with wire cutters.

2. Strip away the insulation with a wire stripping tool. Do not use a knife, except to split cable sheathing.

3. If the wires are solid, remove 1 in. of insulation from the wires. Hold the stripped ends together, side-by-side. With pliers, twist the ends tightly together.

4. Screw a wire nut onto the bare joined ends of the wire.

5. Wrap the wire nut and the insulation below the nut with electrician's tape. Give the splice several wraps, so the splice won't pull apart or bare wire become exposed.

6. If the wires are stranded (many strands), strip off 1 in. of insulation on both wires. Twist the strands tight with your fingers. Hold the wires together — parallel. Then twist the wires together tightly; fold approximately half the splice over. Now screw on a wire nut and secure the nut with electrician's tape.

7. To join a stranded wire to a solid wire, strip off about 1 in. of insulation from the solid wire and about 2 in. of insulation from the stranded wire. Twist the stranded wire with your fingers to make the wire as "solid" or tight as you can. Starting at the base of the solid wire, wrap the stranded wire up the solid wire in a spiral fashion. Then bend over half of the splice with pliers. Screw on a wire nut and wrap the nut and wires with electrician's tape.

BX cable. To cut, use a hacksaw, running the saw blade diagonally across one of the steel "rings" about 6 in. in back of the wires encased inside the cable. Be careful not to cut the wires with the hacksaw; just saw through the top layer of steel. Once the initial cut has been made, take pliers and break up the steel layer, pulling the steel apart. The cut end will be sharp, so watch your fingers. You can buy a plasticlike insulator sleeve that slides inside the cable to cap the wire. This provides a "finished" end to the cable and also insulates the wires at the cut end.

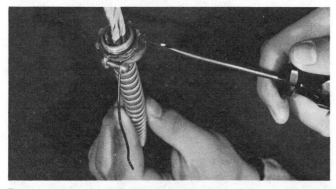

For a two-piece clamp, first expose at least 6 in. of the wires. You may later cut the wire (not cable) to fit after you have inserted cable into the box. Slip clamp on flush to the end of the sheathing, and tighten clamp screws.

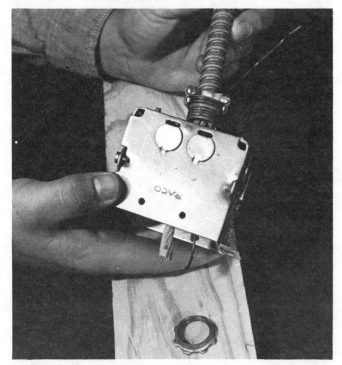

Insert the end of the sheathing through the knockout hole. Slip the metal ring (connector nut at bottom of box) over the wires. Screw the nut on and attach the box. Tighten the nut; tap a nail set with a hammer to turn the nut.

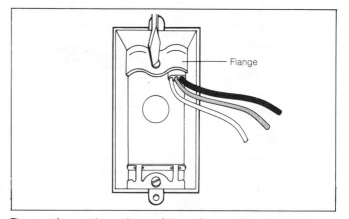

The most frequently used type of clamp for attaching metal cable to a junction box installs inside the box and has extra metal loops. For use with plastic-sheathed cable, use metal snips to cut off the metal strips that hold the loops. Loosely screw the top piece of the clamp inside the box near the knockout. Remove sheathing; strip ends of wires; pull cable in through the knockout hole and under the clamp. The clamp rests on the uncut end of the sheath. Screw clamp tightly against cable; attach box to the wall.

Plastic-insulated cable. One such cable is Romex. To cut, use wire strippers to make the initial cut, squeezing the handles just hard enough to slice the outer layer of insulation. With a razor knife, split the insulation lengthwise until it meets the cut made by the wire strippers.

Peel off the inner insulation, exposing the wires inside the cable. You can cut the excess inner insulation with a knife.

Conduit. To cut, use a hacksaw. Make sure the conduit is held tightly while the cut is made. Smooth the cut end of the conduit, if necessary, with a metal file. Conduit may be bent with an electrician's hickey. You can rent a hickey or, if you have a lot of conduit bending to do, consider buying one.

Wire. To cut, use wire strippers which have a built-in wire cutter, or regular wire cutters. No. 9, 10, 12, and 14 wire is solid, single strand wire. No. 0, 1, 2, 4, 6 wire is stranded. Wire above No. 14, also may be stranded. The strands are extremely fine.

Terminal connections. To make them, loop the wire with long nosed pliers to fit around the screw terminal. If the wire is stranded, first twist the strands tightly with your fingers. Wrap the wire (or hook it) around the screw terminal in the direction the screw will be tightened — usually clockwise.

Grounding Principles

A ground wire channels current to earth. A green jumper connects this bare copper wire in the cable to the ground terminal on the box's metal mounting strap. The mounting strap is in contact with the box via its screws, and also via the screw for the metal cover plate. A 3-prong plug inserted into the receptacle contacts the mounting strap, grounding the device being plugged in. The ground terminal on the box itself also is connected to the cable's ground wire by a second jumper wire. A ground wire usually clamps to a buried 10 ft. (or longer) water pipe but if you do not have access to one then use a steel or copper rod driven 8 ft. minimum into the earth. If the earth is too dry to offer an effective path for current, use two rods. Have an electrician occasionally check this ground system; the soil can become too dry, increasing resistance of the circuit through the earth.

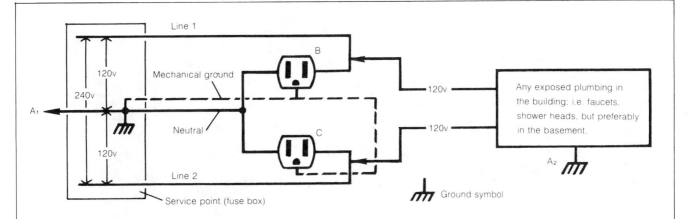

GROUNDING BASICS

Point A connects to a metal rod driven into the earth at the service entrance to the building or to a water pipe in older buildings. The earth, or water pipes which are also underground before they enter the building, will conduct electrical current. Points A and A₂ are common. A human being connected between "B" or "C" to any exposed plumbing will close a circuit and can receive an electrical shock. A human being can be connected to points B or C in several ways. For example:

1 If an appliance with exposed metal also has a 2-wire plug that is defective. Point B or C is making contact with the exposed metal surface; if a person touches the exposed metal he is subject to a shock.

2 The same as above, but with a 3-wire plug using a 3-to-2-wire adapter when the ground wire has been left unconnected.

3 Many cable model radios may have one side of the 2-wire plug connected to the metal chassis. Never place an item like this within reach of any plumbing (if you want to stay alive). Here is a scenario: While standing in the shower, you reach out to change the station on the radio. In the case given, when one side of the 2-wire plug is connected to the metal chassis, you can receive an electrical shock and be unable to release your grasp on the radio. This type of shock would probably be fatal.

What is an electrical shock? Shocks are caused by current flowing through the human body. A fraction of one ampere (a measure of the amount of current) can kill you. If you are not kicked free by the initial shock, your muscles may contract and cause your hand to freeze around the appliance or conductor which you are touching — someone else would have to free you by using an insulated object (such as a wooden chair or a newspaper) to push you away or by turning off the current. These are the reasons why the integrity of the mechanical ground must be carried through to any device that has exposed metal. The third wire mechanical ground is internally hard-wired to the exposed metal of the appliance. In this way, if points B or C come in contact with the exposed surface, a fuse will blow, or sparks will fly. It must be emphasized that by lifting the mechanical ground with three-prong to two prong adapters, the shock protection of the mechanical ground is also suspended.

Adapter safety. When discussing adapters, many owners' manuals, books, and references, indicate that you can use a two-prong adapter if you connect its third wire or metal tab to the center screw which holds the faceplate to the wall outlet box. The center screw that holds the faceplate on an outlet receptacle is NOT ALWAYS grounded. Yet these publications advise connecting the pig-tail ground lead from the adapter to this screw to ground it. Since the nut for this screw in 2-wire outlets is embedded in the plastic of the receptacle and is not connected to anything, proper connection will require you to remove the faceplate and to check for a ground wire. Then secure the adapter's ground wire under the screw that secures the outlet to the metal box. If the metal box is properly grounded, the adapter's ground will then serve its purpose.

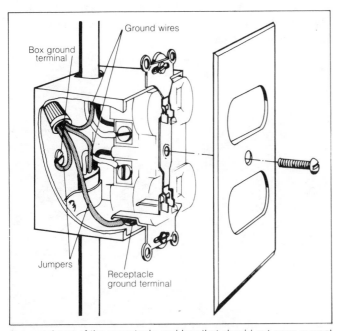

Any metal part of the receptacle and box that should not carry current but which might during a malfunction, is given an emergency route to a ground through the cable's bare copper wire.

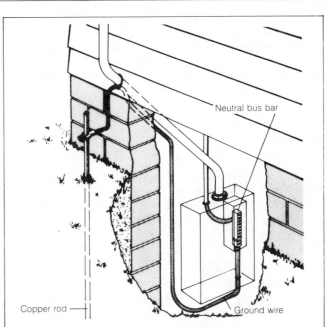

If you do not have access to a buried water pipe 10 ft. or longer, connect ground system to earth by a steel or copper rod driven a min. of 8 ft. into earth.

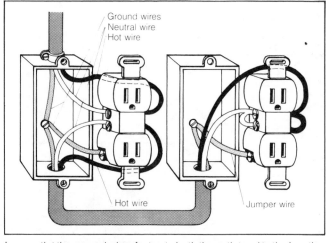

In an outlet the ground wires fasten to both the outlet and to the junction box. This gives a continuous ground throughout the electrical system. At right is an "end of the line" outlet; at left is a line in the middle of the run.

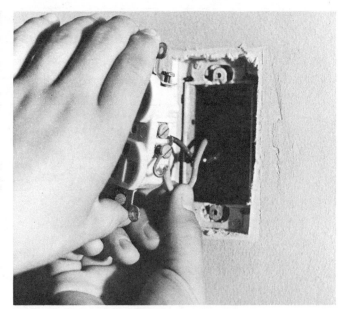

To change an outlet or switch: turn off the power to this area, then remove the cover plate and screws holding the switch or outlet to the junction box. Pull out the switch or outlet; extend the wires.

What Size Extension Cord

You can compare electrical wire with plumbing pipe. For example, the larger the pipe, the more water the pipe can carry. The same applies to electrical wire: the larger the wire, the more electricity it can carry.

Most household extension cords are No. 14, or even No. 16, wire. If the extension cord will power a light, this wire size is usually adequate. However, the cord is not adequate to carry power to a portable electric tool such as a circular saw or electric lawnmower. When you buy an extension cord, match it to the work you want it to do. Never use a lightweight extension cord to power heavy equipment. Hint: the longer the extension cord, the larger the wire.

Aluminum Wire

Your home may be wired with aluminum wire instead of copper wire. If so, you must buy fixtures and electrical parts designed for aluminum wire. These parts are so stamped: "CO/ALR."

Since aluminum wiring expands and contracts as it gets hot and cools, the wire can loosen from terminal screws and other connections. You should check these connections annually for tightness. But turn off the electricity before you make the inspection.

REPAIRS

In each case the first step is to **turn off the electricity.**

Replacing a Wall Switch

Tools and materials. Razor knife with a new blade, screwdriver, long nose pliers, new switch.

STEPS

If the switch or cover plate has been painted, you'll probably have to take a razor knife and cut the paint seal around the plate. Otherwise, prying off the plate can rip the wallcovering around the switch. Use the tip of the razor knife to remove any paint from the screw slots that hold the plate to the switch or mounting bracket.

With a screwdriver, remove the switch plate. Then back out

the screws that hold the switch to the junction box. Pull out the switch to extend the wires and to expose the wires for easier handling.

Here you may see several wires: hot, neutral, and ground wires. The only wires that you have to be concerned with are the ones attached to the switch. Don't tinker with the other wires. Remove the wires attached to the switch from the terminals by unscrewing the terminals and bending the wire loops straight with the long nose pliers.

Back out the screw terminals on the new switch; don't remove these screws. Just loosen them enough for the wire to go around the screws.

Reloop the ends of the wire, using the long nose pliers. Then hook the loops around the screw terminals so the ends of the wires face the direction in which the screw terminals tighten. By doing this, the wire will tighten against the terminals when the screws are tightened.

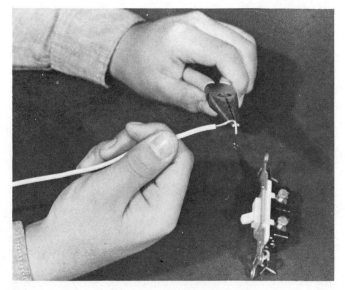

Strip about ½ in. of the insulation off the wires. Bend the end of the wire so that it will hook around the screw terminals of the switch or outlet.

If the terminals in the switch are the push-in, pull-out type, use the tip of the screwdriver to release the wire. The screwdriver is inserted into a release aperture, located next to the terminal aperture. As you press down in the aperture, pull out the wire. The tip of the screwdriver releases a spring, which holds the wire inside the switch.

To hook up the push-in terminal switch, stick the bare end of the wire into the holes from which you released the wire. The wire should be exposed about ½-in. Then carefully fold the wires back into the junction box as you position the new switch in the box. The metal mounting bracket has top and bottom slots through which the mounting screws are inserted. The bracket is slotted so you can vertically align the switch in the junction box, which often is not square with the wall.

On the mounting screws you will find two fiberlike nuts. These are called "plaster" ears and they are used to square and align the switch in the junction box, if you need them for this purpose. If you don't need them, throw them out.

Place the wire on the screw terminals in the direction the screw turns — clockwise. This tightens the wire against the terminal as the screw is turned. Twist stranded wire tight before looping it.

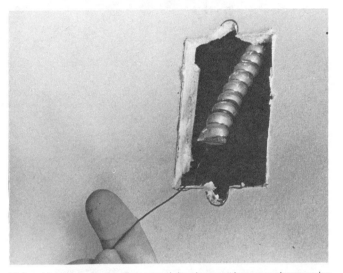

Fish out (reach through hole or conduit using coat hanger or longer wire to which electrical wire has been attached) the BX or Romex cable to go into the junction box. This power wire can originate at a nearby wall switch or outlet; you need not go back to the main service panel (codes permitting).

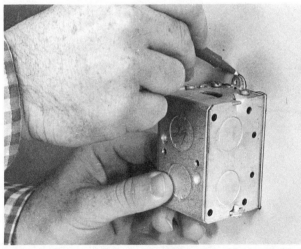

To add an outlet or switch, first trace the outline of the junction box over the spot where you want the outlet or switch. Position it next to a framing member — stud, joist, or rafter — for fastening.

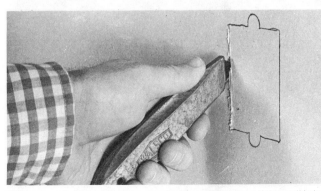

With a razor knife, cut the opening for the junction box. If the wall is lath and plaster, you will have to use a single blade hacksaw in addition to the razor knife. Make the cut as accurate as possible to ease later alignment.

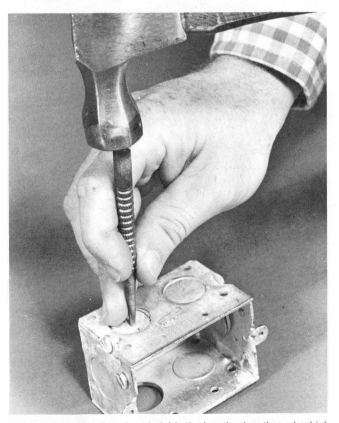

Punch out the slug (knockout hole) in the junction box through which the power wire will run. Junction boxes are designed for single, double — even multiple — switches and outlets.

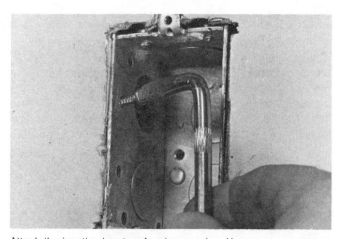

Attach the junction box to a framing member. You can use screws or nails, whichever is easiest to drive. Where a hammer is impossible to swing in the opening, use an offset screwdriver to screw the junction box to a stud.

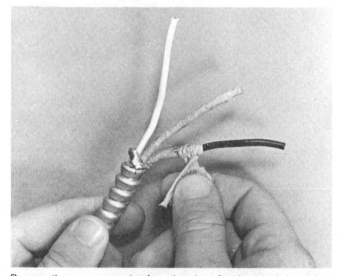

Remove the paper wrapping from the wire, after the metal sheath has been removed. To take off metal casing, bend cable sharply and the casing will crack. Use snips or knife to complete the removal without cutting the wire.

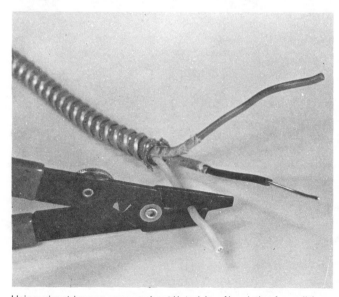

Using wire strippers, remove about ½-to 1-in. of insulation from all three wires. The strippers are notched so they cut to just the depth of the insulation. You then rotate the strippers and pull off the insulation.

Switches are mounted in junction boxes so the toggle faces downward when the switch is "off". Another mounting clue: the information stamped on the mounting plate should be right side up so you can read it.

To complete the new switch installation, screw on the switch plate. If it is crooked on the wall, you will have to readjust the mounting screws that hold the switch to the junction box.

Replacing a Wall Outlet (receptacle)

Tools and materials. Razor knife with a new blade, screwdriver, long nose pliers, new outlet.

STEPS

The procedures involved in changing the outlet are the same as for a wall switch.

Note that black wires are "hot" wires and go to brass-colored terminals. White wires are "neutral" wires and go to silver-

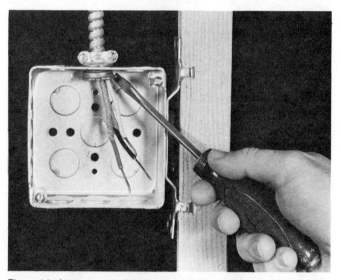

The cable fastens to the junction box with a metal collar. Tighten the collar with a screwdriver. In new construction, junction boxes are held to studs and other framing members with metal prongs; drive prongs in with a hammer.

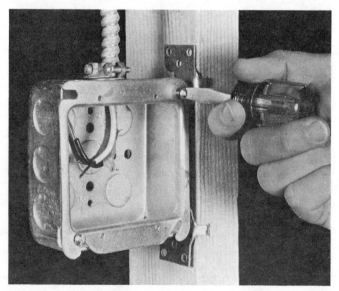

On some junction boxes, a special bracket is necessary to attach switches and outlets. This bracket must be screwed to the junction box after the box has been correctly wired.

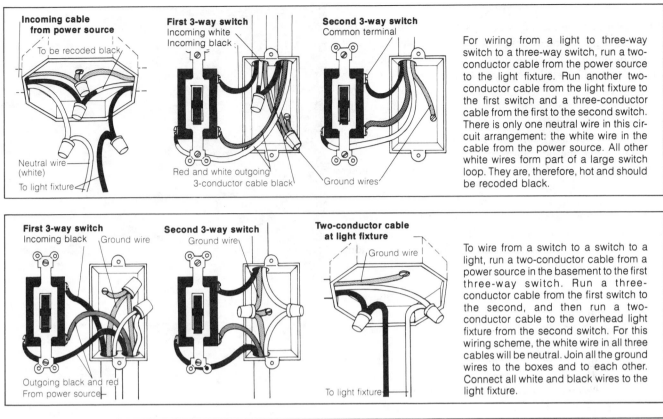

Incoming cable from power source
To be recoded black
Neutral wire (white)
To light fixture

First 3-way switch
Incoming white
Incoming black
Red and white outgoing 3-conductor cable black

Second 3-way switch
Common terminal
Ground wires

For wiring from a light to three-way switch to a three-way switch, run a two-conductor cable from the power source to the light fixture. Run another two-conductor cable from the light fixture to the first switch and a three-conductor cable from the first to the second switch. There is only one neutral wire in this circuit arrangement: the white wire in the cable from the power source. All other white wires form part of a large switch loop. They are, therefore, hot and should be recoded black.

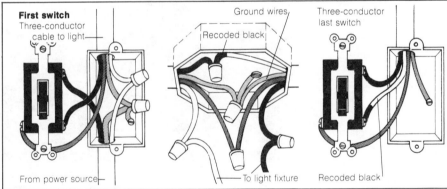

First 3-way switch
Incoming black   Ground wire
Outgoing black and red
From power source

Second 3-way switch
Ground wire

Two-conductor cable at light fixture
Ground wire
To light fixture

To wire from a switch to a switch to a light, run a two-conductor cable from a power source in the basement to the first three-way switch. Run a three-conductor cable from the first switch to the second, and then run a two-conductor cable to the overhead light fixture from the second switch. For this wiring scheme, the white wire in all three cables will be neutral. Join all the ground wires to the boxes and to each other. Connect all white and black wires to the light fixture.

First switch
Three-conductor cable to light
From power source

Ground wires
Recoded black
To light fixture

Three-conductor last switch
Recoded black

When wiring from a switch to a light to a switch (as for a circuit that reaches from a house to a garage) run a two-conductor cable from the power source to the switch in the house. Run a three-conductor cable from this switch to the light fixture, and then run a three-conductor cable from the light fixture to the switch in the garage. The white wire that runs between the power source and the light fixture will be neutral. After the light fixture, the white wire will be used as a hot wire in a switch loop, and should be recoded black.

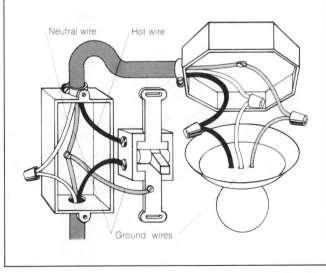

Neutral wire   Hot wire
Ground wires

Ground wires fasten to the junction box and switch as shown. If working with Romex, use the bare middle wire as the ground. The jumper wire from the switch to the box provides a continuous ground.

colored terminals. Green or grey wires are "grounding" wires and are fastened to a grounding terminal on the switch and in the junction box. You may need a short "jumper" wire for this (see illustrations, this chapter).

If you are uneasy about reconnecting the wires to the right terminals on the new outlet, you can tag each wire with a piece of masking tape. Mark the tape to code the wire to the proper terminal.

Installing a Dimmer Switch

There are three types of dimmer switches: single pole; 3-way; line types for lamp cords supplying floor and table lamps. You can buy special lamp sockets with dimmer switches already built-in. The 3-way models are especially made to control light from only one of the 3-way switches; you have to pick the switch you want for the dimmer. This way, the light may be turned on from two points, but dimmed only from one point along the 3-way switching line.

Tools and materials. Razor knife with a new blade, screwdriver, long nose pliers, wire nuts.

STEPS

If the cover plate on the old switch has been painted, break the paint seal with the razor knife, as you would with any wall switch or outlet. Also clean out the screw slot that holds the cover plate to the switch mounting plate on the metal junction box.

Remove the old switch from the junction box, pulling out the folded wires as you pull out the switch. It's a good idea to mark the hot and neutral wires, since there may be several wires running through the junction box.

Some dimmer switches have screw terminals. Other dimmer switches have lead wires. If the switch has lead wires, connect the lead wires to the hot and neutral wires with wire nuts.

If the switch has screw terminals, connect the black wire to the brass-colored screw terminals and the white wire to the silver-colored screw. Loop the ends of the bare wire using long nose pliers, and slip the loops over the terminals in the direction the screws turn.

If the wires are red and black in the junction box, attach the black wire to the black wire of the switch (or the brass colored screw terminal), and the red wire to the other red wires. Use wire nuts for these connections.

Fasten the dimmer switch mounting plate to the junction box and align it. Then screw on the cover plate. The dimmer knob is a "push fit" on the dimmer switch shaft; you simply push the knob on or pull the knob off.

Line dimmer switches are usually spliced into the lamp cord between the plug and the lamp socket. Complete wiring instructions are furnished with these switches.

Replacing a Line Switch

Tools and materials. Screwdriver, new line switch.

STEPS

Unplug the cord. The line switch is in two parts, like a clam shell. Remove the screw that holds the two parts together. One wire will run completely through the switch, unbroken. The other line will be connected to two terminal screws inside the switch. Loosen the terminal screws and remove the wire. Then reconnect the wire to the terminal screws in the direction the screws turn. Since the wire probably will be the stranded type, you will have to twist the strands tight with your fingers so the wires can be looped around the terminal screws.

To complete the job, simply screw the switch together so the parts match. Do not overtighten the screw.

Replacing a Lamp Socket (switch)

Tools and materials. Pliers, screwdriver, glue, razor, knife, new lamp socket assembly.

STEPS

Since lamp switches usually are built into the lamp socket, you will have to replace the entire unit.

Unplug the cord. Remove the felt pad that covers the bottom of the lamp, if there is a felt pad. You can use a razor knife for this, although a long-bladed kitchen knife may be easier since the blade can slide under the pad and lift it without tearing the loose-woven fabric.

At the base of the lamp you will find a nut that holds a long

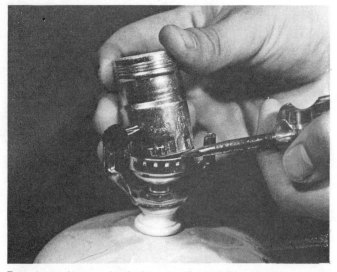
To replace a lamp socket (or lamp cord), you will have to disassemble the socket. Push down on the sides of the socket shell and then pry up on the shell, if necessary.

With outer socket shell removed, socket terminals are exposed. Unscrew the terminals to replace socket or lamp cord. (Note Underwriter's Knot; instructions given in "Replacing A Male Plug", p. 162.)

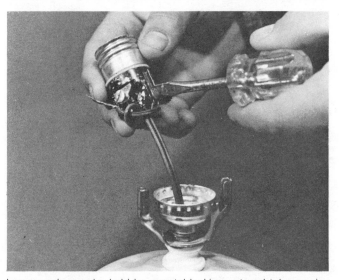
Lamp cords may be held by a metal locking nut and tube running through the lamp, top to bottom. You may have to remove this nut at the bottom of the lamp to pull the cord and socket up for repairs.

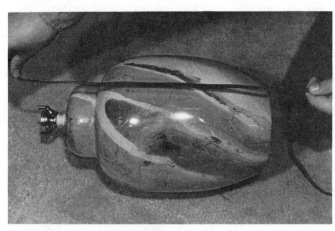

To find out how much lamp cord you need, measure the length of the cord through the lamp, starting from the base over to the socket; then add 6 in. to handle the UL knot and to give some slack.

thin metal tube to a mounting bracket built into the base. The lamp cord runs through this tube. Remove the nut with pliers so you can create slack in the lamp cord. Also, some lamps have a lead base. Remove this base, if possible, so you can have easy access to the lamp cord.

If your lamp is an expensive one, and you do not have to remove the felt pad and mounting nut, try unscrewing the socket of the lamp where it joins the lamp base. Pull up slowly on the socket. If the wire slides out of the base with the socket, pull the wire up about 6 in. This will give you adequate working slack to change the socket. Once changed, the wire can be threaded back into the base and the socket attached to the base.

Pull the metal tube up through the base of the lamp, using the socket as a handle. Now unscrew the socket from the tube; one end of the tube is threaded just for this. Pull about 6 in. of wire through the tube to create working slack.

The lamp socket has four parts: an outer shell, which is manufactured from thin brass or aluminum sheet; a cardboard shell, which is an insulator; the socket, which usually is a combination of metal and plastic; the cap, which is made of the same material as the outer shell. Holding this assembly together are the cap and outer shell. To disassemble the socket, press down on the outer shell where it meets the cap.

Disconnect the wires by backing out the terminal screws on the sides of the socket. Then slide the cap off the wires. Again, identifying or coding the wires is a smart idea.

To hook up the new socket, thread the wires through the cap of the socket. Then attach the wires to the terminal screws, twisting the wires around the screws in the direction the screws turn to tighten.

Slip the insulating sleeve over the socket and then slip on the outer shell, snapping this shell to the cap. Thread the cord back into the metal tube, fasten the socket to the tube, and push the tube back into the base of the lamp.

Replace the nut on the bottom of the tube at the mounting base; replace the weight; reglue the felt pad to the bottom of the lamp.

If you will replace the lamp cord to the socket, you must follow the same procedures as outlined above. However, at the base of the socket, you must tie an Underwriter's knot to support the cord. See the illustration, this chapter, on how to tie this knot.

Grounding Appliances

Tools and materials. Screwdriver, pliers, metal screws, grounding clamps, jumper wire.

STEPS

For junction boxes, connect the ground wire to the inside of the box, not to the grounding post of the switch or outlet. Use a run of jumper wire to connect the switch or outlet to the ground in the junction box. The ground wire from the BX or Romex terminates at this same junction box terminal, although it may "go through" the box to the main circuit breaker. Use a metal screw at the junction box grounding terminal point.

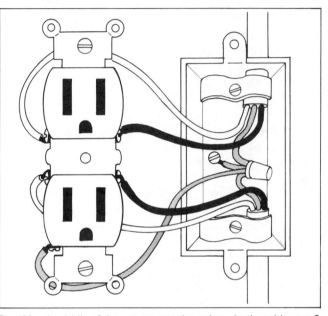

For 120-volt middle-of-the run receptacles using plastic cable, run 2 cables into the box. Connect one 4 in. green jumper to the back of the box and another to the green screw terminal. Use a wire cap to connect jumpers to bare cable wires. Each black cable wire connects to a brass terminal; the white wires attach to the silver terminals.

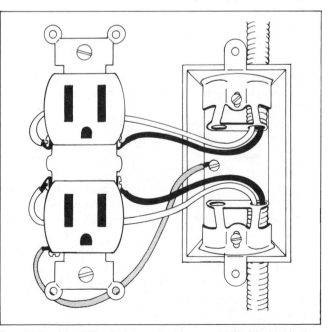

For middle-of-run 120-volt receptacle using armored cable, black wires connect to brass terminals, white wires to silver terminals. Jumper wire goes to box back using machine screw, then to green terminal.

Electric dryers, washers, and other heavy appliances can be grounded to *cold* water pipes near the appliance. Use a grounding clamp for this job; the clamp wraps around the pipe similar to a hose clamp. The wire is attached to the clamp with a screw.

How to Disconnect a Broken Light Bulb

Tools and materials. Paper bag, heavy gloves.

STEPS

Turn off or disconnect the electricity to the light. Remove as much of the broken glass of the bulb as you can with your fingers, wearing a glove to protect your hand. You may be able to remove the base of the bulb by carefully turning the base with fragments of the broken glass.

Wad up a heavy paper bag, making a ball of the paper. Stick this wad into the base of the bulb. Hold onto the light socket (if you can) with your free hand, and then turn out the metal base of the bulb with the wad of paper.

Replacing an Exterior Switch/Outlet (receptacle)

Tools and materials. Screwdriver, long nose pliers, weatherproof switch or outlet (receptacle).

STEPS

The techniques are the same as for changing an exterior switch or outlet as an interior switch or outlet (see those instructions, this chapter).

However, it is extremely important that you purchase switches and outlets made especially for exterior use. These products are so marked on their packages. You can use an interior switch or outlet in an exterior box, *if* the exterior box is fitted with weatherproof gaskets to protect the switches and outlets.

Replacing Fluorescent Tubes

Tools and materials. Heavy gloves, new tubes.

STEPS

Fluorescent tubes have two prongs at each end of the tube. These prongs slip into slots in brackets located at each end of the fixture. Once in position, the tubes are turned to lock in the "sockets" or brackets.

To remove a burned-out tube, you simply twist it until the prongs align with the slot in the brackets. Then pull the tube out of the slots. Installing a new tube is just the reverse of removing it.

If the tube is broken, wear heavy gloves to protect your hands. Bring the tube back to a level position with the fixture, if necessary, and twist the tube to disengage the prongs in the bracket or "socket".

Preheat fluorescent fixtures require a "starter" to heat the electrodes in the tube. Other fluorescent fixtures — rapid start and instant start — receive this heat from the ballast assembly, which is covered by the housing of the light fixture (you can't see the ballast).

The starter looks like an aluminum plug and it is usually located near one end of the fluorescent fixture. To remove the starter, simply twist it out of its socket, like a light bulb.

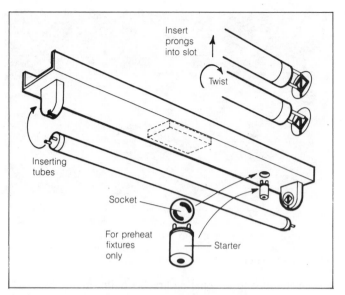

If a fluorescent light fixture malfunctions, first check the main service entry. Test switches for power, and make sure tubes are properly installed in the slots in the end brackets.

Diagnosing Fluorescent Lighting Problems

Problem	Possible Cause/Solution
Hum	Ballast trouble. The ballast may be the wrong type, or the ballast may have been installed improperly. Have a pro check it.
Blinking light tubes	The tube may be ready to fail. Try a new tube. The socket may also be misaligned, or the tube not properly seated in the socket. Other causes: low room temperature (below 50° F.); wrong type of tube; low voltage; malfunctioning ballast.
Tube lights at ends only	Worn or malfunctioning starter. Low room temperature; worn tube.
Flicker	New tubes may have a flicker for several hours. Faulty starter; high voltage; malfunctioning ballast.
No or slow starting	Bad tube. Broken socket. Too much dust and dirt on tube. Wrong type of tube. Malfunctioning starter. Tube not firmly set in sockets. Malfunction of ballast.
No light	Check for blown fuse. Tube may be dead. Bad starter.

Replacing a Male Plug

Tools and materials. Screwdriver, new plug, wire strippers.

STEPS

Many lamp cords have male plugs that are permanently attached to the cords so they can't be replaced. To get around this, cut the cord behind the malfunctioning plug and wire on a new, replaceable plug. This is cheaper than replacing the wire and the plug. Split the insulation down the center with a razor

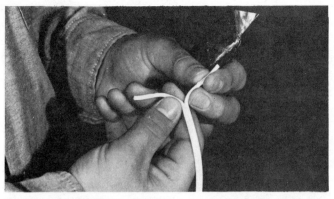

With a razor knife, split the insulation in half between the two "ridges" formed by the encased wires. Be careful not to cut through the insulation so far that you sever the wires.

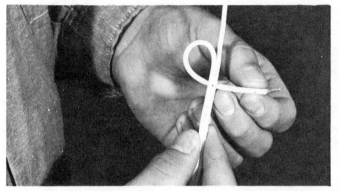

To tie an Underwriter's knot, first form a fairly large loop with one of the wires you split with the razor knife. Keep the loop formations big; they will be easier to work with.

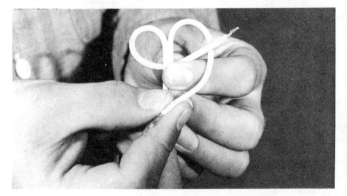

Form another loop with the adjoining wire, so that this second loop is behind the wire that protrudes from the first loop. This is necessary for the knot to be properly tied.

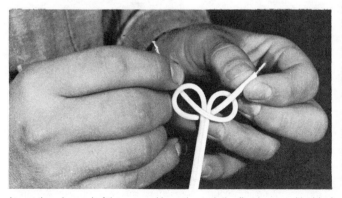

Insert the wire end of the second loop through the first loop and behind it. The wire from the first loop then goes through and in back of the second loop.

Pull the knot tight. The knot should be large enough so it can't pull out of a hole in a plug or lamp base, yet small enough to fit snugly into the base of these components.

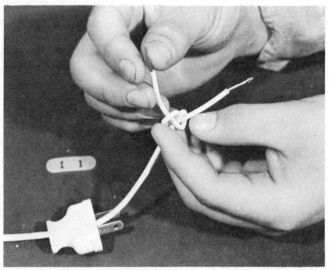

To replace a plug, strip about ½ in. insulation off the ends of the wires. Tie an Underwriter's knot; pull the knot tight after the plug has been slipped onto the wire. Twist the wire strands tight.

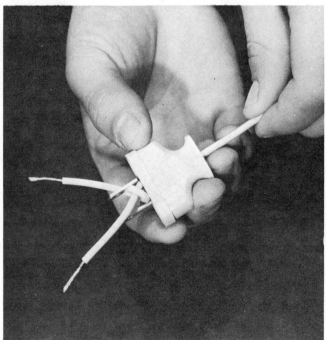

Pull the knot into the base of the plug to fit snugly. Then connect the wires to the screw terminals. Thread the thin fiber insert over the prongs of the plug. Firmly seat the insert in the plug base.

knife, separating the two wires that are encased in insulation. Then strip the wire about 1 inch, starting from the cut end.

Slip the new plug over the end of the wire and tie an Underwriter's knot in the wire (see illustrations, this chapter). The knot keeps the wires from being pulled from the terminal screws when the plug is jerked from the outlet.

Form a loop on the ends of the wire. Then hook the loop around the terminal screws so the loop goes in the direction the screw turns, usually clockwise. The wires that go around the screw terminals should not touch the prongs of the plug. A fiber insert is usually furnished with a new plug. Put this insert over the prongs of the plug so the insert is seated in the base of the plug.

Iron plugs. If not the permanent type, these come in two sections and are held together with screws. To replace a faulty iron plug, remove the screws and the wires from the terminals inside the plug. Then reconnect the wires to the terminals of the new plugs. Assemble the two halves of the plug and screw them together.

If there will be a lot of strain on the plug, you should install a spring coil over the wire and into the top opening of the plug. Some plugs are sold with this spring-coil feature.

Self-connection plugs. Specially slotted, you stick the wire — insulation and all — into the slot and push down on a clamp to make the connection.

Cut the wire as square as possible on the end of the cord before you insert the cord into the slot in the plug. Some plugs require that the insulation be split into two wires before the wires are inserted into the slot. In this case, directions are included with the plug.

Changing a Ceiling Fixture

Tools and materials. Screwdriver, wire strippers, pliers, wire nuts, the new fixture.

STEPS

The junction box is covered by a wide escutcheon plate which is held by a decorative nut. With pliers, remove the decorative nut, which will permit you to drop the escutcheon plate down on the chain or rod that holds the fixture below. Technically, this decorative nut is called a collar.

The collar was screwed to a threaded nipple, which protrudes out from the junction box. The nipple sometimes is called a threaded stud. It is held to the junction box with a strap of metal that spans the junction box. The strap may be fastened with just the nipple or stud, or it may be additionally fastened to the junction box with screws along a slot in the strap. The slot is for adjustment. You may not have to change the nipple or stud and metal strap. The new light probably will fit the old parts since most electrical parts are standard. However, if the old hanging assembly does not work — and a new assembly is included with the lamp — you have only to remove the screws holding the mounting strap and the threaded nipple or stud. Use a screwdriver and/or pliers for these jobs.

The power wires in the junction box probably are hooked to

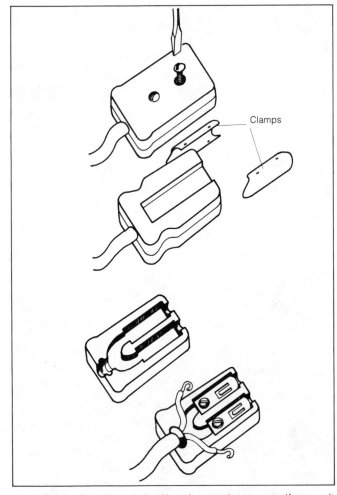

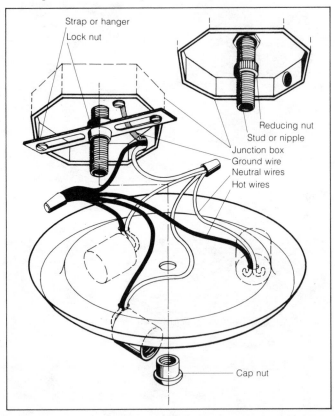

A female plug (usually in clothes' irons) comes in two parts. If you can't disassemble the plug, buy a new cord and substitute. Another solution is to cut the cord behind the plug and splice on a new plug.

Lightweight ceiling fixtures sometimes are attached only to a metal stud projecting from the junction box (above). Heavier ceiling fixtures often add a metal strap to help carry the weight (below).

the wires of the fixture with wire nuts, or are spliced together and wrapped with electrician's tape. Disconnect these wires. Then make any hanger assembly adjustments or changes. Reconnect the wires — black to black; white to white. Also reconnect the ground wire, if present. Use wire nuts for the connections and wrap the wire nuts with electrician's tape.

You'll probably need a helper to hold the light fixture while you remove the old one and install the new one. When the wires have been reconnected, thread the fixture onto the nipple or stud. Then fasten the fixture with the holding nut. Slip the escutcheon plate over the bottom of the nipple or stud and screw on the decorative nut.

To add a switched light fixture, you must run cable from a power source to new fixture outlet and switch boxes. For a new switch in the middle of the run, the cable begins at the power source and runs to the switch and then to the light. The switch wiring is middle of the run, but the light-fixture wiring is end of the run. Use two-conductor cable with ground wire. The hot black wire of the incoming cable connects at the switch to one terminal and the black outgoing wire connects to the other terminal. Join neutral (white) wires with a cap to give an uninterrupted circuit from the light fixture to the service panel. Join uninterrupted ground wires to the metal box and to each other. The hot wire from the switch connects at the light fixture to the fixture's black wire; the white wire connects to the fixture's neutral wire; the bare ground wire connects to the box.

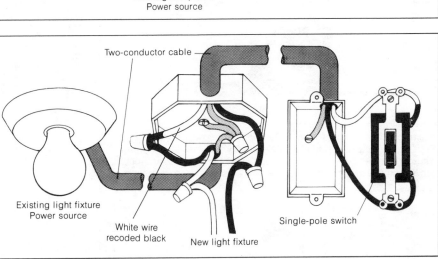

When cable runs to the fixture and then to the switch, fixture wiring is middle of the run and switch wiring is a "switch loop." Use 2-conductor cable with ground. For the light, join the neutral wire from the power source to the white fixture wire. Since you need a hot wire to carry power to the switch and back to the fixture, the black wire of the incoming cable joins to the white outgoing wire for power to the switch. Connect black outgoing wire (for power back from switch) to the black fixture wire. For the loop that carries power to the switch and on to the light, fasten the white wire at the switch to one terminal; fasten the black wire to the other.

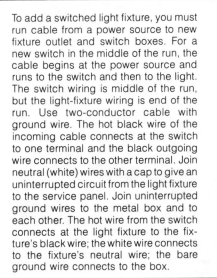

A circuit from an already installed receptacle, to a switch-controlled light fixture, to an unswitched receptacle, is a combination circuit. Run 3-conductor cable from the switch to the light in order to provide the light's switched hot wire and the receptacle's unswitched hot wire. The neutral (white) and ground wires from the incoming cable connect at the switch as shown for middle of the run (above). The incoming cable's black wire connects with a jumper to the switch and to the black wire of the 3-conductor cable. This black wire will run to the receptacle. The red wire found in the 3-conductor cable will carry power from the switch to the fixture's black wire. Join the white wire in the 3-conductor cable to the white fixture wire and to the white wire that runs to the receptacle. Wire the receptacle as for end of the run (see p. 156).

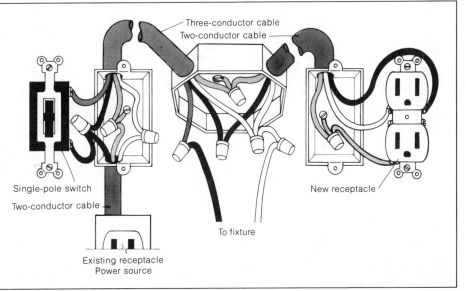

Extending Cable from Old to New Outlet

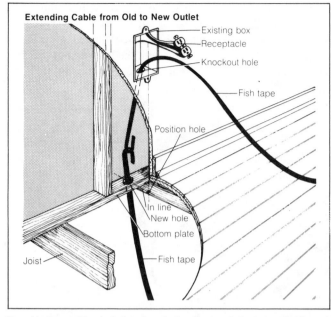

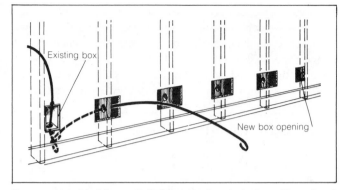

Bore ¹/₁₆ in. position hole into floor below the box to be tapped. Aligned with the hole, drill up through the plate with a ¾ in. spade bit. Use this method to drill a hole in plate below new location. Pull receptacle out from existing box. Through knockout in bottom of box, push a fish tape. Have a helper push another tape up; hook the ends.

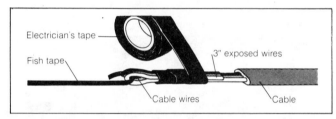

Pull upper tape down through the hole in bottom plate; unhook tapes. Remove 3 in. sheathing from cable end and strip insulation from the wires that are exposed. Loop exposed wires through the tape hook. Tape the looped wires and the hook firmly, using electrician's tape.

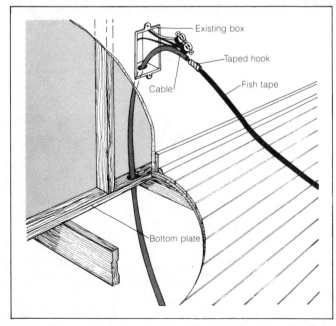

Pull the fish tape back through; detach the hook from the cable. Strip another 8 in. from the cable end. Use an internal clamp to fasten the sheathed edge of the cable to the box. Fasten the cable along basement joists at 4 ft. intervals using cable staples. Fish cable up to the new box and attach; mount the new box in the wall.

For a route behind the wall, first expose the studs. In wallboard, cut a 1 in. high rectangle 1 in. wider than the stud. In plaster, cut with a chisel and saw out underlying lath. Drill a hole in centers of studs. Remove a knockout in bottom of existing box; use fish tapes to pull cable through, as given above.

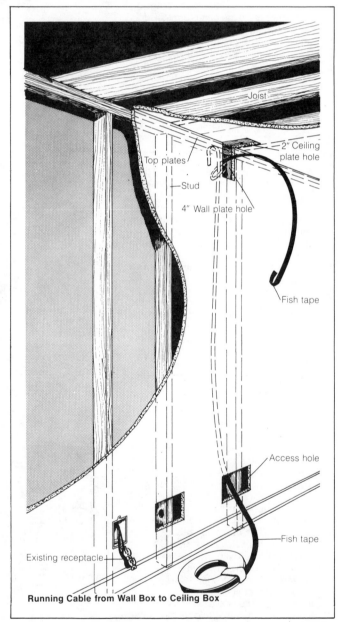

Running Cable from Wall Box to Ceiling Box

Cut ceiling opening between joists. Halfway between these joists, at top of wall, cut ceiling plate and access holes to bring cable horizontally in line with existing box. Push fish tape up to ceiling plate hole. Hook on second fish tape; pull through. Disconnect tapes. Tape hook to cable. Draw cable down behind wall to access (or knockout) hole.

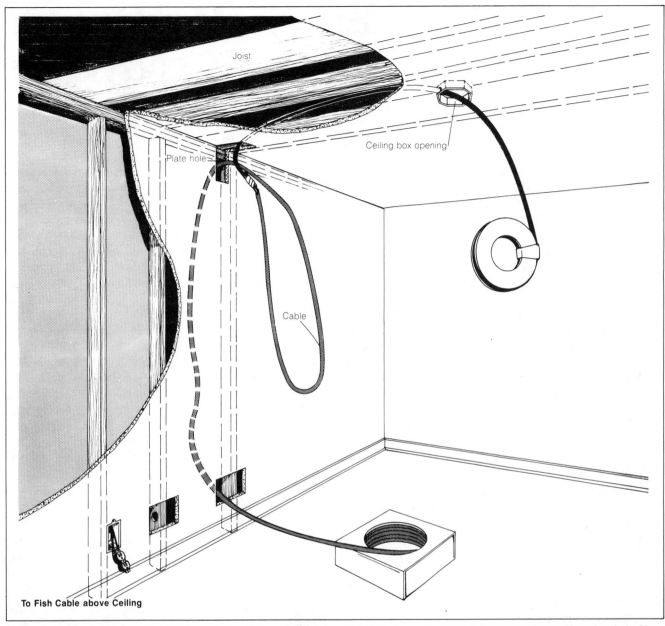

To Fish Cable above Ceiling

Have a helper push the end of the fish tape into the ceiling box opening. Guide it between the joists to just beyond the ceiling plate hole. Use a short, second fish tape to pull first tape down through the hole. Disconnect tapes; attach stripped wires in cable to first fish tape running between ceiling joists. Feed cable into ceiling plate hole and use fish tape to draw cable back to new ceiling box opening.

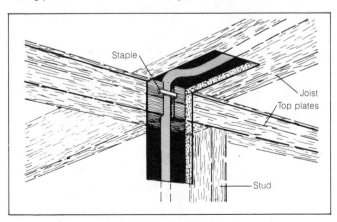

For wall less than ½ in. thick, fasten cable by cutting a channel in top plates. Use keyhole saw for 2 parallel vertical cuts ½ in. deep, ¾ in. apart. Chisel wood out between cuts. Right below edge of top plates, staple cable groove. For wall thicker than ½ in., staple cable to top plates. For either thickness, patch the 2 access holes.

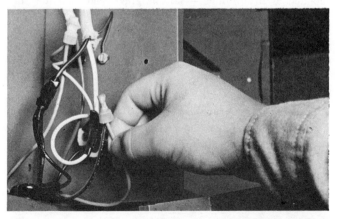

White wires are usually neutral, but in some circuit arrangements they are joined to black (hot) wires to provide another path for current. In these situations the white wire becomes a hot wire, and should be recoded black to prevent chances of later misidentification and possible injury.

8 Exterior Maintenance and Repair

Water can quickly penetrate the finest quality roofing, paint, metal, plastic, stone, brick, concrete, wood, plaster, glass — almost any type of building product. Your only recourse is to stop the moisture before damage can be done. The best way is to put the various components of your home on an annual inspection list, so you can fix any damage before the water can do too much harm. Let your incentive be a comparison of time and money: the longer you delay necessary repairs, the more time and money it will take to make the repairs later.

The exterior of your home is made up of three general building components: the roof; the side walls; the foundation. Of the three, the roof takes the worst beating from weather. From the roof, weather damage continues in a lesser degree to the siding and then to the foundation. It then moves inside to interior ceilings, framing, floors, doors, windows, and other components.

This chapter pinpoints the most important maintenance repairs to the roof, siding, and foundation of a house.

THE ROOF OVER YOUR HEAD

There are four basic types of roofs: gable, hip, shed, and flat. Variations on these basics include: laminated beam; Mansard; folded plate; and, additions such as dormers, skylights, clerestories.

If your roof is flat or has a low pitch, you can make yearly inspections and maintenance repairs to the roof. If the roof has a high pitch, you would be wise to pay a professional to do the work. Steep roofs are dangerous when you are not protected by special safety equipment.

The best roof inspection and repair times are in the early spring, late fall, and on cool mornings during the summer months. Roof coverings — tar and gravel and asphalt — become soft when warmed by the sun. Walking on this soft material can damage it; replacement then becomes necessary, and is often costly.

Ladder Safety

Roof and siding inspection and repairs usually involve a ladder. Although there is always an element of risk, you can be safe on a ladder when you know how to set the ladder, climb it, work on it, and climb down off it.

Start with a good quality ladder. Do not invest in a cheap product with an eye toward a bargain. The extra dollars that you will pay for a quality ladder can save you a lot in the long run and, properly maintained, it will last a lifetime.

Most quality ladders come with tags attached that specify weight load, distance of extension, and other safety and maintenance data. For example, a household grade ladder has a load or weight rating of 200 pounds. A commercial ladder has a

weight rating of 225 pounds; an industrial grade ladder has a rating of 250 pounds. We recommend a commercial/industrial grade ladder, since it is constructed for heavy use. Although more expensive than a household grade ladder, the cost difference is little compared to the higher quality. Be sure the ladder you buy is strong enough to support your weight plus materials that will be hoisted up and down the ladder. It should be long enough to extend at least three rungs over the eaves of the roof, when the ladder is properly set and sloped to the ground. It should be light enough so you can carry it, set it up, and store it properly. To prevent accidents, follow these ladder safety rules.

Do not paint wooden ladders. Paint can hide splits, breaks, and other defects. If you want to put a preservative on the wood, use a clear penetrating sealer. If you find a defect in a wooden ladder (or a metal ladder) such as a split, broken rung or a bent rail, buy a new ladder. Repairs seldom work. When painting, immediately wipe off any fallen paint, caulking, roofing cement or other liquid product that has spilled onto the ladder. The spills will be slippery and can cause an accident.

Lean a stepladder against a wall whenever and wherever you can. When you open a stepladder, make sure the ladder is fully opened, with the tray feature at the front of the ladder pulled completely down and locked. The metal straps running be-

Double-check the locks on ladder extensions. Although they hook automatically, they are not fail-safe. If a lock is damaged, do not use the ladder.

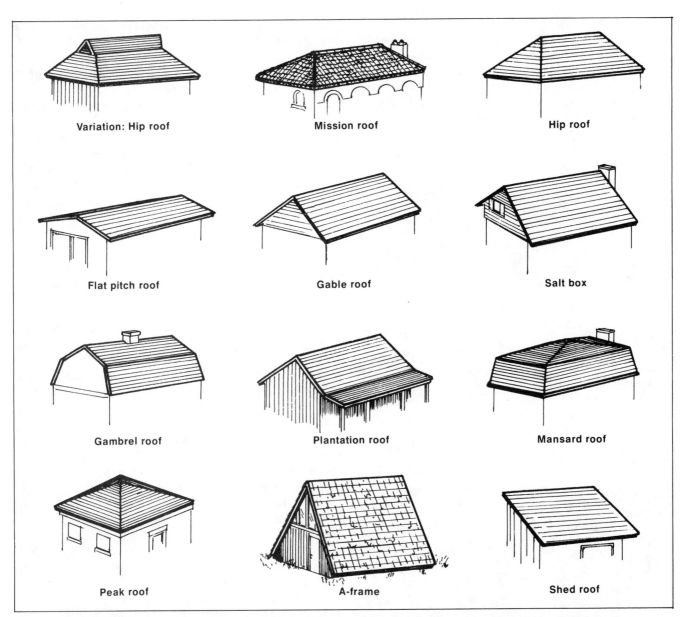

Variation: Hip roof

Mission roof

Hip roof

Flat pitch roof

Gable roof

Salt box

Gambrel roof

Plantation roof

Mansard roof

Peak roof

A-frame

Shed roof

Knowing the style of your roof will help when planning your repair or re-roofing project. Some styles are easier to repair than others.

The legs of the ladder must always be set on a firm footing. If the legs are uneven on a slope, you can prop them level with a piece of scrap wood, concrete block, brick.

tween the front and back parts of the stepladder must be fully extended and locked. Never stand on the next-to-the-top or top step of a stepladder or the top rung of an extension ladder.

Ladders that lean should slope about one-fourth their length from bottom to top. If you set a ladder at too steep an angle, the ladder may pitch backward. If not set at enough of an angle, the ladder may slip out at the bottom from your weight — or, your weight may break the ladder or the extension locks holding the ladder together.

The rails (legs) of the ladder must be on a firm footing, and the ladder must be straight-up-and-down; i.e., it should not pitch to one side or the other. To make sure the ladder is on a firm footing, set the ladder properly. Then stand on the bottom rung of the ladder and "rock" your feet on the rung. Under your weight and the rocking pressure, the ladder should sit square and firmly on the surface. If not, reposition the ladder. If you have set the ladder on sloping ground, you can shore up one leg (or both legs) with a short length of wood (shim). Test the ladder for a firm footing.

Climb the ladder with both hands, one rung at a time. If you have to carry materials up the ladder, and a rope hoist doesn't work or you do not have a helper to hand you materials, lay the material across your forearms and use your hand to hold to the rungs. Keep your hips inside the rails of the ladder. Do not over-reach the length of your arm (as when painting) by standing on one leg on the ladder rungs. Hold on to the ladder with your free hand. Work and then move the ladder. Always wear shoes when working on a ladder.

When working on a roof, make sure the ladder extends at least three rungs above the eaves of the roof. Do not set the

Lean a stepladder against a solid object when you can. When you can't, open and lock the ladder. The paint tray feature on the front of the ladder also must be down.

Raise an extension ladder one rung at a time by hand. Some ladders (like the one shown) have a rope/pulley arrangement for raising the extension. For either model, be sure the hooks are locked.

ladder under the eaves and then attempt to climb over the eaves (and gutter) onto the roof. Make sure the rung hooks on an extension ladder are hooked before you climb onto the extension. Do not lap an extension ladder less than three rungs.

When lifting a ladder, use your arms and legs, not your back. Some ladders have a rope/pulley arrangement for lifting the top extension of an extension ladder. When you are moving a ladder a short distance, you can simply pick it up to move it. Let the rail of one side of the ladder slip into the hollow of your shoulder. Then, with your legs and hands, lift the ladder a couple of inches off the ground and move it. The trick is balance; weight usually is not as big a factor. A 40 ft. industrial/commercial ladder weighs about 90 pounds. In moving a ladder, be careful of overhead obstructions such as power lines and tree branches.

Frequently test the rungs of your ladder for strength and damage by laying the ladder on the ground and walking on the rungs. You usually can tell from this test whether or not the rungs are strong and safe.

Quality ladders have one rung every foot. If the ladder is 16 ft. long, there should be 16 rungs. The bottom rung should be about 7 in. from the ground. The top rung should be about 5 in. from the top end of the rails or legs of the ladder. Ladder rungs should be at least 1¼ in. diameter. Stepladder steps should be about ¾ in. thick and fairly wide to support the soles of your shoes.

Ladder width is important. Buy a ladder that is at least 15 in. wide — even wider if possible. A quality ladder should be at least one foot wide at the top and fan out at the rate of about 1 in. per foot from the top of the ladder to the bottom of it.

Special ladder features include nonskid feet, interlocking rails, automatic extension locks, rope/pulley adjustment, nontwistable rungs "peened" in rails (on metal ladders).

If your budget does not permit you to buy a ladder, you often can rent a ladder for your project at a rent-all outlet. The rental cost usually is not prohibitive.

ROOF INSPECTION

Start roof maintenance with a roof inspection in the fall and again in the early spring. Work from the top of the roof (ridge) to the bottom (eaves and gutter). Checkpoints include:

(1) exposed heads of roofing nails; roof valleys;
(2) damaged or
(3) curled shingles; eaves;
(4) exposed, rusted, and damaged flashing;
(5) cracks and breaks between dissimilar materials such as shingles and siding, flashing at roofing and masonry, metal and wooden frames, and flashing around vents and stacks.

Looking for Roof Leaks

Tools and materials. Short lengths of wire.

STEPS

Go into the attic or attic crawl space on a sunny day. Check the roof sheathing between the rafters. If you spot any points of sunlight coming through the sheathing, stick the wires up through the openings and leave them there. Then climb onto the roof. Where the wires protrude through the roofing, you should look for potential repairs.

This method does not always locate leaks. Water can enter your home in one spot and show up in another spot — often many feet away from the entry point. When it is raining, try to trace the leak from the drip point back to the entry point. Then use a measuring tape for this so you can roughly transfer the distance from the attic space to the roof above. Somewhere in this measurement you will find the leak; it will probably be around flashing.

Leaks often can also be detected by roof damage. Any of the roof checkpoints listed above can be the source of a leak. If you can't get into the attic, or your home does not have an open attic space, you will have to rely on visual inspection of the roof to discover leak points.

Repairing Asphalt Shingles

Tools and materials. Hammer, putty knife, roofing nails, thick asphalt roofing cement; roofing cement available in bulk bucket quantities or in caulking tubes.

STEPS

The most common damage is either curled shingles caused by heat and/or wind or broken shingles caused by wind or walking on the shingles.

For a curled shingle, try sticking down the shingle with a walnut-sized dab of roofing cement placed between the shingle overlap. Gently step on the shingle after you've applied the roofing cement. If this does not work, use the cement plus a roofing nail driven through the layers of shingles into the sheathing. Then cover the roofing nail head with a dab of roofing cement, even though the nail is galvanized.

If the shingle is broken, try putting it back into position with roofing cement and adding a nail or two to hold the shingle down. Run a patch of roofing cement along the edges of the break. Feather the cement out onto the body of the shingle, using a putty knife. This patch is temporary; the shingle should be replaced as soon as possible.

Replacing Asphalt Shingles

Tools and materials. Flat tiling spade or ice chipper, nail

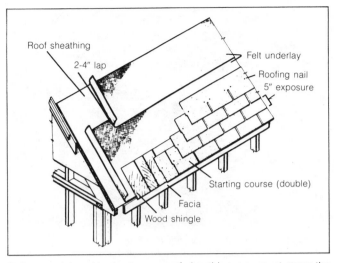

Before applying shingles to new roof sheathing, you must cover the sheathing with roofing felt as additional protection. A layer of wood shingles under the first and double course keeps the edge firm.

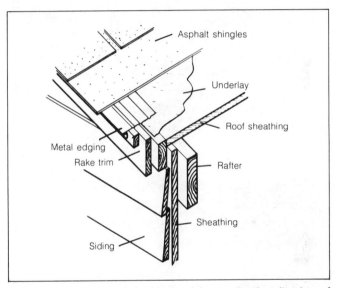

The gable end of your roof requires special protection. Install a piece of metal edging over the roofing felt and adjacent rake trim. Your shingles will rest on this edging and direct rainfall off the roof.

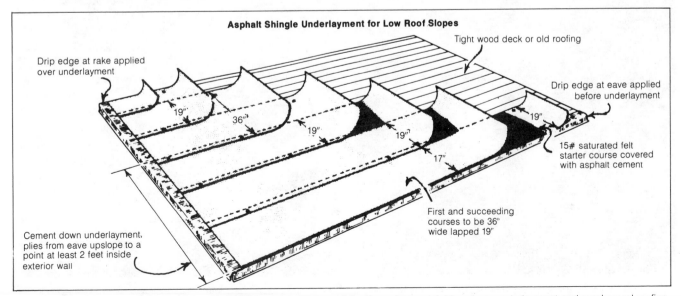

Underlayment for low-slope roofs is easy to apply but must be done carefully. It requires metal drip edges, underlayment and overlapped roofing. Because water tends to puddle on a flat roof, some pitch must be provided and every effort made to avoid unevenness in the surface.

To replace a shingle, lift the shingles above the damaged shingle with an ice chipper (shown) or flat spade. Pull out the nails, insert the new shingle and renail.

puller, hammer, putty knife, razor knife, roofing nails, thick asphalt roofing cement, new shingle.

STEPS

With the spade or chipper, carefully lift the shingle that is above the damaged shingle. This will expose the nails which hold the damaged shingle. If the shingle has been properly nailed you will find three to five nails. Remove these nails and then remove the shingle. Work very carefully so you do not damage the good shingles that surround the damaged shingle.

Set the new shingle in the void that was left by the old shingle. You may have to trim the new shingle with a razor knife so the shingle fits tightly in the space. Nail the new shingle in position, using five nails, placing a nail at the top of each slot and spacing the rest evenly. Then cover the nail heads with dabs of roofing cement. Carefully position the shingle you had loosened above, and hammer down the loosened roofing

Stick down curled shingles or shingles blown up by high winds with a dab or two of roofing cement. Step down gently but firmly on the shingle to embed it in the thick mixture.

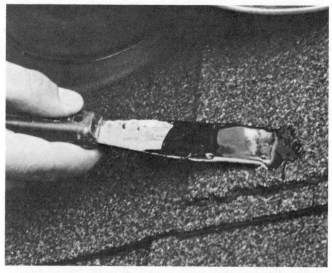

Carefully inspect the roof and cover any exposed roofing nail heads with asphalt roofing cement. If you spot any popped nails, drive them flush and coat the nail heads.

Cap shingles at roof ridges often are blown up by high wind. Stick these shingles down with roofing cement, applied here with a caulking gun. Use plenty of cement.

For a temporary patch for leaks in asphalt and wooden shingles, insert a rectangle of thin aluminum sheet under the shingles, Apply roofing cement to the joints.

nails. If this overlapping shingle is curled, you can add more nails down through the exposed part of it. Cover the nail heads with roofing cement. You may also have to add roofing cement underneath the shingle to keep it from curling.

Check for any breaks around the new shingle and where the surrounding shingles adjoin the new shingle. Fill these breaks with small amounts of roofing cement.

Repairing Wooden Shingles

Tools and materials. Hammer, roofing nails, putty knife, thick asphalt roofing cement, sheet aluminum or galvanized metal, a short length of 1x3.

STEPS

Check the roof thoroughly. If you find too many areas where the shingles have rotted (they will be soggy and split easily when probed with a putty knife), the roof should be replaced or recovered. This is a job that requires a book to itself, and in many cases requires a professional.

If the problem is a split shingle or a loose shingle, try renailing the shingle and filling the split with asphalt roofing cement. Apply the cement to several shingles surrounding the damaged shingle — top, bottom, and at the sides. This will assure that the roof has been tightly sealed at the damaged point. If this

does not work, try inserting and driving a strip of aluminum or galvanized sheet the length of the shingle up under the shingle. The sheet should be wide enough to go under the shingles adjoining the damaged shingle. Place a length of 1x3 against the thin edge of the metal and use the edge of the 1x3 to drive the metal up under the shingle course. When the metal is in place, nail the shingle through the metal and into the roof sheathing. Do this gently; you do not want to bend the metal when you hammer the sheet into position. Apply roofing cement to the nail heads, around the top, bottom, and side cracks of the damaged shingle, and to adjoining shingles around the damaged area.

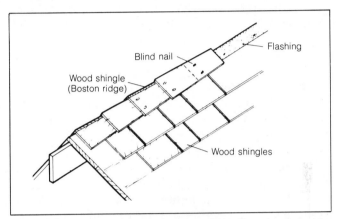

A Boston ridge made with wood shingles which will not bend must be made with metal flashing beneath the shingles over the ridge. Ridge shingles are laid sideways with rising edges butting alternately.

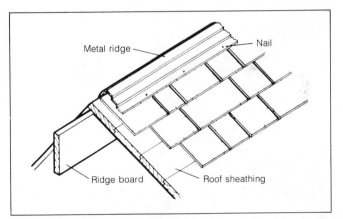

A metal ridge may be used to finish a roof ridge. The metal ridge roll is placed over the completed roofing and nailed down on each side. This provides a continuous strip to divert water down the roof.

Repairing Tar and Gravel (Built-up) Roofs

Tools and materials. Putty knife, razor knife, hammer, roofing nails, thick asphalt roofing cement, household broom.

STEPS

Sweep around the damaged area to clean it, saving any gravel removed from this area; you can use the gravel again.

With a putty knife, clean the damaged spot. If the area has a small bubble between the roofing and sheathing below the roofing, cut the bubble with a razor knife — a clean slit. Then flatten the bubble by stepping lightly, but solidly, down upon it.

Force roofing cement into the slit and under the bubble area, using the tip of the putty knife. When you are finished, nail down the edges of the slit with roofing nails.

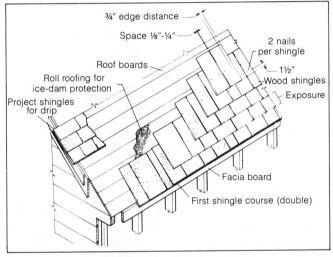

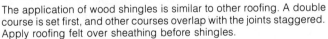

The application of wood shingles is similar to other roofing. A double course is set first, and other courses overlap with the joints staggered. Apply roofing felt over sheathing before shingles.

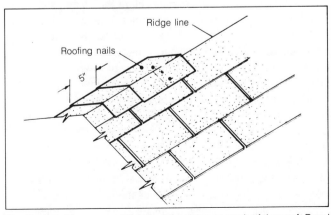

The Boston ridge covers (finishes) the ridge or peak of the roof. Bend asphalt shingles and nail down on either side of the ridge to seal this edge to prevent water leakage under shingles.

Cover the damaged area with a fairly thick coating of roofing cement, smoothing out the cement with a putty knife so the cement is evenly distributed. Then sprinkle the excess gravel you had swept out over the roofing cement, embedding the gravel into the cement with the tip of the broom.

In areas where there is no gravel — usually around the ridge and next to vents and stacks — apply a thick layer of roofing cement and sprinkle gravel over the compound. Seat it with the tip of a broom. You usually can sweep up enough loose gravel on the roof for this, but if not you should buy more gravel rather than create new bare spots while trying to fix the old bare spots.

To remove asphalt roofing compound from tools, use mineral spirits on an old piece of cloth. The broom, however, will be ruined. Use an old broom you won't miss and keep it on hand for future repairs.

Roll Roofing Repairs

Tools and materials. Hammer, razor knife, thick asphalt roofing cement, roofing nails, stiff brush, putty knife, new roll roofing.

STEPS

Roll roofing resembles asphalt shingles, but it comes in rolls like building paper. You'll find most of its damage confined to seams. However, splits in the material can be found anywhere in the roofing, and are usually caused by expansion and contraction.

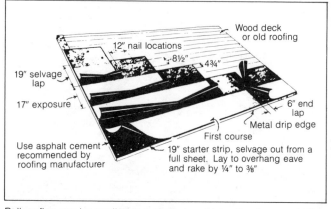

Roll roofing can be applied to a pitched roof as well as to a nearly-flat, low-slope roof if esthetic appearance is not important. The material should be cemented as well as nailed.

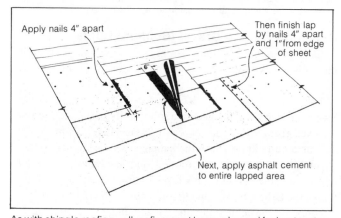

As with shingle roofing, roll roofing must be overlapped for best protection. Nailing should done beneath lapping edges. Sheet ends are also nailed and lapped.

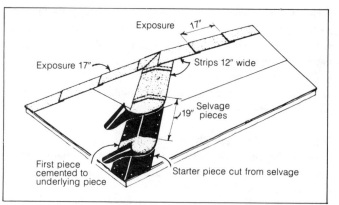

Ridges on pitched roofs covered with roll roofing must be sealed in the same manner as shingled roofs. You may cut pieces from scrap roll roofing to make the ridge pieces.

Sweep the roof around the damaged area. With a razor knife, cut a patch from scrap roll roofing to overlap the damage about 6 in. Test for fit, and then remove it. Apply a fairly thick coating of roofing cement, covering the entire patch.

Embed the patch in the roofing cement, pressing the patch against the old roofing. Don't flatten the patch; just stick it in place. If you can, let the patch set for a couple of days. Then nail down the edges of the patch with roofing nails and coat the nailheads and the edges of the patch with a thin coat of roofing cement.

If the roofing has bubbled, similar to tar & gravel roofing (see above), use the same repair techniques as outlined for tar & gravel roofing, plus the roll roofing patch.

Repairing Metal Roofs

Tools and materials. Hammer, tinsnips, sheet galvanized steel or aluminum (depending on the metal roofing), roofing nails, asphalt roofing compound.

STEPS

Cut a patch of metal to fit over the damage, assuming the damage is small enough for a patch. The patch should always be the same type of metal as the roof: aluminum to aluminum; galvanized steel to galvanized steel; copper to copper. Do not mix metals. This also applies to roofing nails. If the damaged area is large, you may have to replace a section of the roof, which is usually a job for a professional roofer.

Coat the damaged area and the back of the metal patch with a thin layer of asphalt roofing compound. Then press the patch in position over the damaged area. Nail the patch to the roofing with roofing nails spaced about 1 in. apart. Then coat the nailheads and the patch with a thin layer of roofing cement. If this will make the patch unsightly from ground level, let the roofing cement dry for about a month. Then spray the patch with aluminum-colored metal paint — or match the color of the roof. You can buy pressurized spray cans of paint for this.

If the damage is a pinhole leak, drive a roofing nail with a neoprene washer into the hole. Then coat the nailhead with a dab of roofing cement. You can buy roofing nails with neoprene washers molded to the head of the nail.

If the metal is rusty, but not damaged, you can coat the rust with special aluminum paint with an asphalt base; it is made especially for this purpose. Before you apply this coating, clean the rust as best you can with a wire brush. Then sweep the area clean with a broom. You should apply the coating with a roller on a handle extension or with a brush; we do not recommend spraying on the coating. Overspray can lodge on passing and nearby parked cars and on neighbors' homes.

Repairing Plastic Roofs

Tools and materials. Roofing nails with neoprene washers, fiberglass patching kit or a length of similar roofing that may be cut for patches.

STEPS

Plastic roofs are really of reinforced fiberglass. Leaks usually occur at the seams where the roofing overlaps and is fastened to framing members. It is sometimes possible to stop leaks by pulling out the nails at the leak point and replacing these nails with roofing nails that have neoprene washers attached to the heads.

For large patches, it is recommended that you use a fiberglass patching kit — the type used for patching boat hulls. You can buy this kit at a marine supply store, although some home center stores may have patch materials.

If the damage is extensive, you should remove the damaged panels by pulling out the nails that hold the panels in place, and replace the panels with matching new panels. You might also be able to overlay new panels onto the old panels.

Using patches of matching panels is another alternative. Cut the patches with a crosscut saw and anchor them in place with dabs of roofing cement. This technique is not recommended, however, if the patches will show from the top or bottom of the roof.

Slate and Tile Roofs

These roofs are extremely difficult for a homeowner to repair, since walking on the tile or slate can break it very quickly. Again, most tile and slate roofs are high-pitched and the surface is slippery. Therefore, we recommend that you call a professional to make needed repairs.

Roof Flashing Maintenance/Repair

Flashing's role on the roof of a house is to span joints between similar materials — such as shingles, and dissimilar materials — such as shingles and bricks, to prevent leaks. Look for flashing around the chimney, valleys of the roof, vents and stacks, next to skylights, and where dormers or any roof additions meet.

Flashing usually is metal — galvanized sheet, aluminum, copper — although it can be plastic or even strips of asphalt roll roofing. All of this material can rust, corrode, and crack, which will cause problems. However, your biggest troubles usually are due not to the flashing but to the materials adjoining or covering edges of the flashing. Water, driven by wind or through capillary action, can actually flow uphill on the roof and find its way under the flashing, through the roof sheathing, and into your home.

Tools and materials. Hammer, roofing nails, tinsnips, thick asphalt roofing cement, tiling spade or ice scraper, pry bar, new flashing material.

STEPS, MAINTENANCE

Once a year, coat the flashing around the chimney, roof vents and stacks, skylights, and roof additions with a thin layer of asphalt roof coating (cement or liquid). Once every three years, coat the roof valley flashing with roofing cement (or liquid), making sure all nailheads are thoroughly covered and small cracks are filled.

Flashing usually is installed under shingles, although it may be cemented and nailed directly over the shingles. Either way, make sure the nails holding the material are driven flush and have not popped due to settling of the house on its foundation. If you find popped nails, drive the nails flush, add a new nail next to the popped nail, and cover all nailheads with dabs of roofing cement.

Flashing at chimney/roof joints most often extends under the shingles and up the side of the chimney about 6 to 12 in. The top edge of the flashing is bent over and inserted in a mortar

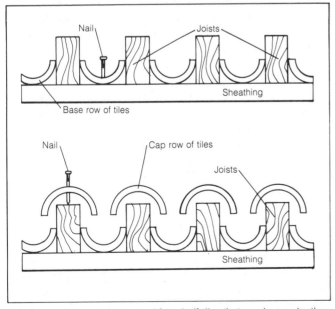

Curved tile roofs are constructed from half-tiles that overlap each other. The base tiles are nailed to the roof sheathing; the cap tiles are nailed to furring strips.

Flashing around chimneys usually needs to be sealed. Use thick asphalt roofing cement and work the cement down into the joint between the chimney and the flashing.

For open seams in flashing, use asphalt cement caulking. The caulking gun provides enough pressure to force the cement down and under the flashing seams.

Seal the flashing around roof vents and stacks. Putty knife application of roofing cement may be easier than the caulking gun technique for hard-to-reach spots.

Fill any voids between roof valley flashing and shingles with roofing cement applied with a caulking gun. The flashing should be cleaned and painted (or coated) with metal paint or roofing cement about every three years.

joint of the chimney. Make sure the flashing is covered with asphalt roofing compound along the shingles and that the metal edge is firmly cemented into the chimney. You may have to re-point the mortar joint in which the flashing is installed (see later in this chapter for details).

At skylights and roof additions, flashing is usually installed under the shingles and up the side of the roof projection similar to a chimney installation. The only difference is that the flashing is nailed to the sheathing, siding, or framing of the projection. Make sure these nails are driven flush with the flashing surface and that the edges of the flashing are covered with roofing cement. Don't skimp on cement; apply plenty of it.

Another critical flashing point is along the eaves of the roof where the roofing material laps over the facia board to which gutters usually are attached. Here, water can work its up way under the shingles, rotting the sheathing and facia. This area often is overlooked, since you would assume that the water would run off the roof into the gutters and be carried away.

With a putty knife, force roofing cement up under the edge of the roofing where it extends over the facia. You may be able to lift the shingles slightly to do this. If the flashing is nailed down over the edge of the facia board, make sure the nails are driven flush with the flashing and the joint is sealed with caulking and paint.

STEPS, REPLACING

If the flashing is nailed over the shingles, use a pry bar and stiff-bladed putty knife to remove the flashing. Pull the roofing nails as you come to them. The flashing probably will be encrusted with roofing cement, so you will have to be careful not to damage the roof when removing the flashing. Once the flashing removal has been started, the rest of the job involves little more than prying up the flashing along the roof valley or around the chimney. You may be able to use the old flashing as a template to make any necessary cuts and match sizes in the new flashing.

If the flashing is under the shingles, you will have to lift the shingles in order to remove and replace the flashing. Use a flat tiling spade or ice scraper to lift the shingles, starting at the top of the shingle courses and working down. Flashing usually extends about 6 in. under the roofing, so you don't have to remove a lot of shingles to get at the flashing.

Once exposed, pry off the old flashing. Use it as a template to cut the new flashing, and nail the new flashing in position. It is a good idea to embed the new flashing in a thin coating of roofing cement applied to the roof sheathing. Coat the joint between the flashing and the roof sheathing with asphalt roofing cement. Dab the cement on the heads of the roofing nails that you used to fasten the flashing to the sheathing.

Replace the shingles, working from the bottom up. Cover with roofing cement the nailheads used to replace the shingles and use a little cement to hold each shingle down as it is replaced.

To replace the flashing along the eaves (often called drip cap), carefully pry up the bottom course of the shingles along the length of the facia. You may have to remove the gutter and gutter hangers in order to do this. Use a hammer and pry bar to remove the gutter, gutter hangers, and damaged flashing. You do not have to remove the shingles from the roof; just pry the

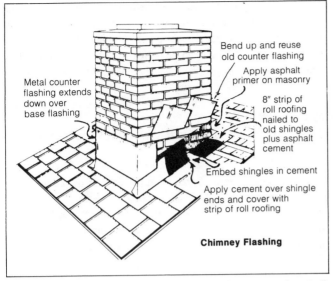

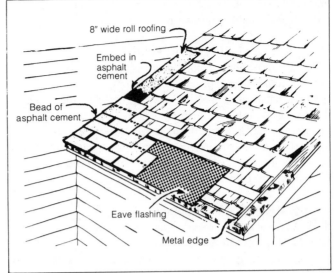

Chimney flashing must be well maintained to seal out water from both the masonry and the interior of the house. The combination of metal flashing, roofing material and cement is a good seal.

New flashing should be applied to roof/wall joints and to roof eaves whenever new asphalt shingles are applied over old. Old flashing is likely to have deteriorated with age.

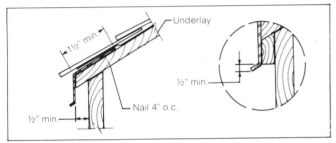

Metal flashing is applied along roof edges as extra protection. Flashing at the eaves is set beneath the roofing felt. Flashing at the rakes is set over the roofing felt.

shingles up enough to remove the old flashing and slide in the new flashing.

The new flashing can be purchased pre-formed; i.e., the necessary crimp in the flashing has already been formed. This flashing is slotted for nails so the flashing can be moved slightly to fit tightly before the nails are driven flush with the top of the flashing.

After the flashing has been nailed in place, cover the nail heads with small amounts of roofing cement, and then reseat the shingles. You may have to use walnut-sized applications of roofing cement to hold the shingles down, since they will have curled slightly when you lifted them.

While you are at this replacement job, check the facia for any water damage or rot. Now is the time to replace the facia if it is damaged. You simply pry off the facia, which is nailed to the ends of framing members (soffit or rafter ends). Give the

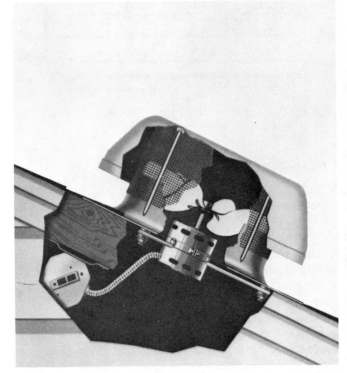

To install base for roof vent, peel back shingles. The bottom of the base sets directly on the roof sheathing. Weatherproof the base joint with insulation tape. Renail the shingles and cover the nails with roofing compound.

Turbine or ventilator fits on top of the vent base, which is held with a clamp or by screws. You may have to turn the turbine or the cover slightly to align it on the base.

new facia two coats of paint on both the front and back side and edges before you nail it in position. This will help prevent rot.

STEPS, REPAIRING

If damage to flashing is not too extensive, you may be able to repair it rather than replace it.

Cut a patch of asphalt roll roofing to cover the damaged flashing. Pre-fit the patch so you know it surrounds all of the damaged area. Then coat the damaged area and the back of the patch with asphalt roofing cement. Embed the patch in the cement at the damaged area and then coat the top and edges of the patch with cement.

Skylight Repair/Maintenance

Skylights can spring leaks around the flashing or around the framing that holds the skylight glass or plastic in position. The skylight also may leak if the glass or plastic is broken or cracked.

Tools and materials. Hammer, roofing nails, razor knife, thick roofing cement, and (depending on type of skylight) dome seals, glass, glazing compound, butyl caulking, paint, paintbrush.

STEPS

Each year inspect the flashing around the skylights on your roof. Give special attention to the glazing around the glass and where the flashing runs up the sides of the skylight framing or the skylight dome seals.

Any cracks in the flashing should be coated with asphalt roofing cement. Nail down any gaps, and drive in any popped nails, in the flashing. If the dome seals are hard (not resilient) when you probe them with a putty knife, the seals probably should be replaced. They usually are held in position with adhesive. Remove the old seal with a putty knife, thoroughly clean out the channel in which the seal is seated, and install the new seal with adhesive recommended by the manufacturer. You will find instructions for this on the packaging of the seals and adhesives.

If the skylights are glazed (like a window), check the mullions for cracked and/or missing glazing and replace the glazing (see Chapter 2). The glazing and mullions of the skylight should be painted every two years. Run the new paint about ⅛ to ¼ in. onto the glass for a good seal.

For cracks in plastic domes, you can sometimes patch the crack with clear butyl caulking compound. Caulking is strictly a stop-gap measure, however. If cracked or broken, the dome should be replaced, since caulking will not withstand the elements long. When you patch the dome, make sure the patch covers both sides of the damaged area.

Broken or cracked glass in skylights can be replaced in the same way as broken or cracked glass in windows. If the glass is fixed in the mullions, however, you should caulk the break in the glass from both sides. Clear butyl caulking works best.

GUTTERS, DOWNSPOUTS, SOFFITS, EAVES

Rain-carrying system is a fancy term for gutters and downspouts (sometimes called "leaders") which divert water from the roof of a house away from the sidewalls and foundation. Some houses do not have this system, relying instead on a roof overhang to protect the house's superstructure. Either way, ex-

cess water must be channeled away from the house to protect its components from rot, decay, flooding basements, mildew, and general dampness. There are four types of gutter/downspout systems, and each has its own set of maintenance and repair problems and procedures. However, the repair methods are similar.

Roof Overhangs

Tools and materials. Shovel, broom, wheelbarrow, dirt, gravel.

STEPS

In an overhang system, water from the roof drips off the edge of the overhang onto a gravel or concrete splash area, or a narrow pathway around the house. The water then is either absorbed by the ground, funneled away through buried tile connected to drains, or directed into sidewalk drains or a driveway.

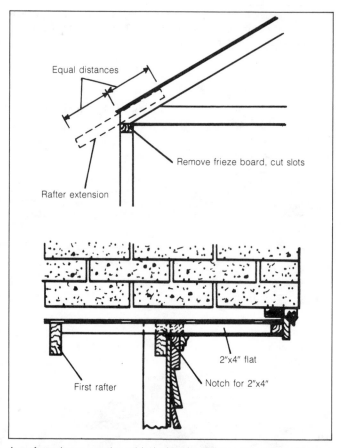

A roof overhang may be added when installing new roofing. Remove the frieze board or fascia and attach a piece of 2x4 to rafters to hold new sheathing, felt and shingles.

There is no repair for this type of system other than replacing the gravel when it washes away or sinks into the ground. The drains must be kept open, and the slope of the ground checked once a year. The slope should be away from the foundation of the house. Add dirt and gravel as needed to the water drip-off area. Drains may be kept open by giving the drain coverings a general sweeping from time to time, because rainstorms cause debris to collect at drain covers.

Roof Sheathing, Lookouts, Eaves

Improper roof drainage and/or roof leaks can cause wooden

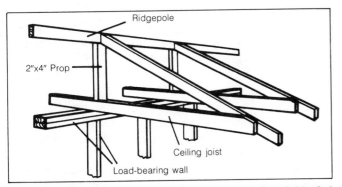

A sagging ridge pole should be repaired before reroofing. Add a 2x4 prop from the ridge pole to an interior load-bearing wall at several points along the length.

framing members along the eaves of a roof to rot. Preventive maintenance is the best course. Faulty gutters usually are the direct cause of rotting wood, not the roofing itself, so look first for any gutter/downspout damage.

To check for rot, push a chisel blade into the wood. If the blade goes into the wood with little or no resistance, rot probably has set in, and replacement is necessary. Fortunately, repairs are not too difficult; you will need more patience than skill. Work will go faster and be safer if you erect a sturdy scaffold next to the repair area, especially if replacing roof sheathing. Other repairs can be made from a ladder.

Tools and materials for sheathing repair. Pry bar, flat spade or wide ice chipper, hammer, crosscut saw, plane, tape measure, 16d galvanized common nails, roofing nails, asphalt roofing cement, asphalt roofing paper, matching patching shingles, wood preservative, paintbrush, matching sheathing.

STEPS

As carefully as possible, remove the gutter and fascia boards. Then, at the top of the patching area on the roof (probably about 4 ft. up from the edge of the roof at the eave) remove the shingles. Use the pry bar, flat spade or ice chipper to lift the shingles and nails. Work carefully so you can re-use shingles that are not damaged.

The sheathing may be plywood or boards nailed to the roof rafters. Since the sheathing is already damaged you can take it out in any way necessary, but make sure that you don't damage the rafters as you rip off the sheathing.

Cut, fit, and trim the new sheathing patch to fit the void. Then coat the patch with wood preservative — both the sides and the edges — before you nail the material to the rafters using 16d galvanized nails.

Cover the exposed new sheathing with asphalt building paper and nail the paper in position with roofing nails. Do not overnail; just use enough fasteners to hold the paper down against the surface of the sheathing.

Now replace the shingles, starting along the eaves and working up the roof. When the shingles are in place and are matched, coat the roofing nail heads with asphalt roofing compound. Then replace the fascia board and gutter. Often, the fascia has rotted. If so, install new fascia, coating its faces and edges with paint.

Tools and materials, lookout repairs. Hammer, 16d galvanized nails, crosscut saw, square, tape measure, jack plane, matching house paint, paintbrush, lumber.

STEPS

"Lookouts" are the 2x4s or 2x6s that support the soffit system. The lookouts stick out from the eaves of the house and usually are spaced 16 in. on center. Since lookouts usually are covered with soffit material, it is difficult to detect rot. The best way is to check the soffit for rot. If there is trouble with the soffit, chances are the lookouts also need repair.

On truss roofs, the lookouts may be the bottom chord of the truss — not a separate framing member. In either case the repair is the same.

Measure, mark, and cut lengths of 2x4s or 2x6s to match the lookouts. The fit shoud be as perfect as you can possibly make it.

Give the new wood and the old lookouts two coats of matching house paint. Then nail the new wood to the lookouts — face-to-face — using 16d common nails. You will need two new lookouts for each damaged lookout. Sandwich the damaged lookout between the new members.

Once this job has been completed, give the entire span another coat of house paint and then nail on the soffit material, if a soffit was used in the construction. You also may have to replace the fascia boards, as explained above.

Tools and materials for replacing gable eaves. Pry bar, hammer, square, tape measure, 10d galvanized nails, crosscut saw, matching house paint, paintbrush, matching trim/molding.

STEPS

Gable eaves sometimes are finished flush with the siding of the house. That is, the eaves do not project or overhang from the roof. The eaves are actually a trim board that is nailed directly to the end rafter of the roof framing. There is a piece of molding nailed to the face of the eave trim board at the roof line. Problems will occur here when water seeps around the molding and under the trim board. This causes rot.

Remove the molding and old trim board with a pry bar and the claws of a hammer.

Measure, mark, and cut the new trim board and molding to fit. Test it in position before you nail it to the face of the rafter.

Give all surfaces of the new trim board, molding, and the face of the rafter, two coats of matching house paint. Then nail on the new trim board and molding and give all materials a top coat of paint.

Wood Gutters

Tools and materials. Hammer, putty knife, aluminum sheet, caulking, asphalt roofing cement, linseed oil, paint, paintbrush, fiberglass, bonding resin, whisk broom.

STEPS

If the gutters are fairly new, give the insides three coats of linseed oil, letting the linseed oil dry between coats. Check that the gutter is clean before you apply the linseed oil.

As an alternative, line the gutters with fiberglass, which is expensive but gives longer protection against rot. Thoroughly clean the gutter, sweeping it out with a whisk broom — if possible, vacuum it. Apply the fiberglass resin to the wood, then embed the fiberglass cloth into the resin. Let the resin dry, and clean the gutter again. Apply two more coats of resin, letting the resin dry and cleaning the gutter between each coat.

For rot in small areas, cut a piece of aluminum sheet to cover the area. Coat the area with asphalt roofing cement and embed the aluminum patch in the cement. When the cement dries, give the top of the patch a coat of cement, feathering the edges into the surrounding wood around the patch.

If the gutter is split slightly, you can repair the split with caulking compound. Thoroughly clean the split with a putty knife and broom, removing any rotting or crumbling wood. Fill the split with caulking compound.

Wooden gutters should be cleaned and painted on the outside of the gutter about every three years — or when the paint starts to crack and peel. Wooden gutters usually have to be painted two to three times more frequently than wood siding of the house.

To repair the outside of the gutter, cut an aluminum patch to cover the damage. Nail the patch to the gutter. Then seal around the edges of the patch with caulking compound, feathering the edges of the caulking onto the metal and the wood. After thoroughly cleaning the surface, give the patch and the gutter two coats of paint.

If the gutter has rotted along its length, it is recommended that you replace the gutter immediately with a new wooden gutter or a metal or plastic model.

Aluminum Gutters

Tools and materials. Putty knife, whisk broom, silicone caulking compound, hammer, pliers, steel wool, wire brush, metal paint, brush, roof compound.

STEPS

Since aluminum does not rust, but will corrode, maintenance is low. Clean the gutters in the spring and in late fall, after the leaves are off the trees. Use a putty knife and whisk broom for this.

Do not paint aluminum gutters until they have been exposed to the elements for about six months. This time period permits the metal to properly oxidize. You can buy aluminum gutters that have been pre-primed and/or pre-finished so the six months' waiting period is eliminated or the painting not even necessary.

If the gutters have corroded, they should be cleaned with steel wool and a wire brush and given two coats of metal paint. If the gutters are old, try coating the insides of them with brushable asphalt roof compound to help protect the metal surfaces.

If the joints of the gutter leak, try bending the connectors to tighten them. Use pliers and a hammer. Then caulk the seam

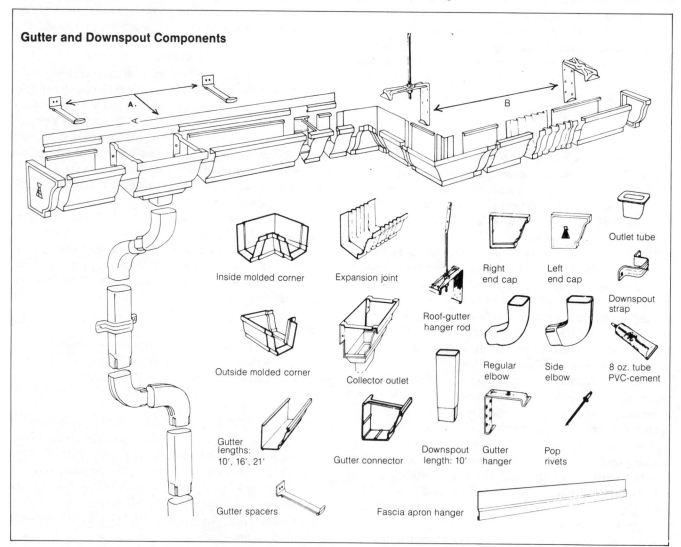

Gutter and Downspout Components

Inside molded corner

Expansion joint

Right end cap

Left end cap

Outlet tube

Roof-gutter hanger rod

Downspout strap

Outside molded corner

Collector outlet

Regular elbow

Side elbow

8 oz. tube PVC-cement

Gutter lengths: 10', 16', 21'

Gutter connector

Downspout length: 10'

Gutter hanger

Pop rivets

Gutter spacers

Fascia apron hanger

Shown are the basic units of gutter and downspout systems. These examples are in vinyl. Repairs to existing gutter/downspout systems must be made in the same material as is now on your home. New systems can be any material of your choice.

Caulk the joints of gutter end caps to prevent leakage. Also caulk the joints of slip connectors on the inside of the gutters. Butyl caulking will last a long time for this repair.

from the inside of the gutter with silicone caulking compound, feathering out the caulking with a putty knife.

Copper Gutters

Tools and materials. Putty knife, whisk broom, steel wool, exterior varnish, paintbrush.

STEPS

With a putty knife and whisk broom clean the gutters in the fall after the leaves are off the trees and in the spring after the final spring thaw.

Copper gutters turn green, a color many homeowners desire. If you want the copper to remain new and shiny instead of turning green, you will have to continually clean the gutters with steel wool and coat the metal with clear spar varnish.

Lengths of copper guttering are joined with solder. If these joints or end caps start to leak, it is best that you call in a professional for repairs since special equipment is necessary.

Plastic Gutters

Tools and materials. Putty knife, whisk broom, metal paint, new hanger brackets, paintbrush.

STEPS

Vinyl or plastic guttering is nearly maintenance-free. Every year in the spring and fall clean the gutters with a putty knife and whisk broom.

Gutter hangers usually are metal and are subject to rust. When you spot rust, paint the hangers with metal paint, or replace the hangers. Replacement may be easier and faster than trying to paint the hangers.

Galvanized Gutters

Tools and materials. Hammer, roofing nails, razor knife, asphalt roll roofing or asphalt building paper, putty knife, thick asphalt roofing cement, paint, paintbrush, garden hose, wire brush, steel wool.

STEPS

Clean the gutters every spring and fall, using a putty knife and whisk broom to remove mud and other debris. Flush out the cleaned gutter with a garden hose.

If the inside of the gutter is beginning to rust, clean the rusty area with a putty knife and wire brush and give the metal two coats of metal paint. Do the same for rust on the outside of the gutters. You may want to paint the metal with metal paint and a top coat of exterior paint that matches the siding or trim on your home.

If the gutter has rusted through the metal, patch this area with asphalt roofing cement, roll roofing or building paper. See the illustrations for patching procedures.

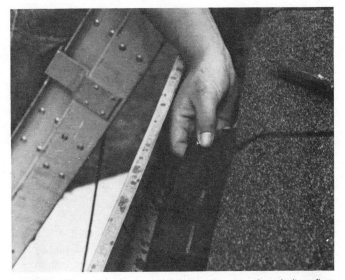

To temporarily patch a gutter, clean the gutter, spread asphalt roofing cement over the hole, and embed a piece of asphalt building paper or roll roofing over the hole.

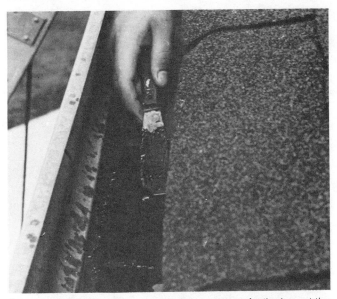

Cover the patch with more asphalt building cement, feathering out the cement at both ends of the patch. For wooden gutters, use fiberglass tape embedded in resin.

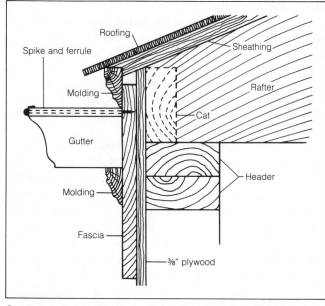

Gutters are installed this way. Molding sometimes is not used above and below the gutter; the spike/ferrule hanger may be substituted with strap gutter hangers.

To repitch gutters so water drains properly, bend the hangers with pliers. If the hangers are spikes/ferrules, pull the spikes, adjust the gutter, and replace the spikes.

Galvanized steel gutters should be coated inside with asphalt roofing cement (thin or brushable mixture) every other year or when close inspection indicates the gutters need a protective coating. If you prefer, you can substitute metal paint for roofing cement.

Gutter hangers are subject to rust and should be painted approximately every two years. The hangers may extend from the gutters up under the shingles, or the hangers may extend over the shingles. You probably will not need to paint the hangers if they go under the shingles, but look for rust and use a putty knife and wire brush to clean any rusty hangers you find. Use a first coat of metal paint. For the second coat, paint color is not critical unless the hangers extend over the shingles. In this case you probably will want a paint color that matches the shingle color so the hangers will blend in with the shingles.

Gutter spikes are another type of gutter hanger. The spikes are long nails, usually aluminum or galvanized steel, that are driven through the lip and back of the gutter into the facia or eave trim board. In some installations, the spikes are threaded through a hollow metal cylinder that extends from the inside front of the gutter to the back of the gutter. This gives the spike hangers more strength and rigidity. The only maintenance necessary is an occasional tap or two with a hammer on the head of the spikes to make sure they are driven flush against the gutter lip.

Adjusting Gutters for Drainage

Tools and materials. Pliers, hammer, bucket, water.

STEPS

All gutters, regardless of type, must be pitched toward downspouts so water can drain from the gutter into the downspout. The right pitch is about 1/16 in. per running foot of gutter. Since this measurement is difficult to determine with a tape measure, the best way to adjust the gutter is pour some water in the gutter and to watch the water flow out.

Hangers should be spaced about every three ft. along the gutter run. If they are not, water may have difficulty in flowing through the gutter. Worse, water may not flow at all, adding lots of weight to the gutter and causing it to sag or break. At the points where the water flows slowly, or stops completely, you will need to adjust the pitch by bending the gutter hangers a little up or down. If the water puddles in one spot, bend the hanger nearest to this spot upward. If the hangers are the strap type, use pliers. If the hangers are the spike type, use a hammer to reposition the hangers.

To adjust the pitch of wooden gutters, you will have to remove the nails that hold the gutter to the facia. Then repitch and renail the gutter to the facia.

Systematic Gutter Cleaning

Tools and materials. Putty knife, whisk broom, garden hose, ladder.

STEPS

Clean the gutters on your house in the fall after the leaves are off the trees, and again in the spring after the last winter freeze and thaw.

Start at the opposite end of the downspout and by hand pick out all the debris in the gutter that you can. With the same ladder setting, scrape the bottom of the gutter with a putty knife, also tossing out as much mud, leaf residue, and granules from the roofing as you can. Brush, then flood this area with a garden hose. Work the entire length of the gutter this way. Then go back at the starting point and hose down the inside of the gutter until the gutter is clean.

Any maintenance work to the gutter — replacing hangers, painting, etc., should be done after the gutter has been cleaned.

Downspout Maintenance and Replacement

Tools and materials. Hammer, pliers, self-tapping metal screws, bradawl, garden hose, ladder.

STEPS, SLIPPED JOINTS

Downspout trouble usually can be found where the downspout connects to the gutter. This joint generally is loose, if it has not slipped completely apart. To take care of this problem, rejoin the downspout with the gutter by punching two or three holes through both the downspout and tail of the gutter, and driving self-tapping metal screws into the holes.

If your home is built of brick, block, or stone, downspout hangers are either metal straps or round hooks with spike ends. When these supports work loose, simply renail the hangers using longer nails. You may want to put up additional hangers for more support to the downspout. For gutter hooks with spike ends, tap the hanger with a hammer to reseat the hanger. If this does not work, pull the hanger out of the mortar joint and reposition the hanger at another nearby mortar joint.

STEPS, CLOGGED DOWNSPOUTS

Position a garden hose in the opening of the gutter and push the hose nozzle down into the downspout. Then turn on the water full blast. Use the hose as a hydraulic ram to break up the obstruction. Snake the hose down into the downspout as the clog moves out.

STEPS, EXCESS WATER

Water should be funneled away from the bottom opening of the downspout so the water does not back up and drain down along the foundation of the house and, possibly, into the basement.

A splashblock, properly sloped away from the foundation may be adequate. You may also need another length of downspout connected to the house downspout to move the water out into the lawn. Another solution is to attach a length of perforated plastic pipe to the bottom opening of the downspout and bury the pipe out in the lawn (see illustration). Other products that you can buy to solve this problem are roll-up plastic lawn soakers that fit the ends of downspouts; plastic splashblocks, and specially designed hoses that fit downspouts.

Dry Wells

If the water problem is too much for a splashblock or plastic pipe to handle, you may want to consider a dry well to absorb the excess moisture.

STEPS

To construct a dry well, dig a hole in your lawn about 10 ft. out from the house foundation. The hole should be deep and large enough to accommodate a 55-gallon steel drum. The top of the drum should be about 15 in. under the surface of the lawn.

Punch lots of holes in the drum; a metal drill in an electric drill will work best. Also punch a hole in the drum to fit the diameter of a plastic or metal pipe that will run underground from the downspout opening to the inside of the drum.

Fill the drum with gravel, old brickbats, broken concrete, and/or masonry debris. Then cover the top of the drum with a metal lid. Tightly pack the dirt you shoveled out for the drum and pipe back around the drum and pipe.

Dry wells should be positioned at all four corners of your house, or where the main downspouts are located. Some downspouts are centered in the gutter run.

If this system does not handle the water problem at your

For cleaning debris from downspouts, use a garden hose as a water jet. You can buy gutter guards and downspout strainers to keep leaves out of the water-carrying system.

A downspout which does not quite reach the ground must have support at the base or the force of the water will eventually dislodge it from the gutter. Bricks make an adequate support if installed firmly.

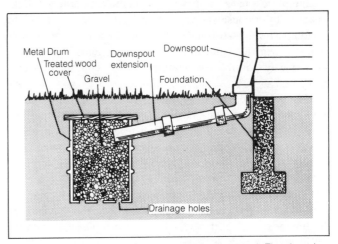

A dry well is a 55-gallon metal drum filled with gravel. The drum has holes drilled into it for drainage. The downspout hooks to the drum.

house, you should consider a central dry-well system, which works similarly to a septic tank hook-up. The planning and installation of this system, however, is best left to a professional landscape architect.

Soffit Repair and Replacement

Tools and materials. Hammer, threaded or cement-coated nails, caulking, square, tape measure, new plywood (depending on the repair), crosscut saw, jack plane, pry bar, paint, paintbrush, ladder.

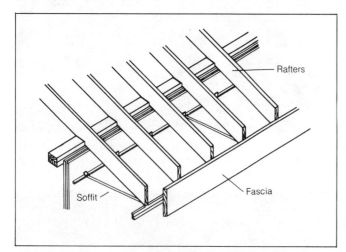

The soffit hides the underside of the rafter overhang. It gives a finished appearance to the overhang and is easy to paint. However, water may back up under the soffit and cause warping, rotting or mildew.

STEPS

If your home has a roof overhang, the overhang probably will be covered with plywood, hardboard, or aluminum. This component is called a soffit. Soffit troubles are almost always caused by water, which seeps from gutters, under the facia, and along the top of the soffit. Wood rot or warp is the result.

The first step is to repair the gutter so it doesn't leak, as above.

If the soffit is not badly damaged, you may be able to caulk the joints and renail the soffit panels to the framing members to which the panels are fastened. The panels usually are installed in 2, 4, or 8 ft. lengths and are nailed to the framing members at 16 or 24 ft. intervals.

To replace a panel, remove any trim molding fastened to the panel and the house siding, and along the fascia. Pry off the molding carefully so you can re-use it. Since the panel will be replaced, rip right into it with a hammer, removing it in the easiest way possible. A hammer/pry bar combination may work best.

Measure and cut the new panel to fit the void, being sure the new panel matches the thickness of the old one. Set the new panel in place, marking in pencil wherever it sticks or binds — if it does stick or bind. Then use a plane to trim the panel to fit. Give the sides and edges of the wood a prime coat of paint. When the paint has dried, nail the panel in place.

Finish by caulking the joints, renailing any trim pieces, and applying a second coat of paint to the wood. You may have to repaint the entire soffit run so the new panel blends in with the old panels.

Metal soffits seldom need replacement. However, if replace-

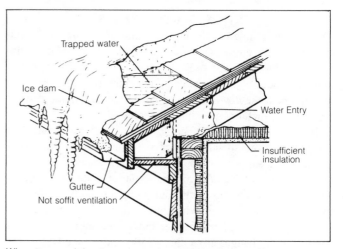

When too much heat escapes a house through the ceiling to the roof, snow melts on the roof surface, is trapped and leaks through the sheathing and into the soffit and the house.

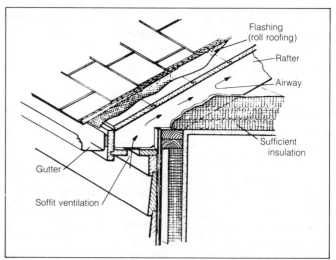

To prevent an ice dam build up during winter snows, insulate underlying ceilings well and provide good soffit ventilation so the snow on the roof will melt from the top down, not from the bottom up.

ment is necessary, you will have to remove an end cap strip that holds the soffit panel in position. This cap usually is nailed to a framing member. The metal soffit panel probably will run in parallel metal channels. At intervals, the panels will be joined by metal divider strips. You simply pull out the damaged panel and slip in the new panel, locking the adjoining panels together with the divider strips. Then nail the end cap back on.

Replacing Soffit Vents

If the attic in your home does not have ventilation, vents should be installed, especially if the attic is, or will be, insulated.

For gable vents at each end of the house, without a vapor barrier for insulation, allow 1 sq. ft. inlet and 1 sq. ft. outlet for every 300 sq. ft. of ceiling area. For gable vents with a vapor barrier (the barrier must face down toward the heated rooms below), allow 1 sq. ft. inlet and 1 sq. ft. outlet for every 600 sq. ft. of attic ceiling area. (See Chapter 4.)

If the attic is vented at both gable ends and along the eaves, allow 1 sq. ft. inlet and 1 sq. ft. outlet for every 600 sq. ft. of ceiling area. This amount should be divided equally between gable vents and soffit vents.

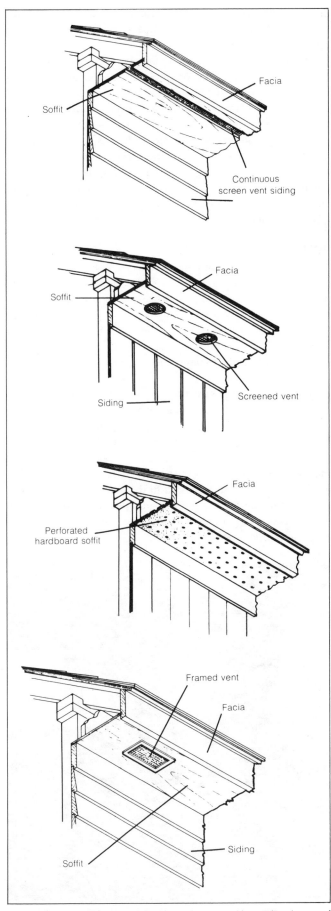

Soffit vents allow air to circulate in attic spaces and lower the chance of ice dam buildup. There are various types of soffit vents available for installation.

Tools and materials. Hammer, screwdriver, keyhole saw, flathead metal screws.

STEPS

Vents are fastened to soffit panels with four to six screws. By removing the screws, the vent can be removed from the panels.

Before you replace a damaged vent with a new one, make sure the opening the vent covers is large enough. If the vent is the standard 6x10 in. product, a tiny hole will not provide enough air passage. Open up this area with a keyhole saw, using the vent as a sawing template or guide.

Some soffit vents are round pieces of aluminum with tiny louvers. These range in size from about 2 in. to 4 in. in diameter. The vents are push fitted into the soffit panels. Use a pry bar to remove the old vent; you just push the new vent into position.

Maintain a tight seal between the chimney cap and flue lining so that water does not seep in and cause damage. The cement wash chimney cap must also be well maintained or pieces will break off.

CHIMNEY REPAIRS

Chimneys should be inspected yearly. Look for broken chimney caps, crumbling mortar joints in the brickwork, and loose or damaged metal flashing at the base of the chimney. Check roof vents for deteriorating roofing compound around the flashing.

Maintenance

To make the roof watertight, metal flashing is bent up the sides of chimneys. The metal then is covered with asphalt roofing cement. This coating has to be renewed every three years or so.

Tools and materials. Baby sledge, cold or brick chisel, mortar mix cement, mixing bucket, tuckpointing trowel, asphalt roofing cement, putty knife, ladder.

Safety. Be safe on the ladder when you climb onto the roof for chimney inspection and repairs. If the roof is steep, let a professional do the job. The ladder should extend above the eaves of the house by three rungs. It also should slope away from the house one fourth the length of the ladder. Make sure the rails on the ladder are on firm ground; have a friend hold the ladder while you are on it.

STEPS

Coat around the flashing with asphalt roofing cement, using a putty knife to trowel the cement onto the flashing. Smooth out

Special plastic fitting is designed to fit the end of a downspout and the opening of a drain. It may also be used to connect the downspout with a length of pipe or tile.

For serious drainage problems, hook the downspout to a section or two of perforated plastic pipe, which can be buried underground. Elbows and other fittings are available for the pipe. The pipe is very inexpensive.

Flexible pipe can be bent to match the downspout opening and clay drainage tile buried in the ground. The pipe is an excellent substitute for clay tile, which often breaks.

the cement with the putty knife, making sure all holes are filled and all nailheads are covered. Use mineral spirits to clean asphalt cement from tools.

To fix mortar damage, remove any loose concrete around the chimney cap with a cold or brick chisel. Cut away the bad concrete, down to good material. Mix up a small batch of mortar mix and trowel it into the break, forming it with a tuckpointing trowel. It is a good idea to soak the surrounding edges of the concrete with water so the old concrete will not absorb all of the moisture from the fresh concrete.

Check the mortar joints, running a cold or brick chisel over the joints. If you spot a bad joint, chip out the damaged mortar and repoint the joint with new mortar and a tuckpointing trowel (see "Tuckpointing Brick & Block," this chapter).

FOUNDATION DRAINAGE

Moisture is a foundation's biggest enemy. Water — in the form of snow, rain, and humidity — can destroy mortar joints in brick and concrete block, rot wooden sills and other foundation-connected framing, and cause other problems such as flooded basements. Occasional holes in the backfill around the foundation will also permit water to seep in, so check periodically and add dirt to any holes you find.

Gutters and Downspouts.

Look for trouble here if your basement is leaking water. Often, faulty gutters and downspouts are serving as funnels to carry the water down against the foundation wall. The result is a damp or wet basement. Repairs or a new rain-carrying system may be the answer. However, in some cases the problem can be handled by adding an extension to the downspout pipe; it just slips over the end of the downspout. Another alternative is to hook a section of perforated plastic pipe to the downspout, and bury the plastic pipe underground

Bury the plastic flexible pipe; then tamp the earth tight around the pipe. Keep the earth sloped away from the foundation of the house for the proper water drainage.

Foundation Seepage

Tools and materials. Since the problem can involve gutters, downspouts, broken concrete joints, tools are related to each job as outlined below.

STEPS

First try patching any interior cracks with hydraulic cement. Clean out the crack with a cold or brick chisel, driving these tools with a baby sledge hammer. Make the cut in the form of an inverted V, if you can. This will help hold the patch in place.

Press the hydraulic cement into the break and smooth it level with the surrounding surface of the foundation wall with a putty knife. You will have to work fast; hydraulic cement sets quickly. Wear gloves for this job, since hydraulic cement creates heat that could injure your skin.

STEPS, WATERPROOFING FOUNDATIONS

If hydraulic cement does not work, and the rain-carrying system is not the problem, there is only one sure way to stop the leaking.

1. Dig a trench around the foundation. The trench should be wide enough for you to fit in it; it should be deep enough to go to the foundation footing.

2. Clean off the foundation wall. Use a wide scraper for this; scrub the wall down with water from a garden hose and a stiff broom or brush.

3. Make a 3-inch-thick bed of medium-sized gravel in the trench. Lay a row of field tile on the gravel around the bottom of the foundation. The tile should have a slight pitch. At one corner of the house, where the tile come together in the downward pitch, run a length of tile out into the lawn about 10 ft. You will need to dig a trench for this, too. Lay the tile on 3 in. of gravel.

4. Coat the foundation walls, from the footing to grade level, with a thick application of asphalt roofing cement. You can apply this with a trowel and brush. Make sure all areas are covered thoroughly.

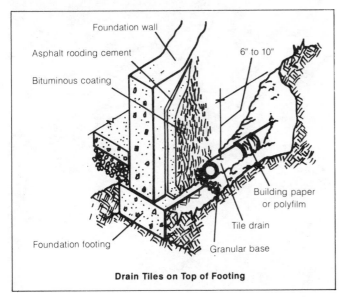

Drain Tiles on Top of Footing

Properly installed drain tile will carry rainwater away from the house foundation and protect against water seepage into foundation and basement. It helps relieve ground water buildup and pressure.

5. Embed a layer of black 4 mil polyfilm into the asphalt roofing cement. Overlap the joints of the polyfilm about 4 in., sticking the joints together with asphalt roofing cement. Give all the polyfilm a thin coating of asphalt roofing cement, brushing the cement onto the polyfilm.

6. Let the job dry for a couple of days. Then backfill the earth from the trench into the trench. Save any leftover dirt. The ground will settle for some time and you will need this dirt to fill small voids.

Window Wells

Tools and materials. Broom, plumbers' snake, asphalt roofing cement, hammer, pliers, screwdriver, nails, putty knife.

STEPS

Most window wells have French-type drains; i.e., the drain empties into a bed of gravel instead of a sewer. It may, however, be connected to the sewer. Keep the top of the drain free of gravel, grass, dirt, and other debris — an occasional sweeping with a broom is all that is needed.

If the drain has become rusted shut, you can replace it with a new drain top. Remove the old one by removing the screws or bolts holding the top and tapping off the tap with a hammer.

Window wells often tip away from the house. You can secure them to the house with nails. If not, fill the gap between the flanges of the metal and the house with asphalt roofing compound. If the gap is a large one, you can force asphalt-impregnated expansion strips into the crack. Then cover the strips with asphalt roofing cement, using a putty knife as a trowel.

EXTERIOR WALLS

Again, water is the cause of most problems with siding, windows, and doors. Freezing and thawing can cause the siding to buckle, separate, crack, and actually pop loose from the sheathing and/or framing members. Doors and windows can stick due to water warp. Laminated wood doors will sometimes delaminate from exposure to the weather.

The best protection is a periodic coat of paint or sealer, usually every 5 to 8 years. It is important, too, to make sure the roof and gutters on the house are in good repair so that excessive moisture is channeled away from the house and does not drip and run down the siding.

How to Patch Split Siding

Tools and materials. Hammer, pry bar, threaded siding nails, caulking and caulking gun, touch-up paint, paintbrush.

STEPS

First, try to renail the siding, pulling the split section together with nails. If nailing doesn't work, pry up the damaged area very carefully and remove the nails holding the siding to the sheathing or framing.

Apply a bead of caulking along the split. Use sufficient caulking, but you need not be lavish. Then lightly tap the split together with a hammer. Have a helper hold the break together while you nail the bottom of the split to the sheathing or framing. The nails pull the split together and hold it secure. Then, with more nails, fasten down all of the damaged area.

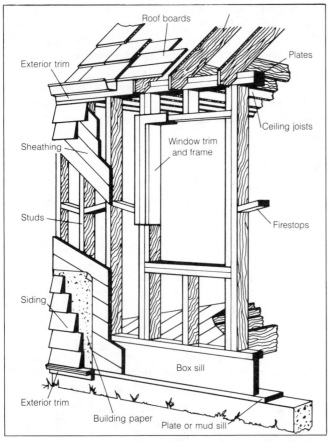

Shown is the anatomy of a typical sidewall of a house, with roofing and gutter detail. Doors are framed similar to windows. Water problems occur mainly at doors, windows, sills.

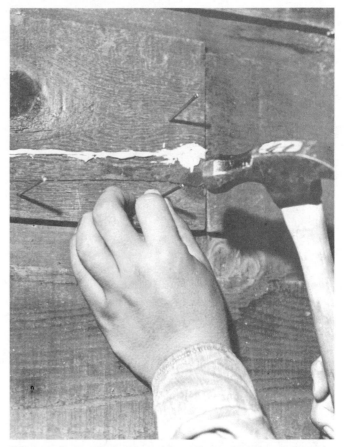

Nail the split along both edges of the split, spacing the nails 2 or 3 in. apart. Threaded nails are best, although you can use 10d or 16d finishing nails.

Siding that has cracked should be filled with caulking compound and then painted or stained. Force in the caulking until the break is full.

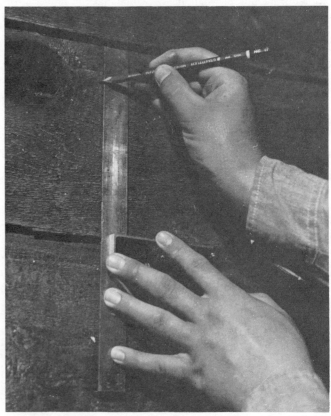

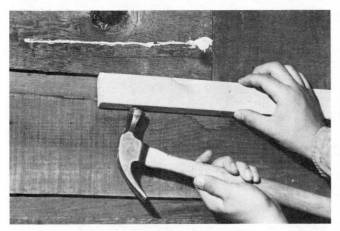

If the split is sagging, fill it with caulking and then force the split back together, using a piece of scrap wood to buffer the hammer blows.

To replace a section of damaged siding, measure, mark, and cut out the damaged section. Square cuts are extremely important so that the new siding will fit snugly.

Complete the job by smoothing the caulking with a water-wetted finger and touch-up the spot with a coat or two of paint.

Patching Drop (Bevel) Siding

Tools and materials. Hammer, pry bar, wooden wedges or thick siding shakes, caulking in gun, hacksaw blade, crosscut saw, tape measure, block plane, square, new matching siding, paint, paintbrush.

STEPS

Drive several wedges up under the bottom edge of the damaged siding board, and the board above it. This will pull the board away from the sheathing or framing. As you do this, you may have to loosen and pry out several nails that hold the board in position. Be careful; you do not want to damage the adjoining siding.

When the gap at the bottom of the siding board is wide enough to accept the width of a hacksaw blade, (or crosscut saw) insert the blade up under the gap and saw the board upward at each end of the board and lift out damaged area. This requires more patience than skill; the hacksaw blade or crosscut saw will be hard to stroke. Wear gloves to protect your hands.

Once cut, the damaged section is easy to pry loose. Since this portion of the board is being replaced, you can risk breaking it. But do not damage the good siding.

Keep the wedges in position. Cut and trim the new siding to match the void. Slide the new piece into place.

When the fit is as perfect as you can get it, remove the wedges and nail the siding in position. Then renail the course of siding above, below, and at each side of the patch. With caulking, seal the joints, and then spot prime and paint (or stain) the new wood. You may have to refinish the entire side of the house if the current paint job has aged more than two years.

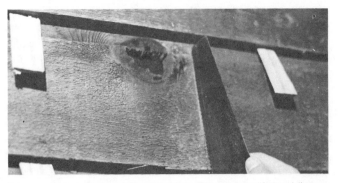

Drive wedges under the damaged siding. The wedges lift the siding so you can cut it with a hacksaw or crosscut saw. You may have to use a chisel, as well as the saw, to cut through the siding. Keep the chisel edge sharp.

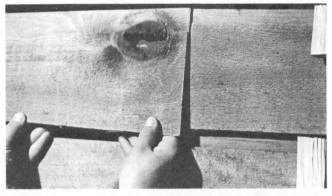

Use the old siding as a template to cut and fit the new siding patch. You may have to use wedges to spread the surrounding siding so the patch may be inserted under the siding above the patch.

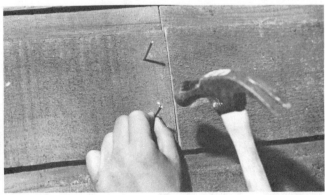

Nail the siding patch to the sheathing, using threaded nails or 10d or 16d finishing nails. You may want to countersink the nail heads and fill the holes. Use wood putty, glazing compound, or caulking for this.

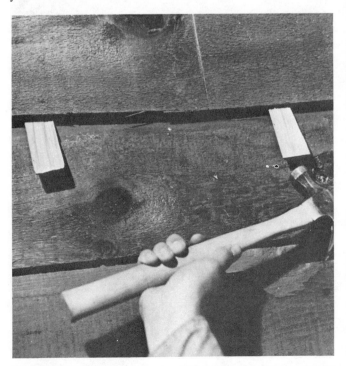

Drive wooden edges along the top of the damaged siding under the course of siding above the damaged siding. You can use cedar shingles for wedges or make wedges from scrap.

Caulk the vertical joints of the patch. If the joints form a crack after the siding has been nailed to the sheathing, caulk the horizontal joints.

Replacing Shingles/Shakes

Tools and materials. Hammer, pry bar, thick-bladed putty knife, chisel, threaded nails, caulking in gun, paint, paintbrush, or paint pad.

STEPS

Shingles and shakes are similar, and their repair or replacement on the side of a house is the same. We will refer to shingles, but the procedures also apply to shakes.

If the damage is slight you may be able to reinforce the

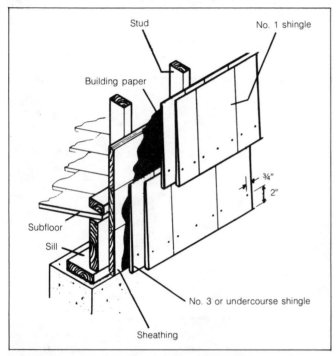

Double course wood shingles are layered so that joints on each course are covered by another course and the overlap from course to course is staggered for a tight seal against the elements.

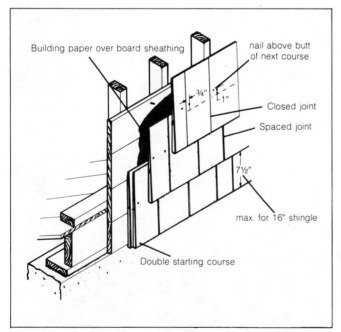

Single course wood shingles are staggered and overlapped like the double course except that the overlap is greater. They may be installed with either a closed or open joint.

damaged shingle with nails around the break. Then caulk the joints and spot paint the damaged area.

If a shingle must be replaced, use a hammer and pry bar to remove the nails holding the shingle in place. These nails will be located above the damaged shingle. Be careful here not to damage the adjoining shingle when you pull out the nails.

Remove the damaged shingle by pulling it down and out. If the replacement shingle will show, you may want to remove a good shingle from the back of the house and use it as the replacement. Then nail in the new shingle to replace the old one. Shingles are very porous, so a newly bought shingle almost never matches those that have weathered.

When painting shingles that are grooved, use a short-bristled brush or painting pad. Work the paint onto the surface with the grooves, not across the grooves.

Repairing Plywood Siding

Tools and materials. Hammer, threaded nails, caulking in gun, hole saw, plywood panel or scrap, paint, paintbrush, tape measure, square, level, crosscut saw, jack plane.

STEPS

Splits, caused by water, are the biggest maintenance problem with plywood siding; repair is easy. Reinforce the split with nails driven around the split. Then force caulking compound into the damaged area. Smooth the caulking and touch up the area with paint or stain.

If the damage is quite small, you may be able to drill it out with a hole saw and then plug this hole with a new piece of matching plywood. Coat the edges of the plug with caulking compound and face-nail the plug to the framing or sheathing. Countersink the nailheads. Caulk nailheads and paint to match.

If the damage is large, you will have to replace the entire

Open joints between dissimilar materials such as siding and concrete should be cleaned and filled with caulking compound or oakum, a ropelike material soaked in resin.

plywood panel. Find the joints, which probably are covered by a batten strip. Remove this strip with a hammer and/or pry bar. Then pry out the panel. Since the panel is already damaged, you don't have to be careful with it when removing it.

Measure, mark, cut, fit, and trim the new panel. Then nail it in position and nail on the batten strips, if there are batten strips. Give the new panel a prime and finish coat of paint or stain.

Repairing Hardboard Siding

Tools and materials. Hammer, threaded nails, caulking in gun, hole saw, hardboard panel or scrap, paint, paintbrush, tape measure, square, level, crosscut saw, medium-grit abrasive, sanding block.

STEPS

You can repair splits in hardboard in much the same way as splits in plywood (see above).

Remove the panel. Cut out the damaged area using a keyhole or crosscut saw. Cut a patch to match the area you have cut out. Set in the patch, nailing as needed. Renail the panel to the house sheating or framing. Coat the edges of the patch with caulking. Then give the entire panel two coats of finish.

To replace a hardboard panel, follow the same instructions given for replacing a plywood panel.

Siding vents let moisture vapor escape from inside your home. This helps prevent peeling paint, since the moisture pops paint on siding as it penetrates the wood. You simply drill a hole in the siding and insert the metal vents.

Repairing Aluminum Siding

Tools and materials. Hammer, pry bar, wooden wedges, plumber's friend.

STEPS

The most common problem with aluminum siding is dents, and they probably won't show if the siding has been properly backed with aluminum siding backer-board. However, for dents that are large but shallow, try pulling them out with a plumber's friend. Stick the suction cup of the plumber's friend over the largest area of the dent, compress the suction cup, and then pull out on the handle. This trick can pop the dent out, although you may have to try several times.

If this does not work, you will have to remove the length of siding and then tap out the dent from the back side of the siding. Follow the same wedge-and-pry techniques for removal of metal siding as for wooden siding.

REMOVING STAINS FROM EXTERIOR MATERIALS

Type of Stain	Removal Technique
Smoke	*From wood:* mild household detergent and water. *From masonry:* Ammonia and water; apply with stiff brush.
Soot	*From wood:* mild household detergent and water; rinse thoroughly. *From masonry:* household detergent and water, or 1 part muriatic acid to 1 part water (commercial chemicals available).
Crayon	*For wood:* remove with blade of a case knife. Then wash area with household detergent and hot water; rinse thoroughly. *For masonry:* remove with case knife, then use stiff wire brush or wire brush attachment for a portable electric drill.
Mud/dirt	Mild household detergent and water; apply with stiff brush. If area is large, work from bottom up. Rinse thoroughly.
Mildew	Use good commercial prep. If repainting, use paint formulated with mildewcide. For small areas, try mixture of lemon juice and water.
Moss	Use hydrated lime and water. Wear heavy gloves; protect face and arms. Scrub with stiff brush; flood the area with water.
Lime salts	Use commercial solution.
Grease	Remove with a case knife and soft, absorbent cloth. Then wash with mild household detergent and water. Rinse thoroughly.

Replacing Vinyl Siding

The methods are the same as for drop (Bevel) siding, this chapter.

Replacing Corrugated Metal Siding

Follow the procedures outlined for replacing plywood siding, this chapter.

Replacing Asbestos-Cement Siding

The methods are the same as for shingles and shakes, and bevel siding, this chapter.

Replacing Block and Brick

If damaged block or brick is over a window or door, under a window, or is stacked — not staggered — it is better to call in a professional. These are critical load-bearing areas; remove the block or brick and the wall could sag or collapse.

Tools and materials. Baby sledge hammer, star drill, cold chisel, brick chisel, premixed mortar mix, mixing container, trowel, tuckpointing trowel, joint strike.

Safety. Wear safety glasses and gloves.

STEPS

With a star drill, brick chisel, and cold chisel, break out the old brick or block, using a baby sledge hammer to drive the cutting tools You may have to use a combination of the tools to remove the old masonry. It is sometimes easier to start at the mortar joints and work the masonry unit out of the wall by prying and chipping on it.

The procedure reads quickly on paper, but it is actually a slow process that takes more patience than skill. Work slowly and chip away in small amounts.

When the old masonry unit is out, clean off any mortar

debris with the cold chisel, but try not to disturb the mortar lines around the other blocks or bricks.

Mix the mortar to a thick consistency.

While you're at this, soak the new block or brick in a bucket of water. Let it absorb as much water as possible.

Wet down the void in the wall where you will insert the new masonry unit. Then, with the trowel, lay down a bed of mortar on the bottom block or brick. Also butter the ends of the new unit with mortar and the top edge of the unit with mortar. Slip the unit into the hole. You will, of course, dislodge some of the mortar as the new unit slides into the hole. This is not a problem, as long as there is enough mortar left for a good bond. If not, rebutter the unit and give it another try.

When the new unit is in place, take a tuckpointing trowel and force as much mortar into the joints as you possibly can. Don't skimp; pack the mortar in tightly. Now strike the joint with the tuckpointing trowel (strike means "to smooth") cleaning away any mortar that may have ended up on an adjoining block or brick.

Let the job set about 30 minutes. Then strike the new joint with a concrete strike or the tuckpointing trowel. The illustrations show the different joints you can make. If possible, pick the one that matches the rest of the joints.

Tuckpointing Brick and Block

Most homes have concrete block or brick work. The mortar joints in these masonry units are subject to expansion and contraction as well as attack by the elements, which can cause the mortar joints to crack and crumble.

Tools and materials. Baby sledge hammer, cold chisel or brick chisel, premixed mortar, mixing container, water, mixing hoe (for big jobs), piece or scrap plywood or board, tuckpointing trowel, joint strike, bucket for clean water.

Safety. Wear safety glasses and gloves.

STEPS

Use the cold chisel or brick chisel and baby sledge hammer to clean out loose and crumbling mortar. Cut the bad mortar down

to the good, but don't overdo it. Just chip away the bad area and stop.

Mix the mortar. If the job is small, a coffee can full of mortar may be enough. If the job is big, mix the mortar in a bucket or regular mixing tub. The mixture should be fairly stiff, but not hard.

Place the mortar on a small piece of board or plywood (this is called a "hawk" and should be small enough for you to handle with one hand). Align the hawk with the mortar joint and push the mortar into the joint with the tuckpointing trowel. Make sure the joint is packed fully with mortar.

If you are working in hot weather, it is a good idea to wet the joint area with water. This will prevent the water from the mortar from soaking too fast into the masonry units and other mortar joints.

Rake the front of the masonry units with the edge of the trowel to remove any new mortar debris. Then strike the joints with the tuckpointing trowel or joint strike. In hot weather, keep the repointed area damp with water for several days. This produces a harder concrete.

Re-point the cleaned joint with mortar, packing the joint full of thick mortar with a tuckpointing trowel (shown). It's smart to wet the joint with water before the mortar is applied.

With a brick chisel or cold chisel remove damaged mortar from brick (or block) joints. Cut the loose material down to the firm mortar. As you are pounding away, be careful that you don't chip or break the bricks or concrete blocks.

When the mortar looks shiny, strike the joint with a concrete strike or the tuckpointing trowel. This step helps seal the surface of the mortar so it can withstand the elements better. A joint strike is inexpensive.

Brick and Block Maintenance

Other than occasional tuckpointing, brick and block need little maintenance. Here are some suggestions on how to keep these masonry materials in good shape.

Remove plants and clinging vines from masonry walls. This vegetation holds moisture that can crumble mortar joints. If you like the appearance of an ivy-covered home, then be prepared to tuckpoint the joints every few years. The joints should be inspected every year.

Mildew can be a masonry problem. You can buy mildewcides to remove the mildew. This involves washing the walls with the solution. You also can buy paint that contains a mildewcide, if the masonry surfaces have been painted.

If your masonry has an accumulation of grime, the best way to remove it is to sandblast the masonry. Some rental outfits offer small sandblasters for rent. But before you get started, make sure that local codes do not prohibit your doing the work. It is also a good idea to check with the neighbors before you

If both neighbors and codes are amenable, the rental agency will furnish you with the necessary equipment and materials, along with instructions. We also recommend that you get bids from a professional sandblasting contractor. It may be to your advantage to have a professional handle this job.

Stains on masonry. Most stains on brick and stone can be removed with strong household detergent, water, and a good stiff scrub brush. If you can't get all the stain off with this treatment, mix 50% muriatic acid with 50% water and scrub this solution on to the surface. Rinse with clear water from a garden hose. Be sure to wear safety glasses and gloves when you apply the acid solution.

How To Patch Stucco

Tools and materials. Hammer, brick chisel, baby sledge hammer, nails, asphalt building paper (55 lb.), chicken wire, staples, latex-based cement, clean sharp sand, mason's trowel, wooden float, straightedge, notched trowel, wide paintbrush, rubber float, garden hose with a spray nozzle, masonry paint, paintbrush, broom.

STEPS

Clean the damaged stucco area with a brick chisel driven by a baby sledge hammer. Then brush away all the debris with an old broom. The area must be as clean as possible, and the damaged stucco cut back to the good, firm stucco.

Line the patch with asphalt building paper, tacking it in position with a couple of nails. Over the paper, cut and fit a piece of chicken wire to match the shape of the patch. Nail the chicken wire to the sheathing in several spots — top, bottom, sides. Do not put in too many nails; the wire has to support the new stucco.

Mix a small batch of latex-based cement (sometimes called bonding cement) with sand. Use one part cement to three parts sand. The consistency should be that of thick mud. With a mason's trowel, spread the mixture into the patch area, working from the bottom of the wire upward.

When the mixture starts to dry, lightly run a notched trowel across the patch. Try to give the surface of the patch a slight tooth so that a second coat of cement can be applied later over the first coat.

Let the patch set for about 10 days. Spray the first patch with water, but do not soak it. Then add a second cement coat — use the same mixture as for the first patch.

With a straightedge that reaches across the patch, level the patch and then smooth it with a wooden float until you see tiny grains of sand on the surface of the patch.

Let the second coat dry for 20 days. Now mix a third batch of patching cement, which should be thinned to the consistency of thick soup. This is a wash coat. Lightly spray the patch with water from the garden hose and apply this last mixture with a mason's trowel. Level the coat with the trowel as you work the mixture over the surface. Completely cover the second base coat with a thin layer of the cement.

When the top coat starts to dry, lightly brush the surface with water. Then, using a rubber float, stroke the surface. Keep the unworked surface damp with water as you work the float. Since the mixture will be drying fast, you will have to work quickly. You have about 25 to 30 minutes in which to float the final surface on the patch. Blend the edges (feather them) into the surrounding stucco so the finish will match.

If the surface will be colored, you can add color to the top coat mixture. As an alternative, you can wait about three months and then give the patch and the entire siding a fresh coat of masonry paint.

DOOR AND WINDOW AREAS
Casing Boards

Tools and materials. Hammer, pry bar, putty knife, crosscut saw, square, tape measure, miter box, butt chisel, new matching casing, glazing compound, paint, paintbrush.

STEPS

Casing is really a trim board — molding — that hides the ends of siding, sheathing, and exposed framing of doors and windows. It is the exterior counterpart of base shoe and crown molding.

Fortunately, casing is easy to replace since it is just nailed adjacent to, over, or around siding, windows, and doors. Pry off the damaged casing using a hammer and pry bar. Measure, mark, and cut the new casing to fit. Then nail it in position, countersinking the nails and filling the nail holes with glazing compound. Prime and paint the new wood.

Around windows and doors, you may have to miter the casing (use a miter box) for a neat, smooth fit.

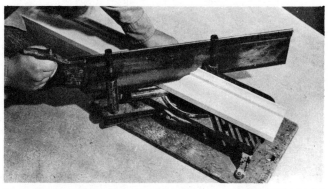

Window and door casing often has a definite pattern that can be matched at home centers. The casing should be mitered, as shown, and carefully fitted around the window or door. Use finishing nails. Fill the joint with caulking compound to deter rot.

Replacing Drip Cap/Water Stop

Tools and materials. Hammer, pry bar, threaded nails, nail set, chisel, scrap 1x4 for pry block, paint, paintbrush, caulking in gun, new molding.

STEPS

Drip cap and water stop is a special molding installed above windows and doors to prevent water from running down the face of these two components. Rot is the big problem since, as the name implies, drip cap and water stop is constantly subjected to water.

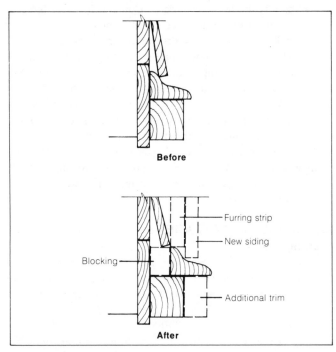

When you install new siding, you have to adjust the drip cap outward with a blocking piece and support it with new trim so that it will do the job for which it is intended.

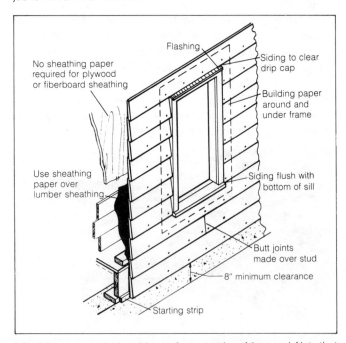

Install flashing on window drip cap for protection of the wood. Note that the bevel siding should come almost to the edge of the frame at the widest part of the board.

The molding is usually nailed to the top window or door casing. Siding butts one edge of it and the back of it is flashed with metal or asphalt flashing.

To remove the old molding, use a hammer, pry bar, and chisel, being very careful not to damage the casing or the siding. The molding probably will be nailed from top to bottom into the casing, or it may be nailed from the face into the sheathing or house framing.

Measure, mark, cut, trim, and fit the new piece of molding. Then give it two coats of paint or penetrating sealer. When this finish has dried, position the molding in the void and face nail it to the sheathing. Then run a bead of caulking at the top, bottom, and edges of the molding, and spot paint all wood as needed.

A pre-fabricated sash can be used to replace an old unit as long as you can remove the sash from the window frame without damage. Inspect the frame after the sash is removed and repair the frame if needed.

Fit the new sash into the frame and install as directed. When it is securely in place, be sure to caulk around the sash unit as well as the frame for air-tight seal.

Replacing Thresholds

Tools and materials. Hammer, threaded or finishing nails, nail set, pry bar, crosscut saw, screwdriver, caulking in gun, paint or stain, paintbrush, wood filler, wooden or metal or metal thermal threshold.

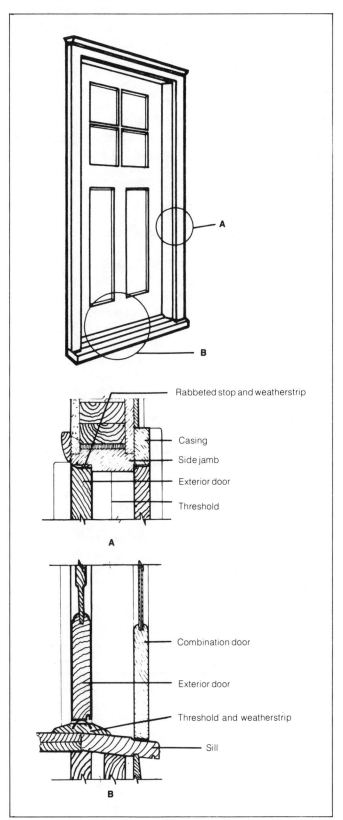

Rabbeted stop and weatherstrip

Casing

Side jamb

Exterior door

Threshold

A

Combination door

Exterior door

Threshold and weatherstrip

Sill

B

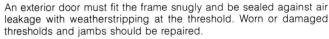

An exterior door must fit the frame snugly and be sealed against air leakage with weatherstripping at the threshold. Worn or damaged thresholds and jambs should be repaired.

STEPS

Use a hammer and pry bar to remove the door stop from the side jambs of the door. Be gentle; you may be able to use the door stop molding again.

If the old threshold is wood, pry it up. If metal, unscrew and pry it up. Measure, mark, cut, and trim the new threshold to fit between the door jambs. The joints should be as tight as possible — (called a "push fit").

If the new threshold is wood (usually oak) give the surface two coats of penetrating sealer before installing it. Run a light bead of caulking compound along the bottom edges of the threshold and tap the threshold in place. Then nail the threshold to the flooring, sheathing, or subflooring. The caulking helps stop moisture and insects from entering the house.

If the threshold is metal (usually aluminum) install it the same way as the wooden threshold, but use a hacksaw to make any necessary cuts. Metal thresholds screw to the sheathing or flooring. Some have a plastic strip running down their center. This strip must be removed in order to set the screws and then replaced after the threshold has been fastened.

In older homes, the threshold may consist of a single piece of wood that extends under the door jambs. To replace, remove the door from its hinges. Remove the door stop from the side jambs, as detailed above.

Once the door stop has been removed, you may be able to pry up the threshold with a chisel or pry bar. If not, you will have to cut the threshold along the jambs and at the front of the casing at the side jambs. Use a crosscut saw or backsaw for this.

Now notch the ends of the new threshold to fit around the side jambs. If you can, use the old threshold as a template for the cut-out. If this is not possible, measure the width of the jambs and transfer this measurement to the threshold. Then measure the depth of the jambs and mark this onto the threshold. The result should be the necessary marks for the notches. The tapered edge of the threshold faces toward the inside of the house; the square edge faces outside.

Give the new threshold two coats of penetrating sealer, after you are sure of the fit. Then run a bead of caulking compound along the edges of the threshold and nail the threshold in place. Countersink the nailheads and fill the holes with wood putty. Apply finish to the threshold. Reposition the door stop and nail it on.

GARAGES AND CARPORTS

These are either a part of the house, attached to the house, or separate from the house. Since garages and carports usually are constructed from the same materials as your house, the same maintenance and repair procedures are used. The exceptions are noted below.

Column and Support Post Maintenance

Tools and materials. Putty knife, broom, caulking compound in gun, paint, paintbrush.

STEPS

Support posts and columns for carports are subject to damage from water, since the supports usually set on a concrete slab and are exposed directly to the weather. Every fall, check the base of the supports to make sure the joint between the support and concrete is sealed. If you spot trouble, clean out the old caulking compound with a putty knife and sweep away the residue. Then carefully force new caulking compound into the joint and spread the compound up the post with a putty knife, feathering the caulking out.

Give the support a coat or two of paint to help protect it, painting over the caulking after it has set for at least two days.

If the supports are metal, use the same caulking and painting techniques detailed above. You should, however, also clean the metal with a wire brush and coat the metal with metal paint.

Garage Door Track Maintenance

Tools and materials. Adjustable wrench or socket wrench set, putty knife, grease, household lubricating oil, wiping cloths, screwdriver and (depending on type of door) hinges, wire turnbuckle, steel wool.

STEPS

If your garage door has tracks in which wheels attach to the sides of the door run, lubricate the tracks about once a year. Wipe grease in the track with a putty knife, and then raise and lower the door several times to distribute the lubricant.

Sticking doors usually are caused by misalignment of the wheels that run in the tracks; or, tracks may be slightly out of alignment with the wheels.

Check the wheels first: they are held to the door with a metal bracket. The screws in this bracket may be loosened so that the bracket can be adjusted for wheel alignment. If the wheels are in alignment, tighten screws as a preventive measure. If you can't tighten the screws, remove them and replace them with longer screws.

If the wheels are in alignment and the brackets are tight, but the door still sticks and binds, adjust the track. Most tracks are held by metal plates that screw to the garage door framing members. The screw slots usually enable you to loosen the screws and slide the bracket and track until they align with the wheels. This is a trial-and-error project.

Other Garage Door Adjustments

Many overhead garage doors are spring-mounted so the door is easy to open and close. If the door becomes difficult to work, or the door does not stay open or closed, you may be able to tighten or loosen the spring. At one end of the spring there will be an adjusting nut. Turn this nut with an adjustable wrench. If you can not easily make the adjustment, call a professional. Some springs require special equipment for adjustment.

Latches and locks. Some garage doors have a bar-type lock: a handle turns a bar that slips into a metal latch plate on one side of the door. Check that the ends of the bar are lubricated with grease, and that the lock mechanism is lubricated with lightweight household oil.

Hinges. Lubricate the hinges on overhead garage doors annually using light household oil. The hinges on outward swinging garage doors also should be oiled once a year.

If the swinging doors are sagging and sticking, you may be able to adjust them by tightening the screws in the hinges. If the screws are loose and won't tighten, replace the screws with longer screws or carriage bolts. You could also add another pair of hinges to the door to help support the weight. Most swinging doors can be made to function with just hinge adjustments, rather than requiring you to plane edges as for entrance and passage doors.

If the hinge treatment does not work, try lifting the sag with a turnbuckle and wire assembly. The assembly stretches diagonally across the door from top hinge to the opposite bottom edge (see Chapter 9).

TERMITES AND INSECTS

The three main chemicals for handling termite and other insect problems are chlordane (mixture), diazinon, and pyrethrum. The chemicals are sold at many home center stores and garden centers. Talk to the dealer about the chemicals and have the dealer suggest the best chemical for you to use. Be sure to follow his directions and the information on the chemical container. These chemicals are dangerous; be careful with them.

Termite Control

Tools and materials. Tiling spade, mixing bucket, chlordane, water.

STEPS

Dig a 6-in.-deep trench around the foundation of your house. Mix a solution of chlordane and water and distribute this mixture in the trench. Then refill the trench with dirt. Remove any scraps of wood and lumber that may be lying on the ground in crawl spaces, under porches, leaning against the house or foundation. Do not overlook firewood stacked against the house or garage. If this is not successful, call a professional.

Controlling Household Pests

Pest	Possible Remedy
Termites	Treat soil under crawl spaces and around perimeter of foundation with chlordane mixture.
Ants	Baygon, malathion, and/or diazinon chemicals applied around the perimeter of the foundation, door sills, and other likely points of entry.
Roaches	Diazinon or baygon.
Silverfish	Chlordane mixture or malathion spray.
Spiders	Buy commercial spray; it probably will contain malathion. Buy spray with residual properties.
Rats	Use rat poison that is not harmful to humans.
Mice	Same as for rats.
Bats	Naphthalene flakes in infested areas.
Moles	Traps. Moles like to eat bugs under your lawn; apply a chemical to kill the bugs. Commercial preparation to kill grubs and worms is applied with regular lawn spreader.
Squirrels	Traps. Plug the entrance holes. Put moth balls and crystals in infested areas such as attics and garages.
Chipmunks	Same as for squirrels.

9 Outdoor Improvements

Home repairs run from lot line to lot line. That is what this chapter is all about: the repair and upkeep of outside areas and structures that enhance the overall beauty and value of your property. Most of these around-the-house items — walks, driveways, decks, patios, retaining walls, and railings — are constructed from strong materials that require only an occasional repair. But don't be careless because the materials are rugged; each area listed here should be checked spring and fall for any weather damage that might develop into costly replacement of materials, including granite, concrete, and steel.

ASPHALT DRIVEWAY REPAIR AND RENEWAL

Most damage to asphalt is progressive. The first signal is a whitish spot on a normally black background. After this initial stage the asphalt will start to fissure and crack. Next will come little, and then big, potholes.

You should renew the asphalt surface about every three years, or when the surface begins to appear whitish, worn or cracked. Depending on the climate in your area this time frame may vary — from 18 months to four or five years. A hard winter, with lots of snow and freezing and thawing, can destroy the asphalt even if it was in good repair before the snow.

Repairing Fissures, Cracks and Potholes

Tools and materials. Liquid asphalt driveway coating, a coating applicator, stiff broom, an oil/grease detergent made especially for cleaning asphalt driveways, a flat spade, a wheelbarrow or large container to hold gummy and grainy debris.

STEPS

Sweep the driveway surface clean. Put the debris in the wheelbarrow or bucket so it won't blow or scatter back onto the surface. With the flat spade, lift any encrusted dirt and grease deposits. You can scrape the surface hard with the spade without fear of damage.

Mix and apply the detergent to the driveway. Use the stiff broom to scrub the mixture into the asphalt. Don't skimp; use plenty of detergent. As you go, rinse away the dirty mixture with clean water.

Once you have finished the cleaning job, let the surface dry thoroughly and then inspect the surface. If you spot any grease or dirt, remove it; the asphalt topping that you will apply will not stick properly to the surface if applied over dirt, grease, overgrown grass patches, moss, grass clippings, and so on. If the driveway needs patching, make the patches before you apply the top coating (discussed below).

Apply the top coat in wide ribbons to about 35 sq. ft. of area at one time. You can pour the coating directly out of the container onto the driveway, which is easier than trying to dip the

Cut overgrown sod at a driveway's edge with a tiling spade. Also use the spade to remove grease, dirt, and mud from the asphalt surface, which must be particularly clean.

Driveway sealer can be applied right out of the bucket; do not thin it with any type of solvent. Plan to cover about 250 sq. ft. per 5-gal. bucket of the top dressing.

applicator into the bucket. Spread the mixture out evenly, using the applicator to distribute the black liquid. Work the topping into the little cracks in the asphalt, then "level" the topping with light, even strokes. The trick is not to leave any puddles of topping on the surface, but to spread it out. Do the entire surface, then wait 24 hours or until the dressing is dry to the touch. If you see any spots that look extra dry, or spots that have been missed, go back over these areas. If most of the surface looks "dry," give the surface another coat. Let the job set at least 36 hours before you drive your car onto the surface.

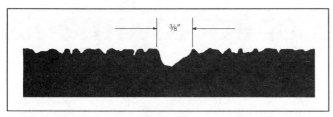

Small fissures in asphalt are normal, but any gap more than ⅜ in. wide should be cleaned and patched with black top mix. A top dressing will fill smaller cracks.

Twist the chisel in your hand as you break out old, crumbling asphalt. Work into the good, hard asphalt, even if you must cut down into the earth; undercut the sides of the hole.

Don't skimp on the blacktop filler. Tamp all of it down into the break in layers, with no overlap onto the surrounding surface at the top of the hole.

Patching

The key is to clean depressions thoroughly, then stick in the filler, tamping down the patch as tightly as you possibly can. Spots eligible for patching include cracks that are ⅜-in. or more wide, potholes, and soft spots in the asphalt surface. You can tell the soft spots because they appear as hollows in the surface and seem "wrinkled." Usually, when you tap a chisel into this surface, the surface will be very soft and it will readily crumble under the hammer blows. It is not necessary to patch

very small cracks, which really are fissures — a normal condition. A general top dressing (discussed above) will fill these breaks better than patching compound.

Tools and materials. Black top mix, sold in premixed bags, a brick or cold chisel, hammer or baby sledge hammer, stiff broom, flat spade, a short piece of 2x4 or 4x4 to tamp the asphalt, a piece of scrap plywood or hardboard, a wheelbarrow or bucket for debris, your car, and work gloves.

STEPS

With the chisel, clean the break in the surface. Remove all of the soft and crumbly asphalt, and cut back into the harder lower layer. You will probably end up with a fairly large crack although it started out very small. But if you do not get all the old, loose material out, the new patch will soon pop out of the break. Or the patch will stay in the break and the area around it will disintegrate.

Asphalt ridges may be the problem rather than cracks. To remove the ridges, you have to chisel out the high spot back to the level spot. This makes a very wide patch, so unless the appearance of the ridge bothers you, don't go to the work of leveling it.

Clean out the break using the stiff broom. You might want to flush out the break area with water from a garden hose. If you do use water, do not apply the patching compound until the area is dry.

Place the patching compound into the break, filling the area slightly above the surrounding surface. If the cavity is large, tamp the mixture as you fill the hole to compact the mixture in layers. Top off the patch by mounding the mixture so it is slightly higher than the normal level.

Now place the scrap hardboard or plywood over the patch and drive your car over the flat wood. The weight of the car will compress the patch into the cavity — like a steam roller. If tight quarters prohibits the car trick, you will have to tamp the patch tight with the 2x4 or 4x4. The patching compound compacts best when the temperature outside is 70 degrees or higher. If you must make repairs in colder weather, preheat the patching compound by leaving it inside your house until warmed up to room temperature.

The more pressure on the newly installed patch the better. Once the job has been completed, sweep the area to remove little chunks of the sticky asphalt. Use mineral spirits to clean tools.

Once you have filled the cavities you may want to add top dressing (discussed above) to finish the project. Let the patches set about two weeks before you brush on the dressing.

CONCRETE REPAIRS

Moisture, freezing and thawing can buckle and crumble concrete driveways, walks, patios, and other on-the-ground placements in a short period of time. You can save yourself lots of work and material expense if you take time to patch concrete when you first notice little cracks and breaks.

Small Patches

Tools and materials. Hammer or baby sledge hammer, brick or cold chisel, stiff broom, wheelbarrow or bucket for debris, water, premixed cement in a bag or bucket, shovel, mixing tub or bucket, trowel, a length of 1x4 or 2x4 to level fairly large patches, safety glasses, heavy work gloves.

Safety. It is recommended that you wear safety glasses and work gloves when you fiddle with concrete repairs. Small chips of concrete can fly through the air when you strike the hard surface with a brick chisel and hammer. The gloves also will protect your hands from this flying debris, as well as give your hands some padding in case you miss the chisel and hit your hand.

STEPS

A flat, on-the-ground patch is easy. Clean the break with the chisel, cutting back to hard concrete. Try to undercut the break so the shape of the cut becomes an inverted V wider at the bottom of the break than at the top of it. This shape forms a narrow rim for the patch and prevents its popping out of the break when the concrete hardens. Flood the break with water and sweep the break clean with the stiff broom. The break should be as free as possible from little chunks and grains of old, broken concrete.

Add the premixed cement (it already contains the necessary sand and gravel) to water. Work this mixture — adding water as you go — until it is about the consistency of thick mud. Blend all of the mixture smoothly with the water, leaving no hard dry pockets of cement. Some concrete patching compounds consist of cement with a latex binder that substitutes for water. Although expensive, this patching compound is excellent for small breaks and chips. Follow the mixing directions on the container to the letter. All the same tools required for premixed cement are used for this type of patch.

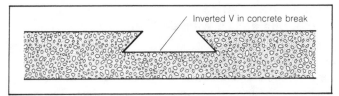

To be sure the concrete patch will remain in the hole, undercut as shown. Concrete cracks must be opened up to receive the patching material; don't fiddle with hairline cracks.

Wet concrete sets fairly rapidly, so you should work fast. Rewet the cleaned break with water. Then press in the concrete mixture with the trowel, compacting the mixture in layers as you go using the sharp edge of the trowel. Fill the whole break with concrete; don't skimp. Level and smooth the patch with the flat surface of the trowel to complete the project. The new concrete will resist rain about two hours after the repair has been made; you can walk on the patch 36 hours after the patch is in position; you can drive your car over the patch about 48 hours after that. The more time, however, the better.

Large Patches

Any patch you can't complete with one bag of premixed concrete — about ⅓ of a cubic foot — can be put into the large patch classification. This includes entire sections of driveways, walks, patios, and floors that have to be replaced to form a patch in or between old concrete.

You have several material choices. You can buy premixed cement, which is fairly expensive for large jobs but convenient. You can mix your own concrete from scratch, using portland cement, sand, gravel, and water. Or, if the patch is large enough, you can buy already-mixed concrete that's delivered to the job site in one of those big cement mixers on balloon tires. There is usually a minimum order for the already-mixed material — 3 cubic yards or more.

Water both cleans and conditions the concrete to receive the patch. If the break is not damp the old concrete will soak the water from the fresh concrete. Use epoxy cement for tiny breaks.

To estimate the amount of concrete you need, find the area of the patch by multiplying the length times the width. Then follow the chart below, figuring about ⅓ cubic foot for each bag of premixed cement.

Area/lxw		Slab Thickness	
	4″	5″	6″
25	.31	.39	.47 Cu. Yd.
50	.62	.77	.93 Cu. Yd.
100	1.20	1.50	1.90 Cu. Yd.
200	2.50	3.10	3.70 Cu. Yd.

If you buy "con-mix" gravel, add 1 part cement to 4 parts con-mix.

To make your own, use these amounts: one cubic yard of concrete includes 6 sacks of Portland cement, 15 cubic feet of fine aggregate, and about 5 gallons of water.

If you buy already-mixed concrete, the retailer will figure out how much concrete you need. Just supply the sales person with the length, width, and thickness of the patch or area you want to fill with concrete.

Tools. Hammer, large sledge hammer, cold or brick chisel, shovel, mixing tub or rental cement mixer, 2x4 screed to "rough" level the patch, 2x6 forming boards, 2x4s sharpened at one end for stakes, 10-penny (10d) double-headed concrete form nails, stiff broom, level, wheelbarrow for debris, pry bar, cement finishing trowel, water, safety glasses, gloves.

STEPS

The hard part comes first; you have to remove the old concrete to make way for the new patch. The best and easiest way is to dig away the earth at the edge of the old concrete. When you have a fairly large hole, try to pry up the slab, even if only an inch or so. Then whack the top surface with the sledge, chipping off as much concrete as you can. Remove the debris and dig some more. Lift, and hammer again at the slab. Repeat this until the old concrete is out.

Another way, although more difficult, is to use a brick or cold chisel to crack the surface of the concrete, working in small sections. Then, with a pry bar, lift out the debris. This can be hard work since the earth below the slab helps hold the concrete firmly. That's why it is easier to lift the slab slightly and chip away at it with the sledge hammer. To ease the work, you may be able to rent an electric hammer which will substitute for the sledge and chisel tools.

If you can't use the edges of the old concrete to support the new mixture while it hardens you may have to form the patch area for the fresh concrete. Use 2x6s for the forms. Align the forms so the top edges match the top surface of the adjoining concrete; you may need to level the forms to achieve this match. Also, you will probably have to dig a small trench along the sides of the patch area in which to insert the form boards.

To support the forms, cut short lengths of 2x4s into stakes. Sharpen one end of these stakes so they are easier to drive into the ground. Once the forms are in position, drive in the stakes at 2-ft. intervals so the tops of the stakes are about ½-in. below the top edge of the forms. Now, with double-headed concrete nails, spike the stakes to the forms. This gives the forms some stability when the concrete is placed.

If the surface supports only light weights, you will not need to reinforce the concrete with reinforcing mesh or rods. If the large patch is in a driveway subject to car or truck weights, use reinforcement. Cut the mesh or rods to fit the patch area. You can elevate the reinforcement within the forms (it shouldn't lay flat on the ground) with half bricks or small stones. Or you can pull up on the reinforcing to position it once the concrete has been placed.

Place the concrete in the forms, tamping it with a shovel to eliminate any voids in the mixture. When the forms are full,

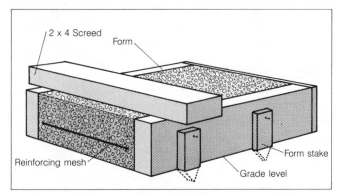

After screeding the fresh concrete surface, it may be further leveled with a wooden float. Follow this with a steel trowel or broom texture. Work fairly fast; concrete sets quickly.

level the fresh concrete surface by "sawing" a length of 2x4 across the top edges of the forms. The 2x4 should be about 4 ft. longer than the width of the forms. As you level the fresh concrete, shovel more concrete into low spots and remove excess concrete that has been pushed to the front of the 2x4 screed. It's sort of a "rob Peter, pay Paul" arrangement. When you have finished the leveling job the concrete will have small ridges on its surface. Wait until the concrete develops a sheen before you begin troweling. To trowel, use wide, sweeping arcs. Watch so the edges of the trowel do not dig into the fresh concrete. Press the face of the trowel into the surface, holding its edge at a slight angle.

Since the new concrete forms a patch, you probably won't need expansion or control joints between the old and new concrete. However, if control joints are necessary, make them by slicing through the fresh concrete with the edge of the trowel at the point where the new concrete meets the old. What you want to do is form a narrow gap so both sections can expand and contract without breaking each other. Or you can use an asphalt expansion strip between sections (see page 000). The strip goes in before the concrete is placed between the form boards.

Keep the concrete damp with water for at least three days after it has been placed. This procedure cures the new concrete, making the patch harder. You can walk on the patch in about 36 hours; don't drive a car or truck on the surface for about 10 days or so.

About 2 weeks after the job is completed you can remove the form boards and replace any dirt and sod removed to make room for the forms.

WALKS AND PATHS
Veneering an Old Walk or Path

"Veneering" is an add-on gimmick to make old, broken-down walks look new again. To veneer a walk you place new concrete over the old walk, using the old walk as a base. The technique is simple; the work is hot and tiring. The cost of veneering is about the same as it would be for a new walk. The advantages are that you save some layout time, rock-busting, and digging.

Tools and materials. Hammer or baby sledge hammer, crosscut saw, level, chalkline, hacksaw, 2x6 form boards, 2x4s for stakes, double-headed 10d concrete nails, 2x4 concrete screed, shovel, trowel, asphalt expansion joints, concrete groover, concrete edger, wooden float, rule, concrete, water,

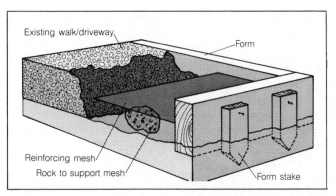

Form and reinforce fairly large concrete patches. Otherwise, weight, wear, and water will cause the patches to break and crumble.

gloves, small reinforcement rods, reinforcement mesh. Since this job usually is a large one, it's smart to either mix your own concrete to save money or buy the already-mixed to save time. Figure out how much material you'll need, using the chart given previously. The concrete veneer should be 4 in. thick.

STEPS

Set the 2x6 form boards along the edge of the old walk so the bottom edge of the forms just touch the edge of the walk. Stake the forms with the 2x4s that are pointed on one end so you can drive them into the ground easily. Nail the 2x4s to the forms — from the outside in — with double-headed concrete nails. As you set the forms, level them in place. To save time leveling, stretch a chalkline along the edge of the forms at about the height the forms will be. This will give you a guide while you

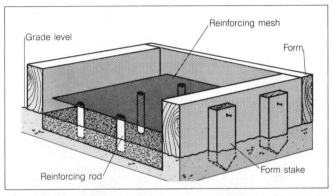

Fresh concrete is placed over old walk to veneer the walk. You use the same construction techniques as used for a new walk.

set the forms. Also, don't forget to drive the stakes about an inch or so below the top edge of the forms. The 2x4 concrete screed has to move freely along the top edges of the forms.

With the hacksaw, cut the reinforcing rods into lengths of approximately 1 ft. Then drive these rods into the surface of the walkway. Use the cracks, holes, and other breaks to sink the rods so they protrude about 2 in. from the walk's surface. The rods will help hold the veneering in position. Space the rods about 2 to 3 ft. apart in any configuration you want. Cut the reinforcing mesh to fit between the forms and tie it to the tops of the rods.

Place the concrete. Work the mixture with a shovel as you go to remove any air pockets and other voids in the concrete. Level the material as much as possible while it is being placed. At four to six ft. intervals, insert an asphalt expansion joint. When about 12 ft. of veneer has been placed, screed the top level with the 2x4, using a see-saw motion. If you find any low spots, fill them. If you find any high spots, remove the excess concrete and use it to fill the low spots.

When the water leaves the surface of the concrete, run the wooden float over the surface. If the float brings water to the surface, the concrete is not ready to trowel. Meanwhile, if the 2x4 screed hasn't leveled the surface to your satisfaction, you can use the float to level the surface. Floating should be done while the concrete is wet. After you use the float, you can trowel the surface.

For a rough surface, you can finish the concrete with the stiff broom. The broom's bristles will form little lines across the concrete for a nonskid surface.

For a professional touch, use a groover to finish control (expansion) joints; the cost of a groover is low. Cut (slice) the concrete with a trowel before using groover.

An edging tool finishes off the edges at the forms and wherever fresh concrete meets dissimilar materials. Run edger and groover after the surface has been finished.

Use an edger to form a neat groove at the control joints where you inserted the asphalt expansion strips. If you want control joints but did not add the expansion strips, cut the concrete with the edge of the trowel. Then use a groover to make a smooth joint.

For a slightly rounded edge, use the edger along the sides of the walks at the forms.

The first day after the job sprinkle the concrete surface with a fine spray from the garden hose. Do this every morning, about noon and in the evening, for five days. This helps the concrete cure so that it hardens properly. After 10 days, you can remove the forms. Keep any heavy weight off the walk for about 30 days.

Raising Sunken Walls and Driveways

The size of the concrete slab determines whether or not you can lift the slab back into a level position. If the slab is too large for you to lift, you have two choices: break out the old slab and put in a new one, or hire a pro with a mudjack. The mud from the mudjack will raise the slab. Highway departments use this technique to lift sunken and uneven roadways.

If the walk or driveway is stone or brick, remove the stones or brick that have sunk and sprinkle sand in the void; now replace the paving unit.

Tools and materials. Hammer, pry bar, length of 2x4 — 10 ft. or so, some bricks or rocks for leverage, coarse gravel, tiling spade.

STEPS

At the sunken area, dig a large hole at the edge of the walk or driveway. You'll have to remove lots of dirt from under the walk or driveway in order to insert the pry bar or 2x4 "lever." This procedure is 75 percent of the job, so spend the time necessary for digging out.

The more dirt you remove, the easier the slab can be lifted. Place the dirt you remove on a sheet of polyfilm. This way, the lawn will be clean after you put the dirt back.

You get the most leverage from a long piece of 2x4 or 2x6 stock, and you may still need several helpers to add weight to the lifting effort. For small jobs, a pry bar often works.

Shove the pry bar or 2x4 into the hole and under the paving unit. At ground level under the pry, place a brick, stone, or thick piece of wood for extra leverage. Then push down on the pry. You may need a helper to lift the paving. If you can't lift it, then dig out more dirt and try again; you may need more leverage blocks.

Once the paving unit has been elevated, have a helper hold down the pry while you scoop and pound in the gravel under the unit until you have added enough to raise it. Release the pry. If you've judged correctly, the paving unit now should be level. If not, lift the unit again and pound more gravel under it until you reach level or the position you want.

Solving Brick and Stone Problems

Since paving bricks and stones are set on a sand base, both often tend to sink and tilt on the base. Normal settling of the ground, moisture — freezing and thawing — and weight can be blamed for the troubles.

Tools and materials. Rubber-headed or rubber-handled hammer, steel trowel, brick chisel or pry bar, level, stiff broom, bag of very fine sand.

Water dislodged these patio bricks by eroding away the sand base underneath the base. In addition to repairing the patio, the rain-carrying system should be checked for needed repairs.

STEPS

Remove the problem paving pieces using the brick chisel or pry bar to lift them off the sand base. If the units are too high, remove a little sand and replace a unit or two and check for level. Repeat this — adding or removing sand and testing — until level is reached. As you set each unit, press it down in the sand and wiggle it back and forth very gently. This will properly seat the brick in the sand. Then tap the surface lightly with a rubber hammer or rubber handle of a regular hammer.

Once the job is finished, the units should be slightly higher than the surrounding surface: about ⅛ to ¼ of an inch. The units will settle to level in a month or two.

Sweep sand into the cracks between the units until the cracks are full. Then sprinkle the area with a fine spray from a garden hose. Sweep more sand into the cracks; sprinkle again. You'll have to do this many, many times until the cracks are completely full. It's amazing how much sand disappears down those seemingly small cracks.

If the brick or stone paving units are cemented together, you'll have to chip away the cement with a brick or cold chisel in order to raise or lower the units. Then follow the sand-leveling procedure described above. Recement the joints using a pointed trowel when the job is completed.

Patience is the key to resetting bricks, blocks or stone on a sand base. You add sand . . . remove sand . . . add sand again, until the units are level and slightly raised next to old, set units.

Level the units as you set them. Otherwise, the job will look wavy when completed. Work with just two or three units at a time. Once set and level, do not jar the units.

Set the units in the sand by lightly tapping each face. If the units were cemented together, you'll have to chip off the concrete with a brick chisel and clean each brick.

Pour about half a sack of very fine sand on the patio surface. Then slowly fill the cracks with the sand. Sprinkle the patio with water and keep filling until the joints are full.

Curb and Gutter Repairs

These breaks are easy to repair with premixed mortar or concrete mix. And since curbs and gutters are not known for their beauty and form, you don't have to be very careful with the patches when smoothing them with a trowel.

Tools and materials. Premixed cement, mixing tub or bucket, hammer or baby sledge hammer, brick chisel, star drill or masonry drill for an electric drill, stiff broom, water, safety glasses, gloves, a piece of ⅛-in. hardboard, ¼x4-in. carriage bolts.

STEPS

Clean the break with the cold chisel or brick chisel, cutting back to the hard concrete. Then, with a garden hose, wash and sweep away the old debris. If the break is a small one, you can fill it immediately with concrete, mixed to the consistency of thick mud. Smooth the surface with a trowel to complete the project.

If the break is on a corner of a curb, you will have to support the patch with carriage bolts.

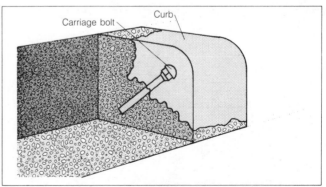

Bolt "peg" technique may be used for broken edges on stairsteps. The peg helps hold the new concrete in the break. You need not set the peg with anchor cement.

Clean with the brick or cold chisel and wash the area; water, and broom. With a star drill or masonry drill, punch a hole in the break. The carriage bolt seats in the hole (see illustration, above). The concrete is formed around the bolt and into the break. You'll have to use a gloved hand to fill the break, since you probably cannot satisfactorily manipulate a trowel in the tight quarters. When the break is full, use the trowel to smooth the surface.

For breaks in straight or curved curbs, use forms to hold the concrete in position while it hardens. With a brick or cold chisel clean the break and wash away any old debris. Lap a piece of hardboard across the break and hold the hardboard in place with a couple of large rocks. You probably will have to make a form for just one side of the gutter, since the earth substitutes as a form on one side. Hardboard makes a good forming material for this repair since you can bend it slightly for curved curbs.

Fill the break with fresh concrete, working it into the break with the trowel. Then smooth the concrete with the trowel. Leave the forms in position for several days while the concrete hardens properly.

When cleaning with a brick or cold chisel — or making holes in concrete with a star or electric drill — be sure to wear safety glasses and gloves.

Walk and Driveway Drainage Systems

The quickest and easiest way to stop erosion along walks and driveways is to install a concrete gutter system to carry away water. The gutters may be recessed into the ground so that they are hidden from view.

Tools and materials. Chalkline, tile spade, trowel, 1x2 wooden stakes, premixed concrete mix (if the job isn't too large; if it is large, consider mixing your own concrete. See "Large Patches," this chapter); a 2-ft. length of 3-in. plastic pipe, garden hose, a wheelbarrow or bucket for debris, 4-in. asphalt expansion strips, small diameter reinforcing rods.

STEPS

Dig a trough along side of the walk or driveway. Make the trough about 6 in. wide and 4 in. deep. To guide your digging operations you can stretch a chalkline along the length of the area where the trough will be.

Just before you get ready to shovel concrete into the void, wet the freshly dug trough with a fine spray from the garden hose. If the earth is fairly damp, you won't have to sprinkle it. At the same time as you place the concrete insert the asphalt expansion strips in the trough next to the walk or driveway. Then lay a reinforcing rod in the center of the trough and elevate it an inch or so with stones or small chunks of brick.

When the fresh concrete is in the trough (you can work in 10 ft. sections), run the plastic pipe along the top surface of the new concrete so you form a half-round "gutter" in the concrete. The hollow pipe will pick up excess concrete; you can empty the pipe when it gets full or heavy.

Use the trowel to add any necessary touches to the newly formed gutter. Keep the concrete wet for about five days by sprinkling it with the garden hose.

REPLACING ISOLATION (EXPANSION) JOINTS

Isolation (or expansion) joints, in concrete, brick, and stone permit similar and dissimilar materials to expand and contract with hot and cold weather and moisture. You will find these joints in walks, driveways, and stairsteps — and where masonry materials meet other materials such as wood and metal. The big problem with expansion joints is the tarlike substance or fiber filler that cracks and dislodges from the joint. This lets in water which, in turn, freezes and thaws so that the materials chip and break. Or sometimes expansion joints are not properly installed, resulting in the slab or steps pulling away from adjoining surfaces and creating a large gap.

For Stone and Brick

Tools and materials. Hammer or baby sledge hammer, brick or cold chisel, asphalt impregnated expansion strips or oakum, premixed mortar mix, mixing tub or bucket, tuckpointing trowel, safety glasses, gloves, an old bucket for debris.

Asphalt expansion strips are usually 4 in. wide and 4 ft. long. You can trim them with a razor knife. Use a buffer block to pound them down into a crack/control joint.

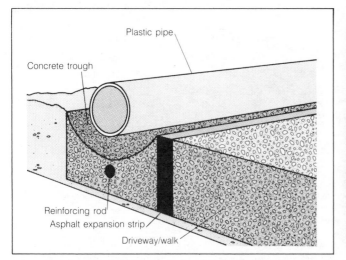

The gutter trough should be about 6 in. wide and 4 to 5 in. deep. You probably won't need mold forms; the walk or driveway provides one side of the "form", and the earth the other side.

STEPS

With a brick chisel or cold chisel, remove all cracked or broken concrete mortar, or tar or fiber, from the joint. You may have to enlarge the joint slightly by chipping back into the solid mortar.

Insert the expansion strip or oakum into the crack, tapping it into position with a hammer or chisel. If the expansion strip you are inserting is stubborn, try pounding against a scrap piece of wood sandwiched between the top of the strip and the hammer. Oakum, a preservative-treated cord material that looks and feels like sticky rope, should be recessed about ½ in. below the surface. Then cap the crack with concrete. This gives a neat job, although you'll probably have to replace the concrete every four to five years.

Fill the joint with concrete after the expansion strip or oakum is in place. A thin tuckpointing trowel is best for this job. Don't use concrete without a "backing" strip.

After the expansion joint fiber material is in place — flush with the surface — fill any little gaps created after chiseling out the old concrete (the best tool for this job is a tuckpointing trowel).

CONCRETE, BRICK, AND WOODEN STAIR REPAIR

Freezing and thawing water can be blamed for most damage to stairsteps constructed of brick, concrete, and wood.

Brick and Concrete Repairs

Tools and materials. Hammer or baby sledge hammer, brick or cold chisel, premixed mortar mix, mixing tub or bucket, water, tuckpointing trowel, safety glasses, gloves, an old bucket for debris.

STEPS

Check the mortar first. If it has crumbled but the bricks or stones are tight, you just have to replace the mortar. Remove the old mortar with a brick or cold chisel and clean the joint with water.

Mix the concrete and pack the joint(s) using the tuckpointing trowel. Be sure the joints are "full" of concrete. Smooth the surface of the joint with the trowel.

If the bricks or stones are loose in the steps, remove the mortar between the joints with the chisel. Then remove the loose bricks or stones. Since both probably will be embedded in concrete, you will have to remove this old concrete using a

chisel. With water, wash away the debris. While you are doing this soak the bricks or stones in a bucket of water so they won't absorb the water from the new concrete when the units are replaced.

Lay a bed of mortar for the units about ½-in. thick — or the thickness of the old mortar. You can use the tuckpointing trowel for this job. Set the masonry units in position, tapping them into the new mortar with the handle of the hammer. Then fill the remaining joints with mortar, smoothing the finish with the tuckpointing trowel. See also "Stone Wall Repairs," this chapter.

Wooden Stair Repair

Rotting and broken treads on wooden steps must be replaced just as soon as you notice the damage.

Tools and materials. Hammer, crosscut saw, pry bar, wooden replacement materials, 16d common nails, wood preservative or exterior paint, paint brush.

STEPS

Remove the damaged boards with the hammer and/or pry bar. If you run into trouble here, try using a wood chisel to split the wood so that you can remove it easily.

Measure and cut the wooden components to size, and then test them in the gaps to check fit and alignment. Give the new wood at least one coat of penetrating wood sealer or paint; two coats would be better. Cover all the wood: ends, edges, faces. The finish helps prevent warp and rot. Nail the wooden members in position, and then give the steps — treads and risers — a coat of finish paint.

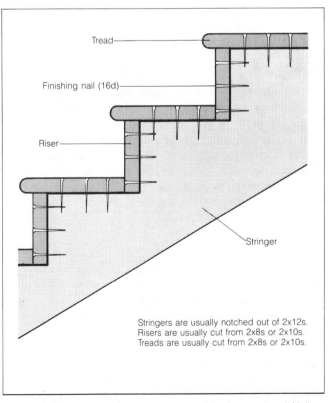

Stringers are usually notched out of 2x12s.
Risers are usually cut from 2x8s or 2x10s.
Treads are usually cut from 2x8s or 2x10s.

Use the old tread as a pattern to measure and cut the new tread. Nail on the tread with 16d common or finishing nails; you may have to remove the tread to replace a damaged riser. Use the same removal, measuring and nailing technique for risers as you would for treads.

If the wood stringers are damaged, they must be replaced. You can disassemble the steps with the pry bar and hammer. Use the old stringers as a pattern to lay out the design on the new wood — probably a 2x10 or 2x12.

If the risers are damaged, which is unlikely, you can remove and replace them after first removing the treads that butt against the risers. Give the new wood a couple of coats of sealer or paint before you reassemble the steps.

Since exterior stairsteps are constantly exposed to bad weather, it is a good idea to check them annually for damage. If the steps are wooden, they should be cleaned and repainted every two to three years.

DECKS, PORCHES AND PATIOS
Replacing Damaged Deck Flooring
Split decking is a common problem because the decking usually is redwood or cedar, which splits easily. Replacing these damaged boards is easy.

Tools and materials. Hammer, pry bar, crosscut saw, new boards, 16d galvanized or aluminum common nails, wood preservative/paint, paint brush.

STEPS
Remove the damaged boards first. If you can get underneath the deck, hammer up on the boards to loosen them. If you cannot get under the deck you may be able to pry the boards up with just the claws of the hammer. If not, use the pry bar. (See "Replacing Porch Floor Boards", below, for more details.)

Cut the new boards to fit and test them for proper fit in the voids. Then give the new wood a couple of coats of wood preservative and/or paint.

Nail the new boards to the deck joists, using two nails at each joint for 2x4s and three nails for 2x6s. If the deck is painted, give the entire deck a coat of fresh paint.

Leveling a Deck or Wooden Patio
A platform that tips is generally caused by a sinking foundation support, where a deck or patio is set just a few inches off the ground. The platform materials usually are 2x4s in a 4x4-ft. section, so the entire unit may be easily removed to expose the pier-type supports of concrete, brick, or concrete block.

Tools and materials (depending on the problem). Hammer, pry bar, scrap wood, cedar shingles, star drill or masonry drill, masonry anchors and bolts, level, tile spade, coarse gravel or rip-rap (a type of crushed gravel).

STEPS
First, try to shim up the sagging platform by sandwiching a cedar shingle or two between the foundation piers and the platform. The shingles serve as small wedges to lift the platform; the platform weight will hold them in position. When the wedges are in place, check for level as you hammer them into position.

If you can't get to the foundation piers with the shingle shims, remove the platform after you determine with the level where the problem is and about how many inches the platform has to be raised to correct the problem.

For brick and concrete block piers (which come out easily) the easiest way to re-establish level is to remove the piers and

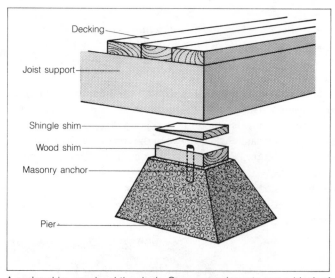

A cedar shim may level the deck. Or you may have to use a block of wood and the cedar shim in combination. An expansion type masonry anchor doesn't require cement to set it properly.

reset them on a gravel base. Tamp the gravel into the hole after you remove the foundation units. Then replace the units and the platform.

If the foundation piers are placed concrete, drill a hole in the top of the piers, using a star drill or masonry drill locked in the jaws of an electric drill. The hole is for the expandable lead type of masonry anchor.

Cut a piece of scrap wood to fit the top of the pier. Drill a hole in the wood to accept the masonry anchor bolt. You may have to countersink or counterbore the wood so the head of the bolt is flush with the wood. Assemble this unit: lead anchor in the hole in the pier; bolt through the scrap wood into the anchor. Tighten the bolt.

Now replace the platform. If the platform still is not level, use cedar shims between the scrap wood and the platform to bring the platform to level.

Replacing Damaged Porch Floor Boards
Porch floor boards rot because porches are built over crawl spaces that hold and transmit moisture to the wood.

Tools and materials. Hammer, pry bar, wood chisel, brace and bit, 10d finishing nails, keyhole saw, wood preservative/paint, paint brush, polyfilm, brickbats, 2x4 scrap, new flooring.

Connect the pilot holes with a saw kerf in the flooring. You then may be able to chisel out the damaged boards. Be careful of flooring nails and the joists underneath, so you don't damage them.

STEPS

With the brace and bit, bore holes in the good wood surrounding the bad wood. Make sure you space the holes to miss the joists underneath the floor boards. The joists support the boards. Then connect the holes with saw cuts, using the keyhole saw for this. The work will go faster if you have an electric jigsaw.

Boards shown at left have tongue and groove; at right, tongue is being squared off of one board in order to fit space left by damaged pieces.

Cut the new boards to fit. Since porch flooring is tongue-and-groove material you will probably have to square off the tongue of one board so all the boards fit properly.

Since the new boards will lap at least two of the joists, add wooden cleats to the sides of the joists to support the flooring. You can use scrap pieces of 2x4s for this; nail the 2x4s to the joists. The top edges of the 2x4s must be flush with the top edges of the joists so the flooring is level.

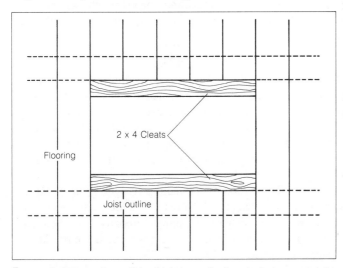

For needed support, use 2-in.-thick scrap for the cleats to support the flooring. Nail on the cleats with 16d or 20d nails; you don't have to clinch the nails to the joists.

Test the new flooring in the space. Then coat it with wood preservative and/or paint. Nail the flooring in place and paint the entire floor. For extra protection, crawl under the space between the porch and ground and spread polyfilm over the ground, using brickbats to hold the polyfilm in place. The polyfilm will help prevent moisture from penetrating the wooden members of the porch.

New flooring will leave a small gap in the saw kerfs. Fill the gaps with water putty; then paint the flooring with porch or deck enamel. If you can, paint the underside of the flooring.

Repair and Maintenance of Wooden, Brick and Steel Columns

Steel columns seldom need replacement. Wooden and brick columns mean trouble; the problem stems from moisture.

Tools and materials (depending on the problem). Hammer, crosscut saw, calking compound, brick or cold chisel, broad wood chisel, premixed mortar mix cement, mixing tub or bucket, tuckpointing trowel, screw jack, wood screws, concrete blocks, scrap wood for base supports and concrete forming, new columns, jackposts, wood preservative/paint, paint brush, safety glasses.

Maintenance is by far the best preventive rot treatment you can give steel, wooden, or brick column supports.

STEPS

For steel columns, check the metal annually, especially at the base of the columns. If the calking around the base where the steel meets concrete is old, cracked, or missing, clean the area with a cold chisel and recalk. Also, remove any rust spots from the steel column with a wire brush and paint the metal, using special metal paint for this. If a steel column has to be replaced, call in a pro to do it. Replacement requires costly special equipment. It also requires expertise.

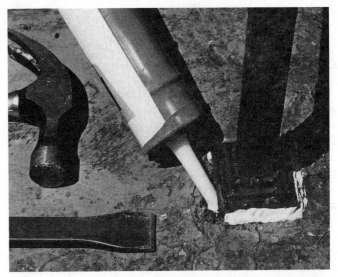

Keep metal column bases calked. Clean away old calking with a brick chisel. If the base is loose, remove it; enlarge the hole and reset the base with anchor cement.

For wooden columns, remove and replace any damaged calking, especially at the base of the columns. Keep the columns painted regularly — usually about every two years and usually around the base where moisture can cause plenty of damage.

For brick columns, check the mortar joints. If you find loose and crumbling mortar, remove it with a brick chisel. Then mix up a batch of mortar mix and tuckpoint the joints (see the chapter on "Exterior Repairs" for details).

If a wooden column has rotted (usually at the base) you have a choice of repairs. You can replace the column, which is a job for a pro, or you may be able to cut away the rot and replace it with new wooden trim or concrete. The replacement repair can be used *only* if there is enough good wood to support the superstructure. If not, the entire column must be replaced.

With a crosscut saw, cut away the rotted wood at the point of the good wood. Then remove the rotted wood with a broad wood chisel. This will leave a notch around the column. Use scrap wood to build concrete forms around the column in a square configuration, or to the height of the notch. You can tack the forms to the flooring to help hold them in position. Run in a couple of large wood screws at the base to help "lock" the concrete to the column.

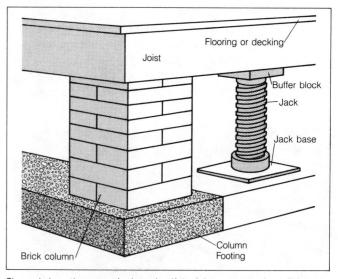

Shown is how the screw jack works. If the joists are rotted, you'll have to have a pro dismantle the porch and replace the joists. Brick columns may be replaced with wood or steel.

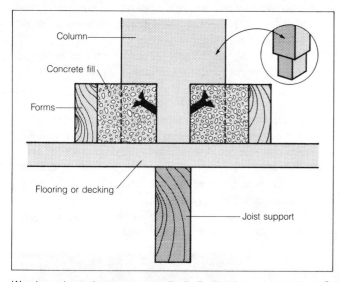

Wooden columns have a concrete "collar" with this repair technique. Or you can build out the damaged or rotted area with new pieces of trim. Cement the new pieces with building adhesive.

Mix the cement into a thick, batter consistency. Then place it in the forms and smooth the surface. Keep the concrete damp for three days — not wet, just damp — and remove the forms after five days.

If the column has not rotted badly, you may be able to use new trim boards and moldings to cover the damage. You will simply have to experiment with this technique to see if it is possible. But before you add new trim to cover the old wood, give the wood a couple of coats of wood preservative. Then fasten on the new wood, after it has been coated with preservative or paint, with nails or building adhesive or a combination of both.

For brick columns beyond tuckpointing repairs, you have two choices: replace the columns, a job for a pro, or support the superstructure with a jackpost, if the jackpost won't show, and make cosmetic repairs to the column.

A jackpost or screw jack is fairly inexpensive. To use it, place a concrete pad or block on the ground near the brick column. Put a preservative-treated block of wood on top of the pad. Sandwich the jack between the bottom block and another buffer block at the top of the jack where the jack meets a supporting joist for the superstructure.

Crank the jack open very, very slowly until the weight is off the column and on the jack.

At this point, if you are lucky, you may be able to repair the brick column by removing loose bricks and setting them in new mortar, replacing brick column supports, or rebuilding the column entirely. If the column has deteriorated so badly that none of these alternatives are possible, you will have to leave the jack in position, and clean and tuckpoint the mortar joints in the bricks. The brick column is now for show; the jack is for support.

Porch and Step Railing Repairs, Wooden

Analyze the job first: can the railings be easily repaired, or should they be replaced? It sometimes is easier to build new railings rather than hold together old ones.

Tools and materials. Hammer, crosscut saw, metal mending plates, nails, calking compound, new (matching) lumber, screws, wood preservative/paint, paint brush, wood chisel, railing brackets.

STEPS

Broken members of wooden railings should be completely replaced. Don't try to splice or patch them with wood. The results would not only be unattractive, but dangerous.

Replacement usually involves removing the damaged member with a hammer. Cut the new member to fit; give it a couple of coats of wood preservative or paint; nail it in position; repaint the entire railing.

If the railing is loose, try nailing it tight. If a railing is supported by a bracket and the bracket is loose, try tightening the screws. If the screws won't tighten properly, back them out of the holes and drive in new, longer screws. If the bracket is broken, replace it.

For loose railings that join posts, use a metal mending plate (angled) screwed to the railing and the post. If decorative posts are doweled into railings and the posts are broken, you can fasten them with angled metal mending plates. Screw one leg of the plate to the post; screw the other leg to the railing. If the post is damaged, saw it off flush at the railing. Then insert a new post, holding it in place at the top and bottom with a mending plate.

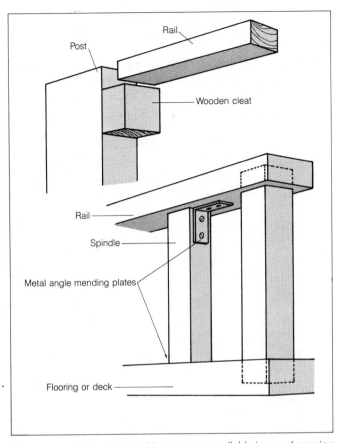

All sorts of metal brackets and hangers are available to mend sagging and broken wooden railings. The least expensive are wooden cleats and metal brackets; renailing also helps.

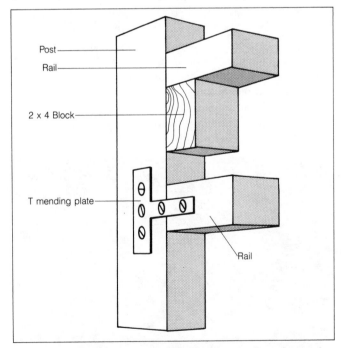

You can buy a variety of hangers to support fence rails and screening. A metal T-shaped mending plate is easy to install to stop wobbling; wooden cleats support rails.

Steel Railings

Steel railings have two big problems: the steel rusts; the steel posts pull out of the concrete.

Tools and materials. Hammer or baby sledge hammer, calk-ing compound, screwdriver, wire brush/steel wool, star drill or masonry drill for an electric drill, masonry anchor cement.

STEPS

To get rid of the rust, wire brush the rusted spots. Then steel wool the metal until the metal is bright and shiny. Coat the metal with special metal primer. Let the primer dry and finish the entire railing with a top coat of metal paint.

To repair loose posts, remove the post from the metal bracket that holds it. Two screws generally have to be loosened so the post can be removed. Then pull out the metal holding bracket, which no longer is anchored in the concrete. If this bracket is damaged, you should replace it with a new bracket. With a star drill or masonry drill in an electric drill, enlarge the hole in the concrete for the metal bracket. Clean the hole as

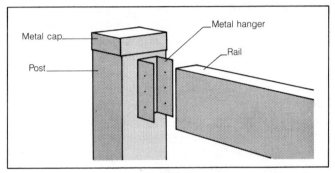

Metal post caps — usually thin aluminum — protect tops of posts from weather. Metal hangers — similar to joist hangers — can be used to strengthen joints between posts and rails.

best you can; a heavy stream of water from a garden hose often works best for this.

When the area is clean and dry, reset the bracket in the hole in the concrete, using masonry anchoring cement. The cement dries fast and hard, so you should work fairly fast. Wait one. day before you secure the metal post in the bracket.

Broken railings and posts sometimes can be welded. This is a job for a pro with a portable welding outfit.

FENCE AND GATE REPAIR AND MAINTENANCE
Replacing and Repairing Damaged Fence Rails

Rails are the horizontal framing members of fences. The rails are fastened to the posts, which are anchored in the ground. Weather stresses are the cause of rail troubles — rot and decay and damage to the rails where they are fastened to the posts.

Maintenance involves nothing more than renailing the rails to the posts when you notice them coming loose, and keeping the rails painted or coated with a good wood preservative.

To replace rails you must remove the screening from the rails, replace the rails, and fasten on the screening.

Tools and materials (for annual maintenance). Wood pre-servative/paint, nails, a paint brush, hammer.

Tools and materials (for replacement). Hammer, pry bar, level, metal hangers (depending on the job), new lumber, nails, preservative/paint, a paint brush, crosscut saw, wood scrap.

STEPS

The point of rot and decay is where the rails meet posts. To replace a rail, you first have to remove the screening or facing from both the top and bottom rail — sometimes a third or middle rail. Use a hammer and/or pry bar. Depending on the design, simple or complicated, you may want to mark the position of the screening on each piece of screening you remove, so you can replace it the same way. As you disassemble the fence, remove any protruding nails from the screening and rails.

Measure, mark, and cut the new rails to fit. Test the fit between the posts. Now give the new rail a couple of coats of wood preservative (if it isn't already treated) or paint. This is easier than trying to cover the wood after the rails have been installed.

Depending on the design of the fence, the rails may fit into notches in the posts; set on cleats; set on hangers (see drawing at "Railing Repairs" above). Level the rails and fasten them in position.

Complete the job by nailing the screening back onto the new rails. At this time, you may want to consider repainting the screening. It's quicker and easier to refinish it before it is nailed to the rails.

Replacing and Repairing Damaged Fence Posts

Look for trouble at the ground (grade) level, where posts rot and decay. Also look at the tops of the posts for weather damage; water is a fence's biggest enemy.

Tools and materials (maintenance). Hammer, nails, wood preservative/paint, 1x4 boards.

STEPS, REPAIR

Check fence posts every spring for damage. If the posts are not painted, give the bottoms of the posts a coat of wood preservative each spring. If the posts are painted, give the posts a coat of paint every two years.

With a hammer, drive in any popped nails; add nails, if necessary, to secure the rails or screening to the posts.

If a fence post is rotted through and is being held only by the rails and screening, you may be able to temporarily repair the post by driving a 1x4 stake down into the ground next to the post. Then nail the stake to the post. The post, however, should

be replaced as soon as possible. If the post is not replaced, damage can result to the rails, screening, and other posts in the assembly.

Tools and materials (replacing a fence post). Tiling spade, pry bar, hammer, level, premixed concrete mix, crosscut saw, wood preservative/paint, a paint bucket, scrap 2x4s or metal hangers, new posts.

STEPS, REPLACEMENT

To replace a post, you will have to remove the rails and screening from the post. You may get away with propping up the fencing while you switch posts. If not, you'll have to remove the entire section of fence.

Dig away the earth around the post, after you saw the post off at the ground level. As you dig, try prying up the post stub. If you are lucky, it may pop up out of the ground. If you are unlucky, you'll have to dig clear to the bottom of the post to remove it.

Set the new post in the old hole. The post should be set into the ground about ⅓ of the length of the post. At this point, you can determine if more digging is in order.

Give the new post a coat of wood preservative or paint, even if the post has been pretreated with preservative. While the finish dries, throw a couple of handfuls of gravel into the hole. You can use old brickbats for this, if you break them with a hammer, or small pieces of stone or old concrete. The rock forms a base for the post and aids water drainage at the bottom of the hole.

Set the post in the hole and have a helper hold the post while you plumb it (make it vertically level) with a level. Pour in the cement mix — right out of the bag — until the cement is about 3 in. deep. Then pour water into the hole and tamp the cement with a piece of scrap 1x2 or 1x3. Then add another layer of cement, water it, and tamp it. Repeat this until the post hole is full of concrete. This technique is easier than mixing the cement and then placing it in the hole around the post.

Let the concrete harden about 3 days before you nail on the rails and the fence screening. At this time, you can saw off the top of the post to level it with the other posts.

Posts that have rotted or are broken at ground level can be supported with 1x4 stakes driven, then, nailed to the posts. Add stakes to two sides; coat them with preservative.

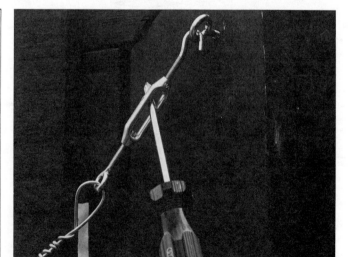

Activate a gate turnbuckle with pliers or a screwdriver after you string the wire from hinge side to latch side diagonally across the gate.

Gate Repairs

Sagging is the No. 1 problem with gates. Inadequate hinges cause the sagging. You may be able to beef up the support to hinges by adding a turnbuckle to the gate.

Tools and materials. Hammer, pliers, nail, two eye screws, 14 gauge wire, a turnbuckle.

STEPS

Position and install an eye screw on the top of the gate above the top hinge. Add another eye screw kitty-cornered from the top eye screw at the bottom of the gate on the latch side. You can punch pilot holes into the wood with a nail for the eye screws. Turn down the eye screws with pliers.

Fasten the wire to the turnbuckle — each end. Then rough measure the wire from the turnbuckle to the top and bottom eye screws. Leave enough wire — about 4 in. — for the wrap at each eye screw.

Now, insert the wire into the eye screws, pulling the wire taut and wrap the wire to make a loop, using the pliers. At this point, the turnbuckle should be turned so the screws in it are barely engaging the threads in the turnbuckle.

After the hookup, turn the turnbuckle with pliers to increase the tension on the wire. This tension "lifts" the gate, eliminating the sag.

Sagging sometimes is caused by an out-of-plumb (vertical level) gate post.

To solve this problem, you may be able to drive a 1x4 stake into the ground next to the gate post and nail the stake to the post, plumbing it at the same time. If this doesn't work, you'll have to remove the post and replace or reset the post. (See "Replacing and Repairing Damaged Fence Posts," this chapter.)

If the gate is damaged, your best bet is to build a new gate. Use the old gate as a pattern for the new one. Take dimensions and lumber sizes from the old gate; assemble it with nails/screws.

Replacing and Maintaining Gate Hardware

When a gate sags, won't open or close properly, or is tough to latch, blame the hardware: hinges and latches. Chances are that the hardware is inadequate for the job it is supposed to do, and is probably too light a weight.

If closing and opening the gate is a problem, try lubricating the hinges with light machine (household) oil or graphite power. If this doesn't work, you'll probably have to replace the old hardware with new, heavier hardware.

Tools and materials. Hammer, pliers, adjustable wrench, drill and drill assortment, hacksaw, chisel, paint, paint brush.

STEPS

Remove the old hardware. The screws and bolts are probably rusted, which means you'll have to cut these fasteners with a hacksaw. If you can, work from the bottom hinges to the top hinges, completely replacing each hinge as you come to it. This way, you won't need help to hold the gate in position while carrying out your replacement project.

Once the new hinges are in place, you may not have to replace the latch. You will probably have to realign it, however, by simply removing the holding screws and repositioning the latch. If this doesn't work, replace the latch.

If loose screws are causing the sagging, opening, or closing problem, try removing the old screws and replacing them with new longer screws. Or, remove the old screws, drill a hole completely through the gate post, and install long bolts through the hinges and the post.

New gate hardware usually is preprimed or painted. If it isn't, give the hardware at least two coats of paint after you install it, to deter rust.

Replacing and Maintaining Fence Screening

Fence screening can be almost any material: wood, plywood, hardboard, screen wire, bamboo, metal slats. And almost always the screening does not cause problems unless rot sets in due to poor maintenance, or because the screening has been damaged.

Tools and materials (depending on the type of screening). Hammer, pry bar, crosscut saw, level, screening to match original.

STEPS

Remove the old screening with the hammer or pry bar. Often small wooden cleats at the top and bottom rail hold the screening in position. You can remove one cleat to slip out the screening. If the screening is boards, prepaint the new boards before you nail them onto the rails and posts. Also, make sure the new screening is plumb (vertically level) as you fasten it into position.

WOOD PRESERVATIVES

There are several types of wood preservatives available. Most of them are inexpensive to moderate in cost. All may be applied to the wood with a paint brush, paint roller, or by dipping the wood into a vat of wood preservative. The latter is the most effective method, but it costs a lot of money to fill a vat with wood preservative that you may not need. The vat technique is best used when you must treat a lot of wood. When applying wood preservative, always have plenty of ventilation. Don't work in a closed room.

Types of preservatives and where they are used include:

Asphalt roofing compound. Buy the liquid, not paste. Use it for any wood that will be buried underground.

Creosote. It comes in liquid form. Use it for any wood that will be buried underground. Ventilate while applying it.

Copper napthenate. Liquid, it may be used on wood that will be buried or exposed above ground.

Pentachlorophenol. Use at least two coats; best for wood that will be buried.

Paint. Use paint for wood that will be exposed above ground. Do not use it for wood that will be buried, unless you simply can't buy another type of preservative.

Stain. Same use as paint. Both paint and stain should be the exterior type.

REPAIRING AND MAINTAINING WALLS
Brick, Block and Stone

Moisture results in crumbling mortar and broken and chipped bricks, blocks, and stones.

Tools and materials. Hammer or baby sledge hammer, brick

Large cracks in brick walls must be cleaned. Then fill large voids with chunks of rock or stone. This provides a "backup" for the new mortar and cuts down on mortar needed.

For fairly even cracks in masonry walls, you can use pieces of asphalt expansion strips trimmed to fit. The edge of this material must be recessed to make room for new mortar.

Fiberglass insulation makes a good crack filler over which mortar is packed. Don't use steel wool or paper; the steel will rust, and the paper will rot, causing the mortar to crumble.

or cold chisel, tuckpointing trowel, premixed mortar mix, oakum, asphalt expansion strips, fiberglass insulation, mixing tub or bucket, shovel, wheelbarrow or bucket for debris.

STEPS

Clean out the old mortar joints with a chisel, making sure all damaged or crumbling mortar is removed. Chip away until you're down to the good, hard concrete.

Mix the cement to a fairly thick consistency; you don't want it to be runny. Then sprinkle the repair area with water and fill the joint with the mortar. Pack the mortar tight into the joint — no voids. Smooth the surface of the joint with the tuckpointing trowel.

If the bricks, blocks, or stones are loose in the old mortar bed, you must remove the units, chisel away the old concrete, and reset the units in new mortar. This is explained in the section on "Tuckpointing, Exterior Repairs." Also see the illustrations, this chapter.

Maintenance of Special-material Retaining Walls

These "special" materials include railroad ties, treated posts, and reinforced concrete. Replacement is seldom necessary but maintenance is a yearly affair.

Tools and materials (depending upon type of wall). Hammer, baby sledge hammer, shovel, gutter spikes, scrap 2x4 or 1x4 for stakes, nails, preservative/paint, paint brush, rip saw, reinforcing rods, star drill, garden hose.

STEPS, RAILROAD TIES & TREATED POSTS

Railroad ties that are stacked can become dislodged. After you restack and realign the ties, spike the ties together using long gutter spikes driven through the edges of the components. If necessary, you can drill a hole through each tie, aligning the holes as you go. Then drive a long piece of reinforcing rod through the holes and into the ground. The top of the rod will be flush with the wood once you have finished the job.

To tuckpoint mortar joints in brick, block, and stone walls, pack in the new mortar so it is tight. Smooth the joint, rounding the corners of the joint to shed any excess water.

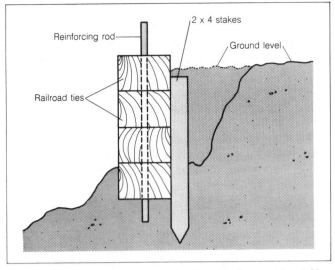

Keep walls built with railroad ties and posts in alignment by staking them with reinforcing rod or wooden stakes. If you can get behind the wall, use stakes; if you can't get behind, use rods.

Weep holes in retaining walls and planters must be cleaned annually — early and late spring. Excess water and moisture are released through these holes, preventing deterioration.

As an alternative, you can reinforce the ties by driving 1x4 or 2x4 stakes in back of the stack and then nailing the stakes to the ties. This technique is easier than the reinforcing rod method, although the backs of the ties are left exposed.

Maintain treated posts the same way as you would railroad ties. Posts often may be spiked together with gutter spikes or 20d common nails. If the backs are exposed, nail a long 2x4 cleat to the posts. Then nail several 2x4 stakes to the cleat, after you have pounded the stakes into the earth.

STEPS, REINFORCED CONCRETE

For cracks in reinforced concrete walls, the treatment is similar to that for cracks in concrete driveways and walks.

Clean out the break with a cold or brick chisel, cutting away the crumbling mortar to the good, hard concrete. Wet the crack

A garden hose makes an excellent hydraulic ram to penetrate dirt lodged in weep holes. Wiggle the hose as you force it into the hole; turn the water on full blast.

Trowel fresh mortar into cracks. Or push the mortar in the crack with your fingers, but be sure to wear gloves. You can smooth the joint with a regular or tuckpointing trowel.

Walls without weep holes should have them to prevent damage from moisture to the wall. Drill holes about every 2 to 3 ft. and line the holes with a short piece of hose.

with water and then fill the break with mortar mix concrete, mixed to a thick consistency. Smooth the surface with a triangular or tuckpointing trowel.

Make sure that all weep and drainage holes in any type of retaining wall are open. These weep holes let water buildup behind the wall escape, preventing damage to the wall.

If the wall does not have weep holes, you'll have to make them with a brace and bit or a star drill.

REPAIRING AND INSTALLING UNDERGROUND SPRINKLING SYSTEMS
Repairs

Grass, grass clippings, and dirt are the troublemakers for spray heads in underground sprinkling systems.

Tools. Special sprinkler head core wrench (usually provided by the manufacturer of the system), screwdriver, pliers, adjustable wrench, fine wire.

STEPS

Turn off the water. Remove the sprinkler head core with the special core wrench or screwdriver or adjustable wrench. The threads turn counterclockwise.

With fine wire — not wood because it can break in the tiny water jets — clean the jets. Then replace the core and turn on the water. Sometimes you may be able to clean the jets without removing the core. Use fine wire for this job. If this treatment does not work, you will have to remove the core to clean it.

If the system does not have cores, unscrew the cap on the sprinkler head. Just loosen it; don't remove it. Then turn on the water full blast. The water pressure probably will flush out any dirt or grass debris. Retighten the cap.

If the piping has leaks, call in a pro to handle this trouble. Special equipment is needed; the equipment is probably too costly for you to buy.

Installation

With the new plastic products, installing an underground sprinkling system is fairly inexpensive (under $100), and not hard.

Tools and materials. Tiling spade, razor knife, pliers, hammer, chalkline, 1x3 stakes, the sprinkler kit, hose, special fittings, level.

Draw a plan of your lawn, showing the placement of the sprinkler system. The best way to do this is on graph paper, each square representing one foot or one yard. Each spray head will sprinkle a circle of grass from 20 to 50 feet in diameter. Choose the type of spray head most suitable for your needs and begin laying out the sprinkling pattern on graph paper. If you have a large lawn, you may need two or more systems to cover the area properly.

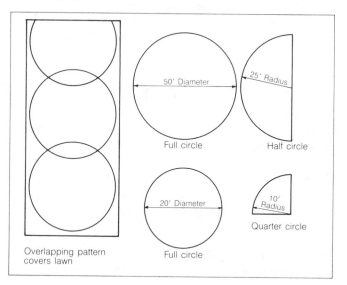

Overlapping pattern covers lawn

50' Diameter — Full circle

25' Radius — Half circle

20' Diameter — Full circle

10' Radius — Quarter circle

This underground sprinkler system kit contains plastic sprinkler heads, tee, elbow, and straight couplings. The connecting hose is a slip fit; the screw caps hold the hose tight without threads.

After laying out and measuring the sprinkling system, cut the hose to fit the couplings. You can use a razor knife or hacksaw for this. Keep the cuts square.

STEPS

With the chalkline and stakes, lay out the lawn for the system, using the graph paper sketch as a guide. Assemble the system, using the various fittings.

Dig a V-shaped trench for the hose and sprinkler heads. The trench should be about 6 in. deep. Just "fold" the sod over it, if you can. You don't need to remove the sod. Then bury the hose, fittings, and sprinkler heads in the trench. The sprinkler heads should be level in the ground. Now connect the system to an outside sillcock.

Since the sprinkler system is plastic, you don't have to drain it in the wintertime. However, you should disconnect the hose from the sillcock.

As the watering season passes by, check the level of the sprinkler heads from time to time. If they tip out of level, dig around the units and reposition them. If the spray jets become clogged with dirt or grass, you can quickly clean them with fine wire; do not use a wooden peg or toothpick in the tiny holes.

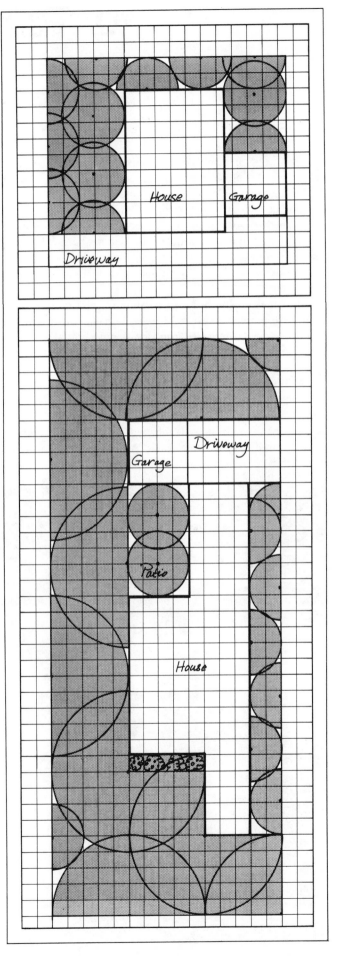

A slit with a tiling spade is usually all that's needed to bury the sprinkler parts. You may want to make a V-shaped trench, however, folding over the sod as you go.

Connect the sprinkler system to an outside sillcock. Or bore a hole through the siding, sheathing, and inside wall and then connect the hose to a water faucet.

10 Painting and Preserving

A house needs not only the decorative advantages that paint offers, but the protective qualities as well. In today's world buying, mixing and applying paint or stain is not difficult for modern technology has made paint lapless, dripless and odorless. Longevity of a paint job has been extended from about four to eight or more years and application has been reduced to rolling, padding, dipping and spraying — in addition to brushing — with tools that are lightweight, easy to use and inexpensive to buy.

Difficulties remain in the preparation of some surfaces, but even these problems have been eased by better paint removal tools, cleaning detergents, caulking compounds and special undercoaters.

HOW TO BUY AND USE PAINTBRUSHES

Like any other product, quality paintbrushes cost more, but they do more: they are easy to use because they are balanced; they are easy to clean; and, they will last for many years if properly used, cleaned and stored. A quality brush can have natural bristles or synthetic bristles. In either case, the brush,

when gripped around the bristles, should feel full of bristles. A natural bristle brush has tiny "flags" at the tips of the bristles. You can see these flags by isolating a single bristle and holding it to the light. The flags let you load the brush with more paint. Synthetic bristles on quality brushes are "exploded" at the tip, a treatment which also permits you to load the brush with more paint.

Make sure the ferrule of the brush (the shiny metal band around the bottom of the handle) is a rust-and-corrosion-resistant metal such as stainless steel, and that the ferrule is screwed or riveted to the handle — no nails.

When buying a paintbrush there is only one inflexible rule: Never buy a pure or natural bristle brush for use in water-based paints. If you should use one in water-based paints, the bristles will bunch and the brush will operate like a long string mop. Use synthetic bristle brushes for water-based paints and natural bristle brushes for oil-based paints.

Before you use any paintbrush, spin the brush in the palms of your hands to flip out any loose bristles and remove any stray bristles by snapping them off against the metal ferrule or

Pure bristle brushes have flags at the tips of the bristles. These flags permit the brush to hold more paint.

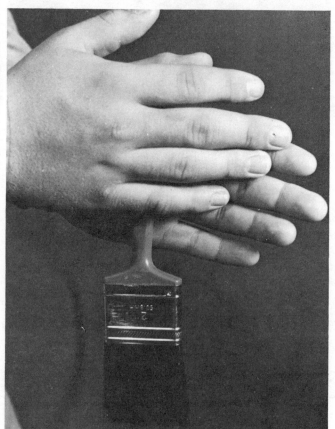

Before using a brand new brush, twirl the brush between the palms of your hands to remove loose bristles.

by carefully cutting them off with a razor knife. The cost range for quality paintbrushes runs from $5 to $20 or more.

Wall and ceiling brushes vary in width from 3 to 6 in., but a 4 in. brush is considered standard because it is easy to use for long periods of time. A wide brush covers more area faster than a narrow brush.

Sash and trim brushes vary in width from ½ to 3 ins. Standard width is 1½ to 2 in., and brushes with angled bristles are designed for painting windows. Most sash brushes have small handles so you can use them like a pencil. This gives greater accuracy when cutting in around moldings, trim, and window mullions.

Round brushes are used for painting round objects such as spindles and railings and are also suitable for stencils and stippling (brush effects in paint), scrolls, and curved surfaces.

For varnish and enamel, use a 2 to 3 in. brush; for masonry, use a wide brush — 6 to 9 in. — because a wide brush holds more paint and covers more surface than a narrow one. This is important when painting large, porous masonry surfaces such as basement walls.

Paint pads do a good job on many surfaces, especially those that are grooved and striated. Paint mitts are suitable for railings and slats, but are usually messy. Artist brushes are essential for very delicate trim, and can be used for minor touch-ups with any type of paint.

How to Buy Rollers

On large, flat surfaces you can spread paint very quickly with a roller. Compared to brush application of paint over a given area, a roller can cut work time in half. For most painting jobs, however, you should team a brush with a roller for best results — use a brush for trim and cutting in walls and ceilings; use a roller for the big surfaces.

Roller handle assemblies are very inexpensive. Size depends on the width of the roller cover needed. If painting ceilings or high side walls, buy an extension handle for the roller which will provide additional reach so you won't have to move the ladder often. This may eliminate use of a ladder altogether.

The best roller frame is the wire or birdcage design because the wires are easier to clean than a solid block frame.

Whatever the material of roller paint trays, usually aluminum or plastic, it is most important that a tray be constructed with ridges across the pan. This will give the roller traction as you load it with paint. If the tray does not have the ridge feature, you can cut a small piece of hardware cloth to fit the bottom of the tray and this wire will provide necessary traction.

You have a wide choice of roller covers — long, short, contoured, and light to heavy nap. For water-thinned paints, buy a roller cover with a plastic sleeve. For oil-thinned paints, buy a cover with a cardboard sleeve. Special rollers which have solid wood frames are available for trim. On these rollers the cover slips over the frame and is secured with either an elastic band or a string tie.

If your painting job will stretch out over several days, buy two roller covers and alternate the covers on work days. In this way, the covers will be dry each time you start painting. Always buy roller covers that match the type of paint you plan to use. This information usually is stamped on the roller cover package.

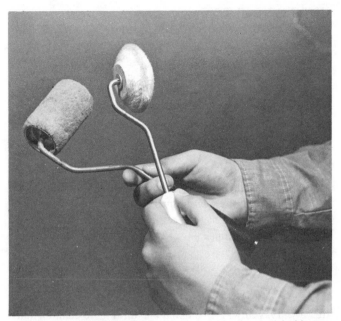

Special roller shapes are sold for trim, windows, doors, or inside corners. The covers usually slip and tie over a solid wood block attached to the roller handle.

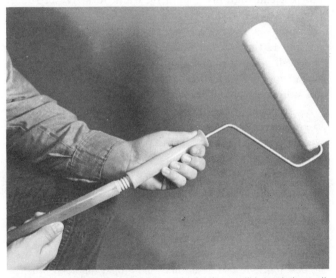

An extension handle for a roller is essential if you will be painting ceilings. Cost is moderate and most extension handles are designed to fit various brands of roller handles. You just screw the handle to the roller.

Dynel/nylon covers. These should be your choice for water-thinned paints. You can also use these covers for oil-thinned paints, but separate covers should be purchased for each type.

Mohair roller covers. Designed for high-gloss enamel and varnish. These are fairly expensive.

Lamb's wool covers. Best for oil-thinned paint, these are also fairly expensive.

Polyurethane foam covers. Used with any paint, these are moderately priced.

Stippling covers. These produce a special design in the paint. Follow manufacturer's directions, but plan on spending some time in practice — patience is also an ingredient.

Use long nap covers for rough and uneven surfaces — brick, stone, concrete, stucco — and short nap covers for smooth surfaces such as gypsumboard, plaster walls and ceilings, wood trim and smooth concrete.

INTERIOR PAINTING

The key to any paint job is preparation. If surfaces to be painted are not clean, patched, sanded or dry, then the time and money spent on paint and painting can be a total loss.

Because the variety of interior paint available is so wide that space does not permit a complete listing, we will classify paint by type to assist you in making an appropriate selection. It is wise to spend some time shopping for paint, keeping in mind that a quality product is readily applied, covers very well, is easy to keep clean and will last for many years.

Interior Paint and Stain Selection

The average cost of a quality interior paint will run from about $10 to $18 per gallon. You are usually assured of a quality paint at mid-price range — $12 to $14 — and less at special sales.

On a fairly normal interior surface, one gallon of paint should cover about 400 sq. ft. of area — do not plan to use less if you expect a professional-looking job. If surfaces are extremely dry, you will need about one-third more paint for satisfactory coverage. To determine how much paint you need, measure the length and width of the surface, translate measures into feet and multiply length by width to arrive at square footage.

Example. A living room wall is 12 ft. long and 8 ft. high; multiply 12 times 8; the answer is 96 sq. ft. Do the same for each wall, plus the ceiling if you plan to paint it. Do not subtract for openings, such as doors and windows, unless most of a wall is a picture window or a doorway.

Be skeptical of "one-coat" paints. One-coat paints usually do not cover as advertised, especially if the paint is applied over a very dry surface, a surface painted a different color or a surface that has been extensively patched with spackling compound. On new wallboard or plaster always use an undercoat or primer which has been formulated to penetrate and seal the surface of new materials and which will provide base for the finish paint. The type of undercoater should be matched to the type of finish paint that you will apply.

Paint chemistry dictates not only the selection of paint for the best job, but also determines the proper thinners, brushes, rollers and clean-up materials to be used. Paint has three basic ingredients: pigment — which adds color and body to the mixture; the vehicle — oil or water — which keeps the pigment in suspension, preventing it from separating or settling to the bottom of the container and hardening; and, thinner — which provides the mixture with consistency. Oil base paint is thinned with mineral spirits; types include resin-based enamels, alkyd enamel and modified-alkyd enamel. Water-thinned paint has latex particles suspended in water; types include PVA or vinyl, rubber and acrylic. Also thinned with water are: thixotropic (dripless), epoxy, urethane and polyurethane paints.

As a rule of thumb, use semigloss, enamel or flat oil-based paint for trim and woodwork. Use a latex-based paint — or one of its cousins — for wall and ceiling surfaces. In kitchens and bathrooms use a semi-gloss enamel, oil or water-based, since this paint surface is easy to wipe clean and helps deter moisture. Buy metal-formulated paint for metal surfaces — such as steel casement windows. For a wood tone, use stain and then protect the surface of the wood with varnish or shel-

lac. On wood paneling, you can use any interior paint but you may have to fill the pores of the wood with wood filler. Then you must sand and prime the surface before top coats are applied to the panels. When you want wood paneling grain to show through, use stain, penetrating wood sealer, varnish and/or shellac. You may also use paste wax and buff the surface. Make sure the paneling is wood, not simulated wood grain, before you apply any finish other than wax. You can paint, varnish and shellac most simulated wood grain finishes, but do not attempt to smooth or buff these surfaces with steel wool, sandpaper or other types of abrasive.

Over masonry, use a flat, semigloss, casein, aluminum or latex paint. We recommend a prime coat on masonry surfaces.

Ceiling tile may be painted with any interior paint. However, paint will cover fissures in the tile, which may destroy any acoustical properties.

Glass may be painted with any interior paint, but three to five coats of paint are necessary to properly cover the shiny surface. Buff with steel wool between each coat, letting each coat dry thoroughly.

There are surfaces that should not be painted. Linoleum, for example, should not be painted. Neither leaded glass nor the leading itself should be painted. If glass is loose in the leading, tighten it with 50/50 solid core solder. Melt the solder with a pencil, or gun type of soldering iron, and flow the solder along the glass next to the lead. Another surface that should not be painted is plastic laminate.

Surface Preparation

Walls, ceilings and trim to be painted should be lightly sanded with fine-grit sandpaper stretched over a sanding block. Surfaces then should be washed with a mild detergent and thoroughly rinsed with fresh water.

If the surfaces have never been painted, sand them with fine-grit sandpaper on a sanding block, vacuum or dust off the residue and apply a prime coat of paint or undercoater. If the surfaces have been painted, but are dry, apply an undercoater, let it thoroughly dry, sand, clean and apply the finish coats.

To cover ink and water stains, apply pigmented shellac to the stain. Let the shellac dry for about one hour, then lightly sand the area with fine-grit sandpaper over a sanding block. Shellac prevents the stain from "bleeding" through the finish coat of paint. Since stain areas are usually small, buy a throw-away brush to apply the pigmented shellac. A brush is cheaper than the cleaner you will need to remove the shellac from a good brush. Some stores sell pigmented shellac in a spray can.

Fill all holes, cracks, and breaks in the surface with spackling compound. Techniques for this are fully explained in Chapter 2.

Surfaces are ready to paint after you: (1) remove all grease and dirt from the surface; (2) lightly sand the surface to remove bumps; (3) remove sanding residue; (4) patch holes and cracks; (5) mask and cover surfaces that you don't want painted, and (6) spot-prime and/or undercoat surfaces that need prepaint treatment.

Spot-Priming

Tools and materials. Paint brush, paint, fine-grit sandpaper, sanding block.

STEPS

Spot-priming can save costs, material and time, since spot-priming does the same job as an undercoater but is done only on small, selected areas that are freshly patched or extremely dry.

About one hour before you start the paint job, coat the spots with the same paint you will use over the entire wall or ceiling surface. Carefully feather the edges of the spot with the tip of a paintbrush so the new paint will blend in with the old. After the paint soaks into the surface and dries, check the spot to see if another coat of paint should be applied to the area. If the spot looks very dry — as if it could absorb more paint — then apply another coat in the same manner. If the spots are especially troublesome and require several coats of primer, lightly sand the areas between coats with fine-grit sandpaper on a block.

When you are satisfied that the spots are properly coated, start the paint job. The new paint will blend in with the pre-primed spots and will appear uniform when dry.

Ceilings

Tools and materials. Paint roller and/or brush, paint, wiping cloths, step ladder, extension handle for paint roller, drop cloths, masking tape, newspapers.

STEPS

Remove all draperies and window shades from the room. Move the furniture to the center of the room, or to one end of the room, or remove from the room. Cover furniture with drop-cloths, securing the edges of the dropcloths to carpeting and/or flooring using masking tape. Paint brushes drip paint and rollers emit a fine spray that settles in a room like dust, so be sure you cover anything that you don't want paint to touch.

If you are painting only the ceiling, or painting the ceiling a different color than the walls, use a brush to paint the ceiling area where it meets side walls and light fixtures. (This is called "cutting in".) You can do this easily if you have a steady hand and a keen eye for straight lines. If not, mask around the ceiling/wall junctions or lights using a 2-in.-wide tape. As insurance against paint stains, you may want to cover the top of any fixtures with newspaper. Fasten the newspaper in place with small strips of masking tape.

Apply paint across the narrow width of the room, working from the unpainted central areas to the just-painted corners. Work completely across the ceiling painting a strip about 3 ft. wide. Start another strip when this is completed. In brief, do not apply paint at random across the ceiling. Start and complete one section before you begin another.

At windows, apply the final brush or roller strokes in the same direction that sunlight enters the room. When painted in this fashion, brush and roller marks won't show when sunlight strikes the surface.

Use a brush to paint ceiling ducts and registers with the same paint used for the ceiling surface. Paint from left to right if you are right-handed; go from right to left if you are left-handed. This trick permits you to work faster and the paint equipment will not get in your way as you apply the paint.

Ceiling color can make a big difference in a room. If you want the ceiling to appear lower, use a dark color; if you want

It is a good idea to strain oil-based paint before you use it. Screen wire makes a good strainer. Always strain paint applied with a spray gun, since straining removes lumps that can clog the nozzle.

"Box" paint by pouring it from bucket-to-bucket several times before use. This thoroughly mixes the paint — especially paint to which you have added tint. Boxing also helps blend paint from a partially used bucket with a brand new bucket of the same finish.

When painting from the original paint container, punch holes around the rim of the bucket so paint lodged in the rim can drip back into the container. We recommend that you use a regular paint bucket instead of using the paint container. In a bucket, you can control the weight and depth of the paint.

Always paint from a dry surface into a wet or freshly painted surface. Use the tip of the brush to smooth laps and brush marks. Dip the bristles into paint only one-third their length, and wipe the handle of the brush often with a clean cloth.

Never dip a brush into paint or stain more than one-third the length of the bristles. Gently slap the sides of the brush against the sides of the bucket after the brush has been dipped into the paint. Do not dip the brush and wipe the bristles across the rim of the bucket.

the ceiling to seem higher, use a light color. White paint has an 80% light-reflecting factor; pale blue 40%, and black about 2%.

How to Paint Walls

Tools and materials. Paint roller and/or brush, paint, wiping cloths, step ladder, extension handle for paint roller, drop cloths, masking tape, newspapers, screwdriver, razor knife.

STEPS

Remove all draperies and window shades from the room. Move furniture out of the room or to the center of the room and cover it with a dropcloth. With wide masking tape and newspaper, go around the baseboard of the room, covering the flooring. One edge of the tape should butt against the baseboard and the opposite edge of the tape should be pressed down against the newspaper. A dropcloth may be laid over the newspaper to complete floor protection. If you do not want to paint them, remove the electrical switch and outlet plates. Use a screwdriver to back out holding screws and a razor knife to pop plates off the wall. Many homeowners do paint switch plates and outlets, because paint hides these plastic or metal rectangles so they then blend in with the wall surface. If you decide to paint them, spot-prime the plates before painting the wall — you may have to spot-prime with two or three coats.

Cut in the ceiling, trim and corners of the wall with a paintbrush, or mask the ceiling for a straight line, if you plan to use a roller on the large surfaces. Run the paint about 6 in. down the wall from the ceiling, up the wall at the base and onto the wall at the corners. Do one complete wall, instead of working catch-up (i.e., making the trim "cuts" as you paint over the large surfaces). This is the fastest method since you will not have to stop and switch equipment.

Work across the wall from left to right, if you are right-handed — the opposite way, if you are left-handed. Do one section at a time, working down from ceiling to baseboard.

When you apply paint with a roller, run the roller in all directions against the wall because this multi-directional application helps distribute paint more evenly. Always apply the paint from the unpainted surface to the just-painted corner and other cut-in areas.

If you are using a wide wall brush to apply the paint, also work from the unpainted surface to the fresh paint. Work the paint evenly; then smooth it with the tip of the brush. At windows, run the roller or stroke the brush across the wall in the direction that light comes through the window — usually horizontally along the wall. If there are any ridges in the paint they will follow the same direction as the light and will not show.

Load paint rollers with paint just short of the dripping point. As you roll on the paint, watch out for roller tracks in the paint surface. Tracks occur at the points where a roller has been set down on the wall prior to rolling out the paint, or where a roller skidded on to the wall.

When using a brush, inspect the wall from time to time for brush marks. These marks are caused by spreading the paint too thin or by starting or stopping the brush on a freshly painted surface.

To remove a loose bristle from freshly-painted surfaces,

Watch out for roller "tracks", exaggerated here for illustration purposes. The tracks are the result of starting and stopping the movement of the roller in fresh paint on the surface being painted. As with a brush, always apply paint from a dry surface to a freshly painted one.

lightly tap the tip of the brush against the loose bristle, gently flicking off the loose bristle. The loose bristle will stick to the paint in the brush so you can then remove it with your fingers.

Paint the trim, windows and doors last. If the doors are flush panel, remove the knobs and paint the panel; a brush is the best painting tool. Do panel inserts first, then paint rails and stiles and finally the edges of the door. Using a brush, paint window mullions first; then paint window stops, casing and sills.

How to Paint Stairwells

Tools and materials. Paint equipment, extension ladder, stepladder, scaffolding board, concrete blocks.

STEPS

The same ceiling and wall painting techniques are used for stairwells (see above). The problem in this project is to reach the ceiling and upper walls of a stairwell. Since we can not see the stairwell in your home, we will list several ladder/scaffolding suggestions that might be adapted for use in your situation.

Stairwell Sandwiched Between Two Walls. One method is to lean an extension ladder on a step, against the wall, and to support it with concrete blocks. However, the safest approach is to build a scaffold on which to rest the ladder. It must be very strong, and placed so it is level on the steps (see illustrations). Attach blocking to ¾ in. plywood with 2 in. No. 8 wood screws. Nail 2x4 legs and braces to the blocks and to each other. Use shims as needed to achieve a firm, level surface.

The standard 5 ft. step ladder needs at least 3 ft.x2 ft. of room; this should be the minimum size of the platform. The actual size of the platform must conform to the requirements of the stairwell. The platform should rest level on the stairs.

Test the platform in its correct position for stability and levelness. Make sure it will not slip off either of the two supporting steps. A slightly unsteady platform will result in a very unsteady step ladder.

If it is necessary to use an extension ladder to reach high places, brace the platform (if possible) against the wall away from the ladder. This will add additional stability.

A drop cloth will be required to protect the steps. Position

the drop cloth once the platform has been set up. The drop cloth should not be under the platform legs; you will need to move it around.

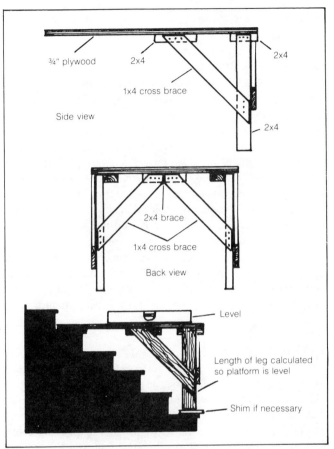

Stairwell that opens onto a landing. You can set an extension on a step and lean the ladder against the wall, but we recommend the scaffolding technique given above.

Landings with two sets of steps. This is found in a split-level house or one with a stairway leading to a landing and then to another floor. Set the ladder on the landing and against the wall. The ladder legs should butt up against the baseboard of the wall so the ladder can't slip from under you. For areas that can't be reached this way, use scaffolding.

How to Apply Texture Paints

Tools and materials. Texture paint, fiber brush, mason's trowel, stippling roller, design cut-outs or pads.

STEPS

Texture paint is a thick mixture of paint that is often used to hide defects in old plaster or gypsumboard. Depending on the paint, it may be applied with a fiber brush, mason's trowel, or heavy stippling roller. The manufacturer's instructions on the container usually specify proper application.

Paint may be textured with various designs after it has been applied to a wall. Some of these are:
(1) swirls — use a wooden mason's float or rubber float, twisting it in the texture paint to make a swirl;
(2) lines — notch a piece of fairly heavy cardboard with pinking shears or regular scissors, and when the paint starts to set, run the notches down or across the wall;

(3) dabbing — as the paint starts to dry, tap it with the flat of a rubber float. Clean the float when the paint starts to bunch on the surface. You also can use wadded newspaper for this effect.

Sand-finish paint is also considered a texture paint. Do not attempt to add sand to make your own.

Interior Paint Cleanup

Tools and materials. Water or mineral spirits (depending on the type of paint you are using), wiping cloths, razor blade, aluminum foil.

STEPS

As you apply the paint, clean up any drips or splatters. If you are using a water-thinned paint, use a water-dampened cloth; if you are using oil-thinned paint, use a cloth dampened with mineral spirits. To clean off water-thinned paints, simply wash in household detergent and water. For oil-thinned paints, clean painting equipment in mineral spirits, preferably outside the house. If weather does not permit outside cleanup, work inside in a well-ventilated room. You will have to rinse the equipment several times in mineral spirits to make sure all paint is out of or off of the equipment. The final rinse should produce clean mineral spirits.

EXTERIOR PAINTING

Because preparation of exterior surfaces for paint is 95% of any exterior paint job, never skimp on preparation.

Equipment you will need for exterior painting is for the most part the same equipment you would need for interior painting. Buying tips outlined earlier apply to exterior painting tools. Ladders are usually even more important for exterior work than interior work.

Wash Your House First

Tools and materials. Long garden hose, car wash brush or scrub brush, bucket, mild household detergent.

STEPS

Remove surface dirt and grime from the siding, soffits, and foundation of the house with water and detergent. After washing the house, you may find that you do not have to paint it for another year or two. Dirt can hide a sound, well-painted surface, but also can hide defects that should be repaired. Wash one side of the house at a time, working from the soffit and eaves down to the bottom of the siding. We recommend a long-handled car wash brush for the scrubbing job, although a regular GI scrub brush works just as well. If the house is extremely dirty — and you will know this when you start to scrub — use a mixture of mild household detergent and water to remove the dirt and grime. Then rinse the surface with water from a garden hose with the nozzle set at full blast. Let the house dry at least two weeks before you apply paint to the clean siding.

Exterior Paint Selection

There are many exterior paints from which to choose, but the choice will narrow down to latex paint, titanium, white lead, shake paint (pigmented stain/sealer), and metal paint. Features of each paint are listed in the paint chart which follows.

Estimating Paint Needs

The basic rule for calculating amounts of paint needed is: If your home has been painted in the last eight years, you will need one gallon of paint for every 450 sq. ft. Plan on one gallon of trim paint — if you will use trim — for every 5 gallons of house paint. If your home is sided with cedar shingles and/or shakes, or is covered with textured siding, add 20% more to the above base figure. This allows for absorption of paint on a porous surface. If your home is sided with narrow lap siding, add 10% more paint to the above base figure. If your home is masonry (block, brick, stucco), add 50% more paint to the above base figure.

To figure out your paint needs, carefully measure the width and height of each exterior wall of your home, then multiply the height by the width. The answer will be the square footage of each wall.

Example: one side of the house measures 20 by 30 feet. Multiplied, the answer is 600 sq. ft. One gallon of paint covers 400 sq. ft. You then would need 1½ gallons of paint to cover this 600 sq. ft. area. The percentages listed above should be added to the base figure of 1½ gallons.

How to Remove Old Paint

Tools and materials. Abrasives, scrapers, paint remover, heat. See "Steps" below to determine the correct tool for the job at hand.

STEPS

Some homeowner/handymen are under the impression that any and all old paint must be removed from siding, trim, windows

Peeling paint almost always is caused by moisture — from damaged roofs, gutters, downspouts, and/or moisture vapor within the house. Find and correct the moisture problem before you repaint the house.

A pullscraper is the best all-around tool for removing damaged paint from wooden and metal surfaces. The scraper, when kept sharp with a file, is suprisingly easy to operate and paint comes off quickly.

A wire brush attachment locked in a power drill chuck also makes fast work of removing loose paint — especially on curved and contoured surfaces such as gutters and downspouts.

and doors before new paint is applied. This is not true. The only time old paint must be removed from a surface is when old paint is peeling, flaking, cracking or not adhering tightly to the surface. The paint is probably not to blame for a damaged surface. The paint has been improperly applied over a dirty or wet surface, or the surface has become wet, causing the paint problem.

Moisture is the biggest enemy of paint. When a paint coating fails, you can almost always trace the problem to moisture. Even with proper ventilation, moisture vapor from foggy bathrooms or steaming kettles finds its way into adjoining rooms. This moisture floats out of the house through walls, ceilings and floors. Some of this vapor settles on and behind painted surfaces, building up pressure. When the pressure is released, it pops the paint, and causes cracking and peeling.

MORAL: To stop paint from peeling, you must stop moisture at its source. This includes moisture vapor (showers, bathtubs, laundry tubs, washers, dryers, dishwashers), cooking, condensation (moisture striking cold surfaces), and water (rain, melted snow, melted ice). Do not overlook trees, bushes, shrubs, flowers, dirt, and other plants or building materials that hold moisture against painted surfaces. Remember: the surface to be painted must be dry before paint is applied. You should also check the venting, roofing, and rain-carrying systems.

You can remove damaged paint with a scraper or putty knife if the damage covers a small area. If the damage covers a fairly large area, the best tool to use is a pull scraper. Keep the edges of the scraper sharp with a cross-cut file, and scrape down to the bare wood. Lightly sand the wood with a medium-grit sandpaper stretched over a sanding block. Then spot-prime the bare wood before you apply top coats of finish to the entire section of siding.

For small areas coarse steel wool may work. In general, however, coarse, and then medium-grit sandpaper works better than steel wool alone. Sandpaper should be used over a sanding block so the abrasive does not dig ridges into material being cleaned.

For large areas, use a power sander. An orbital sander is best, but a disc sander may be used if you are careful not to let

the edge of the disc dig into the material itself. A wire brush locked into a power drill removes peeling paint quickly — but be careful that the brush does not dig into the surface being cleaned. For small areas that will not respond to abrasives and scrapers, try paint remover applied according to the directions on the paint remover container.

As a last resort, old paint can be removed with a blowtorch, propane torch and/or an electric paint remover. The blowtorch and propane torch are dangerous — you could set the house on fire with either — so if you use these tools, be extremely careful. An electric paint remover is reasonably safe, although it can scorch your work if you are not careful. All three tools must be teamed with a scraper and wire brush for paint removal. Heat softens the paint and scrapers and wire brushes remove it from the surface.

Exterior Painting Procedures

Organization makes any job go faster and exterior painting is no exception. By following this checklist your project should move along with all possible speed:

(1) give your house a bath;

(2) estimate paint needs — buy paint and equipment;

(3) repair any building component that is damaged — i.e. roofing, gutters and downspouts, cracked and split siding, crumbling mortar joints, loose boards and casing;

(4) remove window and door screens and all exterior hardware such as house numbers, mailboxes, etc.;

(5) if you plan to paint the foundation or siding which extends to ground level, trim away any vegetation touching the house and pull grass and weeds next to the foundation;

(6) remove damaged and peeling paint;

(7) caulk all open cracks around window and door frames, casing, fascia, soffits, columns, railings;

(8) spot-prime bare wood with a primer compatible with the finish coat of paint that you will apply to the house;

(9) cover plants, shrubs, walks, railings, and other items you do not want damaged by paint, and

(10) paint only one side of the house at a time — complete it before you move to another section.

EXTERIOR PAINT GUIDE

Type	Use	Application	Clean-up	Considerations
Latex	Any surface; prime wood before applying latex.	Brush; roller; paint pad	Water and mild detergent	Flat finish; quick-drying; don't use over oil-based paint unless surface properly primed
Titanium	Any surface; needs primer on new wood surfaces; spot-prime painted wood as needed.	Brush; roller; paint pad; spray gun	Mineral spirits	Gloss finish; durable; long drying time; surfaces must be absolutely dry before use
White lead-based paint	Any surface; needs primer on new wood surfaces; spot-prime painted wood as needed.	Brush; roller; paint pad; spray gun	Mineral spirits	Gloss finish; durable; easy to color tint; good color retention; slow-drying; fair hiding power; discolors from airborne chemicals
Shake paint	Formulated for natural wood.	Brush; roller; paint pad	Mineral spirits	Flat finish; stops bleed-through of wood saps; some fading over time
Trim paint	Any surface, but formulated for trim.	Brush	Mineral spirits	Flat or gloss finish; matching difficulties
Metal paint	For metal, but may be used on other surfaces.	Brush; roller; paint pad	Mineral spirits	Metal must be clean, dry

How to Paint Fascia, Gutters, Soffits

Tools and materials. Ladder, paint, paintbucket, paintbrush or roller, wiping cloths.

STEPS

Thoroughly clean the components. Work across the area starting at the left side and working toward the right if you are right-handed. Reverse the procedure if you are left-handed.

Paint from left to right and from top to bottom. Coat the fascia first, then the gutter and then the soffit. Apply plenty of paint, smoothing it out evenly with the roller or tip of the paintbrush to eliminate lap and brush or roller marks. Paint from dry to wet surfaces.

If the roof overhang is narrow, set the ladder under the soffit and work out over the soffit to the gutter and fascia and then down under the soffit. If the roof overhang is wide, set the ladder against the fascia and/or gutter. Paint these components and then move the ladder across the span. Do not try to over-reach with the paintbrush or roller, but instead move the ladder as you complete an arm's-length section.

Lower the ladder and set it against the house to paint the soffit, if the overhang (fascia, gutter, soffit) cannot be painted in one ladder setting. Complete painting of the fascia, gutter, and soffit before you begin work on the siding.

How to Paint Lapped Siding

Tools and materials. Ladder, paint, paintbucket with a hook attachment, paintbrush or roller (with roller tray attachment), wiping cloths.

STEPS

Thoroughly clean the siding, casings, windows, doors, and attached downspouts (techniques are given earlier in this chapter).

Set the ladder so you will be reaching and working above the top rung of the ladder, then paint across the siding — from left to right — covering three to four courses (laps) of siding at one time. (If you are left-handed, work from right to left.)

After you paint the casing and/or downspout downward as far as you can comfortably reach, then work the paint into the joint formed by the casing and the siding. Work the paint into the joint so it fills all tiny cracks and fissures. Now paint the face of the siding, smoothing paint with the tip of the brush or the roller. When you finish this section of siding, move the ladder to the next section and repeat the painting procedure. Lap edges of the siding before you paint the face of the siding.

Go completely across the side of the house. Then return to the first section you painted, drop the ladder down three rungs, and paint across the house in sections as described above — working from the soffit to the foundation.

How to Paint Grooved Siding

Tools and materials. Ladder, paint, paint bucket, short-bristled paintbrush, paintbrush or roller (with tray), wiping cloths, newspapers, masking tape.

STEPS

The best method is to use a short-bristled brush (stubby) to paint the grooves. Work from left to right, top to bottom, just like on any other siding. Paint the grooves first, making sure the sides and bottoms of the grooves are completely coated with paint. Then with a regular paintbrush or roller, apply the finish to the face of the siding.

Since the grooves form channels for the paint, you can expect excess dripping along the bottom edge of siding. After you paint one section of siding and move on to the next, occasionally go back to the finished job to remove any excess paint with a dry paintbrush. You may have to do this several times

PAINT PROBLEMS AND HOW TO SOLVE THEM

Problem	Possible Cause	Possible Solutions
Peeling	Nearly always moisture	Repair gutters, downspouts, roofing; install vents in siding; remove problem paint, prime wood, apply finish coats
Chalking (comes off on your hand)	Normal conditions	Wash house with water and a mild detergent
Bleeds and stains	Sap pockets, rusty nails and metal components	Coat the spots with 4-lb. cut shellac; coat redwood or cedar with stain-resistant primer; repaint
Checks	New paint applied over paint not yet dry	Remove old paint to bare wood with sandpaper, scrapers, and/or power equipment; prime and finish
Alligatoring	Incompatible paints applied over each other	See "Checks"
Blistering	Usually moisture	Remove paint to bare wood; stop source of moisture; repaint
Paint won't dry	Surface is oily; painting before undercoat is dry	Paint over a clean, dry surface; brush out paint evenly; seal surface with shellac or special aluminum primer
Sags	Too much paint; paint applied over glossy paint	Evenly spread out fresh paint; dull any glossy paint with fine abrasive
Wrinkles	See "Paint Won't Dry"	

until the paint sets. If the siding butts against a foundation — or laps it slightly — mask the foundation with tape and newspapers to keep paint drips from running onto the foundation.

How to Paint Shingles and Shakes

Tools and materials. Ladder, paint, short-bristled paintbrush and/or long nap roller, paint bucket, roller tray, wiping cloths, newspapers, masking tape.

STEPS

Since most shingle and shake siding is striated (grooved) and hangs vertically on the house, the painting strokes should be up and down, not across. However, work from left to right, top to bottom. Paint underside of the shingles where they lap each other and do several courses of shingles at once — just like lap siding. Then, with a short-bristled brush or a long-nap roller, apply the paint to the face of the shingles vertically.

As you go across the siding, return frequently to the area you already have painted. You will find drips of paint along the lapped edges of the shingles. Remove this paint with a dry paintbrush or paint will form icicles along edges of the siding. If shingles lap or butt against the foundation, mask the foundation with tape and newspapers to protect it from drips.

How to Paint Brick and Block

Tools and materials. Brick, wirebrush, whitewash brush or long nap roller, paint, paintbucket or roller tray, ladder, wiping cloths, broom.

STEPS

The best way to clean brick and block is with an abrasive brick and a wire brush. Just before you get ready to paint the surface, go over it lightly with the brick and brush, dusting away any

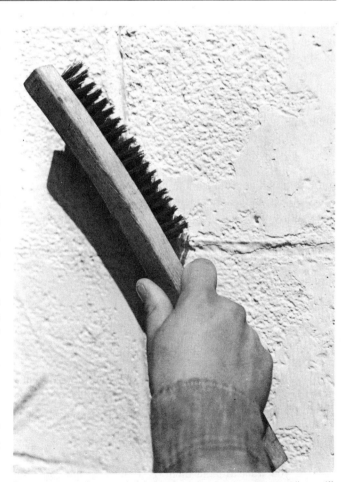

For masonry surfaces — brick, block and stucco — use a medium-stiff wire brush for cleaning away loose paint. You can use a power-driven wire brush on brick and block, but do not use this on stucco; it will cut too fast.

residue with a broom. Use the same procedures for painting brick and block as for regular siding — working from left to right, top to bottom. Do not use Portland cement paint over any brick and block painted with another type of paint.

Because brick and block are very porous, expect to use about 50% more paint on the surface than on a normal wood surface. A whitewash brush is ideal for applying the paint since the surface is rough and will quickly wear out regular bristles. A bristle brush or a roller cover with long nap will also do the job. To paint brick and block well, divide your work into small areas.

When the job is done — but the paint not yet thoroughly dry — the surface may appear blotchy and uneven. If so, let the paint dry completely before you draw any conclusions. If the job is indeed blotchy, another coat is needed. This coat will not require as much paint to cover the same surface — about 50% less than the previous coat — and the job will go much faster. The varied absorption qualities of brick and block are responsible for this problem since some units are more porous than others and require more paint. You usually will be unable to judge this condition until the paint has dried thoroughly.

How to Paint Stucco

Tools and materials. Same as for brick and block.

STEPS

The techniques are the same as for painting brick and block with this one exception — double-coat the surface as you paint it. Although double-coating takes about 10% more paint, the additional paint usually assures you of a smooth, blotch-free job when the paint is dry. Unlike brick and block, stucco has a quite consistent absorption rate so you don't have to double-coat obvious spots as you go — as you automatically do with brick and block. Never use a Portland cement paint over a stucco surface that has been painted with another type of paint.

Use a whitewash brush or a long-nap roller on rough surfaces, as well as plenty of paint. You may find that a brush/roller combination is the best application method. You can also spray stucco, but there are pitfalls as will be explained later in this chapter.

How to Paint Metal

Tools and materials. Metal primer, paint, paintbrush, paint bucket, short-nap roller, roller tray.

STEPS

If the metal is new, prime it with a metal primer. If the metal has been painted and the paint film is solidly bonded to the metal, paint over the metal with regular house paint.

When painting metal watch out for runs and sags (curtains) in the fresh paint. Use a fairly dry brush or roller when you paint metal surfaces.

Painting Special Surfaces

Copper and aluminum. These metals do not rust; they corrode. If you want to paint them, first clean off the corrosion with medium and then fine steel wool. Then apply metal primer to the surfaces. The metal then may be painted with regular house paint.

If your home has copper gutters and you want them to shine, clean them with household copper cleaner and steel wool and then apply two coats of clean exterior varnish. In time, copper gutters may turn black. If so, you will then have to remove the varnish, repolish and revarnish the metal.

Plastic. Do not paint plastic.

Metal railings. Treat the same as any other metal. Clean the surfaces with steel wool, scrapers, wire brushes; prime the metal; apply finish coats of metal paint which you can buy in gloss and flat finishes.

New and bare wood. Wood always needs a prime coat of paint. It is better to give the wood one coat of primer than two coats of finish paint. Never use a primer as a finish coat.

Porch and deck paints. These include alkyd enamel, oil-based porch and deck paint, and varnish. Use these products on porches, steps, and decks — never use regular house paint — because the enamels have been especially formulated to resist wear and tear and standing water (snow, sleet, ice).

Steel and aluminum windows. Use a metal primer and a metal paint. Water-thinned paints can rust metal. You can use a regular house paint over the metal, but the metal must be primed first with a metal primer.

Natural wood trim. Use clear spar varnish — two coats. Do not use a primer.

Screen wire. Use a metal primer and paint applied with a paint pad or a very dry bristle brush. Use regular trim or house paint on the wooden frames, but if the frames are metal, use a metal primer and then a regular house paint trim over the primer.

Use a dry brush — or screen-painting pad — to paint metal screen wire, or the screen ports will clog, as illustrated here. For a smooth job, paint both sides of the screen wire. You may have to give the wire two or three coats of paint.

Plastic screen wire. Do not paint.

Caulking. Any type of paint will adhere.

Glazing compound. Any type paint will adhere.

Concrete walks and driveways. Use a chlorinated rubber paint, latex, or epoxy finish applied with a brush or roller. Follow the manufacturer's instructions to the letter. These directions include removal of all grease, oil, dirt, and other debris.

Spray Painting Basics

Spraying paint is a fast way to paint and the final job looks very professional. However, there are drawbacks to spray paint. The number one drawback is overspray from the spray gun. The paint can float in the air and settle on passing or parked cars, on neighbor's windows, porches, decks, roofs and so on. Some communities have laws against using spray equipment outdoors, so before you do any spraying, check out the codes.

You can buy or rent two types of spray guns: air guns which have a compressor that generates air to spray the paint, and airless guns which flip the paint through the nozzle of the gun and onto the surface. This equipment is best suited for small jobs — not large houses.

Preparation of surfaces to be spray painted are exactly the same as for brush painting, described earlier. Anything you don't want spray painted — windows, doors, railings — must be tightly masked or covered.

Spray paint outside only on a windless day, and never spray around a corner or up over a roof unless the spray is blocked with a covering such as a piece of cardboard or a dropcloth.

To spray paint, the spray gun must be in motion as it starts across the surface to be painted. As you pull the trigger on some spray guns, the first projection will be air followed by paint. The trick is to feather the paint onto the surface as you start spraying the surface, and then to feather the paint off the surface as you complete the arc with your arm. Hold your wrist firmly so the spray gun always remains at right angles to the surface. The heaviest paint concentration will be in the center of the spray pattern and the edges of the pattern will feather out. As you go back and forth across the surface, you will have to lap these feathered edges so the paint will be the same thickness throughout.

This sounds hard to do, but it isn't. However, you should practice until you get the feel of the motion and of the trigger of the spray gun before beginning to spray paint.

To spray angles, spray the surface nearest to the nozzle first. To spray inside corners, spray the adjoining surfaces first. The overspray will paint the corners. At outside corners, point the gun toward the house surface — not around the corner. For gutters, set the ladder high enough so you are shooting the paint downward onto the gutter surface.

Paint for spraying must be specially mixed. Follow the directions on the paint container label, although most rental outlets provide complete instructions with rental spray equipment. As a general rule, use only oil-based paints with pressure-fed spray guns. Use only latex- or rubber-based paints with a pressure-fed, external-mix spray gun.

SPECIAL FINISHES

Home maintenance and repair projects are limited in their use of special finishes. However, you may have an occasion to use a stain or polyurethane finish on a room divider or on paneling in a recreation room or study.

Stains

Sealer-stains are available for one-coat application. There are oil-based wiping stains to be applied with a brush or cloth, then wiped and sealed with shellac or varnish. Or you can choose a water-based stain, which is applied and wiped. Because stain color is important, test the color on a scrap of the same kind of wood that you will stain. Do not be guided solely by color charts in the paint department of a store, for these sample colors are only fairly accurate at best. Without a test, you could be dissatisfied with the final result.

Woods that will be stained or finished with a clear, see-through finish often need to be filled. Wood fillers include wood plastic (it looks like real wood when it dries), wood putty, stick shellac, oak fillers, sawdust mixed with adhesive, and spackling compound that has been toned with a base color.

The staining process requires the following steps:

(1) sand the surface with a medium-grit abrasive;

(2) clean the surface with mineral spirits;

(3) fill the wood, if needed;

(4) sand the surface with fine-grit abrasive once the filler has dried, and clean the surface again with mineral spirits, removing all residue and debris;

(5) apply the stain with a brush, cloth, or pad;

(6) let the stain dry, lightly buff the surface with fine steel wool, and apply additional coats of stain until the desired color and/or tone is reached . . . lightly buff the surface between coats with fine steel wool, and

(7) apply a shellac or varnish to the surface, if needed — two or three coats usually are required. Buff with fine steel wool between coats.

Polyurethane

This finish imparts a "sealed in plastic" look. There are two types of product available: a two-part formula and a one-part formula. We recommend the one-part formula because it is easy to use.

The trick to using this product is to have the wood sanded, filled, sanded, and clean before the finish is applied with a brush or spray gun. The surface of the work must be absolutely bone dry before the finish is applied in a dust-free working area. The work probably will need two coats of finish, but you may not have to sand between coats. Check the manufacturer's directions.

Lacquer

Most lacquers should be sprayed, allowed to dry, and then rubbed with an abrasive for smoothness. Multiple coats of lacquers are usually required — even when brushing on lacquers.

Surfaces to be lacquered must be clean, smooth, dry, and free from any grease. Since lacquer is a very fast-drying product, the chance of dust forming on the surface of the work is greatly reduced, so you may not have to sand between lacquer coats. Let the completed job set about 60 hours before you buff the surface with a very fine steel wool and hard wax. Work in a small area, rubbing the wax while the wax is still wet. The same rubbing and buffing procedures apply to lacquer rubbing compound. Once hard, it is practically impossible to properly finish the surface.

Shellac

A "soft" finish, shellac is fairly easy to apply with a small bristle brush. If the wood must be filled, we recommend a shellac stick filler.

All surfaces to be shellacked should be clean, dry and smooth. Shellac stick is generally melted and flowed into holes, dips, and dings. Then the filler is lightly sanded after it has hardened for an hour or so.

Shellac is thinned with alcohol. For general use, buy a 3- to 4-pound "cut" product (it has been "cut" or thinned with alcohol).

Allow two to three hours drying time between coats of shellac, lightly sanding the surface between coats. You can obtain the type of finish you want — from a high gloss to a dull sheen — by rubbing the shellac with extremely fine steel wool.

Varnish

You can buy polyurethane, vinyl, two-part epoxy, and spar varnishes, depending on the job at hand. All types are generally mar-resistant, but vinyl is extremely scuff-and-mar resistant.

All surfaces must be cleaned, filled and dusted. Varnish is best applied with a brush in a criss-cross manner but be careful not to bubble the varnish by wiping the edge of the brush across the varnish can or along a corner of the work. Always use a new brush for varnish since old varnish brushes have varnish residue adhering to the bristles.

11 Materials and Products

Although space does not permit a listing of all the building products on the market, this chapter will discuss the basic building products that you will need, buy and use frequently.

WOOD

Buying Boards

Boards dimensions are 1 in. thick in nominal size up to 12 in. wide in nominal size. In actual size, boards are ¾ in. thick up to 11½ in. wide.

In other words, when you buy a board you are buying a piece of wood that is ¾ in. wide by ½ in. less than its nominal width. Example: 1x3 is actually ¾ in. by 2½ in. The chart below should end the confusion.

Nominal size (in inches)	Actual size. Boards surfaced 4 sides, dry
1x2	¾x1½
1x3	¾x2½
1x4	¾x3½
1x5	¾x4½
1x6	¾x5½
1x7	¾x6½
1x8	¾x7½
1x10	¾x9½
1x12	¾x11½

If you have a project that calls for a 1x3 in actual measurement, you would have to buy a 2x4 (which really measures 1½ x 3½ in.) and then cut it to the 1x3 in. dimension. You might be able to buy a board of correct size at a millwork shop.

Buying Dimension Lumber

Big boards — 2x4s, 2x6s, 2x10s, etc. — are not called boards but are termed dimension lumber. However, like boards, dimension lumber is not the size that you specify. For example, a 2x4 actually measures 1½ in. by 3½ in. Any dimension lumber larger than the 2 in. nominal size is termed timber.

This chart explains the dimension lumber system.

Nominal Size (in inches)	Actual Size (in inches)
2x2	1½x1½
2x3	1½x2½
2x4	1½x3½
2x6	1½x5½
2x8	1½x7¼
2x10	1¼x9¼
5 in. and thicker	½ in. off nominal size
Shiplap with ⅜-in. lap	
1x4	¾x3⅛
1x6	¾x5⅛
1x8	¾x6⅞

In many communities, a 2x4 is no longer a standard framing member for some codes now permit 2x3s to be used for framing. If you own a new home — one that has been built after 1978 — some of the walls may be framed with 2x3s instead of 2x4s.

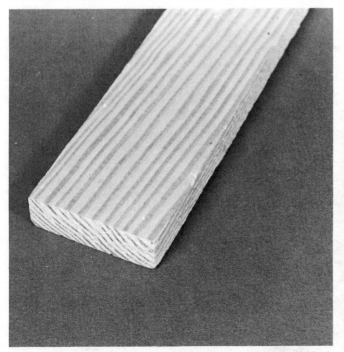

Pay special attention to the graining of boards and lumber. Vertical-grained lumber is not as strong as its flat-grained cousin. It has stability, but a low resistance to warping, bowing, splits and checks.

Flat grained material is stronger than vertical-grained material. Try to pick flat-grained stock for framing members. Note how the grain of the wood runs across the width of the material.

Lumber Grading

All lumber, including boards, dimension lumber and timber, is graded as to quality. As a general rule the better the lumber, the more costly it is. Usually, the larger the lumber (mass), the more expensive it is.

Grading methods can vary. The grade may be indicated in numbers, names, letters or a combination of these. Because this is confusing to laymen, here are some general guidelines. No. 1 is construction grade; No. 2 is standard grade; No. 3 is utility grade and No. 4 is economy grade. The best quality lumber is stamped 1 and 2 clear; lumber with small imperfections is stamped B and Better; lumber with limited imperfections is stamped C select and D select lumber has imperfections that can be hidden with paint.

It might be helpful to know that structural dimension lumber is lumber that is at least 4 inches thick; that select lumber is the strongest you can buy and that common lumber usually has some weaknesses.

BUYING LUMBER

Since the do-it-yourself boom in the mid-1950's, lumber has been priced and sold by the piece. When you go into a home center store to buy a 2x4x8, for example, the price of this "unit" will be stamped on the unit, ie., "$2.44." Taken into consideration in pricing will be the type of wood, the size, the grade and whether the 2x4 is common or select.

Lumber also is divided into two types — hardwood and softwood lumber. Hardwoods include walnut, oak, birch, maple; softwoods include pine, fir, cedar, redwood and hemlock. As a rule, hardwoods cost more than softwoods, but this may depend on the grade of the lumber. A No. 1 softwood may be more costly than birch hardwood.

Pricing schedules are worked out by the retailer in board feet. A "board foot" is the size of a board in nominal inches 1 in. thick, 12 in. wide, and 12 in. long. At one time you had to specify the number of board feet of lumber you wanted. In

some places, this standard of price marking may still be in existence. If so, instead of trying to figure out your needs in board feet, tell the retailer the lineal or running feet, width and thickness of the material you want, and the retailer will figure out the board feet and price for you.

Used Lumber

Sometimes you can buy "used" lumber from a wrecking contractor, farmer, or homeowner selling material which may have been salvaged from a structure being torn down or replaced. Occasionally an owner of used lumber advertises in the newspaper classifieds.

Do not bypass an opportunity to buy this material if you may need it, for used lumber generally is dry and seasoned and is often priced lower than new lumber. Although it may be dirty and appear to be worn, used lumber is just as good — and may be better — than new lumber. Sometimes, under the grime, used lumber turns out to be walnut, cherry, maple or one of the very expensive hardwoods that is almost impossible to locate today.

You also can find bargains in used brick, block, stone, and metal building materials.

Buying plywood

Plywood comes in big sheets of wood — 4x8 ft. standard — which consist of layers of veneer wood, crisscrossed and laminated with adhesive. The face of a panel — called "face" — may have a smooth, blemish-free veneer or it may have blemishes. Plywood is graded and sold according to the condition of the faces. The back of a panel — called "back" — also may have a smooth, blemish-free veneeer, but backs most often are of a lesser quality than faces. Plywood is graded and sold depending on the condition of the backs as well as the faces. Between the face and back of a plywood panel is a series of "plies". The plies are graded and sold as to quality.

Plywood panels are separated into two types, interior and

Veneer core plywood can be recognized by the layers or plies of the core. There are three plies in this plywood sheet, sandwiched between the faces of the panel. The faces are thin wood veneer.

exterior. Interior panels are designated "INT" on a grade stamp on each panel; exterior panels are designated "EXT" on a grade stamp on each panel. Interior panels may be used indoors; exterior panels may be used outdoors or indoors.

Faces and backs of plywood often are intermixed, ie. the face of a panel may be A grade veneer (the best) and the back may be C grade veneer (good). Grading affects pricing. For example an A-A panel (A face/A back) is very expensive; an A-C panel is moderately expensive.

PLYWOOD GRADES AND USES

Grade	Face	Back	Plies	Uses
A-A EXT.	A	A	C	Outdoors; cost may limit use to projects when both sides show
A-B EXT.	A	B	C	Outdoors when both sides show
A-C EXT.	A	C	D	When only one side will show
C-C EXT.	C	C	C	Best for framing construction
B-B EXT.	B	B	B	Utility plywood; for some concrete forming, walks, and other rough use
A-A INT.	A	A	D	Best panel; for cabinets, built-ins, and other construction where both faces will show
A-B INT.	A	B	D	A little less than A-A
A-C INT.	A	C	D	Good face, fair back; for paneling where one side will show
B-D INT.	B	D	D	Utility grade; for rough projects such as underlayment for flooring
C-D	C	D	D	Sheathing grade
CDX	—	—	—	Sheathing grade; usually for exterior use, panels may be used indoors

Veneer letters (A, B, C, and D) specify the grade of the veneer of softwood plywood. Here is what you can expect:

A-veneer. Smooth, sanded, very small, but neatly made; repairs permissible throughout the face.

B-veneer. Smooth, sanded; circular and non-tapered repair

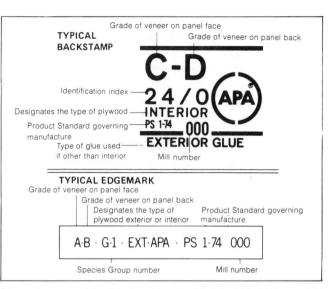

TYPICAL BACKSTAMP

Grade of veneer on panel face
Grade of veneer on panel back

C-D
24/0 (APA)
INTERIOR
PS 1-74
000
EXTERIOR GLUE

Identification index
Designates the type of plywood
Product Standard governing manufacture
Type of glue used if other than interior
Mill number

TYPICAL EDGEMARK
Grade of veneer on panel face
Grade of veneer on panel back
Designates the type of plywood exterior or interior
Product Standard governing manufacture

A·B · G·1 · EXT·APA · PS 1·74 000

Species Group number
Mill number

Plywood approved by the American Plywood Association is marked with this type of stamp. This is your assurance that the product meets rigid standards and is what it claims to be.

plugs and tight knots permissible throughout the face of the panel.

C-veneer. Smooth and sanded; knotholes and some limited splits permissible.

D-veneer. Smooth; knots and knotholes up to 2½ in. in width and ½ inch larger permitted; limited splits acceptable.

N-plywood. Special order veneer with a natural finish . . . the panel veneer will be select all hardwood or all sapwood and will be free of open defects but not all, and some plugs are permitted. This plywood is extremely expensive.

Softwood plywood has both interior and exterior glue bonds and panels are designated by group as to their stiffness and strength. These groups range from 1 to 5; the stiffest and strongest woods are in Group 1.

Hardwood-faced plywood is graded in a different fashion — the grades are A, premium; 1, good; 2, sound; 3, utility; 4,

Particleboard core plywood has a compacted-sawdust look. The core actually is wood fibers held by a resin binder. The face veneers may be laminated to one or to both sides of the panel — the example shown is laminated to just one side.

backing; and SP, specialty grade with decorative features. Hardwood plywood has veneer faces of woods such as maple, birch, walnut, cherry. These panels are expensive.

Both softwood and hardwood plywood panels come in thicknesses of ¼, ⅜, ½, ⅝, ¾, and 1 in. Standard panels measure 4 x 8 ft., although some retailers sell 2x4 ft. and 4x4 ft. pieces. You can special order larger panels.

The plies or cores of plywood can vary but typical construction is that with a series of three plies of veneers laminated together in a crisscross configuration. Other types of cores might be particleboard and lumber. Lumber is solid wood core generally used for hardwood-faced plywood to be fashioned into cabinets and built-ins where edges of the panel will show.

When buying plywood remember to buy exterior type plywood for use outdoors where water and moisture are factors and to buy exterior type plywood for use indoors where high humidity and water are present. For interior use, buy interior type plywood with a water-resistant glue bond. This adhesive will withstand some high humidity and moisture vapor.

BUYING HARDBOARD

Hardboard, often termed "Masonite" — a trade name — is real wood that has been mixed into a fine batter and pressed into sheets under extreme heat and pressure. There are many hardboard manufacturers other than Masonite Corp. but because Masonite was a pioneer in the hardboard industry, the term has become synonymous with hardboard.

You can buy two types of hardboard — standard and tempered. Use standard hardboard where moisture is not a problem and tempered hardboard where moisture conditions are usually present — outdoors for example.

Hardboard panels are available with smooth faces, with one

Lumber core plywood has a solid lumber core to which face veneers are laminated. This material is used for fine cabinets, built-ins and furniture. It may not be readily available at stores selling plywood products.

Particleboard and chipboard have edges that look like this. They may or may not have laminated wood faces. This material is usually used for floor underlayment or sheathing.

smooth face and one rough face, perforated, striated, grooved and embossed. Hardboard paneling is embossed with wood grain patterns so realistic it is difficult to distinguish it from real wood paneling. Special moldings and trim pieces to match or compliment the different hardboard panel designs are available.

Hardboard comes in 4x8 ft. sheets (standard) but larger sizes are available through special order. Thicknesses of the panels are 1/8, 3/16, 1/4, and 5/16 in. Because of the construction of hardboard, it has certain limitations which must be taken into consideration if you plan to use it. Since hardboard panels have no wood grain as do boards, lumber and plywood, hardboard must be fastened to another type of material — you can not fasten another material to hardboard. *Example:* You can nail hardboard to wooden furring strips. You can not nail wooden furring strips to hardwood.

BUYING GYPSUMBOARD

Like plywood and hardboard, gypsumboard is a panel-type building material that replaces plaster-and-lath construction. The panels are composed of gypsum core covered on both faces and all edges with a thick, cardboard-like paper. Standard panels are off-white in color but special panels decorated to be used as paneling are available. You can buy gypsumboard with a moisture-resistant covering, panels designed for use in bathrooms, kitchens, and laundry areas.

Gypsumboard panels are manufactured in 4x8 and 4x10 ft. sizes. Thickness is 3/8, 1/2, and 5/8 in. (standard). You can special order gypsumboard with beveled, eased, square, tongue-and-groove and round edges — and in special thicknesses.

BUYING CHIPBOARD

This is a wood panel product sold under several trade names. Chipboard is called "Aspenite." In appearance, it looks as if large chunks and shavings of wood have been pressed together to form a panel — and it is usually moderately priced.

Chipboard's role in building is roof and wall sheathing, although some homeowners use it for wall paneling. The panels, when finished with a clean penetrating sealer, have a knotty pine appearance.

Available are panels in 1/4, 5/16, 3/8, 7/16, 1/2, 5/8, and 3/4 in. thicknesses by 4x8 ft. face dimensions. Specialty panels include grooved patterns, reverse board and batten and random-grooves. The panels also feature butt and shiplap edges.

Chipboard may be stained or painted but all panel edges must be sealed with finish. When using a roller, choose a medium pile cover and roll it upward on the panel.

BUYING PLASTICS

High-pressure laminate. This product is widely used to surface kitchen countertops. The material is resin-coated paper formed into sheets under extreme pressure and heat.

Standard sizes are 1/32 and 1/16 in. thick in sheets 2x5 to 5x12 ft. — although the larger size may have to be special ordered. The 1/32 in. sheets are the best buy for vertical installation and the 1/16 in. sheets are best for horizontal installation. High pressure laminates are available in a wide range of patterns, designs and solid colors. Some laminates are color keyed to match the colors of brand name appliances.

Fiberglass panels. Usually sold for exterior roofing and screening this material can be used almost anyplace around your home.

Typical panels are corrugated but flat panels and panels that have square instead of round "corrugations" are also available. Corrugations add strength to the panels. A range of colors, patterns, sizes and thicknesses are available as are special rubber-gasket nails to install the panels. For framing purposes, you can buy corrugated molding designed to fit snugly against the corrugated panels.

Polystyrene panels. These are recommended for interior use only and are similar to the fiberglass panels described above.

Acrylic plastic panels. This product is most often used for room dividers, shower doors, recessed ceiling lighting or shelving. The plastic should be supported with wood or metal but it can be attached to itself for support.

The material is best cut with a fine tooth saw, it may be drilled and sandpaper will smooth it. It can be painted with oil-base, enamel or lacquer. Acrylic is an interior product but can be used outside if the surfaces are sealed with a clear finish for weather protection.

Polyfilm. A thin, 2 to 6 mil, plastic sheeting, this material is used as a moisture vapor barrier below concrete slabs, walks, driveways; as a vapor barrier in crawl spaces; as a vapor barrier for insulation; as a paint dropcloth; as a cover for outdoor furniture, etc.

Sheet sizes vary — standard sheets range from 8x10 ft., to 10x50 ft. Basic colors are opaque white and black.

BUYING BRICKS, BLOCKS, AND STONE

These masonry products usually are sold by the unit — one brick, one block and/or one piece of stone makes up a unit. If you have a large project that will utilize a number of these masonry units, you may get a discount for quantity.

Standard bricks measure 2 1/4 in. thick by 3 3/4 in. wide by 8 in. long — paver bricks usually are thicker and brick veneering usually is thinner. A fairly wide range of colors and textures is available.

For projects such as walks, driveways, patios and retaining walls — bricks are graded: Type SW (severe weathering);

Paving bricks, which come in many patterns other than the one illustrated, are durable and can be used for patios, walkways and driveways. The units interlock and can be set in a variety of patterns.

This perforated wall is built to give privacy while allowing a free movement of air. Use the type of brick suited to the project. Even though this wall is not meant to bear loads, it must still be constructed of either SW or MW brick, depending upon the climate.

Concrete block is usually thought of as a plain, utilitarian product; however, there are few limits to the flexibility of concrete. Here is an example of a screen built with concrete block. The pattern was created with a mold and the blocks then set with mortar in the usual way.

Type MW (medium weathering); Type NW (no weathering).

Concrete blocks can be divided into two types — standard blocks which are manufactured from regular concrete, and light aggregate blocks which are made from concrete with a lighter aggregate (sand and gravel). The standard block is heavy and dense; the light block weighs much less and is more porous. Blocks, like many building products, are code specified. Some codes do not permit the use of light aggregate blocks in construction where structural strength is a serious consideration. A standard block measures 7⅝x7⅝x15⅝ in., and usually is sold as an 8x8x16 in. unit. The standard block is called a "stretcher." You can buy other block units in widths of 2, 3, 4, 6, 8, 10, and 12 in. wide, and 4 and 8 in. high. All these full blocks are 16 in. long. Specialty building blocks available include half blocks, bullnose blocks, blocks with solid tops (most blocks have core voids), jamb blocks and partition blocks.

Screen blocks measure 4x4x12 in. (standard) and come in a variety of patterns — shaped outlines, offsets and centered designs. The blocks may be used in combination to create a design, but most often the same block is used when building a divider wall, a screen wall or a decorative garden wall.

Precast patio blocks, used basically as pavers, come in a wide range of sizes and colors — usually green, red, white, black and blue.

Stone types include marble, slate, granite, limestone, sandstone and bluestone. Stone is sold according to the way it is cut. Rubble stones are uncut; ashlar stone is cut on four sides to present a square or rectangular unit and trimmed stone is also cut on four sides. This stone is generally used for thresholds, lintels, window sills etc. Cuts of stone affect the price — dressed stone is cut to your specifications and semi-dressed stone is shaped to rough size, but not to specification. If your project is not too critical as to size requirements, you may be able to sort through piles of semi-dressed stone and find what you need. Undressed stone has had no work done on it.

Phony stone is not phony. It is real stone crushed and reformed with a resin into sheets or individual units such as bricks and stone and in a variety of sizes, shapes, and colors. The material is either nailed up like paneling or set in a mastic made especially for the specific product.

BUYING METAL

There are many types of metal, but the types that will concern you as a homeowner will narrow down to sheet goods — aluminum, galvanized sheet and copper or brass sheet. Tubing is also a popular handyman product.

Sizes range from 1/16 to 1/4 in. thick up to 4x4 ft. squares, although larger sizes are available at specialty shops. You can buy solid rounds of metal (like dowels) as well as thin and thick-wall tubing in a range of diameters and lengths.

Also available are threaded steel rods which may be bent into shapes for special fasteners such as U-bolts, sill connectors and hanger supports.

There is one rule to follow when buying and working with metal — do not mix metals, ie. do not fasten aluminum to galvanized sheet, or copper to aluminum, or any one metal to another. When differing metals touch each other rust and corrosion result.

BUYING GLASS

Because of the large inventory required, many home center stores do not carry replacement glass products. You might have to check telephone advertising pages under "Glass", and if this fails try emergency board-up contractors, auto repair shops, hobby outlets and glazing contractors.

Glass for home construction is manufactured in six different types in a price range from moderate to very expensive and in sizes almost unlimited for standard replacement in windows and doors. Single strength glass is standard for windows and doors; double strength glass is the same — but is a bit stronger.

Tempered glass, best buy for patio doors and screen/storm combination doors, will not shatter into jagged pieces when broken, thus providing a very important safety feature.

Safety glass is similar to tempered glass and should be considered for windows and doors subjected to people traffic. Some types of safety glass have small wires embedded in the glass.

Insulation glass is generally found in patio doors or other installations where large areas of glass are used. The product often is called "thermal" glass.

Specialty glass includes tinted glass, frosted glass and glass blocks — products which are very expensive and are used as special accents. This glass may have to be special ordered, which adds to the price.

When buying replacement glass, we recommend that you take a piece of the broken glass to the store for, with a sample, the store can quickly determine the type of glass you need. Be sure to measure carefully the exact size of the pane you need — don't guess. Trimming bits of glass to fit can be a very difficult job — and an expensive one when the glass breaks.

BUYING FASTENERS

The world of fastening devices is so large and specialized, that in this book we have classed fasteners into categories of nails, screws and bolts. You can buy fasteners for almost all materials you want to join together — this includes adhesives as well as mechanical fasteners such as nails and screws.

Nails. Common nails, finish, galvanized, box, ring-shank, machine, shingle, sheathing, lath, paneling, gypsumboard, tacks and brads are included under this heading. Most stores sell nails in 1 to 5 pound boxes and each box is clearly labeled as to type and size of nail. Some stores sell nails by "bulk", ie. nails are weighed and packaged in a paper bag and you are charged by weight and type of nail.

Common nail sizes are designated by length in inches and by "penny" sizes. "Penny" is indicated by a "d" letter. *Example:* an 8-penny nail is noted as "8d".

The diameter of a nail usually becomes larger as the length increases. Some specialty nails such as brads come in one size, and other specialty nails such as roofing nails are available in only one diameter, but are available in several different lengths.

The most important consideration is that the fastener is appropriate to the job. Shank length and thickness should be long enough and strong enough to hold without causing damage to the wood, block or brick to which you are joining or anchoring other material.

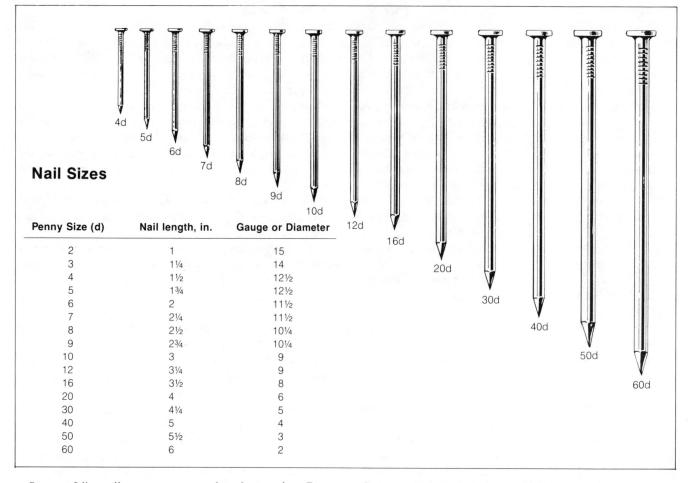

Nail Sizes

Penny Size (d)	Nail length, in.	Gauge or Diameter
2	1	15
3	1¼	14
4	1½	12½
5	1¾	12½
6	2	11½
7	2¼	11½
8	2½	10¼
9	2¾	10¼
10	3	9
12	3¼	9
16	3½	8
20	4	6
30	4¼	5
40	5	4
50	5½	3
60	6	2

Screws. Like nails, screws are numbered as to size. *Example:* a No. 14 screw is 1 to 2¾ in. long. Screws are usually packaged in boxes or polybags and labeled as to number and length — but the sizes are approximate and may vary just a bit.

Screw types include flathead, oval head and roundhead. Slot types are plain, Phillips and stopped (the slot does not extend through the edges of the screw head).

When buying screws — and the same rule applies to nails — figure one third of the length to go through the piece to be fastened, and two-thirds of the length to go into the base material. This formula provides the best holding power. *Example:* When you fasten a ¾ in. thick furring strip to a stud wall, the nail or screw should be 2¼ in. long. Three-quarters of an inch should go through the furring and 1½ in. should go into the stud.

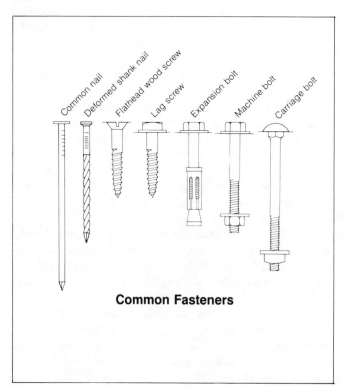

Common Fasteners

SCREW SIZES

Number of Screw	Length in inches
2	¼ to ½
3	¼ to ⅝
4	⅜ to ¾
5	⅜ to ¾
6	⅜ to 1½
7	⅜ to 1½
8	½ to 2
9	⅝ to 2¼
10	⅝ to 2¼
12	⅞ to 2½
14	1 to 2¾
16	1¼ to 3
18	1½ to 4
20	1¾ to 4
24	3½ to 4

Bolts. These are similar to screws, but offer more holding power and fastening ease. Common bolts include machine, carriage, stove and lag. Machine bolts are driven and/or assembled with wrenches; stove bolts are driven and/or assembled with a screwdriver and wrench; carriage bolts are driven and/or assembled with a hammer and wrench and lag bolts (sometimes called lag screws) are driven with a screwdriver or wrench.

Most screws and bolts have matching washers which are sold by type — flat, flush and countersunk.

Screws and bolts are made from a variety of metals — but these fasteners and washers should, when used together, be manufactured of the same metal type: steel, bronze, brass, aluminum, cadmium.

Molly and toggle bolts. These fasteners are designed for hollow wall or hollow core construction. Both are made in a wide range of sizes, lengths and diameters.

The flanges on a Molly bolt are activated when the bolt is inserted into a wall (or hollow core block) and the screw is turned. When flanges are fully opened, they grip the back of the wall or block. The screw then may be removed, inserted through the object to be fastened, and then screwed back into the flange section of the bolt.

A toggle bolt has flanges that are spring loaded. The flanges compress to fit through a pre-drilled hole in a block or wall. Once in place, the flanges spring open and grip the back of the wall or block.

To hang an object with a toggle bolt, drill a hole to fit the diameter of the flanges in a wall or block. Drill another hole the diameter of the toggle screw in the object to be hung. Run the screw through the object to be fastened; then screw on the flange section of the bolt; insert the flange and the screw into the hole in the wall or block and tighten the screw.

When you unscrew the object from the wall, the flange part of the toggle bolt drops from the back into the hollow of the wall so the toggle can not be used again.

Nail and Screw Selection Chart

Type of Fastener	Tools Needed	Prime Use
Flathead screw	Screwdriver, countersink	Joining wood . . . some metals to wood . . . needs pilot hole to prevent splitting
Ovalhead screw	Same as flathead screws	Same as flathead screws
Roundhead screw	Screwdriver	Same as flathead screws
Pan screws	Screwdriver	Same as flathead screws
Self-tapping	Screwdriver	Joining metal . . . needs pilot or starting hole for the threads
Stove bolt	Screwdriver, wrench	Joining wood, metal . . . needs predrilled hole for proper assembly
Carriage bolt	Wrench, hammer	Same as stove bolt . . . head can be countersunk in wood
Machine bolt	Same as stove bolt	Same as stove bolt
Lag bolt (screw)	Wrench, screwdriver	Same as flathead screws and stove bolts
Molly bolt	Screwdriver, drill outfit, hammer	Same as flathead screws . . . for hollow walls . . . needs pre-drilled holes
Toggle bolt	Same as Molly	Same as Molly
Common nails	Hammer, bradawl	Joining wood and some metals . . . may need pilot holes to deter splits
Finishing nails	Hammer, bradawl, nail set	Same as common nails . . . heads usually are countersunk
Box nails	Same as common nails	Same as common nails
Roofing nails	Same as common nails, asphalt roofing cement may be used to seal nailheads to roofing	Same as common nails
Brads	Tack hammer, bradawl, nail set	Joining wood and metal . . . may need starter hole . . . nails may be countersunk
Cut nails	Hammer, drill outfit for pilot holes may be necessary	Flooring . . . elongated head offers decorative effect to joint
Masonry nails	Hammer or baby sledge	Joining wood or metal to masonry
Scaffolding nails	Hammer	For assembling forms . . . double nail head permits easy nail removal
Ringed or annular nails	Hammer	Joining wood or metal . . . tops for gypsumboard . . . nails have screw-holding feature

Toggle bolts have spring-loaded flanges that open and hug the back of a hollow or block wall after the unit has been inserted. Molly bolts are similar to toggles.

BUYING FLOORING

There are six basic types of flooring materials, excluding carpeting. All six must be laid over sheathing which can be plywood, particleboard and hardboard underlayment. Hardboard needs a plywood, particleboard, or sheathing board base.

Flooring may be purchased by the piece or by box or carton. Usually box prices are no lower than piece prices, although some building material retailers will give you a price break on quantity. It is worth an inquiry.

Resilient tile. The choice is vinyl and/or asphalt tile in 12x12 in. squares (standard). Both are available in a wide range of colors, patterns and special designs — such as brick and stone. Life of the flooring is approximately 20 years, but may give more service if properly maintained. Installation and replacement is easy. One disadvantage is that the flooring may discolor and fade somewhat as its lifespan draws to a close.

Hardwood strip flooring. The wood choice is oak, maple and pine in random lengths and widths from 1½ to 3¼ inch. Even these woods may be difficult to locate, although oak is fairly common. The flooring is unfinished, and it is extremely difficult to lay, replace and, sometimes, repair. Life of this flooring is of the same length as the life of the house. Wear resistance is excellent, although in high traffic areas the flooring may, in time, show some wear. This flooring is easy to refinish.

Parquet block flooring. Usually prefinished, this real wood flooring comes in tile form with tongue-and-groove or butt joint edges. Sizes vary and the wood is usually oak. This flooring is as easy to lay as resilient tile and the floor will last the life of the house. Wear resistance is excellent, but wear in high traffic areas can be eliminated with a new finish.

Sheet vinyl flooring. A fairly recent newcomer to the world of building materials, this product is sold in a wide range of colors, designs and special patterns. You can buy it in almost any length — width is 12 ft. (standard). Easy to cut with a scissors, sheet vinyl is as easy to lay as spreading a blanket over the floor. In fact, the material can even be folded like a blanket. Double-faced tape generally is the only floor fastener necessary. Life of this product is about 20 years — the same as resilient title.

Ceramic and mosaic tile. Produced from fired clay and sometimes glass, ceramic and mosaic tile will last the lifetime of a house. It is fairly difficult to set — but easier than hardwood strip flooring. Both products are available in a wide range of colors, patterns and designs, and tile sizes range from one inch squares to 12 inch squares. Standard is 4x4 in. Wear is excellent but some wear will show in high traffic areas such as doorways.

Slate. Generally this material is used as accent flooring, or is laid in an entrance hall or foyer where water would damage wood or resilient tile flooring. It comes in random sizes and may be dark green or grey in color. Slate is fairly easy to install — about like ceramic or mosaic tile. It wears well, although in time, it will show some wear in high traffic areas. You can renew the finish with was or a vinyl coating. However, if you feel that real slate is too expensive or too hard a wearing surface for your needs, there are resilient tiles which look very much like slate and may make a good substitute.

BUYING PANELING

This is simply a selection process. There is such a wide range of paneling surfaces — wood, block and brick tile — that any pre-screening before shopping would be useless. Paneling can be purchased in 4x8 and 4x10 ft. sizes. Thickness ranges from about ⅛ in. to ¼ in.

There is wood-laminated-to-plywood paneling; simulated wood grain laminated to plywood; a particleboard type backing and hardboard. You can buy thick (¼, ½ and ¾ in.) solid wood paneling if you are prepared to spend a good deal more. Moldings are made and prefinished (wood and plastic) to match paneling — inside and outside corners, joint strips, cove, base shoe, crown, chair rail, etc.

BUYING CEILING TILE

Like paneling, ceiling tile has many designs. Sizes are 12x12 in. and 2x4 ft. (standard) and thickness ranges from about ½ to 3 ins. The larger sizes are usually applied to suspended ceilings where metal wall angles, main runners and tees furnish support for the tiles.

Tile is either a fiberboard type material or a thin finish or surface laminated to fiberglass insulation (for suspended ceilings). Most tile is washable and most is fairly easy to replace — especially suspended ceiling tile. You often can buy tile by the piece, although it usually is sold by the carton — 64 sq. ft. to a carton.

Acoustical tile is manufactured with tiny holes or fissures in the tile surface. These holes or fissures help absorb air-borne sound in the room — up to 60 percent of sound striking the tile. Tile may be washed and painted; however, when painted the tile may lose acoustical properties.

Almost all ceiling tile dealers have special instruction sheets available showing how to lay out a room for tile and explaining the mechanics involved in installation. The literature is free.

BUYING READY-MIXED CONCRETE

If you are planning a substantial amount of concrete work, we recommend that you buy the material from a company that mixes concrete for you. You will find these companies in the telephone advertising pages under "Concrete." Ready-mixed concrete is sold by the cubic yard. Usually a minimum order is required — $100 or more — so a project should be large enough to justify this cost.

To place a concrete order, you should be ready to tell the sales person the width, length, and thickness of the job, the time you want delivery, color details, if you want colored concrete and order delivery of concrete reinforcing bars or mesh if necessary. The sales person will estimate all of your needs, give you an approximate delivery time and request payment procedures. The only thing left for you is to get ready for the delivery.

For small jobs, we suggest ready-to-mix concrete, which is available in 40 and 80 lb. sacks. You simply add water and stir. Each bag makes approximately ⅓ cubic yard of concrete. There are several different mixes you can buy: concrete mix for walks, driveways, patios and setting posts; mortar mix, for laying brick and block, making small concrete repairs and tuckpointing mortar joints.

If you want to mix your own concrete, buy Portland cement

in bags and sand. Standard mix is one bag of Portland cement to 3 or 4 bags of sand. Portland cement usually is stocked by home center stores. However, the aggregate you need will have to be purchased from a sand and gravel dealer. You can buy bags of sand at home center stores, but, for large jobs, the cost is prohibitive.

To mix small quantities of concrete, plastic mixing tubs are available at a moderate cost.

CONCRETE MIXES FOR SMALL JOBS

Procedure: Select the proper maximum size of aggregate. Use Mix B, adding just enough water to produce a workable consistency. If the concrete appears to be undersanded, change to Mix A and, if it appears oversanded, change to Mix C.

Maximum size of aggregate, in.	Mix designation	Cement	Approximate weights of solid ingredients per cu ft of concrete, lb			
			Sand*		Coarse aggregate	
			Air entrained concrete†	Concrete without air	Gravel or crushed stone	Iron blast furnace slag
½	A	25	48	51	54	47
	B	25	46	49	56	49
	C	25	44	47	58	51
¾	A	23	45	49	62	54
	B	23	43	47	64	56
	C	23	41	45	66	58
1	A	22	41	45	70	61
	B	22	39	43	72	63
	C	22	37	41	74	65
1½	A	20	41	45	75	65
	B	20	39	43	77	67
	C	20	37	41	79	69
2	A	19	40	45	79	69
	B	19	38	43	81	71
	C	19	36	41	83	72

*Weights are for dry sand. If damp sand is used, increase tabulated weights of sand 2 lb and, if very wet sand is used, 4 lb.

†Air-entrained concrete should be used in all structures which will be exposed to alternate cycles of freezing and thawing. Air entrainment can be obtained by the use of an air-entraining cement or by adding an air-entraining admixture. If an admixture is used, the amount recommended by the manufacturer will, in most cases, produce the desired air content (Source: American Concrete Institute).

BUYING FRAMING HARDWARE

Although there is not a great selection, these items are essential when building a deck or fence.

U brackets. This is galvanized steel bent in a sharp U shape. Nail the bracket to a framing member or decking and insert the post or railing in the bracket. Then nail or screw the bracket to the post.

Joist hangers. Nail these brackets to sills or framing members. Then insert the joists into the metal U and nail the bracket to the joist. This method eliminates toenailing and provides measuring and marking accuracy.

Rail hangers. These are similar to joist hangers, but are used to support the rails of a fence. Nail the bracket or hanger onto the post, and then insert the rail and nail the bracket to the rail.

Post caps. These metal squares — usually aluminum — fit over the tops of square fence posts to protect the wood from weather damage. They are nailed in position.

Bridging. Bridging extends between joists to help support the joists laterally. Wood strips — usually 1x4s — are often used for this purpose. However, you can buy pre-formed metal bridging and nail it to the joists for a neat job with no toenailing.

Truss plates. These plates are metal squares or rectangles that have sharp metal prongs on one side which are used when butt-joining two pieces of framing material. They are driven into the wood with a baby sledge hammer. Home manufacturers use truss plates to assemble roof, floor, and wall trusses and panels. They are exceptionally strong and eliminate weak toenailing.

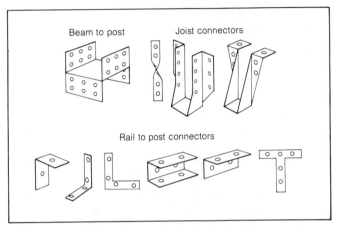

Beam to post   Joist connectors

Rail to post connectors

BUYING INSULATION

A real energy-saver, insulation comes in several forms — blankets, batts, pouring insulation and rigid foam boards (all standard products). Insulation is sold by the square foot, R-rating, and moisture vapor barrier covering. If the material is in blankets or batts, it also is sold by width — 15 ins., or 23 ins. Pouring insulation is sold by weight. Packaged in paper or plastic bags, the material can be fiber or vermiculite (see pages 82 - 87 for additional information about types of insulation and where it is used).

Essential to know about insulation is the importance of R factors. R stands for "resistance" — the larger the R factor number, the better resistance. Three-inch insulation has an R factor of R 11 and 6 in. insulation has an R factor of R 30, which may be sufficient to meet the insulation standards in your area. Insulation dealers are familiar with R-factor information and can tell you about Federal government tax benefits for installing insulation.

Sheets of rigid foam insulation have an R factor of R 2½ to R 4. This information usually is stamped on the insulation package.

Pouring insulation obtains its R factor from its thickness. Most packages provide R factor information according to thickness — 3 to 6 in., in square feet of surface covered. *Example:* one bag of pouring insulation may provide 3½ ins. of coverage over 10 sq. ft., for an R factor of R 11.

BUYING WATERPROOFING

The best waterproofer is to find the leak and repair it. However, you can stop some moisture — not running water — with masonry paint, hydraulic cement and asphalt foundation coating. For basements, the best waterproofer is polyfilm embedded in roofing cement. This procedure is outlined on page 187.

Regular paint is a waterproofer for both interior and exterior surfaces. For this reason, all wood and metal surfaces should be finished with a clear penetrating sealer, paint or varnish for protection from the elements.

BUYING SIDING

Siding falls into seven major classifications, which means that buying siding becomes a matter of taste. Siding, or rather re-siding a house, is a job for a professional, although you probably can handle a small job — such as a garage or room addition.

Replacing siding is a fairly easy chore, too, and this is detailed on pages 187 – 191.

If you are buying siding for repairs, self-installation, or for installation by a professional, the standard choices are:

Brick, block, and stone. This refers to the veneers — not the full masonry units which serve as structural support as well as siding material. Veneers are fastened to sheathing, which is then nailed to framing members; or the old siding must be covered with sheathing and the new veneer attached to the new sheathing. This is a professional project.

Simulated brick and stone panels are made of real stone that has been crushed and reformed in and on fiberglass base panels. These are very realistic, and, when properly installed with nails and a joint grout, it is difficult to tell simulated from real masonry units. The panels are 2x4 ft. (standard), and the system comes with outside corners and special trim pieces for doors and windows.

Wood siding. These products are available in drop, bevel, or lap siding, shiplap, plywood panels, hardboard panels and boards, shakes and shingles. Almost any material that can be used outdoors can be used for siding.

Drop siding measures ¾ in. thick by 6 in. wide (standard). It usually has a small groove cut along one edge which changes the name to rabbeted siding. The siding laps over the siding board below it, thus "lap" siding. The width often is determined by the width of the lap or the depth of the groove or rabbet. *Example:* siding 6 in. wide can be 3 in. wide installed, if the siding course above it is dropped by 3 in.

Bevel siding, also a standard, is tapered from one edge to the other. *Example:* the thin edge is usually ³⁄₁₆ in. thick, the opposite edge ½ to ¾ in. thick. Widths range from 4 to 12 ins.

Plywood siding comes in a selection of designs and textures and because the panels are large — 4x8 and 4x10 ft. they go up quickly. The siding is ⅜ in. thick (standard) and may be applied directly over framing, over sheathing and over existing siding.

Hardboard siding is available as lap siding, in strips, or in regular panels. The material usually is pre-primed (white) and is ready to hang over sheathed walls and old siding. One caution is this — the siding must be painted within 60 days of installation for protection against the weather.

Lap siding sizes range from 4 in. widths up to 16 ft. lengths. Thicknesses are ¼, ³⁄₁₆, and ⅛ ins. (standard). Panel thickness is ¼ in. (standard). Patterns and designs are somewhat limited for most of the siding is either smooth or random-grooved. You can create a board-and-batten effect by nailing wood or hardboard strips over and between panel joints.

Three types of shingles and shakes are available for siding — rebutted-rejoined, machine-grooved and handsplit.

Shingles for siding are sold in cartons of 56 courses of 18-in. shingles per unit and 66 courses of 16 in. shingles per unit. Coverage depends on the amount of lap the shingles are given when they are applied to the sheathing.

Handsplit shingles, more rustic in appearance, are available in three varieties — handsplit/resawn, tapersplit and straightsplit. Sizes are 18, 24, and 32 in. lengths (standard). The products are available in 4, 5, and 6 bundle squares. This depends on packaging in 18 in. and 20 in. "frames".

Shingles for the most part are sold in "squares". One square will cover 100 sq. ft., although in the case of siding, a square of shingles usually will cover more than 100 sq. ft. since the courses have greater laps or exposure than when they are used as a roofing material. You can safely figure 105 sq. ft. of coverage from one square of shingles used for siding.

Aluminum siding. This material is generally pre-finished and comes in a wide range of colors and textures. White is the big seller, although green, red, and yellow are popular. Textures include vertical and horizontal wood grains, stucco, basket-weave and rough "brushed" wood grains.

Panels can be smooth, lapped, V-grooved and board-and-battened. The metal siding usually is installed with "backer board" — strips of insulation sheathing cut to match the widths and thickness of the siding. It is recommended that this backer material be used because it helps reinforce the metal, saves energy and adds some soundproofing qualities.

Steel and corrugated aluminum siding. This is available in several finishes, although a mill finish is the most common. Styles include 1¼ in. and 2½ in. pitch (corrugations) and lengths run 6 to 12 ft. in 1 ft. increments (standard). For outbuildings and roofs, the material may be applied over open framing properly spaced according to the manufacturer's recommendations.

Vinyl siding. Made with polyvinyl chloride plastic, in this siding the color goes completely through the material. The vertical material after installation resembles tongue-and-groove siding.

Asbestos-cement siding. This product comes in "shingle" units, which are usually applied to sheathing with a 1½ in. lap producing a 10½ in. exposure (standard). Asbestos siding panels, 4x8 ft., also are available. Designs include smooth surfaces, striated vertical and wood grain patterns. Colors are available including white. Asbestos-cement siding is highly-resistant to chemical fumes and other air-borne contaminants.

Cautions

Covering old siding with new aluminum or vinyl siding may seem to be a very attractive answer to problems of wear, deterioration, and repainting, but this is not always true. The wearing surfaces are, of course, very durable, but even aluminum siding will need repainting in time, and accidents may cause staining, cutting or denting.

A more serious concern, however, is the fact that the siding may both hide and encourage decomposition of covered wood siding. Aluminum and vinyl are "non-breathing" materials; moisture, once caught under the siding, cannot escape. An older home is usually uninsulated or insulated with blown-in material. There is no vapor barrier between the interior of the house and the insulation. The result is a constant, slow leakage of moist air through the house walls. If the house is covered with impervious siding, the moisture is held between the original wood siding and the new siding. In time, this moisture can cause a great deal of damage to the covered siding, and eventually to the framing of the house.

Special Exterior Sealers and Coatings

To help deter rot and other damage from moisture and sunlight on exterior building materials, you can buy special sealers and coatings at most home center stores and building material outlets. Below is a list of these preservatives, where they are used, and how they are used.

Paint. Use only exterior type paint outdoors. For metal surfaces, such as gutters and exposed flashings, use special metal paint, which may require a primer. This information will be printed on the label of the container.

Do not use paint to protect any wood that will be buried underground or used in an area that is constantly subjected to moisture — such as a crawl space or under an attached porch structure.

Exterior paint may be applied with a brush, roller, paint pad, spray gun, or by dipping.

Stain, Same as paint.

Creosote. This preservative is best used for wood that will be buried underground. You can buy special formulas that may be covered by exterior paint for decorative purposes. Creosote is fairly inexpensive; have plenty of ventilation when you apply the material with a paintbrush or by dipping the wood into a container of creosote.

Asphalt Roofing Compound. There are several formulations of this coating: sealer for asphalt driveways, coatings for roof flashings and foundations. Consistency of the mixtures varies from paint-thin to mud-thick.

Use asphalt for any wood that will be buried underground, inside gutters, over flashings, under shingles. It may be applied with a paintbrush, broom, scraper, putty knife, or with a caulking gun, if purchased in a caulking type cartridge.

Pentachlorophenol. This mixture is excellent for any wood that will be buried underground, although it may be applied to above ground wooden components. Give all surfaces at least two coats of pentachlorophenol — three coats are best.

You can apply the mixture with a paintbrush or by dipping the wood into the mixture. Have lots of ventilation when you work with pentachlorophenol and follow the manufacturer's recommendations for use and cleanup. You'll find these recommendations on the container label.

Copper Napthenate. For exposed or buried wood. After application with a paintbrush or dipping, the mixture will dry with a greenish cast. The wood usually can be painted for decorative purposes, but check the manufacturer's recommendations before you apply it.

Varnish. Spar and/or marine varnish is made for exterior wood and metal surfaces. However, special preparation and finishing schedules must be utilized. These specifications will be on the label of the varnish container.

BUYING ROOFING

Asphalt shingles, the most popular, present a large color selection from which to choose. Sizes and shapes are standardized; weight, however, may be a consideration. The heavier the shingle, the more durable it is. *Example:* a 240 pound shingle is considered better than a 230 pound shingle. The weight refers to 240 (or 230) pounds per square, and a square is 100 sq. ft. Asphalt shingles are sold by the square (100 sq. ft.) but can be bought in ⅓ squares — 33½ sq. ft. If just a few shingles are needed for repairs, you may be able to buy them by the piece. Many home center stores and building material outlets have broken bundles of shingles and are happy to get rid of them on a piece basis. Ask the store manager as to availability and price.

Built-up roofing is more of a construction process than a self-contained product such as shingles. This roofing includes asphalt building paper or felt, hot tar and gravel. This roof is best left to a professional since special equipment is necessary for its construction.

Wooden shingle roofs are handsome but are subject to code and insurance restrictions. Check this out before your planning goes too far. Wooden shingles are also sold by the square — 100 sq. ft. to the square, and by the bundle. See shingles and shakes, this chapter.

Roll roofing is very similar to asphalt shingles, except that this roofing comes in rolls. There is a limited selection of colors, since this material is generally used for outbuildings in rural areas.

Slate and tile roofing are specialty items, and most home center and building material outlets do not handle them. A roofing contractor is your best product source, and we recommend that a contractor make any slate or tile roofing repairs.

BUYING RAIN CARRYING SYSTEMS

There are five different types of gutters and downspouts — wooden, copper, galvanized steel, vinyl, and aluminum. Shapes generally are limited to rounds and rectangles.

Galvanized steel gutters are popular since they are moderately priced. Aluminum gutters are also popular, although slightly more expensive, as are vinyl and copper gutters.

Lengths of galvanized and aluminum gutters are 10 and 21 ft. (standard). Galvanized gutters usually are not pre-painted; aluminum gutters almost always are pre-painted or pre-primed. This includes downspouts or "leaders" as downspouts are sometimes called. Gutter accessories include hangers, spikes and ferrules, inside and outside corners, end caps, slip joint connectors, drop outlets, right or left elbows, double elbows and concrete and plastic splashblocks.

Rain carrying systems and accessories are usually sold by the piece, although some retailers may give you a price if you are remodeling the entire system on your home.

BUYING MOLDINGS

Moldings are used to finish a job — to trim it out. There are hundreds of different sizes and shapes of molding, and the selection is not confined to sizes and shapes. You also have a choice of materials such as wood, plastic and rubber — and a choice of colors and wood-grained patterns. You can buy special moldings that are wood-grained and color-matched to paneling and certain wallcoverings.

Molding is sold by the piece — such as an 8 ft. length (standard) — and by the lineal foot (rather than board foot like lumber). Prices range from very inexpensive to very costly, depending on the type of wood and the pattern or shape of the molding. Widths and lengths of moldings vary; lengths run from 8 ft. to 14 ft. (standard). See pages 000 and 000.

Common moldings include cove, base, chair rail, crown, inside corner, outside corner, quarter-round, joint strips, end strips, drip cap, picture, casing, base, stop, mullion casing, lattice, back band, caps, brick, rounds, half-rounds and hand rails. When buying moldings figure one extra lineal foot to every 20 ft. of molding. This additional material allows for straight and miter cuts.

BUYING ABRASIVES

Abrasive is the new word for "sandpaper", and the word "abrasive" was coined because most sandpaper is not made of sand any longer. Abrasive paper is sold in "open" and "closed" coat papers. Open coat abrasives will not fill with sanding debris as quickly as closed coat abrasives.

The abrasive backing may be of paper or cloth. Weight of the backing is indicated by the letter; A is for lightweight backing; D is for heavyweight backing; J is for a lightweight cloth backing; X is for a heavy-weight cloth backing.

Adhesives are classed or specified by name, letter and/or number. The number system is as follows: very fine — 220 to 600; fine — 120 to 180; medium — 60 to 100; coarse — 36 to 50, and very coarse — 12 to 30.

Aluminum oxide abrasive may be used for wood and plastic — it cuts fast and it wears well. Flint abrasive is very inexpensive and should be used for removing paint and other finishes, sanding sappy or green wood and for rough cuts be-fore smoothing surfaces with aluminum oxide or silicone carbide abrasives.

Garnet abrasive is best suited for smoothing wood. Emery abrasive may be used for wood, although it does not wear well. Silicon carbide abrasive may be used for smoothing plastics, glass and ceramic tile. It is a "hard" abrasive; it wears very well and it is very expensive.

BUYING ADHESIVES

There is a potpourri of adhesives available but the ones concerned with repairs are paneling or builders' adhesive, contact cement and white glue. Most adhesives are fairly inexpensive, and are packaged in caulking type tubes, squirt bottles and buckets. The bucket, or bulk adhesives, usually require a brush or spreader for application.

Common Adhesives

Adhesive	Best Use
Casein	Wood and fabrics
Aliphatic resin	Wood
Epoxy	Wood and metal
Contact	Wood, high pressure laminates, paper, fabrics
Tile cement	Linoleum, resilient tile; check labels for specific use
Casein/latex	Metal, glass, plastic, fabric
Thermoplastic	Wood, fabrics, paper
Thermosetting	Wood, fabrics, paper
Builders' or paneling	Wood, some insulation; check labels for specific use

Abrasives are stamped on the backing with type of abrasive, open/closed coat, size of abrasive grit by name or number or both, weight of backing and type of backing.

Appliance Parts Sources

ALABAMA

**Washer and Refrigeration
Supply Company, Inc.**
R. E. Smith
716 Second Avenue, North
Birmingham, Alabama 35201
Phone: (205) 322-8693

ARIZONA

**Appliance Dealer Supply
Company, Inc.**
Paul Zeller
P.O. Box 2017 (740 West Grant)
Phoenix, Arizona 85007
Phone: (602) 252-7506

**Appliance Parts Company
(Branch-Appl. Parts-Van Nuys)**
2215 East University Drive
Phoenix, Arizona 85034

**Akrit Appliance Supply Co.
(Branch-Akrit Appl.-Albuquerque)**
1132 North Richey Boulevard
Tucson, Arizona 85716

ARKANSAS

Mid-South Appliance Parts Company
Leonard Kremers
1020 West 14th St., P.O. Box 2722
Little Rock, Arkansas 72201
Phone: (501) 376-8351

720 North 11th Street
Fort Smith, Arkansas 72901

CALIFORNIA

**Appliance Parts Company
Division of Washing Machine Parts Co.**
Howard F. Parker, Sr.
15040 Oxnard Street
P. O. Box 2787
Van Nuys, California 91401
Phone: (213) 787-9220

1575 Mable Street
Anaheim, California 92802

372 North Mt. Vernon
Colton, California 92324

14410 Hindry Avenue
Lawndale, California 90260

9870 Baldwin Place
El Monte, California 91731

Cal Sales Corporation
Gene M. Sharpe
641 Monterey Pass Road
Monterey Park, California 91754
Phone: (213) 283-7741

2945 West 5th Street
Oxnard, California 93030

Coast Appliance Parts Company
Leonard A. Ellison
5915 North Kester Avenue
Van Nuys, California 91401
Phone: (213) 782-5770

269 South Arrowhead Avenue
San Bernardino, California 92408

764 14th Street
San Diego, California 92101

8222 Lankershim Boulevard
North Hollywood, Cal. 91605

9817 Inglewood Avenue
Inglewood, California 90301

Electrical Appliance Service Co.
Sabert L. Summers
J. Tribulato
290 Townsend Street
San Francisco, California 94107
Phone: (415) 777-1900

145 Van Ness Street
Fresno, California 93721

4238 Broadway
Oakland, California 94611

1116 "F" Street
Sacramento, California 95814

1140 Lincoln Avenue
San Jose, California 95125

Western Appliance Parts Company
Howard Parker, Jr.
1844 India Street
San Diego, California 92101
Phone: (714) 232-7871

COLORADO

Ray Jones Appliance Parts Company
Aud L. Hanna
376 South Broadway
Denver, Colorado 80209
Phone: (303) 744-6263

1436 North Hancock
Colorado Springs, Col. 80903

1813 East Mulberry Street
Fort Collins, Colorado 80521

**Niles-Noel Incorporated
(Branch-Ray Jones Appl. Parts Co.)**
562 South Broadway
Denver, Colorado 80209

**Akrit Appliance Supply Co.
(Branch-Akrit Appl.-Albuquerque)**
402 Arrawanna Street
Colorado Springs, Col. 80909

CONNECTICUT

Arcand Distributors, Inc.
Richard Arcand
845 Windsor Street
Hartford, Connecticut 06120
Phone: (203) 522-2214

61 Erna Avenue
Milford, Connecticut 06460

American Appliance Parts, Inc.
2516 Whitney Avenue
Hamden, Connecticut 06518
John T. Malatesta

1196 Farmington Avenue
Kensington, Connecticut

10 Boston Avenue
Stratford, Connecticut

Electric Appliance Parts Company
Anthony J. Ciarlo, Jr.
175 Freight Street
Waterbury, Connecticut 06780
Phone: (203) 753-1763

**Westchester Appliance Parts, Inc.
(Branch-All Appliance Parts)**
194 Richmond Avenue
Stamford, Connecticut 06902

DISTRICT OF COLUMBIA

Trible's Incorporated
John R. Trible
2240 25th Place
Washington, D.C. 20018
Phone: (202) 832-9300

FLORIDA

**Marcone Appliance Parts Center
(Branch-Marcone Appl.-St. Louis)**
777 N.W. 79th Street
Miami, Florida 33150

1515 Cypress Street
Tampa, Florida 33606

2108 West Central Boulevard
Orlando, Florida 32805

1019 Rosselle Street
Jacksonville, Florida 32204

GEORGIA

**D & L Appliance Parts Company
(Branch-D & L Appl. Parts-Charlotte)**
5799 New Peachtree Road
Atlanta, Georgia 30340
Phone: (404) 458-8191

**Harris Appliance Parts Company
(Branch-Harris Appl. Pts.-Anderson)**
5129 Montgomery Street
Savannah, Georgia 31405

227 West Dougherty Street
Athens, Georgia 30601

HAWAII

Appliance Parts Company, Inc.
Dave Dumas
P.O. Box 17976
1550 Kalani Street
Honolulu, Hawaii 96817
Phone: (808) 847-3217

731 Kamehameha Highway
Pearl City, Hawaii 96782

3057 Waialae Avenue
Honolulu, Hawaii 96816

118 Hekili Street
Kailua, Hawaii 96734

IDAHO

**IASCO Distributing Company
(Intermountain Appl. Supply Corp.)
(Branch-IASCO Dist. Co.-Utah)**
2895 North Holmes Avenue
Idaho Falls, Idaho 84501

**W. L. May Company, Inc.
(Branch-W. L. May Co.-
Portland, Oregon)**
202 East 33rd Street
Boise, Idaho 83704

ILLINOIS

Automatic Appliance Parts Corp.
Roger Flinn
4441 West Diversey
Chicago, Illinois 60639
Phone: (312) 278-8668

    1506 East Algonquin Road
    Arlington Heights, Illinois 60005

Midwest Appliance Parts Company
Morey Misles
2600 West Diversey
Chicago, Illinois 60647
Phone: (312) 278-1300

C. E. Sundberg Company
Truman Smith
615 West 79th Street
Chicago, Illinois 60620
Phone: (312) 723-2700

INDIANA

Appliance Parts, Inc.
John K. David
P.O. Box 22350
1734 West 15th Street
Indianapolis, Indiana 46222
Phone: (317) 635-3657

Appliance Parts Supply Company
(Branch-Appl. Parts-Toledo)
1241 Wells Street
Fort Wayne, Indiana 46808

Bell Parts Supply
Jule L. Bell
2819 45th Street
Highland, Indiana 46322

Evansville Appliance Parts
Orville N. Joergens
920 West Pennsylvania Street
Evansville, Indiana 47708
Phone: (812) 423-8867

IOWA

The Ricketts Company, Inc.
Mrs. B. L. (Bernice) Ricketts
801 S.E. 14th Street
Des Moines, Iowa 50317
Phone: (515) 244-7236

KENTUCKY

The Collins Company, Inc.
Daniel A. Smith
Appliance Parts Division
819 South Floyd Street
Louisville, Kentucky 40203
Phone: (502) 583-1723

    3071 Breckenridge Lane
    Louisville, Kentucky 40220

    150 Indiana Avenue
    Box 24
    Lexington, Kentucky 40508

LOUISIANA

Bruce's Distributing Company
Bruce J. Sterbenz
509 East 70th Street
Shreveport, Louisiana 71106
Phone: (318) 861-7662

Sunseri's, Inc.
Diego Joseph Sunseri
2254-60 St. Claude Avenue
New Orleans, Louisiana 70117
Phone: (504) WH-4-6762

MAINE

Appliance Parts Company
(Branch-Appl. Parts-Boston)
255 Danforth Street
Portland, Maine 04102

MARYLAND

Trible's Incorporated
(Branch-Tribles, Inc.-Wash., D.C.)
140 Halpine Road
Rockville, Maryland 20852

    2210 North Howard Street
    Baltimore, Maryland 21218

    3533 Fort Meade Road
    Laurel, Maryland 20810

MASSACHUSETTS

Appliance Parts Company, Inc.
Glenn F. Catlow
112 Dartmouth Street
Boston, Massachusetts 02116
Phone: (617) 536-0138

Hall Electric Supply Company, Inc.
(HESCO)
Earl K. Hall, Jr.
33 Brighton Street
Belmont, Massachusetts 02178
Phone: (617) 489-3450

M.G.M.S. Associates, Inc.
Louis P. Miele
22 Water Street
Cambridge, Massachusetts 02141
Phone: (617) 868-8360

Supply Distributors
Victoria Ludlam
50 Revere Beach Parkway
Medford, Massachusetts 02155

MICHIGAN

Servall Company
Kenneth Adler
228 East Baltimore Street
Detroit, Michigan 48202
Phone: (313) TR-2-3655

    26500 Grand River Avenue
    Detroit, Michigan 48240

    24312 Gratiot Avenue
    East Detroit, Michigan 48021

    6619 Schaefer
    Dearborn, Michigan 48126

    630 West Kearsley
    Flint, Michigan 48503

    440 Lake Michigan Drive, N.W.
    Grand Rapids, Michigan 49504

    1100 South Water Street
    Saginaw, Michigan 48601

    412 East Elm Street
    Lansing, Michigan 48912

    4936 Allen Road
    Allen Park, Michigan 48101

MINNESOTA

Appliance Parts, Incorporated
Martin A. Frederick
250 3rd Avenue, North
Minneapolis, Minnesota 55401
Phone: (612) 335-0931

    964 Rice Street
    St. Paul, Minnesota 55117

Dey Appliance Parts
Adolph Dey
P.O. Box 5086
525 North Snelling Avenue
St. Paul, Minnesota 55104
Phone: (612) 647-0717

MISSISSIPPI

Appliance Parts Company, Inc.
Bruce L. Coleman
727 South Gallatin Street
Jackson, Mississippi 39204
Phone: (601) 948-4680

    2214 Lee Street
    Alexandria, Louisiana 71301

MISSOURI

Marcone Appliance Parts Company
Norman Markow
2320 Pine Street
St. Louis, Missouri 63103
Phone: (314) 231-7141

Marcone Appliance Parts Center
(Branch-Marcone Appl. Parts-
St. Louis)
3113 Main Street
Kansas City, Missouri 64111

St. Louis Appliance Parts, Inc.
Joe E. James
2911-13 South Jefferson
St. Louis, Missouri 63118
Phone: (314) 776-1445

NEVADA

Cal Sales Corporation
(Branch-Cal Sales-California)
3453 Industrial Road
Las Vegas, Nevada 89109
Phone: (702) 734-1104

Electrical Appliance Service Co.
(Branch-Electrical Appl. Service-
San Francisco)
611 Kuenzli Street
Reno, Nevada 89502

NEW JERSEY

Jacoby Appliance Parts
Jules R. Jacoby
269 Main Street
Hackensack, New Jersey 07601
Phone: (201) 489-6444/6446

    57 Albany Street
    New Brunswick, N.J. 07101

    1242 Springfield Avenue
    Irvington, New Jersey 07111

    923 North Olden Avenue
    Trenton, New Jersey 08611

Westchester Appliance Parts, Inc.
(Branch-All Appl. Parts-New York)
470 U.S. Highway #46
Teterboro, New Jersey 07608

NEW MEXICO

Akrit Appliance Supply Company
Carlyle L. Otto
2820 Vassar N.E.
Albuquerque, New Mexico 87101
Phone: (505) 345-8651

NEW YORK

All Appliance Parts of New York, Inc.
Arvey Jonas
1345 New York Avenue
Huntington Station, N.Y. 11746
Phone: (516) 427-4600

    600-C Middle Country Road
    Selden, New York 11784

    2850 Sunrise Highway
    Bellmore, New York 11710

    113-02 Atlantic Avenue
    Richmond Hill, N.Y. 11419

    1985 New York Avenue
    Huntington Station, N.Y. 11746

Westchester Appliance Parts
1034 Yonkers Avenue
Yonkers, New York 10714

Buffalo Appliance Parts Co., Inc.
Frank L. Jarmusz
1175 Williams Street
Buffalo, New York 14206
Phone: (716) 856-5005

Nichols Appliance Parts, Inc.
(Branch-Buffalo Appl. Parts-N.Y.)
801 South Salina Street
Syracuse, N.Y. 13202

Rochester Appliance Parts Dist.
(Branch-Buffalo Appl. Parts-N.Y.)
189 North Water Street
Rochester New York 14604

Jacoby Appliance Parts
(Branch-Jacoby Appl. Parts-N.J.)
1023 Allerton Avenue
Bronx, New York 10469

   214 Route 59
   Suffern, New York 10901

   1654 Central Avenue
   Albany, New York 12205

NORTH CAROLINA

D & L Appliance Parts Co., Inc.
Ralph Brackett
2100 Freedom Drive
P.O. Box 1317
Charlotte, North Carolina 28208
Phone: (704) 375-7306

   2811 Firestone Drive
   Greensboro, N. C. 27406

   2324 Atlantic Avenue
   Raleigh, N.C. 27601

Moore and Stewart, Inc.
Denton W. Cruse
316 East Franklin Avenue
Gastonia, N.C. 28052
Phone: (704) 864-8334

OHIO

American Electric Washer Company
Alvin Brouman
1834 East 55th Street
Cleveland, Ohio 44103
Phone: (216) 431-4400

   2801 Detroit Avenue
   Cleveland, Ohio 44113
   988 East Market Street
   Akron, Ohio 44305

Appliance Parts Supply Company
James A. Staebell
235 Broadway Street
Toledo, Ohio 43602
Phone: (419) 244-6741

   1408 Cherry Street
   Toledo, Ohio 43608

Dayton Appliance Parts Company
James Houtz
122 Sears Street
Dayton, Ohio 45402
Phone: (513) 224-3531

Dayco Appliance Parts
338 East Spring Street
Columbus, Ohio 43215

Brand Service Center, Inc.
Paul R. Palmer
808 Elm Street
Cincinnati, Ohio 56202
Phone: (513) 241-3701

   6944 Plainfield Road
   Cincinnati, Ohio 45236

Mason Supply Company
Howard T. Yost
985 Joyce Avenue
Columbus, Ohio 43203
Phone: (614) 253-8607

   3929 Apple Street
   Cincinnati, Ohio 45223

Pearsol Appliance Corporation
Melvin J. Ellis
2319 Gilbert Avenue
Cincinnati, Ohio 45206
Phone: (513) 221-1195

Pearsol Corporation of Ohio
Leonard F. Mandell
1847 East 40th Street
Cleveland, Ohio 44103
Phone: (216) 881-5085

V & V Appliance Parts, Inc.
Victor Lazar
27 West Myrtle Avenue
Youngstown, Ohio 44507
Phone: (216) 743-5144

   553 High Street, N.E.
   Warren, Ohio 44481

OKLAHOMA

Greer Electric Company
Glen Z. Greer, Jr.
1018 South Rockford
Tulsa, Oklahoma 74104
Phone: (918) 587-3346

Pritchard Electric Company, Inc.
Wayne H. Youngblood
3100 North Santa Fe
Oklahoma City, Oklahoma 73101
Phone: (405) 528-0592

OREGON

W. L. May Company, Inc.
Edward Cohn, Jr.
1120 S.E. Madison Street
Portland, Oregon 97214
Phone: (503) 231-9398

   3619 Franklin Boulevard
   Eugene, Oregon 97403

PENNSYLVANIA

Collins Appliance Parts, Inc.
Richard D. Collins, Jr.
1533 Metropolitan Street
Pittsburgh, Pennsylvania 15233
Phone: (412) 321-3700

Parts Distributors Corporation
(Branch-All Appl. Parts-New York)
312 North Easton Road
Willow Grove, Pa. 19090

RHODE ISLAND

Appliance Parts Company, Inc.
(Branch-Appl. Parts-Boston)
316 Cranston Street
Providence, Rhode Island 02907
Phone: (401) 421-6142

Twin City Supply Company
Henry Dziadosz
885 Westminster Street
Providence, R. I. 02903
Phone: (401) 331-5930

SOUTH CAROLINA

G & E Parts Center, Inc.
Sam Lancaster
P.O. Box 2466
2403 South Pine Street
Spartanburg, S. C. 29304
Phone: (803) 585-6277

   P.O. Box 1074
   1212 Bluff Road
   Columbia, S.C. 29202

D & L Appliance Parts, Inc.
(Branch-D & L Appl. Parts-Charlotte)
901 South Cashua Drive
Florence, S. C. 29501

Harris Appliance Parts Co.
Dell Johnson
P.O. Box 611
29 Bypass North
Anderson, S.C. 29621
Phone: (803) 225-7433

   423 Laurens Road
   Greenville, S.C. 29606

SOUTH DAKOTA

Dey Appliance Parts
(Branch-Dey Appl. Parts-St. Paul, Minn.)
300 N. Phillips
Sioux Falls, So. Dakota 57102

TENNESSEE

Brown Appliance Parts Company, Inc.
Mack Brown
857 North Central Avenue
Knoxville, Tennessee 37917
Phone: (615) 525-9363

   2472 Amnicola Highway
   Chattanooga, Tenn. 37406

   125 New Kingsport Hwy.
   Bristol, Tenn. 37620

Curtis Company
Jerry M. Brasher
562 East Street
P.O. Box 4918
Memphis, Tenn. 38104
Phone: (901) 527-1611

Napco, Inc.
Virgil C. Belcher
501 South Second Street
Nashville, Tenn. 37213
Phone: (615) 242-5597

   5002 Charlotte Avenue
   Nashville, Tenn 37209

   111 Old Hickory Blvd.
   Madison, Tenn. 37115

TEXAS

Akrit Appliance Supply Co.
(Branch-Akrit Appl.-Albuquerque)
1805 Montana
El Paso, Texas 79902

   2306 19th Street
   Lubbock, Texas 79401

Pearsol Appliance Company
Mort Mandell
3127 Main Street
Dallas, Texas 75226
Phone: (214) 741-4638

Standard Appliance Parts Corp
Glenn D. Peek
4814 Ayers Street
P.O. Box 7488
Corpus Cristi, Texas 78415
Phone: (512) 853-9823

   1214 West Van Buren
   Harlingen, Texas 78550

Texas Parts & Supply Company
Herbert Mathis
P.O. Box 115
1209 South St. Marys
San Antonio, Texas 78291
Phone: (512) 225-2717

   2820 Guadalupe
   Austin, Texas 78765

Washing Machine Parts Company
Harold Evans
704 North Main Street
Fort Worth, Texas 76106
Phone: (817) ED-2-5343

   3314 Ross Avenue
   Dallas, Texas 75204

Central Supply
Div. of Washing Machine Parts, Inc.
Kenneth D. Buvinghausen
1011 Wood Street, P.O. Box 3385
Houston, Texas 77001
Phone: (713) 224-8491

   5365 College Street
   Beaumont, Texas 77707

1604 South Shaver
Pasadena, Texas 77502

7417 Hillcroft
#2C Houston, Texas 77081

2612 McKinney
Houston, Texas 77003

UTAH

**IASCO Distributing Company
(Intermountain Appl. Supply Corp.)**
Dwayne C. Zenger
825 South West Temple Street
Salt Lake City, Utah 84101
Phone: (801) 328-0505

**Ray Jones Appliance Parts Company
(Branch-Ray Jones-Denver)**
3336 South 300 East
Salt Lake City, Utah 84115

VIRGINIA

Refrigeration Supply Company, Inc.
Edward L. Booth
1657 West Broad Street
Richmond, Virginia 23261
Phone: (804) 359-3275

1736 Allied Street
Charlottesville, Virginia 22901

**Booth Supply Company, Inc.
(Branch-Ref. Supp.-Richmond)**
2621 Florida Avenue
Norfolk, Virginia 23513

926 Vernon Street, Southeast
Roanoke, Virginia 24013

8304 Orcutt Avenue
Hampton, Virginia 23605

**Trible's Inc.
(Branch-Tribles, Inc.-Wash., D.C.)**
7273 East Arlington Blvd.
Falls Church, Va. 22042

Wholesale Parts Distributors, Inc.
Victor L. Via
1141 Lance Road
Norfolk, Virginia 23502
Phone: (804) 461-3888

WASHINGTON

Appliance Parts & Service Company
Harold R. Hansberry
400 9th Avenue, North
Seattle, Washington 98109
Phone: (206) 622-0152

West 917 Mallon
Spokane, Washington 99201

3730 South "G" Street
Tacoma, Washington 98408

WEST VIRGINIA

**Mason Supply Company
(Branch-Mason Supply-
Columbus, Ohio)**
800 Virginia Street, West
Charleston, West Virginia 25303

3rd & Eoff Streets
Wheeling, West Virginia 26003

WISCONSIN

A & E Distributors, Inc.
Walter E. Kuhn
1418 North Erwin Avenue
P.O. Box 8045
Green Bay, Wisconsin 54308
Phone: (414) 437-8215

Power Equipment
Frank Morella
2373 South Kinnickinnic Avenue
Milwaukee, Wisconsin 53207
Phone: (414) 744-3210

CANADA

Mossman's Appliance Parts, Ltd.
John Mossman
1465 Gerrard Street E.
Toronto, Ontario, Canada
M4L2A2
Phone: (416) 461-1147

746 Ellice Avenue
Winnipeg, Manitoba, Canada
R3G OB6

Waugh & MacKewn Limited

Myrle Hickey
1025 Elias Street
P.O. Box 2277 STN. A
London, Ontario, Canada
N6A 4E9
Phone: (519) 432-1115

5325 Crowley Avenue
Montreal, Quebec, Canada
H4A 2C6

3913 Manchester Road
Calgary, Alberts, Canada
T2G 4A1

2285-A Gladwin Cres.
Ottawa, Ontario, Canada
K1B 4K9

ACKNOWLEDGMENTS
The manufacturers and associations listed below generously supplied illustrative material and information.

AFCO, Industries, Inc.
Alexandria, Louisiana 71301

American Concrete Institute
P.O. Box 19150
Detroit, Michigan 48219

American Plywood Association
P.O. Box 1119A
Tacoma, Washington 98401

Andersen Corporation
Bayport, Minnesota 55003

**Asphalt Roofing
Manufacturers Association**
Suite 702
1800 Massachusetts Avenue NW
Washington, D.C. 20036

Brick Institute of America
1750 Old Meadow Road
McLean, Virginia 22101

Formica Corporation
Wayne, New Jersey 07470

Hobart Manufacturing Co.
Troy, Ohio 45373

Home Ventilating Institute
4300L Lincoln Avenue
Rolling Meadows, Illinois 60008

Kool-O-Matic Corp.
1831 Terminal Road
Niles, Michigan 49120

Leigh Products, Inc.
Coopersville, Michigan 49404

**National Concrete
Masonry Association**
2302 Horse Pen Road
Herndon, Virginia 22070

**National Mineral
Wool Association**
c/o John Baer Company
355 Lexington Avenue
New York, New York 10017

Nutone Division
Madison & Red Bank Roads
Cincinnati, Ohio 45227

**Owens-Corning
Fiberglas Corporation**
Fiberglas Tower
Toledo, Ohio 43659

Portland Cement Association
5420 Old Orchard Road
Skokie, Illinois 60077

Season • all Industries, Inc.
Indiana, Pennsylvania 15701

Metric Conversions

LUMBER

Sizes: Metric cross-sections are so close to their nearest Imperial sizes, as noted below, that for most purposes they may be considered equivalents.

Lengths: Metric lengths are based on a 300mm module which is slightly shorter in length than an Imperial foot. It will therefore be important to check your requirements accurately to the nearest inch and consult the table below to find the metric length required.

Areas: The metric area is a square metre. Use the following conversion factors when converting from Imperial data: 100 sq. feet = 9.290 sq. metres.

METRIC SIZES SHOWN BESIDE NEAREST IMPERIAL EQUIVALENT

mm	Inches	mm	Inches
16 x 75	⅝ x 3	44 x 150	1¾ x 6
16 x 100	⅝ x 4	44 x 175	1¾ x 7
16 x 125	⅝ x 5	44 x 200	1¾ x 8
16 x 150	⅝ x 6	44 x 225	1¾ x 9
19 x 75	¾ x 3	44 x 250	1¾ x 10
19 x 100	¾ x 4	44 x 300	1¾ x 12
19 x 125	¾ x 5	50 x 75	2 x 3
19 x 150	¾ x 6	50 x 100	2 x 4
22 x 75	⅞ x 3	50 x 125	2 x 5
22 x 100	⅞ x 4	50 x 150	2 x 6
22 x 125	⅞ x 5	50 x 175	2 x 7
22 x 150	⅞ x 6	50 x 200	2 x 8
25 x 75	1 x 3	50 x 225	2 x 9
25 x 100	1 x 4	50 x 250	2 x 10
25 x 125	1 x 5	50 x 300	2 x 12
25 x 150	1 x 6	63 x 100	2½ x 4
25 x 175	1 x 7	63 x 125	2½ x 5
25 x 200	1 x 8	63 x 150	2½ x 6
25 x 225	1 x 9	63 x 175	2½ x 7
25 x 250	1 x 10	63 x 200	2½ x 8
25 x 300	1 x 12	63 x 225	2½ x 9
32 x 75	1¼ x 3	75 x 100	3 x 4
32 x 100	1¼ x 4	75 x 125	3 x 5
32 x 125	1¼ x 5	75 x 150	3 x 6
32 x 150	1¼ x 6	75 x 175	3 x 7
32 x 175	1¼ x 7	75 x 200	3 x 8
32 x 200	1¼ x 8	75 x 225	3 x 9
32 x 225	1¼ x 9	75 x 250	3 x 10
32 x 250	1¼ x 10	75 x 300	3 x 12
32 x 300	1¼ x 12	100 x 100	4 x 4
38 x 75	1½ x 3	100 x 150	4 x 6
38 x 100	1½ x 4	100 x 200	4 x 8
38 x 125	1½ x 5	100 x 250	4 x 10
38 x 150	1½ x 6	100 x 300	4 x 12
38 x 175	1½ x 7	150 x 150	6 x 6
38 x 200	1½ x 8	150 x 200	6 x 8
38 x 225	1½ x 9	150 x 300	6 x 12
44 x 75	1¾ x 3	200 x 200	8 x 8
44 x 100	1¾ x 4	250 x 250	10 x 10
44 x 125	1¾ x 5	300 x 300	12 x 12

METRIC LENGTHS

Lengths Metres	Equiv. Ft. & Inches
1.8m	5' 10⅞"
2.1m	6' 10⅝"
2.4m	7' 10½"
2.7m	8' 10¼"
3.0m	9' 10⅛"
3.3m	10' 9⅞"
3.6m	11' 9¾"
3.9m	12' 9½"
4.2m	13' 9⅜"
4.5m	14' 9⅓"
4.8m	15' 9"
5.1m	16' 8¾"
5.4m	17' 8⅝"
5.7m	18' 8⅜"
6.0m	19' 8¼"
6.3m	20' 8"
6.6m	21' 7⅞"
6.9m	22' 7⅝"
7.2m	23' 7½"
7.5m	24' 7¼"
7.8m	25' 7⅛"

All the dimensions are based on 1 inch = 25 mm.

NOMINAL SIZE (This is what you order.)	ACTUAL SIZE (This is what you get.)
Inches	Inches
1 x 1	¾ x ¾
1 x 2	¾ x 1½
1 x 3	¾ x 2½
1 x 4	¾ x 3½
1 x 6	¾ x 5½
1 x 8	¾ x 7¼
1 x 10	¾ x 9¼
1 x 12	¾ x 11¼
2 x 2	1¾ x 1¾
2 x 3	1½ x 2½
2 x 4	1½ x 3½
2 x 6	1½ x 5½
2 x 8	1½ x 7¼
2 x 10	1½ x 9¼
2 x 12	1½ x 11¼

PIPE FITTINGS

Only fittings for use with copper pipe are affected by metrication: metric compression fittings are interchangeable with Imperial in some sizes, but require adaptors in others.

INTERCHANGEABLE SIZES		SIZES REQUIRING ADAPTORS	
mm	Inches	mm	Inches
12	⅜	22	¾
15	½	35	1¼
28	1	42	1½
54	2		

Metric capillary (soldered) fittings are not directly interchangeable with imperial sizes but adaptors are available. Pipe fittings which use screwed threads to make the joint remain unchanged. The British Standard Pipe (BSP) thread form has now been accepted internationally and its dimensions will not physically change. These screwed fittings are commonly used for joining iron or steel pipes, for connections on taps, basin and bath waste outlets and on boilers, radiators, pumps etc. Fittings for use with lead pipe are joined by soldering and for this purpose the metric and inch sizes are interchangeable.

(Information courtesy Metrication Board, Millbank Tower, Millbank, London SW1P 4QU)

WOOD SCREWS

SCREW GAUGE NO.	NOMINAL DIAMETER		LENGTH	
	Inch	mm	Inch	mm
0	0.060	1.52	³⁄₁₆	4.8
1	0.070	1.78	¼	6.4
2	0.082	2.08	⁵⁄₁₆	7.9
3	0.094	2.39	⅜	9.5
4	0.0108	2.74	⁷⁄₁₆	11.1
5	0.122	3.10	½	12.7
6	0.136	3.45	⅝	15.9
7	0.150	3.81	¾	19.1
8	0.164	4.17	⅞	22.2
9	0.178	4.52	1	25.4
10	0.192	4.88	1¼	31.8
12	0.220	5.59	1½	38.1
14	0.248	6.30	1¾	44.5
16	0.276	7.01	2	50.8
18	0.304	7.72	2¼	57.2
20	0.332	8.43	2½	63.5
24	0.388	9.86	2¾	69.9
28	0.444	11.28	3	76.2
32	0.5	12.7	3¼	82.6
			3½	88.9
			4	101.6
			4½	114.3
			5	127.0
			6	152.4

Dimensions taken from BS1210; metric conversions are approximate.

BRICKS AND BLOCKS

Bricks

Standard metric brick measures 215 mm x 65 mm x 112.5. Metric brick can be used with older, standard brick by increasing the mortaring in the joints. The sizes are substantially the same, the metric brick being slightly smaller (3.6 mm less in length, 1.8 mm in width, and 1.2 mm in depth).

Concrete Block

Standard sizes

390 x 90 mm
390 x 190 mm
440 x 190 mm
440 x 215 mm
440 x 290 mm

Repair block for replacement of block in old installations is available in these sizes:
448 x 219 (including mortar joints)
397 x 194 (including mortar joints)

NAILS

NUMBER PER POUND OR KILO

Size	Weight Unit	Common	Casing	Box	Finishing
2d	Pound	876	1010	1010	1351
	Kilo	1927	2222	2222	2972
3d	Pound	586	635	635	807
	Kilo	1289	1397	1397	1775
4d	Pound	316	473	473	548
	Kilo	695	1041	1041	1206
5d	Pound	271	406	406	500
	Kilo	596	893	893	1100
6d	Pound	181	236	236	309
	Kilo	398	591	519	680
7d	Pound	161	210	210	238
	Kilo	354	462	462	524
8d	Pound	106	145	145	189
	Kilo	233	319	319	416
9d	Pound	96	132	132	172
	Kilo	211	290	290	398
10d	Pound	69	94	94	121
	Kilo	152	207	207	266
12d	Pound	64	88	88	113
	Kilo	141	194	194	249
16d	Pound	49	71	71	90
	Kilo	108	156	156	198
20d	Pound	31	52	52	62
	Kilo	68	114	114	136
30d	Pound	24	46	46	
	Kilo	53	101	101	
40d	Pound	18	35	35	
	Kilo	37	77	77	
50d	Pound	14			
	Kilo	31			
60d	Pound	11			
	Kilo	24			

LENGTH AND DIAMETER IN INCHES AND CENTIMETERS

Size	Length Inches	Length Centimeters	Diameter Inches	Diameter Centimeters*
2d	1	2.5	.068	.17
3d	1/2	3.2	.102	.26
4d	1/4	3.8	.102	.26
5d	1/6	4.4	.102	.26
6d	2	5.1	.115	.29
7d	2/2	5.7	.115	.29
8d	2/4	6.4	.131	.33
9d	2/6	7.0	.131	.33
10d	3	7.6	.148	.38
12d	3/2	8.3	.148	.38
16d	3/4	8.9	.148	.38
20d	4	10.2	.203	.51
30d	4/4	11.4	.220	.58
40d	5	12.7	.238	.60
50d	5/4	14.0	.257	.66
60d	6	15.2	.277	.70

*Exact conversion

Helpful U.S. Government Publications

INVESTMENT & CONSTRUCTION

Buying Lots from Developers
043G. $1.00. 28 pp. 1976.
What to ask about a property and contract before you sign; information the developer must give you under law.

Can I Really Get Free or Cheap Public Land?
632 G. Free. 12 pp. 1978.
What public lands are still available for purchase or homesteading; how to go about it.

Designs for Low-Cost Wood Homes
044G. $1.30. 30 pp. 1978.
Sketches and model floor plans; how to select economical, durable materials; order forms for working plans.

Drainage Around the Home.
045G. $.60. 6 pp. 1977.
How to identify drainage problems caused by flooding, seasonal high water tables, or density of the soil.

Finding and Keeping a Healthy House
091G. $1.25. 20 pp. 1978.
How to identify and protect your home from water damage, wood decay, and destructive insects such as termites, beetles, and carpenter ants.

Having Problems Paying Your Mortgage?
683G. Free. 5 pp. 1979.
Steps to take if you are having trouble making your mortgage payments on time; where to go for help.

Home Buyer's Vocabulary.
655G. Free. 14 pp. 1978.
Defines terms you need to understand when buying.

Home Buying Veteran
600G. Free. 36 pp. 1977.
Useful for non-veterans as well; choosing a neighborhood, a lot, a house; checklist for inspecting a house; financing.

House Construction; How To Reduce Costs
049G. $.80. 16 pp. 1977.
How to save in location, style, interior arrangements, and selection of materials and utilities.

Move in ... with a Graduated Payment Mortgage
656G. Free. 2 pp. 1978.
How this new program enables you to buy a home and make lower monthly payments during the first few years of your mortgage.

Questions and Answers on Condominiums
602G. Free. 48 pp. 1979
What to ask before buying.

Remodeling a House ?   Will It Be Worthwhile?
670G. Free. 9 pp. 1978.
What to consider when deciding whether a wood-frame house is worth restoring.

Rent or Buy?
051G. $.80. 32 pp. 1979.
How to compare costs and returns of renting with owning a home; includes charts for estimating the monthly costs of each.

Selecting and Financing a Home
052G. $1.10. 23 pp. 1977.
Brief comparison of renting with buying; how to figure what you can afford; how to apply for a loan; what to look for in homeowners insurance.

Selling Property: Brokers, Title, Closing, and Taxes
671G. Free. 7 pp. 1978.
Advantages and disadvantages of using a real estate broker; some costs of selling; tax implications.

Settlement Costs
053G. $1.00. 40 pp. 1978.
What they are; documents to expect; sample forms and worksheets to compare costs; how to avoid unfair practices when purchasing a home.

When You Move: Do's and Don'ts
603G. Free. 6 pp. 1974.
Planning, what to expect during the move, and how to handle a loss or damage claim; tips for the do-it-yourselfer.

Wise Home Buying
657G. Free. 28 pp. 1978.
Discusses choosing a real estate broker, locating a house, inspecting an old house, and financing the purchase of a home.

Wood-Frame House Construction
054G. $4.25. 223 pp. 1975.
Comprehensive, illustrated handbook of detailed instructions and basic principles for building and insulating.

ENERGY CONSIDERATIONS

Buying Solar
055G. $1.85. 80 pp. 1976.
How solar energy can be used to heat and cool your house and heat your water; advantages of the different types of equipment and systems; designing a system; how to estimate costs and savings.

The Energy-Wise Home Buyer.
109G. $2.00. 59 pp. 1979.
Twelve energy features to look for in a home; detailed energy checklists; comprehensive charts and maps for figuring your energy needs and costs.

Firewood for Your Fireplace
047G. $.60. 7 pp. 1978.
Burning characteristics of various woods, where and how to buy firewood, and tips on safe fireplace use.

How To Improve the Efficiency of Your Oil-Fired Furnace
605G. Free. 12 pp. 1978.
What you and the service technician should check; adjustments that will cut costs.

Tips for Energy Savers
610G. Free. 46 pp. 1978.
How to save energy and money on home heating, cooling, lighting, appliances, etc.; how much insulation you need; lists annual electricity use for appliances.

MAINTENANCE

Controlling Household Pests
064G. $.50. 30 pp. 1977.
Procedures and proper pesticides for controlling rats, cockroaches, termites, clothes moths, carpet beetles, etc.

Corrosion
057G. $.80. 8 pp. 1978.
Causes of common corrosion problems; how to prevent and remove rust, tarnish, and other corrosion from silver and other metals.

Family Work and Storage Areas Outside the Home
672G. Free. 11 pp. 1978.
How to use the space you have more efficiently; build different types of storage sheds; and get financing.

How To Prevent and Remove Mildew
077G. $.90. 12 pp. 1978.
What it is; how to prevent and remove it from different surfaces; and how to get rid of dampness and musty odors.

Painting—Inside and Out
092G. $1.30. 32 pp. 1978.
Directions for doing a top-quality paint job, including surface preparation, paint selection, application, use of natural finishes; also lists references.

People and Fire
093G. $1.40. 27 pp. 1977.
Latest ideas on fire safety for homes, apartments, and mobile homes; includes household fire safety checklist and electrical troubleshooting guide.

Protecting Your Housing Investment
616G. Free. 32 pp. 1979.
Maintenance of heating systems, plumbing, and building structure; treatment of special problems such as pest control and moisture.

Index

removal, 72-73
Cracks, 170
Crawl-spaces, insulating, 86
Creosote, 211, 241
Crosscut saws, 13, 179, 189, 191, 193, 195
Current, 151
Curb repairs, 203-204
Cutting in, 219

Dampness, 178
Decay, 178, 209
Decking, roof, 168
Dimmer switch, 159
Disc faucets, repairing, 105
Dishwasher, 64, 142, 143
Disposals, food, 66, 144, 145
Diverters, repairing, 99, 108
  bathtub spout, 108
Dome seals, skylight, 178
Door and window areas, 193-195
  casings, 193
  door stop, 195
  drip cap, 194
  jambs, 195
  molding, 193-194
  thresholds, 195
  thermal, 195
  water stop, 194
Doorbell maintenance and repair, 145-146
Dormers, 168
Doorknobs, installing, 54
Doors, 50-54, 89, 90, 196
  garage, 196
  weatherstripping, 89, 90
Downspout, 43, 178, 182
Draft diverter, gas furnace, 130
Drains, 108, 115, 129, 128, 187
  blockage at opening, 115
  closers, 129
  connection repairs, 128
  French type, 129
Drainage, ground level, 183
Drainage systems, 179, 180, 181, 182, 204
Drapery rods, 45
Drip cap, 176, 178
Driveways, 197-200
Driveway sealer, 197
Drills, 26
  star drill, 191, 203, 206
Drop cloth, 219, 220
Drop siding, repairing, 189
Drum trap, 116
Dry well, 183-184
Ducting, 6, 74, 75, 94, 132-133
  oil furnace, 6
  anatomy, 132-133

Eaves, 170, 177, 178-179
  gable, 179
Electric drills, 26
Electric furnaces and ducting, 134
Electric range, 64
Electrical breakdowns, troubleshooting, 156, 157, 158, 159, 160, 162, 163, 164, 165, 166
Electrical code, 149
Electrical system, 149, 150, 151
  breaker, 151
  testing voltage, 151
Electrician's tape, 153, 165, 166
Electric paint remover, 223

Enamel, 217, 218
  semi-gloss, 218
End filler strip, 69
Epoxy materials, 113
Escutcheon plate, 164, 165
Estimating paint quantities, 218, 222
Excess water pressure, 128
Expansion fasteners, 10
Expansion joints, 201, 204
Extension cord, 156
Exterior paint, 222-227
  chart, 224
  latex, 222
  metal paint, 222
  porch and deck, 226
  portland cement, 226
  shake (pigmented stain), 222
  titanium, 222
  white lead, 222

Fascia, 176, 179, 223, 224
Fasteners, 235-237
Faucets, repairing, 99-108
  cap washers, 102
  cartridge, 105-106
  disc, 105
  gaskets, 103
  new models, 103-104
  o-rings, 103
  old fashioned model, 101
  rotating ball, 107-108
  stem washers, 99-102
  tipping valve, 103
  valve seats, 103
Feather (technique), 171, 219
Fences, 209-211
Fiberglass, 175, 179, 233
  patching kit, 175
  resin, 179
Field tile, 187
Files, 20
Filters, 93, 94, 97, 131, 133, 146-147
  air conditioning, 97
  changing gas furnace, 131
  furnace, 93-94
  gas furnace, 131
  lawnmower, 146, 147
  oil furnace, maintenance, 133
Fireplaces, 42, 43
Fish tape, 166-167
Fitting, replacing, 121
Fixtures, light, 164, 165, 166, 167
Flashing, 175
Flange butt insulation, 82
Flaking, 133
  pipe, 133
  tool, 133
Flashing, 170, 175-178, 194
  Asphalt, 194
Float, 193, 221
  mason's wooden, 221
  rubber, 193, 221
Float ball, replacing (toilet), 111
Flooding basements, 178
Floor plan, 63
Flooring, 9, 54, 55, 56, 57, 58, 59, 60, 63, 75-80, 238
  hardwood, 238
  kitchen, 76-80
  parquet block, 238
  preparation, 67

sheet vinyl, 238
Fluorescent tubes, 162
Flush handle and tank, toilet, 109, 113
Foil-faced fiberglass insulation, 82
Footing, 187
Foundation, 43, 168, 186, 187
  drainage, 186-187
Frames (shingles), 240
Framing hardware, 239
Framing members, 177, 229
Frozen pipes, 127
Fuel tanks, oil furnace, maintaining, 133
Furnace, 93, 94, 129-133, 134
  burners, 93
  coal convectors, 133
  electric, 134
  filters, 93-94
  gas, 129-133
  hot water, 134
  maintenance, 94
  oil, 132-133
  repairs, 93-98
  thermostat adjustment, 131
  troubleshooting chart, 131
Furring strips, 10, 86-87
Fuse, 149, 150, 151, 155
  box, 155
  cartridge, 151
  service entry, 149
  socket, 150
  time delay, 150
  type S, 151

Gable eaves, 179
Galvanized metal, 173-175, 181-182, 235
  flashing, 175
  gutters, 181-182
  roof, 174
  sheet, 235
Garage door, 90, 196
Garage door opener, 146
  diagram, 146
  problems, 146
Garages and carports, 195-196
  columns, 195-196
  doors, 196
  door track (misalignment), 196
  hinges, 196
  latches/locks, 196
  support posts, 195-196
Garbage disposal problems, 144-145
Gas burners, furnace, 93
Gas furnace, 129-133
  air shutters, 130-131
  anatomy, 129-130
  blowers, 133
  ducts, 132-133
  filters, 131
  gas odor, 130
  manual controls, 132
  motors, pulleys and belts, 132
  pilot light, 129, 130
  registers, 132-133
  repairs, 129-133
  reset buttons, 132
Gas line leaks, 131
Gas, odor, 130
Gaskets, 104, 162
  faucet, 104
Gates, 209-211
Glass, 47, 48, 218, 235